When Ballet Became French

When Ballet Became French

Modern Ballet and the Cultural Politics of France, 1909–1939

Ilyana Karthas

McGill-Queen's University Press
Montreal & Kingston • London • Chicago

ISBN 978-0-7735-4605-9 (cloth)
ISBN 978-0-7735-9780-8 (ePDF)
ISBN 978-0-7735-9781-5 (ePUB)

Legal deposit third quarter 2015
Bibliothèque nationale du Québec

Printed in Canada on acid-free paper that is 100% ancient forest free (100% post-consumer recycled), processed chlorine free

McGill-Queen's University Press acknowledges the support of the Canada Council for the Arts for our publishing program. We also acknowledge the financial support of the Government of Canada through the Canada Book Fund for our publishing activities.

Library and Archives Canada Cataloguing in Publication

Karthas, Ilyana, 1972–, author
When ballet became French : modern ballet and the cultural politics of France, 1909–1939 / Ilyana Karthas.

Includes bibliographical references and index. Issued in print and electronic formats.
ISBN 978-0-7735-4605-9 (bound). – ISBN 978-0-7735-9780-8 (ePDF).
– ISBN 978-0-7735-9781-5 (ePUB)

1. France – Social life and customs – 20th century. 2. Ballet – Social aspects – France. 3. Ballet – Political aspects – France. 4. Ballet – France – History – 20th century. 5. France – Civilization – 20th century. 6. France – History – 20th century. I. Title.

DC33.7.K378 2015 944.081 C2015-902208-8
C2015-902209-6

Set in 10.5/13 New Baskerville, with Bodoni. Interior design and typesetting by James Leahy.

This book is dedicated to my son Dylan and daughter Sofia

Contents

Illustrations

Acknowledgments

Research for this book was supported by generous grants from Brown University, Columbia University's Council for European Studies Florence Gould Foundation, and the University of Missouri-Columbia's Research Council Board. Special thanks go to the staff at the Bibliothèque-musée de l'Opéra, Bibliothèque de la ville de Paris, Bibliothèque Nationale de France, Archives Nationales de France, NYPL Performing Arts Library, University of Missouri-Columbia's Ellis Library, Columbia University's Butler Library, and the San Francisco Performing Arts Library. At the Paris Opéra, I was given the rare opportunity of a rooftop view of the boulevard de l'Opèra – I will never forget it! I am grateful to the École des Hautes Études (EHESS) for its sponsorship while I was residing in France, and, specifically, to Christophe Prochasson for offering me the opportunity to attend his seminars. Thanks go to my dear friend Kerstin Duell for opening the world of Parisian tango to me. My Parisian community – Virginie, Evelyne, Avigail, and Angie – made my stay incredibly rich, inspiring, and unforgettable.

Many teachers, colleagues, and friends offered me invaluable guidance over the course of this project. My deepest gratitude goes to my doctoral dissertation supervisor and mentor, Carolyn J. Dean, who believed in this project and my abilities from the outset, and who has become a dear friend. I am indebted to Jane Garnett at Oxford University and Deborah Valenze at Barnard College for their continual guidance, inspiration, and mentorship, which I cherish. My sincere thanks go to those who took the time to read over my chapters and/or offered incredibly helpful insights regarding my project. These include my colleagues Linda Reeder, Theodore Koditschek, Jonathan Sperber, Catherine Rymph, and Martha Kelly, as well as

James H. Johnston and Bill Weber, both of whom share my passion for the arts. I would like to thank my fellow panellists, commentators, chairs, and attendees at the many conferences at which I presented my work. Their feedback and enthusiastic support for this project helped me to refine my arguments and strengthen the manuscript. These include Linda L. Clark, Elinor Accampo, Karen Offen, Leora Auslander, Sarah Fried-Gintis, David Shafer, and Richard Sonn. My thanks go to Judith Surkis, Mary Louise Roberts, and Simonetta Falasca-Zamponi for their advice and interest in this project. My book has benefited from the advice, discussions, and steadfast support from my colleagues in MU's Department of Art History, Department of Romance Languages, and Department of Women's and Gender Studies, including Michael Yonan, Kristin Schwain, Jim van Dyke, Carol Lazzaro-Weis, Flore Zéphir, Joan Hermsen, and Elisa Glick. A special thanks to Matthew Dye, who helped me with many translations. I would also like to thank the late Kermit Champa, with whom I had the privilege of working at Brown University. His passion for art, music, and dance encouraged me to pursue an interdisciplinary approach and to weather its challenges. My gratitude to Mary Gluck at Brown, who helped shape my approach to intellectual and cultural history and who played a crucial role in the way that I teach it. Ulle Holt's dissertation was a real asset to this project, and our conversations during my graduate years on the Ballets Russes and French culture were a pleasure and inspiration. I would like to thank Ann Youmans for all her help in preparing my manuscript for publication, my copy editor James Leahy, managing editor Ryan Van Huijstee, cover designer David Drummond, and my editor at McGill-Queen's University Press, Jonathan Crago, for his enthusiasm for this project, his skill, patience, and generosity with his time. Finally, I would like to thank Peter Stearns for inviting me to contribute an article to the *Journal of Social History* (45, no. 4 [Summer 2012]: 960–89). Drawn from sections of chapter 7, this article offered me the opportunity to show the richness of dance as a subject of analysis for historical research.

Thanks to my dear friends, Jenny Carson, Christine Knauer, and Catherine Polan Orzech, whose unwavering support has meant the world to me. J.A. Fernandez – there are no words to describe my gratitude (Fokine!). This book would not have been completed without the incredible support and unrelenting encouragement of my family. I am extremely grateful to my parents, Loula and George, who first exposed me to the beauty of art and music, and never dissuaded me from the paths that I have chosen – whether it be a career in ballet or academe. My sister Diana continually inspires me to develop my creative imagination and not give up. Most of all, I would like to thank my husband Mark Thompson, without whose patience, support, and love, this book never would have been written. I was raised in a family that was passionate about the arts. This book is dedicated to my children Dylan and Sofia, who I hope will always find inspiration in the arts and experience the joy that the arts bring to one's life.

When Ballet Became French

Introduction

At the Sixth Impressionist Exhibition in 1881, the French painter Edgar Degas presented for the first and last time a sculpture entitled *Little Dancer Aged Fourteen.* The statuette caused an uproar, generating polemics and divisions among critics. Two-thirds life size and adorned with a horse hair wig, a green satin ribbon, a tattered mid-thigh tulle and gauze tutu, a silk bodice, and pink ballet slippers, it outraged many spectators' sense of propriety. Unlike the dreamy, idealistic representations of Romantic ballerinas, it was violently criticized for its excessive realism and for the expression of "bestial boldness" of the ballet girl who was said more to resemble a "girl-monkey" than a sylph. Her body toughened by exercise, with tired eyes, chin up, and shoulders back, spectators found her "repulsive," "frightening … a flower of precocious depravity."[1] One critic remarked, "wishing to present us with a statuette of a dancer, [Degas] has chosen amongst the most odiously ugly; he makes it the standard of horror and bestiality … Yes, certainly, at the very bottom of the barrel of the dance school, there are some poor girls who look like this monster … but what good are they in terms of statuary? Put them in a museum of zoology, of anthropology, of physiology, all right: but in a museum of art, really!"[2] The "realness" of the piece even incited anthropological and anatomical treatises to make reference to the statuette, comparing it to monkeys and rats.[3] Joris-Karl Huysmans, a more sympathetic critic, recollected that at the exhibition "one hear[d] fathers cry: 'God forbid my daughter should become a dancer.'"[4]

This so-called monster was actually one of three sisters, all training to become ballerinas and all sketched by Degas. Born to working-class Belgian parents in France, the adolescent girl, Marie van Goethem, lived near the painter's studio and attended classes at the Paris

Opéra's ballet school. According to Martine Kahane, curator of the Bibliothèque-Musée de l'Opéra, Marie passed all her early ballet exams and was promoted from the ranks of "petits-rats" or "flowers of the gutter" to join the corps de ballet at fifteen, a year after Degas made the sculpture. Only two years later, she was dismissed, most likely because she was late or absent from the ballet too often.[5] Her mother, Madame van Goethem, a widow who worked as a laundress, probably had been prostituting her daughters.[6] Marie's older sister Antoinette was arrested for stealing money from her lover's wallet at the bar Le Chat Noir and served a three-month jail sentence, as did Marie for pickpocketing one of her customers.[7] Only Charlotte, the youngest sister, continued her career as a dancer, becoming a soloist with the Paris Opéra Ballet and later a professor at the ballet school at the Opéra.[8] She retired in 1933.

I begin with Degas's *Little Dancer Aged Fourteen*, its reception, and a brief account of the lives of his models to demonstrate how criticism reflected and shaped contemporary French values, specifically, late nineteenth-century French values associated with working-class female bodies.[9] Ballet dancers were seen primarily as workers and minimally as artists in their own right. Degas depicted the ballet he observed in the 1880s: it was primarily a working-class profession and an art form in decline. In his work, the ballet dancer was not a metaphoric symbol of nobility, grace, or poetry, but, first and foremost, a sexual being, a worker, and a titillating subject. To the French public of 1881, the ballet had come to represent a modern space of cross-class sexual exchange, a world of display and male possession, and an eroded French art form.[10] As these critics imply, the fin-de-siècle ballet signified a degenerative (national) body. How then did ballet rise from this lowly status? Why was ballet re-embraced by French society, and, moreover, how did dance become a means of marking qualities of national belonging?

Interdisciplinary in its approach, *When Ballet Became French: Modern Ballet and the Cultural Politics of France, 1909–1939*, addresses the ways in which ballet served as cultural force in early twentieth-century France. It seeks to show how ballet became a cultural phenomenon that was able to attain the power to raise vital cultural questions of the day. The book explores the relationship between the status of an art, the production of meaning that surrounded it, and the specific historical cultural context in which it was produced. While it traces the cultural project to revive ballet in France, the book's primary aim is to explore the ways in which critics engaged in discussion of ballet and why they turned to ballet to assert modern cultural values. In this respect, this is a book about the reception of ballet and how criticism shaped and reflected the public's understanding of the art and what it meant to be French. This work examines the meaning of a specific body of literature, ballet commentary, and seeks to explain how it served to mediate between French values and ballet aesthetics. In offering such a study, I hope to demonstrate the richness of using dance as a source for the study of cultural and political history and to show how ballet played a major role in articulating French values in a period of momentous change.

This book analyzes discourse on ballet. It examines what was written about ballet by journalists, commentators, intellectuals, and critics writing in newspapers, periodicals, and books in Paris between 1909 and 1939, focusing on commentary on ballet published in respectable bourgeois journals. Increasingly, analysis of ballet appeared in journals such as *La Revue Musicale, La Nouvelle Revue Française, Le Figaro, Le Temps,* and *Comœdia* – all with a predominantly middle-class readership.[11] These periodicals and newspapers contained reviews and articles catering to theatre, opera, and ballet audiences. These audiences themselves were changing at the turn of the century, and, in turn, journals' readership also changed. The voices in this book are those of journalists, professional critics, intellectuals, prominent artists, musicologists, and dance specialists who published commentary on ballet in these journals in this period. These include figures such as Henri Prunières, Jacques Rivière, Pierre Lalo, Robert Brussel, André Levinson, Auguste Rodin, Jean Cocteau, Valentine Gross, Julie Sazonova, and Serge Lifar. Before André Levinson, a Russian émigré who appeared on the Parisian scene in the 1920s, there were no dance experts writing for such papers in France. Nonetheless, critics writing for Parisian newspapers and journals managed to reshape Parisian attitudes towards ballet through their analyses and editorials. Some educated the public on new developments in modern ballet and established criteria against which to measure the art just as they did with modern music, opera, art, and literature. In doing so, they cultivated, once again, a public taste for ballet.

However, most discussions of ballet offered a wide range of opinions about not only ballet, but also French cultural life. This book reveals how early twentieth-century discourse on ballet in France functioned as a nexus that drew together a myriad of cultural anxieties, including those about the nation, modernity, modern art, gender identity, sexuality, the body, race, and health. It addresses why prominent critics and intellectuals used ballet as a means of redefining France's self-image at a time of profound change in European society and worldwide. Moreover, it investigates why ballet revitalized in a particular way in France. This book shows how, in their project to revitalize French ballet, critics used the medium of ballet as a battleground to forge coherent ideas about national identity, modern aesthetics, and gender norms. In doing so, it demonstrates how an examination of rhetoric on ballet offers a unique vantage point through which to analyze the ways in which national identity, modern aesthetics, and gender ideologies intersect and are inextricably linked. By focusing on the figure of the critic, this book renders explicit the processes that cultural historians often assume, namely *how* aesthetics take on broader social and political significance. Rather than taking that relation to be transparent or necessary, I illustrate how significant cultural labour is involved in the production of these meanings.

Jeffrey H. Jackson's recent study of music and modern life in interwar Paris offers an example of this approach to the study of the performing arts. In his book *Making Jazz French: Music and Modern Life in Interwar Paris* (2003), Jackson examines how the French embraced and reconfigured American jazz in France. Rather than being a study on jazz music itself, it offers a critical analysis of what jazz meant to French people during the interwar period. Jackson's materials centre on commentary on jazz published in newspapers, periodicals, and books in order to understand the reception of jazz in France. This study is concerned with issues similar to those raised by Jackson, namely, the questions France faced at the turn of the century and, later, during the interwar years: "What kind of nation would France be? Was French identity based on a set of deep-rooted traditions, or was it compatible with the cutting-edge changes of the twentieth century?" What was the relationship between French identity and modern life?[12] In other words, France faced the dilemma of how to reconcile tradition with modernity and rapid change. These questions resonate in discussions of ballet in the early twentieth century just as they do in discussions of jazz music, modern art, classical music, and modern literature. Many intellectual figures endeavoured to revitalize French ballet and to make it compatible with modern French national culture. In the process, debates surfaced in major bourgeois journals and newspapers over whether French ballet could reflect French bourgeois values and modern tastes.

There are a number of excellent histories that examine cultural institutions as a vehicle through which to study broader shifts in society and politics.[13] Some employ multi-disciplinary investigation by incorporating theoretical tools from art history, gender and feminist studies, film studies, literary criticism, and post-structuralism. There are three monographs that are particularly innovative in offering a historical study of cultural and artistic forms. James Johnson's *Listening in Paris: A Cultural History* (1995) investigates the political and social influences upon public response to music and, ultimately, reveals why French audiences became silent. Lenard R. Berlanstein's *Daughters of Eve: A Cultural History of the French Theatre Women from the Old Regime to the Fin de Siècle* (2001) examines how the French incorporated women performers (i.e., actresses) into their culture in the modern period and how French theatre women became the embodiment of republican values by the end of the nineteenth century. In looking at the cultural institution of theatre, Berlanstein analyzes actresses as "cultural sites where social, class, political and gendered forces intersected in such a way to produce meanings that helped explain social organization."[14] Inspired by the interdisciplinary teachings of Carl E. Schorske, Deborah Silverman's book *Art Nouveau in Fin-de-Siècle France: Politics, Psychology, and Style* (1989) explores the connections between visual form and historical change within a specific national culture: that of France in the late nineteenth century. She treats art nouveau as a historical phenomenon that is part of the broader cultural and political history of fin-de-siècle France. These studies have informed and inspired the approach taken in this book by offering new ways of exploring the relationship between art(s) and society. Firmly grounded in historical analyses, they reveal the ways in which the shaping of aesthetics, culture, and national identity are interconnected.

One particular cultural medium that moved through the early twentieth century and emerged as a dominant force to express anxieties about national identity, modernity, and gender has not yet been explored by cultural historians: ballet. As this book will reveal, many of the cultural transformations occurring in France and across much of Europe in this period not only played an instrumental role in ballet's revival in the West, but also were expressed and shaped within the critical debates that surrounded ballet. In the case of France, these changes were reflected in new assertions of nationalism, modernism, aesthetic tastes, and definitions of gender. In other words, engagement with ballet offered critics and intellectuals a different context in which to address (construct or contest) modern French cultural identities.

It is with these considerations in mind that this book deals with discourse on ballet from 1909 to 1939. I have chosen this period because the Ballets Russes' arrival in Paris in 1909 ignited extensive discussion among prominent critics and intellectuals about the function and role of ballet in modern society. From 1909 through 1939, critics from respectable journals such as *La Revue Musicale* (Henry Prunières), *La Nouvelle Revue Française* (Jacques Rivière), *Le Figaro* (Robert Brussell), *Le Temps* (Pierre Lalo), and *Comœdia* (André Levinson) – all with a predominantly bourgeois readership – were writing about and reviewing ballet. Their analyses and editorials, wide ranging as they were, reshaped Parisian attitudes about ballet. Their new engagement in reviewing ballet not only elevated the reputation of the art form by forging new definitions and understandings of it, but also offered them an opportunity either to reinforce traditional French values or to challenge them.

It is clear that, by 1939, ballet's status as a cultural and artistic institution had improved significantly and its reputation had been stabilized and de-eroticized. By this point, we find prestigious bourgeois journals devoting, for the first time, entire issues to articles on ballet and dance. For example, *La Revue Musicale* devoted an issue in 1938 to articles on ballet and choreography. This reveals the extent to which ballet was now taken seriously as an art form. By 1939, we find rhetoric on ballet pronouncing its artistic worth, acknowledging its autonomy as an art form independent from music, pantomime, and decor, and emphasizing its worthiness to receive state funding. The financing of the Paris Opéra, formerly controlled by subscribers, was transferred over to the state in 1939, indicating the French nation's investment in ballet as a symbol of cultural pre-eminence. The RTLN (Réunion des Théâtres Lyriques Nationaux, established in January 1939) brought together the Paris Opéra and Opéra-Comique and was devoted to financing and cultivating both state institutions. Moreover, by this time, French dancers achieved a national and international celebrity status that reflected a renewed professionalism of female dancers and an acceptance of male dancers. In sum, by 1939, French ballet had become a symbol of Frenchness worthy, once again, of embodying French grandeur.

The year 1939, of course, also brings the reader to the eve of the Second World War and the ensuing defeat and occupation of France. A study of ballet's continuing ascendance after 1939 thus would entail examining a far different context. Under occupation, the Paris Opéra necessarily served a different function. It could no longer be a site for French republican national pre-eminence. Alan Riding's book *And the Show Went On: Cultural Life in Nazi-Occupied Paris* (2010) demonstrates well this new context. Historians such as Patrice Higonnet (who works on culture and politics) and Charles Rearick (who works on the cultural history of Europe) have shown how Paris was the cultural capital of the world between 1918 and 1939, further making the case for bracketing the era of this study. By the 1940s, Paris was no longer a magnet for artists and writers from around the world as it had been in this earlier period. After all, it was occupied. Émigrés would not go to Nazi-occupied Paris. Audiences changed at the Paris Opéra (many Germans attended performances), and journals were under heavy censorship and taken over by those of the Far Right. What is clear in this period is that ballet (and the Paris Opéra) had already gained a positive reputation, one that the Germans acknowledged. Paris Opéra ballet director Serge Lifar was allowed to create new works, and several talented ballet dancers rose from the Paris Opéra ranks and attained celebrity status. Furthermore, Lifar took his troupe on tour in 1940 to avoid the recruitment of his male dancers to the war effort, which reveals that the Paris Opéra had an international reputation by then.[15]

Not only do the war years constitute a distinct period, but the legacy of ballet's development in the years 1909–38 proved to be an enduring one. The major role that writer André Malraux (France's first Minister of Cultural Affairs from 1959 and 1969) played in French cultural policy also benefited ballet.[16] In 1982, the Ministry of Culture's Direction de la Musique et de Danse became the first autonomous body to determine state dance policy and funding. The Division de la Danse quadrupled national funding for dance between

1982 and 1986. However, the Paris Opéra ballet's revival in the 1980s would not have come about if Lifar had not paved the way in the 1930s, and, in turn, Lifar would not have been as successful if a public taste for and understanding of ballet had not been not revitalized and cultivated by intellectuals in the teens and twenties. The years between 1909 and 1939 were thus a critical moment when the French decided to recognize ballet, once again, as a legitimate and valuable art form after a long period of decline.

BALLET AND FRENCH IDENTITY

While this is not a social or cultural history of ballet, a consideration of ballet's evolution as an art form and the various cultural roles that it served in the past is crucial to understanding commentary on ballet in the early twentieth century. The longer history of ballet is important to this study because early twentieth-century critics consistently referred to it in their attempts to make French ballet compatible to modern life. Consequently, critics' assumptions concerning the history of ballet may not correspond exactly to the realities of ballet's past. They made selective use of the past to support their arguments. As Benedict Anderson's *Imagined Communities: Reflections on the Origin and Spread of Nationalism* (1983) addresses, nations invent and mythologize the past to create unified and coherent national and cultural values.[17] Critics also created an "imagined past" as they attempted to renegotiate ballet's identity as a modern art form.

Historically, ballet has played a central role in the expression of French identity and cultural pre-eminence. The earliest form of ballet in France, "court ballet," appeared in the sixteenth century.[18] It was performed by the nobility and served above all as a spectacle through which to glorify the state. The elevation of ballet's status in France began in 1661 when Louis XIV (r. 1643–1715) established the first of his many academies, the Académie Royale de Danse, an official school of dance, located outside the royal premises. The Paris Opéra was created shortly after as a state institution to house professional dancers, musicians, and singers. Increasingly, dancers were drawn from commoners, who were able to imitate the grace of the aristocratic body on stage. Professional ballet began, moreover, as an exclusively male institution. At first, all dancers were male and female roles were performed by boys *en travesti*. Increasingly, however, a few women joined as professionals in the course of the eighteenth century.

During the French Enlightenment, the nature and function of ballet were discussed at length by the philosophes. The decorative use of ballet within opera, influenced by the rococo style and associated with aristocratic decadence, came under attack at this time. Philosophes, such as Diderot and Rousseau, argued that dance should signify something other than its technical movements (deemed as merely decorative) and that, in doing so, ballet could achieve a similar narrative role as poetry or song. In other words, ballet should appeal to the mind rather than the senses. This new aesthetic taste for dance manifested itself in the choreography of Jean Georges Noverre. Noverre conceived ballet now as primarily expressive, rather than merely decorative. In doing so, ballet became a legitimate vehicle for narrative and dramatic expression. Ballet survived the French Revolution, in part, because it was recognized as an expressive art form that could embody republican values.[19]

An equally significant aspect of ballet's development in France as a pre-eminent cultural institution was its involvement in transnational artistic exchange, in this case between Russia and France. As ballet became officially a national art form under Louis XIV in France, Russia was beginning to open its doors to the West. The Eurocentricity of Peter the Great and later Catherine the Great resulted in Russia's embrace of Western art techniques and styles which held Russian art to European standards and ideals. This Russian adoption of European art forms included those of ballet.[20] This is best exemplified in the reformations of French choreographer Marius Petipa (1818–1910). Having studied under the legendary French court dancer and choreographer Auguste Vestris (referred as the *dieu de la danse*), Marius Petipa is known as the father of classical ballet and the inheritor of the French ballet tradition.[21] Discouraged with the decline of ballet in the mid-nineteenth century, Petipa left his homeland in 1845. Already established as an exceptional dancer in France, Belgium, and Spain, Petipa moved to St Petersburg in 1847. There, he was offered first a one-year contract as principal dancer at the Imperial Theatre. He was then named choreographer-in-chief in 1862 (a position he held for nearly fifty years), and he became premier ballet master of the Imperial Theatre in 1869.[22]

Petipa arrived in a country desperately searching for its own national artistic style: a Russia that attempted to reconcile its eighteenth-century dependence on European culture (ideals, art, literature) with its new aspirations to reaffirm a distinct Russian national identity. In other words, there existed in Russia an internal conflict with parts looking to the West (St Petersburg) and others looking to the East (Moscow). Petipa found a Russia that was searching for a distinct national style and art forms it could claim for itself. Ballet in its decline in the West offered Russia a perfect vehicle through which to develop a distinct national art. Petipa not only elevated the Russian ballet to international fame, but also laid the foundation for twentieth-century ballet. His classicism, which integrated the purity of the French school with Italian virtuosity, was fused into a Russian national style.[23]

Over the course of the nineteenth century, with the rise of the bourgeoisie, French ballet was transformed into a private enterprise. Similar to the current state of ballet, it was subsidized by the government but became increasingly dependent on private support. The Opéra was increasingly funded by private sources with only a partial royal subsidy in the 1830s during the July Monarchy (1830–48). The subsidy demonstrated the continuing importance attached to ballet as an important symbol of French high culture. In 1831, when Louis-Désiré Véron (founder of *Revue de Paris*) took over the private management of the Paris Opéra, his six-year contract emphasized his obligation to the state: "The entrepreneur will maintain the Opéra in all the pomp and luxury expected of national theatre." In fact, Véron declared in his memoir, "the July Revolution is the triumph of the bourgeoisie … the Opéra will become its Versailles, it will rush *en masse* there to replace the *grands seigneurs* [lords, princes] and the exiles of the court."[24] The Revolution of 1830 brought the bourgeoisie to power, and the Opéra would now signify their new status. At this time, audiences comprised some aristocrats, but mostly government officials, professionals, and businessmen. In 1833, a group of 'ballet admirers" established the Jockey Club, a gentlemen's club located next door to the Paris Opéra. Véron also opened the Foyer de la Danse, a warm-up space in which young dancers could "mingle" with such "admirers." Thus with the privatization of the Opéra came the commodification of its dancers (libertinism at its best). Not surprisingly, sexual desirability became as much a marker of a dancer's success as talent.[25] From this point on, ballet would be thrown into the commercial marketplace, dependent on profits, public tastes, successful marketing, and, of course, criticism. Reviews of ballerinas catered to the male gaze, male desires, and male expectations by emphasizing dancers' sensuality, personality, and physical appearance.[26]

By the late nineteenth century, ballet no longer catered to an exclusively haute-bourgeois audience. While ballet existed throughout Western Europe, it was absorbed into popular entertainment. Ballet as its own production (i.e., not merely performed within an opera) was performed less in the opera houses or legitimate theatres as in the 1840s, and more often in the music halls and "palaces of varieties" of Paris. For example, only a handful of ballets were produced at the Paris Opéra between 1875 and 1905, with its dancers appearing in Opéra *divertissements*, while hundreds were produced at the Folies-Bergère and other music halls. By the 1890s, the lines between "high art" represented by the Opéra and the Opéra-Comique and the leading music halls became less rigid. The fact that choreographers and composers moved between the Opéra-Comique and the Folies Bergère reveals ballet's decline as an exclusive high art for the haute-bourgeoisie.[27] Such theatrical spaces attracted a wider audience by allotting space to poorer classes. Dance historian Ivor Guest notes that "filling the cheaper parts of the houses in ever increasing numbers were clerks and shop assistants, soldiers and workers, who lacked artistic pretensions and cultural background, and were unimpressed by academic conventions and classical allusions."[28] In other words, there was a disintegration of a discriminating audience. Ballet declined into a primarily eroticized entertainment. As such, men all but disappeared from the ballet stage and women took on men's roles *en travesti*, which intensified the erotic aspect of ballet performances. By the late nineteenth century, ballet had evolved into a feminized, eroticized, and often popular entertainment.

Thus, when Serge Diaghilev introduced the Russian ballet to Western Europe in 1909, he did so at a time when ballet, at its peak in Russia, was in decline in Western Europe. Without a doubt, Serge Diaghilev's introduction of his innovative Russian ballet company into France had a significant impact on ballet across Europe and America. Diaghilev aimed to expose modern Russian national culture to the West through ballet.[29] Diaghilev was part of a late nineteenth-century Russian "revival" movement that had grown out of the conflict between those who believed that Russia should define itself in Western terms and those who thought that a return to and rediscovery of Russian heritage was best for the nation. This movement can be seen as a rejection of the policies of Peter the Great, with his emphasis on secularization and Westernization, as well as an affirmation of national heritage. During the last decades of the nineteenth century, as revival artists searched for new modes of expression, a new cultural movement called the World of Art led to the appearance of the Russian avant-garde.[30] As a core member of the World of Art group, Serge Diaghilev decided to open a window to Russia in Paris.

The Ballets Russes could not have come to Paris at a better time, and Diaghilev, as a creative visionary, would have been fully aware of this. Paris was perceived as the cultural capital of Europe at the end of the nineteenth and beginning of the twentieth centuries. During the Belle Époque or "Golden Age" (1871–1914), Paris emerged as the cultural capital of the Western world and was perceived as the epitome of modernity. In this period, Paris, known as the "City of Light," drew in a variety of entertainments, witnessed innovations in theatre, and hosted a number of grand exhibitions. It would become the world capital of fashion, art, literature, and entertainment. Thus the capital emanated a new cultural and intellectual energy. If one was a writer or artist, Paris was the place to be.[31]

The Belle Époque can also be seen as the dawn of consumer society and mass culture. Although Haussmanization had expelled the *classes laborieuses* to the fringes of the city, leaving central Paris overwhelmingly middle class, spaces of consumption were available to all. Café-concerts, music halls, dance palaces, and cabarets were mostly inexpensive and often drew in members of various social classes. Such spectacles in Paris, in the words of Johannes Willms, were "society's way of coping with the deeply disturbing alienation of modern life."[32] Places like Montmartre and the Moulin Rouge soon gained a reputation far beyond France's borders. The grand expositions held in Paris served as spectacles as well as national propaganda and often served as markers of historical change.[33] The exposition of 1878 represented the apparent political stability of the republic, the victory of the republic over supporters of royalist restoration; the 1889 exposition coincided with the centennial of the French Revolution; and the 1900 exposition was held not only at the beginning of a new century, but also after the conclusion of the Dreyfus affair.[34] Each exposition drew in hordes of foreign tourists, who then carried the reputation of Paris (or a mythologized version of it) with them across the globe.

Cautiously presenting first Russian art, then Russian music, and later Russian opera to Parisian crowds, Diaghilev made his breakthrough in the Parisian scene with his Russian ballet troupe. Aware that Paris was a place in which there existed different definitions of what was modern, Diaghilev offered his own vision of modernism through dance production. He brought to Paris a reinvented "Russian" form of ballet that experimented with modernism. Debuting the work of Russian choreographer and dancer Michel Fokine in 1909, Diaghilev had secured a continuing program of productions in Paris by 1911. By 1914, he had managed to both forge and sustain a new cultivated and heterogeneous ballet audience consisting of not only the aristocracy, but also the "haute bourgeoisie" and demimonde.[35] The financial backers of the Ballets Russes (a significant portion from the aristocracy) came from the "liberal" Right: philosophically and economically liberal but, unlike those of the Left, conservative in basic social conceptions. These included many female figures who controlled the Paris social and intellectual scene in the late nineteenth and early twentieth centuries, such as the Marquise de Ganay (née Haber), the Comtesse de Greffuhle, the Comtesse de Béarn, the Comtesse de Chévigne, and the Princesse de Polignac (née Winnaretta Singer – the American sewing machine heiress who married into the French aristocracy).[36]

The Ballets Russes also managed to permeate both high and popular culture as an entertainment. Ballets Russes productions were performed in both traditional and non-traditional venues –on the variety and concert stage and at the Paris Opéra. Diaghilev's company was able to influence not only haute couture fashion but also popular trends across Europe. In fact, the first mass-media ballet stars led to the emergence of a "ballet consciousness" on both sides of the Atlantic through their endorsements of beauty products; creations of fashion in hair, hats, and coats; participation in feature films; and even having social dances named after them. This is important because it reveals that ballet, like art, literature, fashion, music, and film, penetrated many aspects of daily life and thereby shaped ideals of femininity and masculinity. The "celebrity status" of the prima ballerina or ballerino (e.g., Anna Pavlova, Tamara Karsavina, Vaslav Nijinsky, or Serge Lifar) was used in the popular marketing and publicity of the ballet company and in order to promote the ballet as an important cultural institution.[37] This in itself was a modern concept of advertising for ballet production.

Diaghilev not only contributed to the revitalization of ballet as a reputable cultural institution in France, but also revolutionized it as a performing art that fused together painting, music, dance, and drama. His company created innovations in choreography, set and costume design, and music and altered perceptions of musical theatre, ballet, and the dramatic stage. Diaghilev eventually managed to attract artistic collaborations with artists and designers such as Picasso, Dalí, Miró, Derain, Dufy, Matisse, Stravinsky, Gucci, and Chanel. Each collaborator contributed to the broadening of the concept of ballet and brought about a new conception of theatre and dance divorced from traditional ballet. Collaborators such as Jean Cocteau went beyond the boundaries of what a ballet was considered to be in the early 1900s by proposing new ways in which music, sets, and movements could be used in ballets.

Diaghilev's Russian ballet company also managed to re-establish the male dancer as a figure of importance in ballet as well as to revive masculine beauty in dance, although in an entirely new way.[38] Innovations in choreography for the male dancer brought virility and a new athleticism to the male dancer role. In addition to a newfound virtuosity for the male dancer, the very "Russianness" of Diaghilev's male dancers presented them as less tainted by civilization and more in touch with their "natural masculinity." If the attribute of grace returned as an important criterion for ballet dancers, it did so with a particular gender distinction. The recognition of the virtuosity of Russian male dancers occurred at a time when French masculinity was in crisis. Furthermore, the new appreciation for athleticism of male dancers reflects the physical culture movement emerging in this period. At the same time, male dancers such as Nijinsky were often described as androgynous in that they displayed a spectacle of male sexuality and expressed sensuality and sensitivity (conventionally feminine) yet with extraordinary strength and dynamism (conventionally masculine). An examination of the changing status of the male dancer thus offers a unique opportunity to consider shifting notions about masculinity and male sexuality.[39]

As one can see, the history of ballet in France is complex yet rich territory for historical research. Ballet originated in France, developed further in Russia, and was modernized on its return to the country of origin. In this respect, ballet is an excellent example of a powerful artistic and cultural exchange between nations. French dancer and choreographer Marius Petipa brought to Russia the artistry of French classical ballet, and, later, Serge Diaghilev brought to France Russian innovations in ballet production. With its mythologized representation of Russia, its virtuosic dancers, its incorporation of symphonic music, and its collaborations with the avant-garde, French audiences became captivated again by ballet performance, as presented by a foreign (i.e., Russian) troupe. Within this context, ballet's history is complicated further by the fact that ballet re-entered the cultural consciousness of Western Europe and gained international allure between 1909 and 1938 – a period when notions about the body, athleticism, nationalism, race, gender, sexuality, politics, and the arts were being radically rethought and transformed not only in France, but also internationally. Certainly, these transformations influenced the reception of the Ballets Russes in Paris and abroad, and allowed for a new appreciation for the art of ballet.

With such a rich history, it is not surprising that early twentieth-century critics and intellectuals found so much to talk about in their discussions of ballet after the arrival of the Ballets Russes. Thereafter, ballet criticism played a key role in the course ballet took in France. In fact, the lasting success of the Ballets Russes was indebted to the overwhelming number of positive critical reviews. Indeed criticism had a particularly important influence on artistic productions at the turn of the century. As Wesley Shrum points out in *Fringe and Fortune: The Role of Critics in High and Popular Art* (1996), criticism of the performing arts tends to interact with the art directly "either through the performers, by changing their orientation to their work; or through the audience, by promoting exposure and knowledge."[40] In other words, critical reviews that occur before the end of the performance run can potentially influence the creative process of revising it. However, criticism can also shut down a production. Thus we find a "triangle of mediation" among critics, artists, and spectators.[41]

Ballet criticism must be seen in this light. The French press played a crucial role in the lasting success and praise of the Ballets Russes troupe by attempting to reintegrate ballet as an acceptable art form in France at a time when ballet was in severe decline. Ballet audiences and financial supporters (subscribers) read and engaged in the debates and discussions that surfaced in reviews. Moreover, the successful reception of the Ballets Russes in Paris offered the company the credibility it needed to later tour around the globe and to establish regular programs in Paris and Monte Carlo.

Émigrés also played a crucial role in shaping public opinion of ballet in France. For example, Russian émigrés contributed not only to the cultural life of France, but also to the development of French modern aesthetics. In their capacities as critics, artists, directors, and patrons, they cultivated a public taste for ballet (and, one can argue, for dance in general). Diaghilev and Fokine brought a "new ballet" to Paris that was infused with modernism; Nijinsky demonstrated that male dancers could be both graceful, beautiful, and athletic; Debussy, Roerich, Satie, and Stravinsky's symphonic music became a permanent feature of ballet production; and the designs of Léon Bakst and Natalia Goncharova inspired Parisian fashion. Russian émigré André Levinson, considered the first professional dance critic, embarked on a crusade to educate the public on ballet and the workings of the Paris Opéra Academy. In fact, as we will see, Levinson played a key role in the French quest to reclaim ballet. Russian émigré Serge Lifar was also committed to remaking French ballet and eventually managed to revitalize the Paris Opéra ballet. In tracing the dedicated efforts of these two émigrés, I highlight the role of foreigners in the construction of national symbols. Through an analysis of the dance writings of Levinson and Lifar, this study shows the ways in which émigrés served as effective vehicles for the transfer of foreign aesthetics and how their commentary offers a unique perspective on the transformations, anxieties, and offerings of Parisian life in this period. By examining the role of the émigré in shaping French modern tastes, this study reveals the hybridity of modern European culture and aesthetics (the internationalization of modern aesthetics) as well as the diasporic tendencies of early twentieth-century Europe. My approach to this study is, therefore, predicated on an understanding of the interaction among an international circle of public intellectuals, the theatregoing public, and contemporary attitudes concerning nation, politics, gender, and art.

POLITICS, MODERNITY, AND ANXIETY FROM THE FIN DE SIÈCLE TO THE INTERWAR YEARS

This book is about France, about what the arrival of a foreign troupe, the Ballets Russes, meant to the people at the turn of the century and why the revitalization of French ballet became so important to them. It is critical to consider the timing of the Ballets Russes' arrival to answer these questions. At the turn of the nineteenth century, French ballet was at its deepest state of decline as an exclusively haute-bourgeois institution. This apparent decline of ballet accompanied a more generalized crisis in French culture. At the end of the nineteenth century, France's Second Empire had suddenly fallen, the country was bitterly divided over the Dreyfus affair, and the French struggled to deal with the anxieties prompted by changing gender identities. France experienced a destabilization of culture that fostered both anxieties and coping mechanisms. Historians have pointed out the ways in which the fin de siècle was a period of either "cultural crisis" or a "belle époque."[42] Some historians, such as Mary Louise Roberts, have shown how it was both simultaneously. Certainly, during the fin de siècle, anxieties arose over depopulation, racial degeneration, feminism (the "New Woman"), labour unrest, political scandals, sexual transgressions, and the overall health of the French nation. At the same time, Paris was growing an international reputation as a major cultural centre as the "City of Light." The Belle Époque was a period of tremendous artistic production, creativity, mass consumption, popular entertainment, innovation, and pleasure. As Roberts rightly notes, there existed "a mix of crisis and amusement."[43] This cultural contradiction was reflected in the response to the arrival of the Ballets Russes. While this foreign company fuelled fears of national degeneration already circulating in France, it also nourished Paris's reputation as a vibrant and dynamic cultural and artistic centre.

At the end of the nineteenth century and in the early twentieth century, French cultural identity was fragile. This was a time when France questioned its traditions and sought to redefine what cultural values were French. As historians have highlighted, there was a transformation of political culture during and after the Dreyfus affair. The scandal prompted by Dreyfus's trial and ultimate exoneration raised questions about French identity and the nation's political and moral values. Culture became an important political battleground in which these issues were contested. It was within this context that during the Third Republic republicans turned to cultural production to delineate a coherent French identity. While they attempted to transform grand opera and dramatic theatre to serve new republican interests and tastes at the end of the century, it was not until the arrival of the Ballets Russes to the Parisian scene that they began to consider the cultural role that the ballet could play in the Third Republic. While the republic was more or less secure politically by the early years of the twentieth century, culture remained contested ground – especially, after the First World War. The domain of culture thus became "a form of political intervention" and cultural criticism a means through which to assert a pure and true essence of France on the part of the Left and the Right. Writers of the Far Right especially aimed "to prove that the Left had no monopoly on 'intelligence'" in France.[44] From the Dreyfus affair to the end of the Second World War, the Right increasingly focused its attention on the arena of culture and on the project of constructing the idea of a "True France." These critics believed that their construction of a coherent and hegemonic French identity would lead to national renewal.[45] This attempt to create a distinct and exclusive identity for France became the chief strategy for conservative cultural thought and practice. Thus the French (particularly, the political Right) turned to culture and the arts in an attempt to delineate a hegemonic national identity.

Music and art historians have shown how prominent members of both the Left and the Far Right were deeply concerned with the relationship between national ideology and artistic values.[46] They have addressed the ways in which nationalist objectives helped to transform "the criteria of aesthetic legitimacy and thus critical standards."[47] In other words, turning to the arts to express national qualities involved a renegotiation of aesthetic standards. For example, both art critics and nationalist writers argued for a return to tradition and an embrace of classicism as the French national style.[48] They then identified "Classic Masters" as exemplars of a unified tradition based on a national mythology of the nation. In doing so, they "inscribed their works and styles with a 'national' significance."[49]

Recent scholarship on music has shown the way in which music and politics were entangled at the end of the nineteenth century in France. In particular, Jane F. Fulcher's innovative study of French cultural politics and music addresses the decisive moment during and after the Dreyfus affair when musical culture became particularly politicized.[50] However, analysis of the impact of nationalist cultural initiatives on discussions of French ballet in this period has not yet been addressed by historical scholarship. Just as the music world became polarized by politics, ballet rhetoric, as we shall see, became equally penetrated by political ideologies, at times just as overtly and directly.

This study, however, does not attempt to "fit" culture into narrow political categories. I have, therefore, avoided framing my central questions too rigidly in terms of French politics or even French national identity. Dance in the early twentieth century touched many levels of society, and, as I show, critics certainly responded in ways that bear on themes of politics and nationalism. However, my discussion of Diaghilev, the Ballets Russes, and the symbolists shows implicitly, and at times explicitly, that there were important cultural currents that rejected such associations for "true art": for example, Diaghilev's formulation of the only relevant nationalism being unconscious, or Mallarmé's notion of art being for the elite and not the vulgar masses. The role that politics, ideologies, and nationalism played in the promotion of ballet is thus only one part of a broader story that examines the development of French cultural and artistic values in the early twentieth century. In other words, fashioning ballet for a republican France was merely one problematic with which critics of ballet were faced. This more expansive analysis of ballet commentary enriches the relevance (and accuracy) of my discussions of dance while also allowing me to include the more narrow political responses of critics.

Thus it is important to address the nebulous relationship between national character and republican political form. While political factions often claimed particular values as their own, they also embraced similar ones, for example, the reverence of physical culture and neoclassicism during the interwar period. While I make clear that critics, including Russian émigrés Levinson and Lifar, explicitly asserted ballet as French (national character), I argue that their visions of French ballet *corresponded* with republican values (regardless of whether or not they were fervent republicans).[51] For example, Levinson's and Lifar's formalistic approach to ballet and campaigns to reveal ballet dancers as professional artists demonstrate the ways in which critics, implicitly or explicitly, attempted to "fit" dancers within French post–First World War trends of femininity and masculinity. Levinson's and Lifar's portrayal of modern ballet dancers as disciplined, dedicated, hard-working "impresarios" paralleled republican values of the interwar period that emphasized professionalism, industriousness, unity, sportsmanship, and secularism (for example, Levinson and Lifar do not bestow any religious value upon ballet, unlike Isadora Duncan). Levinson's classicism aligned him with the classical revival movements in the late 1910s and 1920s, with the efforts of the highly influential republican journal *La Nouvelle Revue Française*, run by André Gide, Henri Ghéon, and Jacques Rivière, all of whom wanted to restore classical values such as clarity and purity to French art and criticism. In this context, we can see how Levinson's rhetoric on ballet related to the intellectual currents of the day that were espoused by republicans.

What is clear is that critics drew upon (whether explicitly or implicitly) both national and republican values to promote and legitimize ballet and its dancers. In this respect, I contend that critics "refashioned ballet *for* a modern democratic republic" rather than arguing that they "refashioned ballet *as* a modern democratic form." In the former case, the political intentions of dance experts are less significant than their ability to promote a ballet that appealed to modern tastes and to advocate for governmental support (at the time, in the hands of a republican government). For example, while some French critics lamented that a superior ballet troupe was impossible in a democratic country (due to its aristocratic tradition), Levinson insisted that ballet was apolitical and could thus coexist with any political ideology. In doing so, Levinson was able to separate ballet from its traditional political affiliations (monarchical), while heralding its national (French) artistic origins. Moreover, he suggested that ballet could flourish in a democratic republic and that it did not necessarily depend on a court for its success. In 1939, it was a republican government that took over the financing of the Paris Opéra ballet, France's leading ballet company. This is significant because it shows how the French republican government could reconfigure an institution once deeply associated with aristocratic culture and customs. The following pages reveal the process by which French ballet was deemed compatible with a French republic by 1939 and how that compatibility was, in part, shaped by foreigners.

As this book explores how cultural anxiety in France informed critics' desire to reclaim ballet as French and to reshape it as a modern art form, it also explores the reasons why attitudes towards the French professional dancer's body (female and male) changed from those who stigmatized it as degenerative and monstrous to those who celebrated it for its artistry, athleticism, and representation of French republican identities. Unlike French music, which was experiencing a revival at the end of the nineteenth century (e.g., Debussy, Fauré, and others), French ballet was in a state of serious decline. First, ballet was no longer exclusively performed at the Opéra, but was now also found in the music halls and boulevard theatres. Second, its components (choreography, set design, and music) had eroded into mediocrity. Third, ballet was now perceived as an erotic entertainment for the bourgeoisie and petite bourgeoisie. The absence of men on stage, which necessitated the use of cross-dressing by female dancers, and the increasing shortening of the tutu to reveal the knees, all fuelled the eroticization of ballet performance. With increased anxieties concerning the degenerative body, the female dancer became an object of scorn for some critics. The reception of Degas's now-famous statuette *Little Dancer Aged Fourteen*, at the Sixth Impressionist Exhibition in 1881 is a good example of the polemics generated by the image of a dancer at an art exhibition. As we have seen, the statue was described by some as a "girl-monkey," a "monster," and "repulsive," belonging in a museum of zoology rather than an art exhibition.[52] In this state of decline, ballet was not recognized for its potential to symbolize republican values. The key to understanding why and how critics reshaped perceptions of ballet and its dancers lies in the changing attitudes in France towards the performing body, the dancing body, and the body in general.

At the end of the nineteenth century, there was a shift in the way bodies, particularly women's bodies, were presented on French stage. Female actresses, for example, gained a new professionalism and acquired a new aura of glamour. As Lenard Berlanstein has shown, theatre actresses in France came to signify republican ideas of femininity between 1880 and 1914. Rather than existing as symbols of temptation ("daughters of Eve") or as unruly women who had power over men, actresses were seen as capable of representing republican femininity on the French stage. One major factor for this change was the transformation of theatre audiences from predominantly male to both female and male, a phenomenon that occurred also in ballet audiences. As Berlanstein suggests, female audience members also consumed images of actresses but in an entirely different way. Berlanstein reveals how journalists had to "sanitize" actresses' lives to make them models of propriety.[53] Actresses gained the power to influence trends in fashion, inspire literature, and even to endorse mass-produced products. Sarah Bernhardt, for example, endorsed Peale beauty products and La Diaphane hair products and perfume.[54] We find a similar phenomenon occurring in the 1900s with the Ballets Russes' ballerinas and later in the 1930s and 1940s with the Paris Opéra's *étoiles* (stars). Thus the theatre, like the department store, became a space in which women could be active consumers. In the process, the new status of the leading actress as an "upright" bourgeois woman became a "marketable commodity."[55] In sum, the French found a way to reconcile femininity and achievement or, in the words of Berlanstein, "normalize achieving women."[56] This would play a central role in how critics discussed ballet dancers and their attempts to de-eroticize and legitimize them as professional artists.

The shift in French social and cultural attitudes towards social dancing in the early twentieth century is also important to consider. This shift deeply affected the reputation, popularity, and appreciation of ballet. In fact, this period witnessed a renaissance of dance as a public social pastime. For example, the jazz movement in Paris necessitated the establishment of dance halls and dance schools and reshaped national consciousness of dance, particularly, gender and sexuality in dance. It should be noted, however, that the connotations of this development in popular dance and ballet are not necessarily the same. In turn, the 1920s saw a profusion of ballets inspired by jazz, with ballet dancers even doing the Charleston on pointe.[57] Furthermore, the audience for ballet and social dancing overlapped for the first time (e.g., in 1911 and 1912: ballet and tango). By the 1930s, Paris had become *the* dance centre of Europe – with free dance, modern dance, and social dance all in circulation. This new exposure to dance certainly influenced critical responses to ballet.

Furthermore, new attitudes towards athleticism began to surface in France at the turn of the century. For the first time, exercise was encouraged for young girls rather than being seen as threatening to their reproductive health.[58] By the interwar years, sports columns appeared with increasing regularity in daily newspapers and journals, sports heroes and heroines were celebrated, and recreational sports such as tennis, hiking, cycling, golf, and European football all became popularized and commercialized. This new interest in athleticism and the body both substantiated and disrupted traditional gender boundaries. For example, French sports heroine Suzanne Lenglen, who was a nine-time champion at Wimbledon, gained national as well as international renown in the competitive sport of tennis. As she demonstrated her athletic talents, she also showcased the latest feminine styles in fashion. We will see how rhetoric on ballet celebrated this physical culture movement by emphasizing dancers' athleticism and femininity.

OLD TRADITIONS, MODERN ALTERNATIVES

Thus the turn of the twentieth century signifies a period of transition for the French. The new pace of modern life with its unprecedented changes brought a sense of instability, anxiety, yet also fascination. In attempting to assimilate with modernity, France was compelled to attempt to reconcile its past with its present. Historian Charles Rearick in *The French in Love and War* (1997) captures eloquently the amalgam of old traditions and modern visions circulating in France in the early twentieth century. In this period, he writes, "a Paris-centered popular culture supplied the nation with a mix of old familiar identities and attractive new alternatives." As people chose from "the gamut of cultural options and 'distractions,'" they found ways of "dealing with the anxieties and pains that both new and old ways of living brought." In this way, as Rearick points out, "they shaped meaning for their lives in some of the most extraordinarily dangerous times of this century."[59] Such visions fall within the greater desire among the French for stability yet transformation. As this study will show, intellectuals used ballet as a platform upon which to work out definitions of French modern identity (particularly, the reconciliation of tradition and modernity) in this period of instability.

Among the "gamut of cultural options," there were certainly many foreign images that circulated in France, particularly within the cosmopolitan milieu of interwar Paris. No doubt, Paris in this period was a hotbed (even *the* hotbed) of cultural transnationalism. Indeed, as scholars have shown, transnational forces played a decisive role in the construction of modern identity in this period.[60] These transnational dynamics were part and parcel of the reconfiguration of French ballet. As we will see, both the history of the Franco-Russian alliance in the late nineteenth century and the permanent emigration as a result of the Russian Revolution played an outsized role in the reshaping of "French" ballet. Furthermore, many of the processes and movements that account for the national transformation of French ballet – modernist aesthetics, the "modern girl," athleticism and new body politics, new forms of professional and work discipline, the cinema, and new kinds of celebrity – had important international and transnational dimensions. Thus transnational trends as well as local and national ones played a significant role in reshaping attitudes towards ballet and its dancers.

While transnational forces contributed to the shaping of modern French culture, they also propelled the French to locate distinctly national cultural forms, particularly in the interwar years. For example, at the turn of the century, Frenchmen were heavily influenced by the image of the "rugged man" put forth by Theodore Roosevelt and reasserted their own French version of the strong, healthy, and sportive French male body. Similarly, during the interwar years, modern ideas about French womanhood were influenced by transnational trends, such as the new images of women that circulated in Hollywood (e.g., images of Marlene Dietrich). This certainly contributed to the shaping of modern French women's identities while also inspiring a distinct French version of emancipated womanhood (in a country that had withheld suffrage after the First World War). In highlighting the connections between the national and the international in the case of ballet, I trace not only how foreign influences paved the way for new images of ballet and its dancers, but also how these very transnational forces incited Parisian critics to assert their own distinctly "French" vision of them. By showing how transnational influences are mediated by claims of national authenticity in the case of ballet in France, this study uses concepts of transnationalism, while also deconstructing them in order to reveal the ways they reinforced the national.

In a desperate attempt to revive high culture, France turned to ballet to serve as an important tool for the project of national and cultural renewal. The intellectual project to revive French ballet, however, faced several challenges and problems that intellectuals had to address. In France, critical discussions of ballet often centred on whether or not ballet's historical roots could be reconciled with modern life; tradition with modern values and tastes. Critics pondered how a decadent art, captive to traditions and sexual and gender stereotypes could be transformed into a modernist art form that combined the best of traditional French technique with contemporary innovations in choreography, set design, music, and staging. Debates raged over whether French ballet could serve as a republican cultural institution. Discussions also took place about the aesthetic function of ballet and whether it should serve as a collaborative art or as a purely choreographic one. Critics debated how a French modern aesthetic might be forged. Lastly, criticism of ballet reflected the changing attitudes towards the body (particularly, the performing body) and served as a vehicle through which critics could attempt to "professionalize" both the male and female dancer. Thus the challenges that intellectuals faced in reviving French ballet rested on ballet's connection to politics, modern aesthetics, gender identity, and the body.

The following chapters reveal the ways in which discourse on ballet was part of a broader quest on the part of the French to delineate French modern values at a time when French values were ambiguous and unstable. Discussions of ballet on the part of bourgeois critics and intellectuals revolved around three central themes: national identity, modern aesthetics, and gender ideology. For the purpose of organization, this book presents these themes as a series of layers, each one building upon the next with the understanding that all are interconnected. Each chapter presents criticism that exemplifies how critics and choreographers alike were experimenting in shaping new criteria for ballet and working out of contemporary cultural contexts. In addition, each chapter will show how constructions of gender and ballet were (as they still are) tightly bound to each other.

Chapter 1 traces the development of ballet criticism in bourgeois newspapers and journals in the nineteenth and early twentieth centuries. It discusses the prominent journals in which ballet commentary appeared, some of the major critics reviewing and writing on the ballet, and those institutions and agendas directing them. This chapter analyzes the role that criticism played in French culture in this period, its position as a "mediator" between the French public and art forms, and its influence in shaping public opinion and French values. While ballet criticism published in bourgeois journals began as the domain of men, it eventually fell into the hands of women as ballet aesthetics were valued differently and as women were increasingly recognized for their expertise in dance as accomplished artists themselves. I demonstrate this shift by analyzing the link between the types of critics who held authority over ballet (as reviewers and commentators) and the changing status of the art form. Chapter 1 aims to bring to light the broad range of Parisian critics and intellectuals writing on ballet by the early twentieth century and how the status of their positions helped to cultivate a new public taste for ballet.

Chapter 2 introduces the response of critics and intellectuals to the Ballets Russes upon its arrival in 1909. While the Ballets Russes' use of symphonic music initially drew prominent music critics to review ballet in bourgeois journals, the company's ability to fuse tradition with modernism also intrigued critics. The Ballets Russes reflected its inheritance of French classical technique (through the classical training of its Russian dancers) and its rebellion against classical tradition (through its modernist productions). Critics became absorbed in this duality. Moreover, while the Ballets Russes performed "classical" Romantic ballets (e.g., *Swan Lake*, *Les sylphides*, and *Giselle*), it also performed avant-garde ballets that dismantled practically everything the French public associated with classical ballet: its aristocratic and courtly traditional associations; its solidarity as a feminine art form and female space; its use of tutus, pointe shoes, and straightbacks. Even its music changed. Intellectuals and critics in France began to ponder whether French ballet could embrace the new nationalist and artistic possibilities of ballet exemplified by the Ballets Russes. Critics debated whether French ballet could reconcile its courtly tradition with modern life. While some critics thought ballet could be "democratized" to serve the republic, others were more pessimistic, seeing ballet as an art of the past that could only serve the needs of a court. By contextualizing critical responses to the Ballets Russes within the cultural anxieties of early twentieth-century France, we can understand what compelled critics and intellectuals to inquire whether French ballet could also embody both tradition and modernity and become, once, again, a quintessential representation of the haute-bourgeoisie.

Chapter 3 analyzes the process by which critics, intellectuals, and dance figures re-envisioned ballet to serve French modern tastes and the tensions involved in reconciling tradition with modernity, and foreign influence with French tradition. Intellectuals struggled to reconcile ballet's various historical incarnations with its original French roots while at the same time attempting to make it compatible with modern French republican values. By contextualizing commentary on ballet within the greater search on the part of the French to create a coherent French national identity, we can see the way in which ballet served as a cultural force in shaping Frenchness in this period. This analysis of ballet commentary also illuminates the connections between the national and the transnational by tracing how transnational influences are interpreted in national and local contexts. The chapter reveals the ways in which Opéra directors Jacques Rouché and Serge Lifar managed to reform the Paris Opéra and revive French ballet and how their writings about and actions dealing with ballet reflected the society around them.

Chapter 4 details how the arrival of the Ballets Russes in Paris incited a plethora of commentary about ballet's nature as an art form. It situates critical responses to the Ballets Russes' "new ballet" within broader discussions about modern aesthetics and French tastes. In doing so, we will see that commentary on ballet was both a reflection of and a powerful force in shaping the artistic climate of France in the early twentieth century. The chapter begins by tracing the aesthetic development of ballet in France from its origins to its institutional and aesthetic decay in the nineteenth century. Through a historical contextualization of nineteenth-century ballet criticism, we will see the reasons why ballet languished as a high cultural form and thus lost its respectability as an art form by the end of the nineteenth century. The chapter then turns to the marvel of the Ballets Russes and how it intoxicated Parisian spectators with its Russian modernism and collaborative visions of ballet production. The chapter presents the modern aesthetic of ballet put forth by the Ballets Russes, analyzes the response by critics and intellectuals, and introduces the debates that it spawned over the direction ballet was taking. The arrival of the Ballets Russes incited many artistic and intellectual figures to reconsider the artistic potential of ballet. Echoing the aesthetic concerns raised during the Enlightenment over whether the purpose of dance was to express ideas or to be merely decorative, early twentieth-century critics engaged in similar discussions of whether modern ballet should be valued for its ability to express ideas, its collaborative potential (e.g., its dependence on symphonic music and dramatic expression), or its autonomous formal qualities (e.g., choreography and dancing). As this chapter will show, these dialogues were deeply shaped by changing attitudes regarding art's relation to nationalism, modernism, and the body. They were also influenced by transnational trends in modern aesthetics.

Chapter 5 revisits the dance writings of the leading personalities involved in refashioning ballet for a modern democratic state. It examines the use of ballet to delineate a coherent French national identity, but now through the debates over its aesthetic nature. Through an analysis of ballet commentary, we will see how intellectual and artistic figures attempted to create a distinct French style that could reflect French classical tradition yet suit modern tastes. Modern conceptions of ballet espoused by some bourgeois critics differed from those of the Ballets Russes. The very reduction of choreographic autonomy imposed by the Ballets Russes, for example, had stimulated inquiries into the true nature of dance. By examining the aesthetic debates that arose in major bourgeois journals and newspapers, this chapter shows how a new "dance for dance's sake" ideology surfaced in France that found itself deeply invested in French cultural politics. Thus, similar to what was happening in French music and art, French ballet fell within the broader French trend of self-fashioning. Chapter 5 describes the efforts of Serge Lifar, director of the Paris Opéra ballet, to develop a prestigious national French style of ballet grounded on the vocabulary and discipline of the Russian tradition. The implementation of a distinctly French modern ballet aesthetic (one based in choreographic autonomy and corporeal expression) can, therefore, be envisioned as having self-consciously played a role in the rhetoric of the regeneration of a nation.

Yet the modernization of French ballet aesthetics posed specific problems for the French. The origins of ballet in France were associated with the ancien régime and, therefore, aristocratic decadence; modern ballet was developed by the Russians; Russian ballet gave the male dancer, once again, a new centrality upon the ballet stage. Did ballet's new association with Russian culture impede its connection to French identity or stigmatize it as an exotic world of femininity, androgyny, or homosexuality? Could the French renegotiate modern ballet aesthetics to suit the needs of republican France? While ballet production consisted of multiple aesthetic forms (music, design, choreography), it also revolved around the body of the dancer. Because of this, the politics of the body (especially, the performing body) would play a decisive role in the efforts of critics to reconceptualize and regenerate it. Why and how did intellectuals attempt to de-eroticize ballet dancers? Critics often pondered over whether French female and male dancers could embody republican virtues and thus earn respectability. They debated whether some form of French masculinity could be restored upon the ballet stage and whether the female dancer could embody some form of republican womanhood. Thus ballet would raise some different and challenging questions for those who considered how to regenerate it as a symbol of French cultural pre-eminence.

Between 1909 and 1938, prominent critics as well as dance figures, such as Serge Diaghilev, Michel Fokine, André Levinson, and Serge Lifar, engaged in discussions over the roles of men and women in ballet as they attempted to improve ballet's reputation. In fact, the artistic legitimacy of the male and female dancer was an issue frequently raised by early twentieth-century observers. This is not surprising as the reputation of dancers fluctuated throughout ballet's history in France. In retrospect, the image of the male dancer began as a chivalric and noble ideal of elite masculinity in the seventeenth and eighteenth centuries, became regarded increasingly as an embarrassment in the nineteenth century, then regained a strong presence and legitimate role on the ballet stage in the early twentieth century. Equally interesting (but not surprising) is the fluctuating image of the female dancer from having little or no presence in the ballet milieu in the seventeenth and eighteenth centuries, to becoming the epitome of femininity in the early nineteenth century, to losing all respectability in the late nineteenth century, and finally to acquiring mass adoration and emulation in the early twentieth century.[61]

Critics and intellectuals were instrumental in not only strengthening the professional status of the ballet dancer (both female and male) and the art of ballet, but also renegotiating traditional notions of the body, gender, and sexuality in French culture. They debated whether the twentieth-century dancer could embody republican ideologies of gender. In the early twentieth century, French republican attributes such as fitness/health, strength, virility, discipline/hard work, and elegance were increasingly attached to both the female and male dancer. As many critics attempted to masculinize male dancers in their reviews, they also promoted a new professionalism of the female dancer, emphasizing the amount of discipline and hard work involved in attaining technical virtuosity. In the delineation of clear gender identities on the ballet stage, the binary opposition of femininity and masculinity could be sustained (at least superficially). Thus intellectuals and critics attempted to renegotiate traditional perceptions of female and male dancers in order to make ballet an acceptable representation of republican France.

Chapters 6 and 7 explore how ballet was used as a source through which to assert a variety of notions concerning gender, the body, modernism, and the nation. These chapters look at the relationship between national ideology, modernism, professionalism, the body, gender, and the ballet. The development of a new rhetoric about male and female ballet dancers was crucial to the revitalization of ballet as a high-art form. Both chapter 6 and chapter 7 investigate several interlocking factors involved in the renegotiation of gender in modern ballet. Each addresses the changing meanings of attributes attached to ballet dancing and dancers over the years; the Ballets Russes' modernization of ballet and the new qualities of virtuosity and professionalism it presented and inspired; the ways in which intellectuals, such as André Levinson and Serge Lifar, helped to professionalize the dancing body; and finally, the transfiguration of gender ideologies and attitudes towards the corporeal body during the course of the early twentieth century, particularly in the 1920s and 1930s. As we will see, body politics played a central role in raising the status of ballet and transforming it into a vessel for showcasing French cultural pre-eminence. These body politics were shaped by both national and transnational forces. These final chapters contextualize the dancing body within the new emphasis on athleticism being embraced by the French in the 1920s. For example, we find critics increasingly emphasizing dancers' athleticism, technical grace, and virtuosity, avoiding insinuations of the sexual availability of female dancers and stressing the masculine strength of male dancers. Furthermore, these chapters examine how tastes for neoclassicism helped to foster a reconceptualization of the female and male professional dancing body. The neoclassical revival in the 1920s and 1930s, the new fervor for athleticism in both men and women, and the new comfort with the body all opened a space for a new modern aesthetic of ballet, the return of the male dancer, and a revitalized national institution: the Paris Opéra ballet.

Chapter 6 delineates how ballet was used in the early twentieth century as a vehicle through which to assert ideas about French masculinity, male corporeality, and male beauty. It examines critical discourse on ballet that engaged in debates over the place of men in ballet. There were several factors involved in the French public's acceptance of the male dancer on the French stage. These included the Ballets Russes' "new ballet," republican ideologies of gender (here masculinity), the physical culture movement and the new attitudes towards the body that it forged, and critics' and choregraphers' extensive efforts to reinstate the male dancer and to revive the beauty of the masculine form in ballet. The chapter contextualizes commentary on the male dancer within shifting ideologies concerning French masculine identity that were occurring in the early twentieth century, particularly after the First World War.

Chapter 7 continues a gender analysis of commentary on ballet but now through an examination of the female dancer. When the Ballets Russes arrived in Paris in 1909, the artistic legitimacy of the female dancer was on unstable ground as was ballet's position as a high art exclusive to the haute-bourgeoisie. This chapter considers the work of critics, intellectuals, and dance experts as they attempted to renegotiate traditional ideas about femininity, female corporeality, and women's roles in ballet. Through their laborious efforts to de-eroticize ballet, they contributed to the professionalization of the female ballet dancer in France and thus rendered the female dancer capable of embodying republican womanhood. This was possible for a number of reasons: the appearance of the Ballets Russes and the new heterogeneous audience that it fostered; the extensive commentary that the Russian company instigated; the destabilization of traditional ideologies of gender, particularly after the First World War; new attitudes towards the female body and professional achievement; and bureaucratic changes at the Opéra. As we will see, the ballet was a cultural force through which to assert ideas about women in an age of momentous change.

The French articulated a distinct national and modern identity for themselves by way of a new modern aesthetic of dance. This process was complex and multifaceted, resulting in the exposure to new forms of dance; a growing critical dialogue and debate on dance; a physical culture movement; nationalist fervour; and transformations in French aesthetics, changing gender identities, and the search for a modern national identity. Criticism of ballet engaged reactions to this revitalized art form within broader dialogues concerning modern French culture and society.

1

Parisian Intellectuals, the Press, and the Ballet

Art does not develop independently of criticism … A work of criticism inevitably reflects a response at a particular historical moment and in light of particular commitments and interests.[1]

– Francis Frascina and Charles Harrison

As the above quote suggests, criticism plays a vital role in the shaping of an art form. Criticism tells us the extent to which an art form is valued and the function it serves in a given society and time. In doing so, it reveals the cultural, political, and social weight that an art form carries in a given period. Yet critical discourse on art can also provide a great deal of information about the cultural and political climate in which it is produced. This chapter introduces the ways in which criticism served as a mediator between artistic forms and French cultural identity. The rise of the printed press in France served as the most useful instrument for the dissemination not only of critical views on the arts, but also of particular notions about France. The following chapter examines the development of ballet discourse in the periodical press from the nineteenth century through the interwar years. An understanding of the rise and politicization of "cultural criticism" is essential to analyzing this development.[2] By examining the growth and politicization of ballet criticism in France, we can see how ballet in this period was increasingly considered as not only a newsworthy element of Parisian cultural life, but also an important artistic presence in a nation that wanted to be seen as modern.

This chapter introduces many of the Parisian critics who helped to cultivate a new public taste for ballet and contributed to the reshaping of the genre. It begins by analyzing how cultural criticism emerged in French press journalism and why it was used by the

French as a vehicle for political expression in the nineteenth century. It then turns to the prominent bourgeois journals and critics involved in reviewing and discussing ballet in the early twentieth century. The chapter reveals the major periodicals and newspapers in which ballet reviews appeared; the types of critics who reviewed the ballet; the central figures involved in the promotion of ballet and their political and cultural agendas; and the imagined audience to which ballet reviews were directed. The chapter's central aim is to show the connection between the types of critics who held authority over ballet (as reviewers and commentators) and the changing status of the art form. Examining who is reviewing and writing on the ballet often reveals the status of ballet in a given period. For example, Enlightenment philosophers' engagement of dance as a subject of discussion tells us that dance held an important social and cultural role in France in the eighteenth century. When dramatic critics reviewed ballet during the Romantic era when there was an increasing privatization of the Opéra where it was mostly performed, we discover a change in the way ballet and its dancers were judged. These critics were compelled to cater to the tastes of the Opéra's male subscribers. The introduction of symphonic music in ballet and the interest that it inspired among music critics helped to elevate ballet's status as an art at the turn of the twentieth century. Furthermore, when large-distribution bourgeois daily papers such as *Le Figaro*, *Le Temps*, and *Comœdia* decided to commission "dance experts" (Russian émigrés no less) to review and comment on ballet in the 1920s, we can see a new legitimacy and importance given to ballet as an art form in France.[3]

Studies on art criticism have shed light on the various roles criticism played in modern France. On one level, criticism served to measure a work of art's worth, originality, intent, prominence, innovation, or disruption of paradigms, to reflect "broader changes in style, and to point out the qualities that a work or artist shared with a specific "period style."[4] However, criticism also served as a social and discursive practice. As art historians such as T.J. Clark emphasize, criticism supplied a connection between art and the socio-political relations of a given historical moment.[5] They have stressed "the complex role that art criticism played in negotiating the relationship between culture, on the one hand, and a range of social and ideological formations, on the other."[6] As Michael R. Orwicz asserts, "criticism acquires the status of sign, illuminating or reflecting a body of deeper social concerns that are somehow 'revealed' in what often tends to be labeled as 'the critics' 'anxieties,' 'confusion' or 'silences' when confronting [art]."[7] In this light, criticism is not merely a response to art, but also an effect of other cultural and social processes. This book rests on the understanding that criticism, as discourse, is "a historically constituted representational and signifying practice."[8] Criticism is permeated by political, social, economic, and cultural conditions that shape "its content, form, and the very object of criticism."[9] The language of criticism thus becomes a key site that draws in a multiplicity of discourses – aesthetic, cultural, social, political, sexual, scientific, literary, and so forth. As we will see throughout this book, criticism on ballet served as a vortex into which a variety of contested, controversial, or celebrated values could be drawn. Through an analysis of ballet criticism, the book reveals how ballet emerged as a cultural force in early twentieth-century France. We will see in subsequent chapters how critical discourse on ballet reflected, substantiated, and, at times, challenged French values, many of which were in flux and ambiguous, especially after the First World War.

THE POLITICIZATION OF CULTURAL CRITICISM

The rise of cultural criticism is important to consider as its politicization grew out of censorship of the press at the turn of the nineteenth century. In other words, cultural criticism became a surrogate for overt political criticism. In the early years of the nineteenth century, when there were systems of censorship and surveillance of the Parisian press, the new press laws exempted from censorship "any journals devoted exclusively to the sciences, the arts, literature, commerce, or announcements and advertisements."[10] As art historian Susan L. Siegfried points out, this reveals that anything "cultural" was seen as "politically neutral" and "non-threatening." This period witnessed a proliferation of specialized cultural, scientific, and commercial journals. Siegfried notes that "with more than sixty journals under publication during the Napoleonic period, fewer than one third carried political news." The thirteen newspapers that were officially licensed to print political news "expanded their coverage to include articles on theatre, literature, the arts, the sciences, philosophy, and religion."[11] Thus we find a new variety of news coverage where the "cultural supplement" or the *feuilleton* was appended into a separate section of the newspaper, distinct from the "important" political and military news.[12] This is an indication that "culture" was deemed distinct from political life and foreign affairs.

The nineteenth-century *Journal des Débats* adopted this formula. However, the *feuilleton* proved to be anything but politically neutral. The *Journal des Débats* gained quite a reputation for its *feuilleton* and the politics that emanated from its pages. One of its most celebrated critics was Julien-Louis Geoffroy. Geoffroy's criticism covered such a wide range of the arts that he was eventually adorned the title of "king of the feuilleton." Geoffroy's criticism offers a good example of the ways in which the *feuilleton* became infused with politics. Geoffroy began his career under the *ancien régime*, writing for the royalist newspaper the *Ami du Roi* (Friend of the King) established in 1790.[13] His criticism of the arts in the *Journal des Débats* often embraced political sentiment, in this case, royalist bias. In many of his writings, Geoffroy glorified seventeenth-century French culture and claimed that the best French literature and theatre had been produced under the absolute monarchy of Louis XIV. As Siegfried points out, this sentiment, while reviving an image of absolutist authority (desired by Napoleon), was "much to the dismay of Bonapartists who insisted on the Revolutionary origins of the regime."[14]

Another *Débats* critic, Jean-Baptiste-Bon Boutard, became the most influential professional art critic in the early nineteenth century. In fact, his articles were referred to as "the Gospel of the feuilleton ... the divine feuilleton ... the infallible feuilleton."[15] His criticism also offers an example of the politicization of aesthetic values in the *feuilleton* in the early years of the nineteenth century. Also keeping a low profile during the French Revolution, Boutard revealed his conservative politics through his criticism in the *feuilleton*. In his articles, he attacked the "left-liberal leanings" of the aesthetic criticism of Enlightenment philosophers such as Denis Diderot.[16] Thus political criticism was expressed under the guise of cultural criticism within the pages of the *feuilleton*. As Siegfried notes, criticism of culture published in this period in journals such as the *Journal des Débats*, the *Mercure de France*, the *Publiciste*, and *La Presse* served "as a surrogate for the free expression of political opinion."[17] The *Journal des Débats* became a model for this new type of professional journalism that served as a forum for the exchange of ideas, accountable to the reading public.

Eventually, the *Journal des Débats* acquired the most extensive circulation of all French daily papers.[18] However, the journal, like many other papers, was also shaped by a new and highly competitive free market of publishing.

Journals and newspapers, especially mass-circulating presses, were driven by market strategies that affected what topics were covered and, moreover, how they were conveyed. The pressures of the market motivated many papers, including the *Journal des Débats,* to encourage specialization in reporting, including that in the *feuilleton.* As a result, the credentials of the critic shifted. Increasingly, the authority of critics rested on their extensive exposure and even minimal practice of the art that they were reviewing. As Siegfried notes regarding art critics, "after 1800 we begin to see a new breed of art critic; not merely a man of letters who dabbled in criticism in art, this new critic had some kind of professional artistic training, while not necessarily a practicing artist himself."[19]

The evolution of specialization in journalism is deeply connected to the status of the art form that was the object of criticism.[20] In the early nineteenth century, painting, sculpture, and architecture were perceived as the loftiest of arts, and thus, with the rise of press journalism, "experts" were soon brought in to critically review them. By the 1830s, art criticism had developed into a highly specialized field. Music at the turn of the century, however, was deemed only slightly more respectable than dance. Dramatic critic Geoffroy, who wrote on both dance and music, referred to music as "a mere distraction, judged not by the soul, but only the ear." According to Geoffroy, "music was also along with dance, an art which could easily be manipulated by the state in service of a showcase genre, that of grand opera."[21] Thus Geoffroy saw music and most of its composers as "lacking the dignity of artistic autonomy." Artistic autonomy, according to many literary critics, rested on an art's ability to represent something outside of its formal qualities. As one critic asked, "From where, then, does the anonymous writer wish the musician to take the bases of his art, if it is not in the relation of sounds with the soul? Does he want music to be merely an insignificant song whose only goal is to amuse the ear for a while?" He then answered, "I consent to this only if music is not called an art, and that it is given, at most, the title of trade."[22]

This attitude towards music in France, however, was short-lived. The specialization of music criticism followed in the wake of the development of serious art criticism. In the late 1820s, music criticism transferred from the hands of literary critics (such as Geoffroy) to those of trained musicians who were familiar with the technical language of music. François-Henri-Joseph Blaze (known as Castil-Blaze), wrote for the musical *feuilleton* in the *Journal des Débats* between 1820 and 1832. He was trained in music at the Conservatoire de Paris and became a composer and musicologist. Castil-Blaze is often regarded as the first French music critic to have studied music. Music scholar Katherine Ellis asserts that Castil-Blaze's first article for the journal *Chronique Musicale* (7 December 1820) marks a critical moment when "French music criticism took a decisive turn towards professional status."[23] Throughout the 1820s and 1830s, figures such as Castil-Blaze and Françoise-Joseph Fétis, who was also trained as a musician, insisted that music not be judged by the irrelevant standards of men of letters. Fétis, an ambitious music critic, founded the musical journal *La Revue Musicale* in 1827 that covered a wide range of articles on music and musical life.[24] As the aesthetic of music became increasingly recognized for its technical and theoretical aspects, musicologists and music historians were commissioned to review not only music, but also opera, which was steadily being seen as a genre in its own right (particularly between 1830 and 1848). Other specialized music journals followed, including the long-running weekly *Ménestrel* (1833–1940), the prestigious *Revue et Gazette Musicale de Paris* (1834–80), and *La France Musicale* (1837–60), yet these journals reached a limited audience. Thus music aspired to gain a new voice equal to the advances made in literature or painting. The new music critic, like the art critic, would have some kind of professional artistic training. For example, musicographer Jean Lucien Adolphe Jullien (1845–1932) and conductor Alfred Bruneau (1857–1934), both of whom studied at the Paris Conservatory, contributed articles and reviews on contemporary music and opera for France's most prestigious music journals in the second half of the nineteenth century.

While this may well have been the case for art, literary, and, eventually, music critics, it was not the case for ballet critics, for whom it was "unheard of … to participate in a ballet class."[25] During the nineteenth century, reviews of ballet appeared in a variety of publications and under a variety of headings. They were featured most often in theatre, opera, and music columns of the *feuilleton* in newspapers and journals such as the *Journal des Débats*, *La Presse: Dramatique, Musicale et*

Littéraire, and *Le Moniteur*, all of which catered to a bourgeois readership. Ballet reviews were often written by dramatic critics who were literary figures (e.g., nineteenth-century poet Théophile Gautier) who had no technical training in dance. A cartoon of Gautier illustrates this point well (fig. 1.1). Not being practitioners of ballet, these critics had to confine their critical comments to what they knew best. The authority and legitimacy of critics of ballet relied on their ability to judge the literary, dramatic, or musical aspects of ballets rather than choreographic and technical ones. Reviews included detailed descriptions of plots, costumes, scenery, and the erotic charge of bodily display. Often critics were preoccupied in highlighting female dancers' "beauty," "physical voluptuousness," and "revealing costumes."[26] Serious considerations of ballet choreography in reviews were scarce and few. As a result, most nineteenth-century reviews and publications on ballet remained limited either to an overstressing of the role of the individual dancer or to glamour-slanted publicity. Therefore, unlike that of art and music, the aesthetic judgment of ballet fell almost exclusively in the hands of spectators and amateurs in the art of dance. This raises questions of the extent to which ballet criticism remained masculine, undeveloped, and lay outside "specialization" in reporting. Clearly, it did not correspond with the shifting criteria for reviewing art, literature, and music. It would take much longer for the genre of dance to be recognized for its artistic autonomy and to necessitate trained experts to review it. As we will see, this phenomenon occurred only in the early twentieth century.

At the end of the nineteenth century, press journalism would transform significantly and cultural criticism would take on a new dynamism. The Third Republic was central to the further politicization of cultural criticism in press journalism in France. In the 1870s, the Third Republic was by no means secure and the *idée républicaine* was far from being a cohesive concept.[27] The Third Republic did manage, however, to establish a free press in 1881. Republicanism and freedom of the press had become strongly intertwined in French politics over the course the century.[28] The republican commitment to the press can be seen, in the words of historian Dominique Kalifa, "in the significant role newspapers played in France's nineteenth century revolutions, and from French democracy's need for public information, civic education, and a diversity of ideas."[29] Thus parliamentary

Figure 1.1 This 1858 caricature from *Le Charivari* satirizes Gautier as a critic without professional dance expertise. The caption reads, “Monsieur Théophile Gautier himself demonstrating to Madame Ferraris the various steps of his ballet, which she has only to interpret for the public.”

deputies of the Third Republic recognized that the press was essential to the republic. While the press could serve as a vehicle through which politics could be freely expressed, it could also be used to delineate a French republican identity.

However, the relationship between the republic and the press was not as loyal as it appears, as it catered initially more to market demands than to political agendas.[30] The commercialization of the press placed new constraints on newspapers and changed their priorities.[31] Drawing in as many readers as possible became the primary objectives of presses. "The press is an industry," Albert Thibaudet wrote at the time, "before becoming a vocation."[32] This was a time when press journalism flourished. There were 2,685 periodicals in Paris alone in 1899, and, of course, the rise of the penny press across the nation (e.g., *Le Petit Parisian, Le Matin, Le Journal*) was extremely popular.[33] Although market-driven, newspapers still played an important role in encouraging democratic debate, through the guarantee of the pluralism of opinion, and, in general, supported the republic.[34] The commercialization of the press is significant because journalists were compelled to meet the demands of popular tastes to lure in profits.

However, in the last years of the century, the French press became infused with politics. The political crisis of the Dreyfus affair, beginning in 1894 and continuing until 1906, polarized the press along political lines. Novelist Émile Zola, then one of the most popular writers in France, asserted forcefully that Alfred Dreyfus was indeed innocent and a victim of corruption and anti-Semitism in the highest levels of the army. Zola published his denunciation, "*J'accuse*," in the French daily newspaper *L'Aurore* on 13 January 1898. Those who agreed with him issued a declaration of support, the "Manifesto of the Intellectuals," which was signed by nearly 7,000 writers, artists, and academics.[35] Such responses spurred a counterreaction on the part of the Far Right (e.g., Maurice Barrès). No longer a simple case of espionage, the case grew into an *affaire* that split the country. The pro-Dreyfusards consisted largely of pro-republicans who included writers, artists, and intellectuals, and the anti-Dreyfusards comprised many anti-Semites, loyal supporters of the French army, and embittered monarchists still reluctant to accept the Third Republic. Two conceptions of France emerged, creating debates, once again, over the authority of the army, Church, and nation. As Jane Fulcher writes, "political leagues, demonstrations, and petitions now thrust their way into French public life, politicizing new social groups and rending most sectors of society in France.[36] The Dreyfus affair reveals how the press was used as a vehicle through which to express competing political and cultural values. Thereafter, press journalism continued to embrace this rhetoric of politics. In fact, newspapers then (and, one can argue, still today) often clearly defined their political leanings whether it was to represent a monarchist position, a conservative republican, a radical republican, or a socialist position.

With the closure of the Dreyfus affair, which resulted in his pardon in 1899 and his exoneration in 1906, nationalists set their sights on the art world. France's artistic achievements would thus become the ideal means for furthering their concept of French identity. The highly distinguished art historian Eugène Müntz wrote in his article "L'art et la morale," "it is indispensible that painters and sculptors take account not only of the aspirations of an elite but those of the entire nation."[37] He asserted that artists could "speak a language capable of being understood by all" and could thus "apply themselves to exalting with force and clearness the sentiments which sleep in the heart of the most humble of their fellow citizens."[38] As nationalists helped to fuse French nationalist ideology with artistic values, art became a powerful tool with which to forge a "mythology" of the nation.[39]

Like art criticism, music criticism also engaged in such cultural polemics. The Dreyfus affair had also split the world of music. Wagnerism became linked with the affair and with anti-Semitism, and French composer Claude Debussy was linked to republican nationalism. Hailing the work of Debussy, critic Henri Baüer exclaimed in *Le Figaro,* "Finally someone who will liberate French music from Wagnerian oppression."[40] Music critic Pierre Lalo, writing in the most important paper in Paris, *Le Temps,* urged young composers "to emancipate themselves from the tyranny of the Wagnerian formula."[41] Although Claude Debussy claimed his neutrality among his pro-Dreyfusard friends, he became an object of attack by anti-Dreyfusards. Those from the other side criticized Debussy for ignoring the laws of musical elements and declared his music as "synonymous with 'anarchy,' 'disorder' and 'confusion'" in which the "notes only repel and detest each other."[42] Music critic Émile Vuillermoz went so far as to point out the similar initials of the names Achille-Claude Debussy and Alfred Dreyfus.[43] As music historian Jane Fulcher points out, by

1910 the polarization of politics had infiltrated music criticism, with "the Action Française as well as the Socialist Left playing lead roles."[44] In the early years of the twentieth century, the question of what constituted the "authentic" French tradition became the subject of critical debates among music critics. The particular controversy between two prominent music critics, Louis Laloy and Camille Mauclair, represents well the ways French politics penetrated the genre of music. Mauclair's politically provocative essay "La réaction nationaliste en art et l'importance de l'homme de lettres" ("The Nationalist Reaction in Art and the Importance of Men of Letters"), which appeared in the journal *Revue Mondiale* (15 January 1905), addressed directly questions of national identity and tradition. Referring to the quest on the part of politics and art to locate "origins," he explained how artistic styles had developed specific political associations in France and stressed that a political message could be encoded in style. In other words, he observed that artistic style could signify political and national meanings. Both Laloy and Mauclair wrote for musical and political journals. Among their commitments to publish reviews of music, they also reviewed the ballet. Like their music reviews, their ballet reviews were infused with political meanings. Their ballet criticism thus offers valuable insight into the cultural politics of early twentieth-century France.

THE PRESS, THE CRITICS, AND THE BALLET

In 1845, the actor Edmond Got noted, "The newspapers! Journalism! These are the powers of the moment! The greatest preoccupations of theatre is what will be said on Monday [the day reviews appeared]."[45] Got's observation reflected the dependence of theatre on critical reviews by the mid-nineteenth-century.[46] The ballet was no less vulnerable to critical opinion. In the second half of the nineteenth century, the bourgeois newspapers that had the most abundant coverage of Parisian theatrical and musical life were journals like *Le Figaro* and *Le Temps* – newspapers with a large circulation without being mass-circulation dailies. Their readership consisted mostly of the urban middle classes with above-average education and wealth. *Le Figaro* and *Le Temps* were thus founded to appeal to the better-educated, more affluent reader. *Le Figaro* (weekly from 1854, daily from 1866) and *Le Temps* (est. 1861) were both read by opinion leaders of all parties and exercised an influence far beyond that of the mass press.[47] Moreover, these journals, and others like them, played a crucial role in shaping public opinion on not just politics, but also art, music, dance, and theatre.

Le Figaro, begun as a literary paper in the 1820s and 1830s, had participated in the press campaigns leading to the fall of the Bourbon dynasty. It featured the work of George Sand, Honoré de Balzac, Gérard de Nerval, and other writers of the Romantic era. By 1866, when it became a daily, its literary and erudite style attracted contributions from figures such as Émile Zola, Pierre Loti, Paul Verlaine, and Marcel Proust. Its book and theatre reviews were of the highest quality and two of its strongest features. One can argue that *Le Figaro* was the most influential of all the newspapers in opera circles because of its subscription list, which included members of the aristocracy, wealthy bourgeoisie, diplomats, and high-ranking officers.

For its part, *Le Temps* appealed to an elite different from that of *Le Figaro* in that it was more liberal, Protestant, and to some extent more serious. Founded in 1861, it became one of the most important and prestigious national daily newspapers of the French Republic. It also gained a strong reputation for its coverage of foreign affairs through its extensive network of correspondents. Politically, *Le Temps* was moderate, but, according to Clyde Thogmartin, it appealed especially to the *républicains d'empire*, those republicans in support of France's imperial mission. Under the Third Republic, *Le Temps* was regarded as the "semi-official" voice of the government in foreign policy.[48]

It is within the pages of *Le Figaro* and *Le Temps* that we find numerous reviews of ballet and dance between 1909 and 1938, but now within their music columns. The Ballets Russes' innovative use of symphonic music and "Russian" national motifs attracted music critics to review ballet. Critics were excited about the new central role music played in ballet production and were intrigued by the correspondence of music with choreography and decor. They were also fascinated by the potential of ballet to represent national sentiment. This new conception of ballet sparked dialogues about art, politics, and the ballet among music critics. By the 1920s, *Le Temps* regularly alternated ballet reviews and discussions on dance within its music columns. Music critic Pierre Lalo systematically and enthusiastically wrote on ballet and music for the paper.

In 1909, the premier group of the Russian ballet, the Ballets Russes, immediately captured the attention of prominent critics and intellectuals in France, who thereafter redirected their attention to the ballet and reconsidered ballet's aesthetic worth. The Russian company had presented ballet in an entirely new way as a dynamic collaborative art form that incorporated symphonic music, experimented with modernism, and embodied an exotic "Russianness." The positive reception of the foreign company by Parisian critics (particularly music critics) in many ways reflects the cultural climate of France in the Belle Époque, when the French public thirsted for anything new, modern, and foreign. Many of such critics, however, did not have the expertise to evaluate dancing. In fact, there remained no professional dance critics, but only literary, opera, or theatre critics who also reviewed ballet performances (not yet separated from opera or an opera evening). They were educated, but not experts on dance.

When reviewing the Ballets Russes, these "non-experts" were faced with a complicated artistic medium – a newly developed and modern artistic mode of representation that entailed an examination of dramatic expression, symphonic music, avant-garde design and decor, and, of course, choreography. Critics writing on ballet, whether literary or music, did not understand choreographic terminology or the specificities behind technical virtuosity. Therefore, it is not surprising to find less discussion on choreography and dancers' execution of steps and more analysis of decor, costumes, musical scores, and, more generally, French cultural values. Critics and intellectuals writing about ballet in this period often related ballet to their particular specialty, whether music or theatre, or to the dominant ideologies and tastes of the day. The fact that French bourgeois periodicals and newspapers such as *Le Figaro, Le Temps, Comœdia, La Revue Musicale,* and *La Nouvelle Revue Française* (*NRF*) eventually brought in specialists on dance as well as designated specific sections or columns for discussions on dance reveals a growing regard, appreciation, and interest in dance as an artistic form among the haute-bourgeoisie.[49] However, even by the 1920s, when ballet reviews and ballet criticism appeared consistently in either music or dance sections and even on front pages of respectable newspapers, there still remained very few specialists on dance, the exceptions being André Levinson and Fernand Divoire in France, and Cyril Beaumont and Arnold Haskell in England.

Those non-specialists writing on the ballet came from a wide range of backgrounds and education. It is in the early ballet reviews in *La Nouvelle Revue Française,* known for its Leftist politics and literary experimentation, that we see early signs of a serious renewed interest in the art of ballet by intellectuals.[50] The journal was founded in 1909 by André Gide, Henri Vangeon (Ghéon), Jean Schlumberger, and Jacques Copeau – all members of the Parisian literary avant-garde. All six founders at one time or another wrote on the ballet in the form of either a review or commentary. In 1910, just a year after the Ballets Russes unveiled itself to the Parisian public, Henri Ghéon (1875–1944) published a fourteen-page article on the early ballets of the Ballets Russes: *Schéhérazade, Firebird,* and *Giselle,* including a section devoted to specific Russian dancers. Ghéon, whose career in the theatre was built on rewriting medieval miracle plays, hailed the Ballets Russes' new incorporation of symphonic music, its renovation of decor, and the "réincarnation du 'danseur'" and commended the Ballets Russes for transfiguring ballet into a new genre.[51] French author and writer André Gide (1869–1951), who won the Nobel Prize in Literature in 1947, also became enthralled and greatly inspired by the Ballets Russes' new approach to ballet. Heavily influenced by the symbolists (especially Mallarmé), he sought within his own prose to derive life and substance from ballet's form alone. In his reviews of the Ballets Russes, Gide often praised the "new ballet's" conception as a collaborative art rather than an aesthetically pure art form of movement. In other words, he perceived ballet not in terms of choreographic autonomy, but rather by the way in which movement could serve as poetic inspiration.

Jacques Rivière (1886–1925) is another figure who concerned himself with the developments in ballet in France. After writing many articles and reviews for the journal, Rivière took over the running of *La Nouvelle Revue Française* in 1919. In this capacity, he was a supporter of new and experimental ideas. As his biographer Karen Levy points out, "Rivière led the *NRF* through what was without question one of the stormiest, most chaotic periods of change when many contradictory voices were all clamouring, not only to be heard, but to dominate the literary, intellectual, and social scene."[52] She also notes that "when others of his generation were reacting indignantly to the anarchic tactics of the Dadaists and later the Surrealists, Rivière expressed his gratitude to them for having dared to shake the foundations of language and attack the very concept of literature itself." "Although he opposed many of their attitudes," she writes, "he nevertheless recognized the necessity for asking the radical questions which they posed."[53] Rivière's responses after the premiere of the Ballets Russes' *Le sacre du printemps* [The Rite of Spring] are most revealing of his open mind and appreciation for novelty. In *Sacre,* he enthusiastically located the invention of "a whole new technique": "One could rightly object that I seek a whole new technique in what has been invented and makes sense only for a well-determined single work. I might be told that this choreography that is so angular is only intended to represent the still unformed and clumsy gesticulations of primitive beings. And this music that is so stifled is created only to paint the heavy anguish of spring."[54] He went on to capture the birth of twentieth-century music and dance:

> I should answer that it is exactly the characteristic of masterpieces to create for their use an expression that is so complete, so useful and so new that it quite naturally becomes a general technique. Nothing good is invented in a vacuum. To have new ideas with a somewhat strange import, one must work at some very precise objective, one must want to express something in a way which cannot be confused with anything else. It is just as one strives for the particular, as one concentrates all of his creative faculties on the same small point, that the truly expansive innovations burst forth as if they had been kept under too great a pressure. True fecundity is born of extreme urgency.[55]

Essentially, Rivière points out that the discoveries of both Stravinsky and Nijinsky should be understood and appreciated beyond the "absurd" subject of the work. Rivière dedicated twenty-five pages to contemporary ballet in this 1913 review, and his arguments are fundamental to the revitalization of discourse on ballet in France.

Thus, even before Rivière became editor of *NRF,* he contributed many articles and reviews of ballet to the journal, often focusing specifically on the innovative productions of the Ballets Russes. His landmark article "Of the Ballets Russes and of Fokine" even raised some critical questions about the genre. Here Rivière proclaimed adamantly that it was the dancing, rather than the musical score, decor, set designs, or costumes that made the Ballets Russes truly unique. Rivière was the first critic to make this observation. His familiarity with French dance terminology (e.g., *penché, tendu, arabesque*) in this article reveals his investment as a critic of ballet.[56] In another early article, Rivière had announced that the Ballets Russes' production of *Petrushka* was a masterpiece and pointed out that Michel Fokine, its choreographer, was a true genius.[57]

While Rivière stood alone in his focus on dancing and choreography, music critics also helped to reshape public opinion on ballet. Writing in both music journals such as *La Revue Musicale* and generalized journals such as *Le Temps, Le Figaro*, and *La Nouvelle Revue Française*, music critics frequently expressed their admiration for contemporary ballet scores and their fascination with the new relationship between music and dance.[58] The use of Debussy's music in the ballets of the Ballets Russes such as *L'après-midi d'un faune* (1912) and *Jeux* (1913) played a significant role in increasing the attention paid to France's own talented composers as well as the use of symphonic music in ballet. By the turn of the twentieth century, the music of Claude Debussy (1862–1918) had become a symbol of national sentiment and French pride. A native of France, Debussy was known as a harmonic innovator who embraced the impressionistic style of evoking a mood or an atmosphere with his music. His innovations were based on subtle inflections of French language and poetry. The Ballets Russes' collaboration with French composers thus provided a new context in which to discuss ballet. Discussions on ballet now fell into a broader discourse on French nationalism, music, and aesthetics. The review of ballet by music critics helped to elevate its worth as an art by drawing its discussion into more serious contexts.

In fact, many prominent music critics wrote frequently on ballet and promoted ballet as a serious art. Pierre Lalo (1866–1943), son of the composer Edouard Lalo,[59] wrote regular columns on ballet for *Le Temps* from 1898 until 1914. A student of literature, classics, philosophy, and modern languages, Lalo went on to become a well-known music critic writing also for *La Revue de Paris, Journal des Débats, Courier Musical*, and *Comœdia*. His articles are characterized by conservatism, wit, sarcasm, and astuteness. He was a firm advocate of the music of Debussy, but hostile to Ravel (a hostility that lasted for nearly forty years) and other composers, such as Delage and Honegger. Eventually, Lalo became a member of the governing bodies of the Paris

Conservatoire and Radiodiffusion Française. The fact that Lalo was an important and highly visible voice in the music world who was committed to his columns on ballet reveals the new level of consideration that ballet was receiving. Moreover, Lalo was particularly supportive of the Ballets Russes' use of male dancers. As we will see, his ballet reviews played a crucial role in restoring the artistic integrity of male ballet dancers in France. Collectively, Lalo's reviews provide much information on how ballet was understood, reconceptualized, and translated to serve modern tastes.

Louis Laloy (1874–1944) is another prominent music critic and scholar who wrote frequently on ballet. He was one of the most important and influential musicologists and music critics in France in the early twentieth century. Proficient in eight languages (French, English, German, Russian, Italian, Greek, Latin, and Mandarin Chinese), Laloy was one of the first doctoral candidates in music history at the Sorbonne and eventually taught music history there. He served as a music critic for journals such as *La Revue Musicale*, the *Grand Revue*, the *Gazette des Beaux-Arts*, the *Revue des Deux Mondes*, and *Comœdia*. After serving as an editor for the prestigious *La Revue Musicale* (1901–12) from 1901 to 1905, he founded his own musical journal, *Le Mercure Musical*, which was closely associated with the *Mercure de France*, a socially conservative but aesthetically liberal (Liberal Right) journal. Over the course of his career, Laloy published concert reviews, scholarly articles, and monographs on a variety of subjects, not necessarily limiting himself to music. Laloy's circle of friends comprised an eclectic group of composers, writers, artists, poets, and performers. These included André Breton, Jean Cocteau, Sidonie-Gabrielle Colette, André Gide, Auguste Rodin, and Igor Stravinsky.[60] He was a close friend of Claude Debussy, writing the composer's first French biography. His seminal 1910 essay on Debussy attempted to explain how the composer's work was impressionist and how both painting and poetry were essential to understanding his music.[61] Laloy was thus exposed to a community of artists whose works aimed at modern innovation and experimentation. As a staunch defender of French contemporary music, Laloy did not limit his artistic interests to music. He also wrote enthusiastically about ballet, particularly French ballet. In his article "La danse à l'Opéra" of 1927, Laloy hailed the corps de ballet of the Opéra as a unique institution in Europe "by right of its seniority and brilliance of its tradition." He commended the extensive "training of the human body [that] carried with … painstaking methods … absolute perfection in the prescribed movements."[62] As we will see, Laloy played a key role in pointing out the discipline, hard work, and athletic strength demanded in the training of the dancers at the Opéra. In fact, Laloy was actively engaged in the world of ballet. From 1914, Laloy served as secretary-general of the Paris Opéra, was given the charge of producing the program for Diaghilev's Monte Carlo season of ballets in 1924, and wrote a short book, *La danse à l'Opéra,* in 1927. In 1936, Laloy was appointed professor of the history of music at the Paris Conservatoire, where he taught until 1941.

La Revue Musicale (1920–40), another musical journal in which we find regular reviews of ballet in the early twentieth century, was considered one of the best journals of music history and criticism. This journal is not to be confused with *La Revue Musicale* (1901–12), of which Laloy was an editor, or the three others of the same title. Founded by musicologist Henry Prunières (1886–1942), its objective was to support innovations in modern music.[63] As it gained a national and international reputation, music critics, musicologists, and composers all contributed to its pages. Prunières emphasized the importance of "educating the French public in order to help them develop musical understanding." He once explained in an interview, "It seems to me that the duty of any music critic worthy of the title is to make every effort to dispel the public's ignorance and its absurd biases." He continued to point out how the music critic should "inspire simultaneously a love for the art of the past, which is above suspicion, and the art of the present, an *a priori* abomination. It was with this in mind that I founded *La revue musicale* in 1920."[64] The launch of the journal was extremely successful, attracting over 1,300 subscribers within its first three months of publication.[65]

La Revue Musicale would serve as a particularly important tool in reviving the reputation of ballet in France. Part of Prunières's vision for the journal was to stress the interconnections among a variety of arts, including that of dance, and to expose a broad range of aesthetic styles, theories, and genres. In 1938, *La Revue Musicale* devoted an entire issue to the topic of ballet. Entitled "Le ballet contemporain" (Contemporary Ballet), its articles included "Souvenir de Diaghilev" (In Memory of Diaghilev) by Pierre Michaut; "La danse et la music" (Dance and Music) by dancer, choreographer, and ballet historian

Serge Lifar; "Pour ou contre un chorégraphie autonome" (For or Against an Autonomy of Choreography) and "Le décor de ballet" (Ballet Decor) both by André Boll; "Poésie de la danse" (Poetry of the Dance) by Roger Lannes; "Avenir du ballet" (Ballet's Future) by Fernand Divoire; and "Questions chorégraphiques" (Choreographic Questions) by dancer Julie Sazonova.[66] Thus Prunières's mission to "dispel the public's ignorance and its absurd biases" extended beyond those attached to music to include also those that surrounded the art of dance.

THE ÉMIGRÉS

Émigrés made an extraordinary impact on French cultural life in the early twentieth century, particularly Russian émigrés. Recent studies have shown the ways in which Russian émigré communities interacted with French society. Leonid Livak notes in *Russian Émigrés in the Intellectual and Literary Life of Interwar France: A Bibliographical Essay* (2010) that while Russian emigration to France was numerically less than that of Poles, Italians, and Spanish (roughly 100,000 to 150,000 in this period), "Russians left the deepest impressions on the French hosts thanks to the visibility of their cultural elite."[67] According to Livak, this was because Russian exiles included a larger number of "educated, culturally ambitious, and politically active individuals" than other immigrant groups.[68] One contemporary observer went so far to remark frankly, "Almost all of Russia's brain will stay in France for a while. Let us recognize and appreciate this fact."[69]

Indeed, Russian émigrés had a profound influence on the shaping of art and culture in early twentieth-century France. Their contributions reveal the internationalization of French cultural production in the early twentieth century. Russian émigrés played a decisive role in fostering new perceptions about ballet in France. In fact, many would participate in the cultural project to revive ballet in France, particularly the cultural elites who emigrated from Russia in the wake of the revolution. Russians made extraordinary contributions to the revitalization of ballet in France in their capacity as patrons, critics, intellectuals, artists, composers, designers, dancers, and choreographers. Referring to the Ballets Russes and its impact on the world of ballet, Roberts H. Johnston acknowledges in *New Mecca, New Babylon: Paris and the Russian Exiles, 1920–1945* (1988) that "no other facet of Russian cultural creativity could marshal a comparable roster."[70]

The influx of Russians who settled in Paris must be understood within the context of Russian emigration to France, the émigré experience in Paris, and the politics of that population. During the nineteenth century, both France and England served as asylums for political refugees fleeing repressive regimes. For example, many Polish and Russian exiles formed permanent communities in Paris and London. The 1891 Franco-Russian Alliance paved the way for the relatively warm welcome and privileged status of the Russian émigré community. After the First World War, France took in more refugees than any other country in the Western world. As James E. Hassell notes, "more people found haven in France during the twenties than in any other country, including the United States."[71] France was rather generous when it came to Russian emigration. Marc Raeff's study *Russia Abroad: A Cultural History of Russian Emigration, 1919–1939* (1990) reveals that émigrés were issued working permits relatively easily in France, with the exception of those hoping to work in the "liberal" professions, such as lawyers, doctors, and teachers as these occupations required French citizenship or veteran status in the French army. Naturalization became gradually easier to attain, particularly in the 1930s.[72] Many Russians, however, did not wish to become naturalized as French citizens, believing that their sojourn in France was a temporary one. Eager to increase its labour force in mining, industry, and in the reconstruction of areas devastated by the First World War, the French took in a large number of Russian labourers in the 1920s. However, when the French were hit by the Depression in the 1930s, their eagerness dissipated as there was less need of foreign labour. As a result, permits were more difficult to renew and penal measures were implemented for any Russian who violated the law – expulsion or imprisonment were two of such measures. Policies relaxed under the government of Léon Blum when émigrés were able to join labour unions.[73] The diversity of those who emigrated to France is also worth noting. As Raeff shows, "Russia Abroad" in Paris included a "representation of all shades of political ideologies and all trends of styles."[74]

Most of the Russian cultural elites who emigrated to France settled in Paris. As Livak notes, these included large numbers of "educated, politically active, and culturally ambitious people" who sought to maintain an intellectual and cultural life for themselves. Paris was appealing to them for a number of reasons. First, the alternative urban centres of Prague, Sofia, Belgrade, and Berlin were no match for Paris's offerings as an international cultural hub. Second, Paris supplied numerous and wide-ranging newspapers and journals. Parisian Russian literary intelligentsia established Russian daily newspapers and periodicals and wrote articles in French for leading Parisian newspapers and journals. Third, Parisian culture offered a flexibility when it came to subject matter and a vibrant avant-garde community. As Roberts H. Johnston asserts, Paris was a city "where no topic was forbidden, no fashion unexplored."[75] The émigré writer Vassily Yanovsky described Paris as having "the special French air of freedom" where "everything may be weighed anew, overhauled and understood in a new way."[76]

France would have been a familiar place for those Russian exiles who were members of the professional, affluent, and cultured bourgeoisie, particularly the intelligentsia. The history of transnational cultural exchange between France and Russia exposed Russian intellectuals to French art, music, literature, poetry, and ballet. Like the cultivated cosmopolitan elites, many intellectuals were also fluent in the French language, which enabled them to contribute articles to French journals and to integrate within French artistic and literary circles, particularly the avant-garde. For members of the Russian aristocracy, many of whom would become patrons of the arts in France, France was "literally" a familiar place. Since the middle of the nineteenth century, the French Riviera had been a favoured vacation spot of wealthy Russians, including the royal family.

The years 1920 to 1924 witnessed the increasing visibility of Russian exiles in the French press. A few of them managed to establish successfully themselves as authorities in specialized fields. For example, critic Boris de Schloezer (1881–1969) became an authority on modern music (he published a notable monograph on Stravinsky in 1929) and contributed several favourable reviews of the Ballets Russes to the *NRF*. In the late 1930s, Schloezer wrote a particular impressive article for the *NRF*, simply entitled "Ballets," which hailed the dancing of Serge Lifar as "marvellous" and "impeccable."[77] Articles such as these helped to reshape public perceptions of the male dancer. Over the course of his career, Schloezer played a significant role in French cultural and musical life.

Another émigré and intellectual who had a tremendous impact on culture and the arts in the 1920s was André Levinson (1887–1933).

Central to the course of ballet in France, he established a prolific career as a dance and foreign-literature critic. In fact, it is safe to say that André Levinson was seen as the chief role model for other critics in France, especially when it came to analyzing choreographic elements that were unfamiliar to music and literary critics. As a journalist remarked in introducing his column in *Le Figaro* in 1922, Levinson's authority as the great critical specialist of the study of dance was without dispute and the value of his advice on dance was peerless.[78]

Born in St Petersburg, Russia, in 1887, Andréi Yakovlevich Levinson was exposed to ballet as a child – growing up near the Mariinsky (later Kirov) Theatre. Educated at the Imperial University, he studied psychology, philosophy, philology, Greek, Latin, Romance languages, and the history of art.[79] Certainly, he was aware of the rising Russian nationalist movements in art, music, and dance at the turn of the century. Moreover, Levinson experienced a culture in which the art of ballet was at its peak and well esteemed as a state art form. In 1913, Levinson joined the faculty of the Imperial University as a professor of French literature and translated French texts such as those of Stéphane Mallarmé and André Gide into Russian. Working as a literary critic, he wrote weekly columns for *Rech'*, an important liberal St Petersburg newspaper.[80] Like many other Russian intellectuals who moved to Paris in the early twentieth century, Levinson was fleeing from the Bolshevik Revolution. As Lynn Garafola notes, Levinson's emigration was deeply political since he held "fiercely anti-Soviet views."[81]

Not long after his move to Paris in 1921, Levinson became an increasingly important figure in Parisian artistic circles and eventually became a faculty member of the Sorbonne, where he taught Russian literature and lectured on dance and art. He was well respected among intellectuals and was given a regular column on dance in the daily newspaper *Comœdia* by 1922. Founded in 1906, *Comœdia* was a respectable journal that was dedicated entirely to reviews and articles about art, the theatre, and literature. It catered to the theatre crowd and to arts lovers. Between 1922 and 1923, *Comœdia* published a series of vibrant articles, many contributed by Levinson, in response to Paris Opéra director Jacques Rouché's launching of "La Saison Francaise" – an Opéra season dedicated to French ballet. The season stimulated lengthy critical discussions in *Comœdia* about the state of ballet in France not only on the part of Levinson, but also among a variety of figures, particularly the intellectual André Rigaud. In his reviews of the 1922–23 season, Rigaud expressed his enthusiasm and support for Rouché's season of French ballet. In one article, Rigaud asked rhetorically and boldly: "Why doesn't Paris have French ballets?"[82] It is this very question that Levinson frequently addressed.

In addition to *Comœdia*, Levinson contributed articles on dance to *Le Figaro*, *Le Temps*, and *La Revue Musicale*. Music and literary critics writing on ballet in such journals acknowledged Levinson as an "expert" and adorned him with the utmost respect. Among all critics writing on ballet in early twentieth-century Paris, Levinson was the only one who really understood the language of ballet – specifically its choreographic elements and terminology. He took it upon himself to educate not only the public, but also other critics who might use him as both a model and an interlocutor with whom they could refine their ideas. In 1924, music critic and scholar Louis Laloy wrote that Levinson was "in all the senses of the ordinal number, the first choreographic critic of our times."[83] In recognition of his key role in dance criticism, Levinson was awarded the Légion d'Honneur (the French Republic's highest honour) in 1928 and was naturalized as a French citizen in 1932, one year before his death.

Levinson wrote at a time when dance criticism was still experimental and constantly changing in France. Eventually, he established a new foundation for examining ballet – one that included an analysis of choreography (the dance itself). As critic and as historian, Levinson had a profound influence on dance criticism and dance history. His first book on dance, *Masters of Ballet* (*Mastera baleta*) was published in St Petersburg in 1914. The book traced and examined the history of attitudes towards the art of ballet. His later writings include articles and books covering a wide area of subjects from individual dancers and painters, the aesthetics of dance, dance productions, Spanish dance, to music and ballet. He also published a series of historical essays on Jean-Georges Noverre, Salvatore Vigano, Auguste Vestris, and Carlo Blasis. Apart from his numerous reviews and criticism, other works include his *Ballet Old and New* (1917), *The Idea of the Dance: From Aristotle to Mallarmé* (1927), *La danse d'aujourd'hui* (1929), and *Serge Lifar: Destin d'un danseur* (ca. 1933) – a text focusing on the life and career of Serge Lifar and his work in Paris during the 1920s and 1930s.[84]

Additionally, Levinson was one of the first to write about the relationship between modern music and dance in his article "Stravinsky and the Dance" (1924) as well as in "Ballet, Painting, Music" (1917).[85] In these articles, Levinson criticized the Ballets Russes for its devaluation of classical choreography for the sake of music. While he supported the use of symphonic music in ballet rather than the earlier "manufactured [music] in mass production by the official composers Minkus and Pugni," Levinson argued that the use of symphonic music in the Ballets Russes' productions did not conform to the concerns of ballet. For example, Levinson argued that "the merits of [the Ballets Russes' *Firebird*] lay completely outside the realm of choreography."[86] According to Levinson (and rightly so), Fokine's dance aesthetic rejected many of the conventions of balletic forms in order to comply to "ready-made musical forms."[87] Both André Levinson and Serge Lifar argued that it was not enough to add symphonic music to ballet, but rather that symphonic music should adapt itself to classical dance movement and choreographic expression.[88]

In many of his articles and books, Levinson stressed the importance of maintaining ballet tradition. In fact, he took a particularly steadfast position on the preservation of classical ballet – especially the classical style of ballet developed by French dancer Marius Petipa. Unlike musical scores or photographic preservation of the visual arts, before video, there were fewer means of documenting a ballet performance. Ballet choreography was most commonly passed along from generation to generation through demonstrations offered by the dancers, choreographers, or directors themselves. Dance notation was scarcely used and less often understood. Levinson set out this predicament of ballet preservation most eloquently, writing that "the only way to preserve the precious choreographic works of the past is to continue their performance and experiments." "The forms of dance must be guarded vigilantly," he wrote, "just like the fire at the vestal sanctuary. Once extinguished, it will not flare up again."[89] As we will see, Levinson engaged in the French nationalist project of cultural renewal by proposing a revival of French ballet through a reassertion of French classicism in dance aesthetics.

Although unquestionably of seminal significance in the evolution of twentieth-century ballet criticism, Levinson by no means stands alone. In fact, no overview, regardless of how brief, of ballet criticism could aspire to be complete unless to Levinson's contributions we add those of the many-sided and versatile Serge Lifar, himself the subject of one of Levinson's books. Serge Lifar (1905–1986) can be seen under a variety of guises: as a dancer, choreographer, artistic director, critic/reviewer, intellectual, dance historian, lecturer, and author. As an expert critic and historian of ballet, Lifar's writings on dance were critical to its reconception as a modern art form in France. Like Levinson, Lifar became an authoritative voice on dance. As such, he was invited to publish numerous articles in various newspapers, periodicals, and journals as well as to give lectures on dance. Born Sergei Mikhailovich Serdkin in Kiev in 1905, at the age of fifteen, he enrolled at the school of the Kiev Opera Ballet run by Bronislava Nijinska. He arrived in Paris as a member of the Ballets Russes company in 1923. Within the Ballets Russes social circles, he befriended leading members of the Parisian intellectual and artistic avant-garde. He noted in his autobiography that "Gide, Valéry, Giraudoux, Claudel, and Mauriac became definitely my friends. Cocteau, Picasso and Braque were so already – and I mention only a few."[90] Establishing himself in Paris as a choreographer and star dancer, he was soon engaged as the ballet master and director at the Paris Opéra Ballet, where he remained in charge until 1957.

Lifar's ambitions at the Paris Opéra ballet were to establish ballet as an autonomous art, to restore a sense of national pride in it, and to develop a distinctly French style of modern ballet. In 1932, when he was awarded the title of *professeur de danse*, he began reforms of the Opéra's school to enable its dancers to perform the more modern ballets, particularly his own. Lifar believed that choreography was more important than the music and decor in a ballet, and he argued that since ballet technique has its own innate formal values, its choreography should not derive from music. In an article published in *La Revue Musicale* in 1938, entitled "La danse et la musique," Lifar stated that it was his desire to "liberate dance from the cage where music holds it captive."[91] French writer Louis Viardot's observations at the time reveal the predicament that Lifar faced: "People do not dance in a ballet all the time; some time is taken up with miming, acting, the passions."[92] Viardot's words reveal the extent to which ballets used pantomime and acting as a means for expression. Lifar, however, aimed to manifest such "expressive qualities" through the dance (choreography) itself. Conveying drama through choreography rather than through mime or music, Lifar created more than fifty ballets on themes from myth, legend, and history and, contrary to Paris Opéra custom, gave leading rather than supporting roles to men. His famous ballet *Icare* (1935) was unusual in that it was choreographed originally without music, and only later was a percussive score added to accompany the dancing.

Lifar's ideas on dance manifested themselves in articles and choreographic works from the 1920s to the 1960s. Among many of his writings on dance, *La Danse* (1965) is a seminal work in its argument for dance as an autonomous art form. Most famous is his *Le manifeste du chorégraphie* published in 1935, which first outlined what would become the official French national style of ballet. Lifar proclaimed that "for a ballet the Dance must have the first word and the last."[93] Other publications by Lifar on dance and ballet include: *Pensées sur la danse* (1946), which featured a preface by Paul Valéry and drawings by Aristide Maillol; *Traité de danse académique* (1949); *Traité de chorégraphie* (1952); *Méditations sur la danse* (1952), *Le livre de la danse* (1954); *La musique par la danse* (1955); and *Au service de la danse: À la recherché d'une science: La chorélogie* (1958). Ultimately, Lifar was able to successfully unite both French and Russian classical ballet traditions as he reconceptualized ballet for a modern era.[94] As choreographer, critic, and historian, Lifar also legitimized dance as a profession and established choreography as its own autonomous art form. According to Lifar, choreography was a type of science that could be studied to the highest degree. He once wrote, "Choreography has become a science: a chair in Chorélogie at the Sorbonne has existed since 1955."[95]

FEMALE CRITICS

Lest we leave the reader with the impression that rhetoric of ballet was shaped only by men, it is important to point out that female critics are by no means absent. Before 1900, most critical discourses on ballet published in reputable Parisian journals were written by men with only a few exceptions. This is not surprising, as ballet had fallen into decline during the nineteenth century and, by the end of the century, had gained a reputation as an eroticized art for its almost exclusively male audiences. I argue that, by the 1930s, women's increasing visibility as critics and reviewers of ballet emerged as a result of the increasing value attached to the formalist aspects of dance and choreography. As specialists like Levinson and Lifar drew attention to the formal aspects of dance in their reviews for major bourgeois newspapers and journals, dance criticism became "professionalized" in the sense that standards and credentials were finally established for reviewing ballet. The criteria for reviewing ballet, which previously could be met by the amateur/spectator, now relied on the understanding of dance training and technique.

In the realm of art, women's central obstacle had been their exclusion from formal artistic training. Historically, women artists were banned from the Royal Academy of Painting and Sculpture in the seventeenth and eighteenth centuries (with a few exceptions) and, in the nineteenth century, barred from life-drawing classes in both private and public institutions.[96] By the 1880s, women were still excluded from the state-sponsored École des Beaux Arts (School of Fine Arts, established as the Académie Royale de Peinture et de Sculpture in 1648), the primary training facility for the inner circle of artists who would most likely receive both state and private patronage. Women found other avenues of artistic training, such as private lessons (if one had the means and the connections) or the state-sponsored art school, the École Gratuit de Dessin pour les Jeunes Filles (est. 1803), which provided artistic training for talented women without money. With the efforts of the sculptor Mme Léon Bertaux and the Union des Femmes Peintres et Sculpteurs that she founded in 1881, the École des Beaux Arts finally granted women access in 1897. By this time an "art for art's sake" ideology had already taken hold in French aesthetics. In other words, art critics turned their attention to the formal qualities of art. As trained artists in their own right, women could gain the credibility to critically discuss the formal aspects of art.[97] In late nineteenth-century Europe, women were also gaining access to professional journalism and contributing increasingly to the press. By the 1870s, women were regularly publishing art journalism. For example, French republican Maria Deraismes wrote art criticism, including the publication of a long defence of woman artist Éva Gonzales, whose works were rejected by the Salon jury in 1874. Practising artist Marie Bashkirtseff, writing under the pen name of "Pauline Orell," contributed art criticism to the feminist journal *La Citoyenne*, including many reviews of the Salon. Judith Gautier, who regularly published art criticism for over twenty years, was one of the few women art critics in France to write under her own name instead of a male pseudonym. The increasing visibility of women art critics was by no means limited to France as the female art critic Elizabeth Robins Pennell observed in 1891: "Women have ... gone very thoroughly into journalism. You only have to go to one of the press views in a London art exhibition to find out how many are art critics."[98]

A similar shift occurred in music. By the end of the nineteenth century and beginning of the twentieth century, composers had gained the authority to review music alongside musicologists, particularly at a time when a "music for music's sake" ideology was slowly being embraced. Even though women were allowed to study music at the Paris Conservatoire by the nineteenth century, female musicians had other restrictions. In the music world, for example, women had less opportunity than men to interact with orchestras and opera companies and to develop their technique. Moreover, specific musical instruments were deemed more "appropriate" for women to play. For example, Anna "Nanneri" Mozart, who was a virtuoso violinist, was discouraged by her father from performing the violin publicly and limited to her role as piano accompanist for her brother Wolfgang Amadeus. This situation remained relatively unchanged by the 1880s. As Linda Clark points out in *Women and Achievement in the Nineteenth Century* (2008), there was an assumption that women students would become teachers and performers and not composers or conductors. "They were expected to study voice, piano, or harp, rather than advanced musical theory," she writes. "String, wind, or brass instruments were long considered unsuitable for women.[99] Furthermore, to compose, let alone to be heard, a woman needed to conquer social restrictions and taboos. Women needed to find the time and space for such artistic activities without jeopardizing their domestic responsibilities. Clara Schumann, for example, while well respected by her male peers, was herself often reluctant to perform in public. In 1870, she wrote to her friend, the composer-violinist Joseph Joachim, for advice regarding an invitation for her to perform in the Beethoven centennial celebrations in Vienna (Liszt and Wagner conducting): "I am turning to you with a request to that effect; what shall I do? ... I, as a woman, cannot act as you do." She continued, "It would seem arrogant if I, as contrasted with men, were to express my opinion openly. I must invent a lie! But what shall I say?" Joachim's reply was, "I find the fact that you are a woman has nothing to do with it, or it may be the very reason for you to stay away. In any case, you are, as far as art is concerned, 'man enough.'"[100]

The implications of women undertaking music criticism were significant, just as they were in art. Criticism implied authority of the mind, wisdom, and judgment, and, moreover, the ability to disperse specialized knowledge to readers – all attributes still deemed as exclusively male. Nevertheless, women did manage to contribute to musical discourse by the early twentieth century. For example, the pioneering female musicologist Marie Bobillier (pseud. Michel Brenet, 1858–1918) published many important articles and over twenty monographs (e.g., on Haydn, 1910) in the late nineteenth and early twentieth centuries, making a significant contribution to music scholarship. In fact, she often included discussions of the careers of women musicians in her works, providing an indispensable history of women in the music world. Musician-writer Marie Lipsius (pseud. La Mara, 1837–1927), who knew Liszt and Wagner, also wrote over twenty books and many essays on music.[101]

Women's situation in the world of ballet was different in that training was wholly accessible, but often at the expense of respectability. As critic Joris-Karl Huysmans recollected at Degas's first and only exhibition of the statuette *Little Dancer Aged Fourteen* in 1881, "one hear[d] fathers cry: 'God forbid my daughter should become a dancer.'"[102] It is in the comments of impressionist Pierre-Auguste Renoir, however, that we gain insight into the politics of women as artists and intellectuals (i.e., their involvement in cultural production). In 1888, he made a distinction between women "as creators" and "as performers in the arts."[103] Renoir claimed "women are monsters who are authors, lawyers and politicians, like George Sand … and other bores who are nothing more than five-legged beasts." He continued, "the woman who is an artist is merely ridiculous, but I feel that it is acceptable for a woman to be a singer or dancer." Performing women, according to Renoir, were acceptable (and not immoral) because their "artistry" was grounded in display rather than invention. "Gracefulness," he wrote, "is a woman's domain and even her duty."[104] Renoir's comments reveal the inferior status of the performing arts in relation to the visual arts in this period. Singing and dancing as performative and bodily were deemed more trivial. Thus creativity (i.e., intellectual effort of the mind) was deemed a masculine domain while performance (bodily skill) was considered a feminine one. Renoir did not seem to have an opinion of female ballet choreographers (few as they were at the time).

As has already been suggested, with the arrival of the Ballets Russes and its "fusion" of symphonic music, modern art, set design, decor, and exotic costumes, ballet performance could be judged in a variety of ways. The modern ballet troupe attracted discussions among not only music, literary, and art critics, but also artists and poets. Auguste Rodin, André Gide, and Jean Cocteau all wrote on ballet and all were greatly inspired by the Ballets Russes. Rodin, for example, in his writings on dance, admired the beauty of the male form in the ballets of the Ballets Russes. French artist, costume designer, and later radio broadcaster Valentine Gross (Hugo) (1887–1968) also contributed to discourse on ballet. She consistently attended Ballets Russes performances (she attended four performances of *Le sacre du printemps* in 1913) and for six years sketched the Ballets Russes dancers. She was particularly inspired by Ballets Russes dancers Vaslav Nijinsky and Tamara Karsavina of whom she exhibited a collection of sketches. In fact, the Galerie Montaigne sponsored an exposition of Gross's sketches in the foyer of the Champs-Élysées theatre on the tumultuous opening night of Stravinsky's famed ballet *Sacre.*

Gross had planned to collaborate with the Ballets Russes as a designer in 1914 on the ballet *Parade* alongside composer Erik Satie and poet Jean Cocteau but did not participate in the eventual production of 1917. However, she later collaborated with the ballet company as a designer in 1921 on the production of *Les mariés de la Tour Eiffel.* Gross's circle of friends included a number of prominent artists including Erik Satie, Jean Cocteau, and Roger de la Fresnaye. In the 1930s, she befriended several surrealists, including Salvador Dalí, Max Ernst, René Char, Tristan Tzara, and Nusch and Paul Éluard.

Gross contributed several reviews and articles on ballet to Parisian journals and newspapers.[105] Her writings capture much of the spirit and complexity of the European avant-garde from the 1920s to the 1950s. In 1913, Gross contributed an article to *Comœdia* that attempted to capture the tumultuous atmosphere of the premiere of *Le sacre du printemps.* She wrote, "The theatre seemed to be shaken by an earthquake ... It seemed to shudder. People shouted insults, howled and whistled, drowning the music. There was slapping and even punching. The dancers could not hear the music. Diaghilev thundered orders from his box. There was something wonderful about the titanic struggle which must have been going on in order to keep these inaudible musicians and these deafened dancers together, in obedience to the laws of their invisible choreographer. The ballet was astoundingly beautiful."[106] In her articles and sketches, Gross also made great efforts to make the male dancer more acceptable. Her numerous drawings of Nijinsky attempted to capture his grace, dynamism, and masculine beauty of form.[107]

Thus women, like men, were captivated by the Ballets Russes and managed to find the opportunity and authority to engage in discourses about it. As the innovations of the Ballets Russes, with its reconception of ballet as a collaborative and expressive art form, raised questions over the very function of ballet, the nature of reviewing ballet came under scrutiny. As ballet became increasing valued as a primarily choreographic art form, the credentials of the dance critic changed. British dance critic A.V. Coton's description of the critic's function is particularly insightful in this respect. In his book, *A Prejudice for Ballet* (1938), he writes:

> The critic is the most frequently misunderstood and unappreciated of all persons engaged in the production and elaboration of the complex processes constituting an art-form. The necessity of his function is continually being denied by everyone but himself. Actually the critic is recognized by the artist as the disseminator of information, the explorer into strange territory, and the obliging guide to all strangers coming into first contact with the form discussed ... The first-rate critic needs to be a writer of higher than journalistic standards, a man with a wide knowledge of the whole technique of the art-form discussed, and, whenever possible, something of a practitioner of the form.[108]

Although Coton's definition of the critic seems somewhat idealistic in its list of requirements, it does reveal an aim to establish his or her intrinsic worth in a living body of art. Coton's notion that the practitioner him/herself may serve as a competent reviewer of ballet is significant in that we find several female dancers reviewing ballet in the 1930s in France. Coton is a valuable source because he attempts to establish a new standard of ballet criticism. In fact, this was a subject that he revisited throughout his lifetime. Coton boldly criticized music critics for solely judging ballet as a form of expression of music. He noted that "no music critics had the faintest notion of what went on in the ballet school, how dancers were formed, or how a choreographer set to work, and the failure of at least half of all the Diaghilev ballets to get over the footlights what they had to put over is directly attributable to this particular perversion of criticism."[109] Writing in 1938, Coton remarked joyfully on the blossoming of balletomane critics of ballet. He noted that "in the space of a very few short years this strange new art of ballet (concerning which, at first, few people were at all sure about its 'artness') has risen to the position of the most effectively publicized, financially secured, and completely misunderstood art-form in general circulating in the civilization of Western Europe."[110]

In the early twentieth century, especially with the exposure to the Ballets Russes in Paris, women were slowly acknowledged for their expertise to write on ballet as ballet dancers and choreographers, and even as members of the ballet audience and patrons of the ballet. However, as some critics began to point out (e.g., Jacques Rivière), the actual dancing (choreography) was often neglected in reviews. As dance became increasingly valued and judged for its choreographic (formal) elements (ca. 1930), women as accomplished dancers could provide valuable insight into these elements of choreography (just as Coton demanded of dance critics). Writer and critic Irène Lidova is one such example. She was a dancer herself, studying under Russian instructors Olga Preobrajenska and Victor Gsovsky. Until 1938, Lidova was on the staff of the journal *Vu*, contributing regular studies of dancers. In 1941, she organized the first recital of the Paris Opéra's étoiles Roland Petit and Janine Charat. Also in 1941, she arranged a series of recitals in Paris for Petit, Charat, Jean Babilée, Skorik, Colette Marchand, and other dancers from the Paris Opéra ballet. In this way, Lidova served a valuable role in exposing the new Paris Opéra talents to Parisian audiences. From 1945 to 1946, she served as general secretary to the Paris-based company Les Ballets des Champs-Élysées, and later she joined Roland Petit's company Ballets de Paris. Eventually, she became French correspondent for the English magazine *Dance News*. Another female writer and critic of ballet was P.W. Manchester. She was founder and editor of the magazine *Ballet-Today* (1946) and secretary of the Ballets Rambert from 1944 to 1946. Although she was English, she served as an English correspondent for *La Revue de la Danse* – a specialized periodical on dance that circulated in France.

Julie Sazonova seems to have been the most visible female critic writing on dance in France in the early twentieth century. She wrote articles regularly in *La Nouvelle Revue Française* and *La Revue Musicale.* Her article "Questions chorégraphiques" was one of seven articles devoted to contemporary ballet in the March 1938 issue of *La Revue Musicale.* Sazonova's article appears next to those by Pierre Michaut, Serge Lifar, André Boll, Roger Lannes, and Fernand Divoire – all of whom had built reputations in Paris as "experts on dance." In her article, Sazonova engaged in the growing debate concerning the nature of dance. In her affirmation of dance's French historical past, she traced the "golden age" of classical ballet in its development under Gaétan and Auguste Vestris and the reforms of Noverre. Like Levinson, Sazonova perceived French classical dance as the purest form of ballet. In this article, she expressed her concerns with the increasing "athletics" of ballet (specifically, fouettés) and its fast pace in contrast to "the fundamental perfection of classical dance: the grace and expression of slow movement."[111] She wrote: "The true concept of dance seems to be more and more rare, the beautiful race of the great masters from whom we could renew this art is exhausted, and the choreographic scene is threatened to be invaded by the young record holders of both sexes who think they are artists because they know how to turn well and to whip the foot in a fouetté, without beauty, without style. It is a great time to put an end to this engagement, to recall in us the real sense of choreographic art and to look to retrieve the principles that inspire the great creators."[112] This passage reveals one of several attitudes towards the modernization of ballet and its future development in France. Other articles, such as "La saison chorégraphique: Ballets Joos, Ballets 1933, Ballets de Monte Carlo" in *La Nouvelle Revue Française* (1933), reveal Sazonova's encouragement of the male dancer and his potential as a legitimate performing artist.[113]

In addition to female critics and writers of ballet, we find also a growing collection of books on dance and dancers published by former female ballet dancers (e.g., autobiographies, biographies, and dance studies). Lydia Sokolova's *Dancing for Diaghilev: The Memoirs of Lydia Sokolova* (1960) is an example of a work that reflects the breadth of knowledge and authority on dance and ballet that a woman could attain as a professional dancer. Her memoirs provided much information on the Diaghilevian years; the reception of the Ballets Russes, the nature of its collaborations, financial difficulties, international tours, aesthetics, and intimate workings/operations. After the 1930s, we find an increasing number of autobiographies written by female dancers such as Isadora Duncan (*My Life*, 1927), Tamara Karsavina (*Theatre Street*, 1930), Ninette de Valois (*Come Dance with Me: A Memoir, 1898–1956*, 1957), and books on dance such as Isadora Duncan's *The Art of Dance* (ca. 1928).[114]

Coton's observation that ballet is a misunderstood art form is echoed in current scholarship on the aesthetics of dance. Dance scholar Selma Jeanne Cohen captures best the lasting dilemmas of accessing and understanding dance:

> As yet we have been offered little in the way of comprehensive theories of dance. Yet this most complex of all the arts is also the one most in need of aesthetic analysis. Existing in the dimensions of both time and space, involving not only creator, work, and audience, but performer as well, dance presents a formidable challenge to the most expert of philosophical minds. But in this case such an expertise alone is not enough, for the problems that require a sense of physicality, a grasp of kinesthesia without which any theory of dance must remain hopelessly isolated from reality. Neither dancer nor philosopher can do the job alone.[115]

Cohen highlights the need for both practical and theoretical understandings of dance. In fact, in the case of France, the philosopher André Levinson and the dancer Serge Lifar together, in their own ways, managed to configure a distinct national dance style and to reform and revitalize the Paris Opéra ballet.

2

The "Russian Season" in Paris and the Politics of Transnational Artistic Exchange

Cultural grandeur has always been important to the French. On 5 January 1875, the French president Marshall MacMahon formally inaugurated Charles Garnier's new opera house, which would become known as the Opéra Garnier. The structure was flanked by four intersecting streets – the rue Halévy, rue Auber, rue Scribe, and rue Gluck (an homage to French composers, save Gluck) – and would be showcased by Baron Haussmann's grand avenue de l'Opéra (completed in 1879) that would culminate at its front doors. Those in attendance at the inauguration gala included the Lord Mayor of London, a number of crowned heads of Europe, and other prominent political, financial, and artistic figures. The grand gala opened with excerpts from several operas and a popular scene from the ballet *Le corsaire*. Spectators were, however, more enraptured by the splendours of the building than the artistic performances. One of the largest and most expensive monuments commissioned during the Second Empire of Napoleon III, the Opéra Garnier was adorned with gold leaf, coloured marble, paintings and sculpture created by famous artists of the period, and palatial marble staircases. With its glittering mirrors, ornate chandeliers, opulent architecture, and lavish furnishings, the new Opéra captured a sense of the luxury of the Second Empire, which had dissolved a few years before the building was finished. Although the site was originally designed to link the court with new bourgeois public areas, as Mary McAuliffe suggests, "few at opening night probably remembered … or even cared, that the Avenue de l'Opéra was originally intended as a fast and direct route from the emperor's residence in the Tuileries Palace to the new Opéra."[1] Under the Third Republic, the grandiose Opéra Garnier would become a powerful symbol of the rise of the bourgeoisie, the French

Republic, and the restoration of France's cultural pre-eminence, of which the revitalization of ballet would take part.

The occasion of the inauguration of the Opéra Garnier, referred to then as the Palais Garnier, is significant to this study in a number of respects. The building is a physical embodiment of the connection between national culture and the arts. Although Garnier's project was conceived during the Second Empire, it was completed under the Third Republic, indicating the continuing need for a site of socialization of the dominant class and a state symbol. The new opera house served as an extravagant space for the social display of the wealthy, powerful, and fashionable. However, the meanings attached to the Opéra went beyond those of socialization among the elite or even the artistic productions performed there. The decision to complete the luxurious Opéra Garnier reflects the need on the part of the French to recover a sense of high culture after the Franco-Prussian War. The national opera house's splendour was intrinsically linked to the position of Paris among the great capital cities of Europe, many still under monarchical rule. In order to compete with the opera houses of other European cities, Paris's new opera house needed to be a marvel. In this respect, the Opéra Garnier served in the project of cultural recovery at the end of the nineteenth century. It continued to be an important marker of French identity and France's cultural grandeur. Additionally, the fact that the École de Danse continued to reside in the national opera house, now the Opéra Garnier, while ballet was at a low point, reveals that ballet retained a status deemed worthy of the opera stage (even though it still mainly served as a mere divertissement to opera, "background entertainment," or a means through which the haute bourgeosie could practise libertinism). Today, the Opéra Garnier features primarily ballet with opera mostly staged at the newer Opéra de Paris-Bastille.

Thus the launching of the Opéra Garnier under the Third Republic is a good example of the way in which the French refashioned cultural institutions and the arts. Originating as a symbol of the Second Empire, the opera house became a symbol of the Third Republic – a similar phenomenon that occurred during the French Revolution after it had been a symbol of the absolutist court. For some, however, the Palais Garnier and Paris's other opera houses remained symbols of the frivolity of the Second Empire. They perceived the new opera house and its new audience, now the haute bourgeoisie, as replacing

Figure 2.1 Édouard Detaille, *Inauguration of the Paris Opera House, January 5, 1875*. This painting demonstrates how the bourgeoisie had replaced the aristocrats as the key audience at the Paris Opéra by the second half of the nineteenth century.

"a fading court culture."[2] French writer Édouard Dujardin was pessimistic about the artistic integrity of the Opéra, observing in 1885, "elegant restrooms, sumptuous décors, and ballets – that is the Opéra.

Art is to be found in the concert hall."[3] His statement suggests that the ballet was not considered "art." The fact that the ballet was placed in the same category as restrooms speaks for itself.

Dujardin's observation suggests that the artistic legitimacy of the Opéra was compromised. He implies that the national opera house did not represent French artistic pre-eminence. By using ballet production as a means through which to demonstrate the Opéra's artistic failings, he captures the degradation of ballet by the mid-1880s. What motivated the French to revitalize ballet at the Opéra? How did it affect the grandeur of the Opéra Garnier? This chapter offers the first layer within which to situate the cultural project to revive ballet in France in the early twentieth century: critics' understanding of the relationship between ballet and national culture, a discussion that was launched with the arrival of the Ballets Russes. Between 1909 and 1938, many critics writing on ballet increasingly addressed (whether implicitly or explicitly) the relationship between ballet and politics. Their commentary offers a unique perspective of the politics of national identity in early twentieth-century France. The chapter begins by presenting the political social, economic, and cultural landscape of fin-de-siècle and Belle Époque France in order to explain why the Russian troupe was welcomed so enthusiastically on the part of Parisian audiences and many critics. It then turns to the ways in which critics and intellectuals responded to the Russian company upon its arrival in 1909 and explores the motivations behind such critical responses. There are four central issues that preoccupied critics in their discussions of the Ballets Russes: the embodiment of Russian national and exotic themes in ballet; the virtuosity of the Ballets Russes dancers (both female and male); the company's "fusion of arts" and use of modernism; and the origins of ballet in France. The chapter reveals how the Russian ballet played an important role in the process of reincorporating ballet as a high art into the French cultural landscape. As the Ballets Russes continued to overshadow the French ballet at the Opéra, critics began to consider ballet's potential to carry a modern "republican" French identity and to regain its status and grandeur as a French cultural institution. Through an examination of critical responses to the Ballets Russes, this chapter shows how commentary on ballet served as an expression of the cultural anxieties of early twentieth-century France regarding cultural production and national identity.

THE CULTURAL LANDSCAPE

Before considering the spectacular arrival and reception of the Ballets Russes in Paris, one must first recall where France stood as a nation at the turn of the century. The Franco-Prussian War (1870–71) and the civil war in Paris that followed in its wake had produced a rupture in the cultural life of the nation. Inciting war with the Prussians in the hopes of imperial expansion, the French Empire suffered a humiliating defeat at the hands of the Germans. With the collapse of the Second Empire, the loss of two provinces, Alsace and Lorraine, and the payment of 5 billion francs by 1873, there was widespread hostility towards Germany. For some, "La Revanche" or "revenge" became the motto of the day. For example, Charles Maurras, founder of the Action Française (est. 1898), expresed his view of the deep penetration of vengeance in French cultural life, observing that "from 1871 to 1898, La Revanche was the queen of France; it was, in the years in which we lived, a luminous formula."[4] While there was no open policy of revenge established by the governments of France in this period, Maurras's statement captures well the embitterment of the French towards Germany.

The French defeat in the Franco-Prussian War dealt a serious blow not only to French national pride, but also to the standing of France in Europe. While they were deeply wounded by the loss of Alsace-Lorraine to Germany, the new German nation, moreover, seemed on the verge of eclipsing France in every measure of international power and prestige. In this period, Germany was on the rise and stronger than France in terms of industry (coal and steel manufacturing), population (higher birth rates), military (more men serving in the army), and cultural production. Furthermore, for the first time in their history, the French were unable to keep Germany disunited. Isolated diplomatically and feeling vulnerable in the shadow of a strong and unified Germany, France experienced cultural anxieties about where it stood among other European nations, and these doubts manifested themselves in a variety of ways. Thus the defeat by Prussia deeply affected France's national self-image. This self-image continued to be strongly influenced by the French view of Germany as rival, enemy, or model.[5]

Increasingly, France measured itself against Germany, economically, culturally, and artistically. Fears of mediocrity rose as Germany spawned an increasing number of promising novelists, intellectuals, and writers. During the 1870s, the German language steadily gained prominence as a foreign language in the scholarly world thanks to the distinction of German universities at the time, successfully replacing Latin as the dominant language in all major European and North American universities. Indeed, research in the sciences began to be published in German. France responded to this cultural challenge by attempting to locate, foster, and celebrate its own talents. The growing need to reassert their cultural pre-eminence prompted the French to turn to the arts, modernism, and cosmopolitanism. The founding of the Société Nationale de Musique, just one year after the Franco-Prussian War, is a good example of this tendency in the realm of music. Soon Claude Debussy supplanted Richard Wagner as the icon for modern classical music in France. Furthermore, France inherited a new relationship between art and modernism, and by the turn of the century a wave of modernism turned Paris into a mecca for artistic culture.

The French sense of inferiority was exacerbated by internal problems. The Dreyfus affair and a series of other scandals rocked the fragile republic.[6] All suggested that the young Third Republic was in danger of collapse. The Dreyfus affair was particularly bitter, polarizing monarchists and republicans, Catholics and secularists, Jews and anti-Semites. This case, and the incidents it spawned, also reflect the level of anxiety about France's international status vis-à-vis Germany. The hesitant exoneration of Dreyfus further underlines France's inability to heal its internal divisions. Historian Gordan Wright epitomizes the affair accurately when describing it as "the shame and glory of modern France."[7] As we will see, such polemics shaped the crucial context in which ballet was discussed in France.

France's internal problems and international insecurity drove the French to seek allies. Demoralized by defeat and burdened by a low birth rate and vulnerable army, France searched for alliances in the east (Russia) and the north (Britain). The monarchist Right inclined toward Russia, and constitutional monarchists and the radical Left toward Britain.[8] A near military conflict in Egypt temporarily ruled Britain out, leaving Russia as the prime candidate. With Russia as an ally on the eastern frontier, the French government hoped to deal with the threat from Germany in the east. As a consequence, 1891 witnessed the surprising spectacle of republican France allying with reactionary, monarchist Russia. The Franco-Russian entente was established and France emerged from diplomatic isolation. This agreement was strengthened with a military pact signed in 1894, and, in 1899, in an effort to further reinforce ties with Russia, an accord was negotiated over the balance of power in Europe. It was agreed that should the Austro-Hungarian Empire become a threat to Russia, France would intervene, and should France need help recovering Alsace-Lorraine, Russia would come to its aid. The pact also involved a provision for collaborative action should either side come under attack by Britain. The Franco-Russian entente was strengthened still further by a series of sizable loans made by the French to the Russians.

But the alliance between republican France and imperialist Russia was a tricky one. In fact, the French government had been severely criticized by French liberals for its decision to extend financial credit to the czarist regime during the 1905 revolution. Liberals argued that this decision enabled Czar Nicholas II to remain on the throne and to postpone his acceptance of constitutional reform. Furthermore, financiers were worried about Russia's ability to repay its debts or even to provide military support in a time of crisis. Such worries were exacerbated by traditional French prejudices against Russia that had existed well before the Franco-Prussian War. "Russia is a barbaric country," cautioned ardent republican Alphonse de Lamartine in 1855, "and Europe must beware of her."[9] As we will see, such anxieties over Franco-Russian cultural and artistic exchange would surface in early twentieth-century ballet commentary.

The improving, yet complex, official relationship between France and Russia created an atmosphere conducive to cultural exchange. By the end of the nineteenth century, economic and cultural exchanges between France and Russia were officially encouraged in order to strengthen this unlikely partnership. For example, a number of Franco-Russian musical associations were founded in 1891. These associations provided performance opportunities for Russian composers in Paris. Similarly, the Imperial Academy of Arts began sending their students to France, where, eventually, they formed the Association des Peintures Russes de Paris in 1896. Modern Russian art was included in France's fifth world's fair, the prestigious and profitable Exposition Universelle of 1900. While none of the Russian paintings were acquired by French museums or managed to captivate French

Figure 2.2 "Entente Fraternelle." The Franco-Russian Entente, 1893.

spectactors, Russian sparkling wine defeated all the French entries to claim the internationally coveted "Grand Prix de Champagne"![10] Also as part of the Exposition Universelle, the Pont Alexandre III was opened by Czar Nicholas II in honour of the former Czar Alexander III. One of the most ornate bridges in Paris, it was constructed from steel and stone with four gilt-topped pillars in the art nouveau style. The bridge was situated symbolically between the Grand Palais and Les Invalides (a military building) to further cement ties between Russia and France.

It is within this landscape of political and cultural exchange that Serge Diaghilev took on Paris. In 1906, he organized the Salon d'Automne's section for Russian artists that included the works of Bakst, Larionov, Levitskii, Vrubel, Korovin, Maliavin, Somov, and Grabar. In 1907, Diaghilev presented a series of concerts of Russian music at the Paris Opéra. With these concerts, he introduced to Paris the music of Rimsky-Korsakov, Scriabin, Rachmaninov, and

Glazunov – all Russian nationalist composers. The following year, he presented French audiences with the Russian opera *Boris Godunov* (based upon Pushkin's tragedy), which was performed also at the Paris Opéra.

MAY 1909

In 1909, Diaghilev introduced his ballet troupe, the Ballets Russes, to Parisian audiences at the Théâtre du Châtelet. Diaghilev, rather strategically, presented the ballet *Le pavillon d'Armide* in his opening of the 1909 season. While the creative artists involved were all Russians – the sets and decor by Alexandre Benois, the music by Nicholas Tcherepnine, the choreography by Michel Fokine, and the dancing by Anna Pavlova and Vaslav Nijinsky – *Le pavillon d'Armide* was an homage to seventeenth- and eighteenth-century French culture. By presenting an obviously "French" ballet, the Russians honoured French tradition and demonstrated their understanding of French culture. Benois noted that the ballet "was meant to demonstrate to the French public our understanding and interpretation of that 'most' French epoch, the eighteenth century."[11] The Ballets Russes presented both canonical French-inspired classical ballets, such as *La sylphide* and *Giselle*, and exotic "Russian-" and "Oriental-" themed works which fused Western and Eastern aesthetics. It was the latter that appealed most to Parisian audiences. While it began as a summer theatre, the Russian ballet became a permanent company in Paris in 1911. They would continue to perform at the Châtelet but also at the Opéra Garnier. The company's favourable reception and success led to two decades of performances and worldwide tours. In the last years of its existence (1922–29), the Ballets Russes established its base in Monte Carlo, Monaco – a mecca for the elite and leisure classes.[12]

From all of Diaghilev's "presentations" of Russian modern art, his debut of the Ballets Russes was the most successful. This was due to a number of factors. The Ballets Russes entered the Parisian scene when the French public was thirsting for anything new and modern. Parisians were enormously receptive to new artistic impressions. It was also a time when all things foreign were fashionable in France. In fact, there was a particular passion for all things Russian. This was prompted by the influx of Russian expatriates in Paris at the turn of the century. With the French translations of Russian literary works such as those of Tolstoy and Dostoevsky and the travel accounts of Russia by Dumas and Balzac gaining popularity, the French public was offered a variety of avenues into Russian society and culture. In fact, a "Russomania" spread among Parisians for Russian literature, painting, music, or fashion.[13] This Russomania rested on a perception of Russia as exotic. One expatriate, Russian painter Alexander Benois, who designed sets for the Ballets Russes, wrote regularly for the Russian press in Paris and often reported on the Parisians' fascination with Russian culture. Benois offered critical insight into the sources of the Parisian fervour for Russian culture at this time, writing that "it was Russian culture which triumphed in Paris, the whole essence of Russian art, its conviction, its freshness, its spontaneity … Our primitive wildness, our simplicity revealed itself in Paris as something more refined, developed, and subtle than the French themselves could do."[14] Former Ballets Russes dancer Lydia Sokolova (née Hilda Munnings) reminisced in her memoir that "when the Russian Ballet had first come to Europe, what thrilled Parisian audiences was not that they danced ballet, but that they were so Russian."[15]

Thus, unlike the modern works of art presented at the 1900 Exposition Universelle and the 1906 Salon d'Autumne, which were thought to be too Western influenced, the Ballets Russes presented a sensationalism, primitivism, and exoticism that satisfied Parisian tastes at the time. As Benois noted, the immediate attraction of the Ballet Russes was its "barbarism," opulence, sado-eroticism, sensationalism, and, in his words, the "spontaneity to become absorbed, just as children are completely absorbed in their play, in the God-like play which is art." He described this "play" as a "secret which has been lost on the Western stage, where everything is technique, everything is consciousness, everything is artificial, and from which have gradually disappeared the mysterious charm of self-oblivion, the great Dionysiac intoxication, the driving force of art."[16] Here Benois draws upon the polarization between "authentic" primitivism and purity, and the damaging artificiality of decadent oversophistication. This is an assumption that some critics would reiterate in their reviews of the Ballets Russes. For example, critic Lise-Léon Blum observed in 1914, "The Russian are children at play and their games are not our own … the Russians are back and still we do not tire of them … perhaps it is because they confuse us." She explained, "nothing is more foreign to our senses than these violent outbursts, frenzied and intensive dances, instinctive candor and unbridled fantasy ... The simple truth is that the Russians enchant us because they excite us. They are a young race ... [a] beautiful stranger ... And those who like them best are the most cultivated and the most jaded."[17] Critic Jean Perros once exclaimed, "Primitivisme! Primitivisme ... the Russians had come and finally, we were seeing the light." He then noted that the company had offered Paris "youth, candour, and truth," an "innocent soul," "youthful sensibility," and "ingenuous feelings." He concluded that their "simplicity, ardour, and devotion in the presence of nature ... explained their art and made it admirable."[18] This opposition between primitivity and the overly civilized also rested on the naturalist idea concerning the corporal body; namely, that the Russians, being less "civilized" than the French and closer to a natural state, were more "in touch" with their bodies and thus naturally better dancers.

Indeed, Ballets Russes productions (particularly those performed between 1909 and 1918) exploited Western European interests in expressionism, orientalism, symbolism, primitivism, and, to a greater extent, exoticism. As Benois described, they often conveyed an intoxicating fantasy of Russia as a wild, untamed place. This "fantasy" became an extraordinary cultural force in France. Sokolova recollected that "classical ballet was not new to Paris: Russian exotism was."[19] Sokolova suggests here that what initially captivated Parisian audiences was not the ballet dancing, but rather the exotic display of Russia. The French fascination with Russians as exotic "Others," however, was not as new as Sokolova would have us believe. The Russian stereotype held its roots in the nineteenth century, particularly in the fin de siècle. Defining "Others" was often a way of asserting a certain identity for France or, more generally, Europe. In fact, those Russians who did not reproduce an exotic Otherness were deemed often as uninteresting. In 1903, the reviewer and composer Alfred Bruneau criticized Tchaikovsky's work as "devoid of the Russian character that pleases and attracts us in the music of the New Slavic School, developed to hollow and empty excess in a bloated and faceless style, his works astonish without overtly interesting us."[20] Bruneau's critique is informative as it implies that, according to the French, a Russian composer's identity was dependent on an exotic group identity. Moreover, the lack of exoticism in Russian music made its composer "faceless." Clearly, to be a successful Russian artist and composer in France at this time, the mask of exoticism needed to be worn.

As we can see, Diaghilev's mythologization of Russians as exotic was not entirely original. He tapped into a French taste already rampant among Parisians. In fact, many Russian émigrés used a stereotype of "Otherness" to promote their success and acceptance in French society. Benois, in providing the image of Russians as retaining the "mysterious charms of self-oblivion" and "great Dionysian intoxication" may very well have fallen into the Russian tendency of parading themselves as Other. Diaghilev established a "Russian" repertoire created deliberately for a French audience. Therefore, it was imperative that set and costume designs, musical scores, stories, and choreography all emanate the stereotype of Russia as "exotic." As Richard Taruskin remarks, "not until 1921 would Diaghilev dare present Chaikovsky in any way but tiny doses to his audience; and when he did … he nearly lost his shirt."[21] Diaghilev knew that Tchaikovsky's transparent Western influences would not meet French tastes for the foreign in the Belle Époque. Strategically, Diaghilev drew upon a coherent mythology of Russia as primitive, exotic, and "Other."

Diaghilev's myth of Russia must be understood within the context of the polarization of national identity in Russia. Historically, Russia had been divided between the Western-looking St Petersburg (constructed by Peter the Great) and a Moscow that spurned the West and celebrated an authentic Slavic identity. Therefore, Russian national culture identity was no straightforward matter. It was a complex hybrid of East and West. The Ballets Russes navigated this seemingly conflicted national culture by uniquely asserting its own myth of Russia. Diaghilev linked "Russian" culture with a modernized style of ballet. *Firebird, Le festin, Schéhérazade, Prince Igor,* and *Sacre du printemps* are some of the ballets that revealed the potential for ballet to carry a powerful national image while offering a modern edge. A "Russian" national ideology was projected not only by the themes of the Ballets Russes' ballets, but also by the music, decor, set design, and costumes (even when its ballets did not draw explicitly upon Russian national subjects or themes).[22]

Diaghilev's presentation of *Firebird* (1910) performed at the Paris Opéra is a particularly good example of the exportation of a myth of Russia through ballet production. Loosely drawn from Russian fables, *Firebird* is the story of magic and love. The ballet tells the story of Prince Ivan's journey to win the heart and hand of his beloved princess Tsarevna, who is imprisoned in the Eastern-styled court of the evil tyrant Kostcheï. With the help of the exotic Firebird, Ivan is able to get past the magician-king and free his love. In this celebration of Russian folklore (expressly designed for a non-Russian audience), Diaghilev offered his own invention of Russian tradition by introducing orientalist and exotic elements into the ballet. Dance scholar Sally Banes describes the production of *Firebird* as "an insoluble mix of Russian and orientalist imagery," which not only concerned national ideology, but also served as the ultimate symbol of Russianness in its folkloric and exotic theme.[23] Ballets Russes dancer Lydia Sokolova commented similarly on Diaghilev's particular vision of Russia in the ballet: "Diaghilev, who in ballets like *L'Oiseau de Feu* [*Firebird*] and Petroushka 'revealed Russia to itself and to the world,' was by no means committed exclusively to the art of his own country – how could he be without degenerating into a mere purveyor of local colour, a hawker of peasant arts and crafts?"[24] In other words, Diaghilev incorporated styles extending beyond Russian art in order to sensationalize ballet. Thus we can see how ballet became a site for the assertion of a specific type of Russian national identity and, in this case, an identity much debated within Russia.[25]

Furthermore, while the Ballets Russes productions embraced the ambiguity and complexity of Russian national identity, they also challenged the traditions of ballet itself.[26] *Firebird*, for example, offered an alternative style of ballet, one that abandoned the formal symmetry of classical ballet and instituted free movement and pantomime in order to produce a more powerful dramatic effect. As its choreographer, Michael Fokine, noted, "In the composition of the dances I used three methods vastly different both in character and technique." The evil kingdom included movements that were at times "grotesque, angular, and ugly, and at times, comical," with its monsters "crawling on all fours and leaping like frogs." Instead of wearing classical pointe shoes, the princesses danced barefoot with natural, graceful, soft movements and some accent of the Russian folk dance. While only the dance of the Firebird was staged en pointe, "jumps … predominated in the choreography," which was "highly technical."[27] With an accompanying score by Igor Stravinsky that incorporated its own "exotic" Middle Eastern keys, *Firebird* was an instant success. Similarly, the turned-in, slouched, heavy movements in ballets like *Petrushka* and *Le sacre du printemps* and the "angular, entwined gestures and twisted torsos" of *Schéhérazade* and *Les orientales* created, in the words of dance scholar Sally Banes, "an alternative bodily canon" in ballet, which distinguished itself as Russian.[28] Vigorous and athletic steps, like those found in traditional Russian character dancing, were also integrated into the choreography. Traditionally, character dancing played a minor and, at times, inferior role in classical ballet productions. Fokine, in breaking the rules of traditional ballet, such as expanding character dancing, reconfigured ballet into something modern, versatile, and very "Russian." In fact, character dancing in ballets became and remains today primarily associated with Russian or Slavic culture.[29]

While scholars such as Banes do offer insight on the Ballets Russes' productions, they do not provide enough of a historical analysis of the ways in which dance criticism responded to the Ballets Russes. By historicizing what the critics were saying, one can gain perspective into how the French responded and absorbed the novelties of the Ballets Russes, and also locate the cultural shifts occurring in France in the early twentieth century. Much work regarding the impact of the Ballets Russes has tended to place too much emphasis on the innovations and transgressions of the Ballets Russes and their effect on French audiences. This project moves beyond such work in that it reveals how the presence of the Ballets Russes initiated a more complex dialogue on the function and value of ballet and its relation to nationalism, modern aesthetics, and gender. For example, the Ballets Russes played a part in inspiring the French to locate their own national qualities in ballet and to shape their own distinct national style. In doing so, they managed to revitalize their own national ballet as well as to legitimize criticism on dance. By historicizing the material on the Ballets Russes, one can also see the way in which ballet played an integral part in the political, social, cultural, and artistic shifts occurring in France in the early twentieth century. In the following pages, we will see how ballet became a site for the assertion of a specific type of Russian national identity and what that identity meant to the French.

Such innovations in ballet production (that is, exoticism, character dancing, pantomime) initiated a wealth of discussions on the nature of ballet. For the first time in decades, criticism of the ballet became legitimized and the artistic qualities of ballet production were taken more seriously. It is within the context established by the preceding pages that we can now explore the ways in which critics responded to this Russian modern ballet. There are four issues that preoccupied critics above all in their discussions of the Ballets Russes: the presentation of Russian national and exotic themes in ballet; the new "modern" style of Russian ballet; its virtuosic female and male dancers; and the origins of ballet as inherently French. Such discussions compelled critics to reflect upon the status of their own French ballet. Some even began to consider ballet's potential to reflect a modern republican French identity and to regain its status and grandeur as a French cultural institution. While critics expressed their enthusiasm for the Ballets Russes in their reviews, they also revealed their anxieties about foreign influence on French art and culture. We will see in the following pages how the Ballets Russes played a part in inspiring the French to locate and assert their own national qualities.

Press journalism in France responded to the Ballets Russes' "national" motifs and "new ballet" in various ways. Early reviews of *Le festin* (1909), *Firebird* (1910), *Schéhérazade* (1910), and *Petrushka* (1910) reveal that the idea of an exotic Russianness and its link to a new, modern form of ballet were powerfully promulgated by critics. According to one critic, *Firebird* "embodie[d] all the picturesque, strange, and invincible charm of the tales of Slav mythology."[30] Another critic attempted to link specific choreographic elements of the new ballet to intrinsic Russian qualities: "The third point particularly emphasized by the 'new ballet's' propagandists is the group principle. 'Group action,' about which several years ago all and sundry were holding forth, is ostensibly drawn from the depths of the Russian national soul (like the Slavophile's 'tribal community' of old) and in theatrical terms the predominance of the 'ensemble' has come to the fore as a basic principle of new ballet."[31] Here critic André Levinson is referring to the Ballets Russes' abandonment of the tradition of having one star dancer or couple before a corps de ballet backdrop. He associates the new ensemble work or "group action" and "new ballet" of the Ballets Russes with the Russian national soul. Thus, Levinson alludes to the association here of "new ballet" with Russian culture, and "classical ballet" with the older, Romantic French tradition.

In a review dating from 1910, critic Robert Brussel acclaimed the exotic *Firebird* as the most complete and beautiful performance of all the shows presented by the Ballets Russes. He stated that it represented the future of "a completely new orientation of the art of dance." For Brussel, it was the poetic vision, innovation, and vivacity that made the "new ballet" of the Ballets Russes so revolutionary: "Before *Firebird* we have known many pleasant and brilliant ballets, ornamented with interesting or mediocre music, sometimes of high quality, but always subjected to the demands of an old-fashioned tradition ... *Firebird* is perhaps the first which was liberated completely from these obstacles; the music, the fabrication, the decor and direction of choreography, equally maintain an interest." Here Brussel commends the Ballets Russes for introducing a balance of artistic elements (that is, the decor, choreography, and music) in their productions, an indication that Wagner's concept of "Gesamtkunstwerk" or "a total work of art" (i.e., a fusion of arts) had not yet been completely driven from French tastes by 1910. In *Firebird*, he was also enthralled with the Russian ballet's ability to capture Slavic poetic qualities: "The poem formed the material for a very rich and very complete lyrical drama, a rare event for a ballet; it is alive, expressive, and everywhere full of the most fresh poetry. It has borrowed one of a number of tales from Slavic mythology, and in particular those of the immortal Kotcheï: Ivan Tzarevich, chasing the marvellous bird made of gold and of flame, penetrates the secret domain of Kotcheï."[32] Thus it was for its ability to embody poetry and to balance other art forms, Brussel argued, that *Firebird* represented a turning point for ballet in the West. The Ballets Russes, in his opinion, was transforming the art of ballet into something new, more versatile, and poetic, but, moreover, exotic.

According to music critic Pierre Lalo, it was the dramatic intensity of movements and incorporation of character dancing in the ballets of the Ballets Russes that made the "new ballet" particularly exciting and appealing. In his *Le Temps* review of the ballet *Prince Igor* (1909), he attempted to explain why the Russian character dances were so attractive to the French public: "The character dances, which for the Russians have less prestige, are those that attract us the most. Russia, due to the extreme diversity of the races that compose it and its relatively recent civilization, has innumerable types of popular dances that have not yet lost their flavour and primitive meaning. Many of these dances are employed in the ballet, to which they communicate, as much through their multiciplicity as by the vehemence of their steps and figures, a variety of looks and an intensity of life that are extraordinary."[33] Lalo, like many others, located the Ballets Russes' splendour not only within its use of popular and "primitive" motifs and its diversity of traditions, but also within its incorportion of powerful movements in ballet. For example, Lalo interpreted the opening scene of *Prince Igor* as a war dance. He described the dramatic intensity of the ballet as "a violent and natural action of savages energized by rhythm, movement, and force," which was executed in what seemed to him to be "an indistinct style of hygienic exercise."[34] Lalo went on to describe the dancing as an extraordinary mixture of "frenetic gestures and forms where the fury of movement carried a sort of dizziness and Dionysian Madness." Here we are reminded of painter Alexander Benois's description of the Ballets Russes as embodying a "primitive wildness" and "great Dionysiac intoxication."

Lalo's excitement about the intensity of character dancing and its allure as primitive is not particularly new. In fact, we find similar critical responses to flamenco dancing, a type of Spanish character dancing, that was performed in Paris at the turn of the century. One critic, writing in the prestigious music journal *Le Ménestrel*, asserted that "the drunken rhythms" of flamenco were "so boisterous" that it took "such a strong hold of its victims and spectators [actors and spectators alike] prey to this special fever ... The public utters furious cries." He began his article by referring to the Spanish dancers as the "degenerate descendants of ancient Greece."[35] Another critic, Jean Lorrain, wrote in the nationalist paper *L'Écho de Paris*, that flamenco was "a sort of hysterical unconscious frenzy." Clearly, Russian character dancing and Spanish flamenco dancing elicited similar critical responses on the part of critics. As we can see from such commentary, Parisians were both attracted and hostile to foreign dance. Futhermore, the descriptions of the Ballets Russes' "new ballet" as a "fury of movements," "frenetic," and full of "dizziness" starkly contrasted with France's Romantic "old ballet," which was composed, fragile, ethereal, feminine, and refined.

Lalo's reaction to *Prince Igor* captures well the French vision of Russians as less rational, less civilized, and less in control. We find similar responses in the realm of music. In his review of a piece by Russian composer Glazunov in 1889, music critic Adolphe Jullien used words such as "rare instinct," "strangest rhythms," "violence," "an expressive and tender melancholy," "an exaggerated use of color," "a veritable abuse of developments or orchestral combinations," and above all, "the absence of an underlying plan."[36] Another critic writing about Russian music at the Exposition Universelle went so far as to remark that it was not a good idea for the French public to "absorb Russian music in extreme doses."[37] Here a critic mimics the tone of a doctor. Clearly, when it came to music, refinement, control, and rationalism were still deemed by critics as essential to a composer's success in France. According to some music critics, Russian composers lacked measure, planning, and control. As Lalo's review indicates, the Ballets Russes also exhibited a lack of control in their dancing and, in their irrational state, even exhibited a "Dionysian madness." Nonetheless, the Ballets Russes was successful in captivating Parisian audiences with their exploitation of Otherness and, in doing so, drew critics' interest to ballet production.

As we will see, Lalo's overall tone was one that resonated within many French reviews of the Ballets Russes. Lalo's remarks on Russia's "relatively recent civilization" and "their primitive flavour" are not surprising given the predominant attitudes of the French towards foreigners in this period, particularly Russians and Jews.[38] In a period when fears of national degeneration were high in France, foreigners were a means against which to delineate French superiority. A letter that appeared in *L'Action Française* on 6 January 1909 offers a good example of such rhetoric. The contibutor remarked, "[a] horde of Russians, men and women, has invaded the schools, especially the Faculties of Medicine and Letters. These individuals are ridiculously dressed, speak hardly any French, and affect a rudeness toward their French comrades that is typical of their native land ... The whole educational machine built by our fathers is now functioning for the benefit of the foreigner."[39] While revealing French anxieties about foreigners invading French institutions, this letter also expresses the French expection that foreigners, here Russians, assimilate to French culture. According to this writer, Russians should learn to speak French well, to dress "appropriately," have good "French" taste, and converse in a rational, French manner. Here Russians are perceived as the antithesis of the French. Yet, as we have already seen, in the world of art and entertainment, this very difference was what appealed to the French. Thus while Russian exoticism was alluring in the realms of literature, art, fashion, and cuisine, it still incited anxieties over the invasion of French culture by foreigners.

At a time of increasing anti-Semitism, Jews were also targeted as "exotic," "barbaric," and "invasive." Thus when critics were not attributing "Russianness" to the orientalist flavour of the Ballets Russes, they were often referring to the "Jewishness" of Leon Bakst's decor. Referring to the sets of Bakst, painter and critic Maurice Denis once noted in his diary, "Saison Russes: les ballets juifs" [Russian Season: the Jewish Ballets].[40] Denis may very well be referring here to the large number of Jewish patrons, collaborators, and members of the audience of the Ballets Russes.[41] In fact, the novelist Paul Morand went so far as to say that it was the "great Israelite audience that established the success of the Russian ballet."[42] However, by linking the Ballets Russes to Jewishness, Denis also emphasizes that the Russian company belonged to a different cultural world. Art critic André Warnod was more direct, stating forthrightly: "Bakst is Jewish and this explains the sensuality of his art and his prodigious talent for assimilation."[43] At the turn of the century, qualities of Jews were not merely regarded as socially constructed but biologically bound. Jews were often stereotyped as lustful, excessive, shrewd, duplicious, and sensual.[44] In his book *L'éducation de la volonté* (1893), hygienic reformer Jules Payot observed that in young men, sensuality was one of the most significant obstacles to masculine autonomy.[45] Thus by drawing attention to Bakst's Jewish origins and the sensuality of his art, Warnod emphasizes Bakst's Otherness and potential effeminacy – sensuality being an impediment to masculinity. According to both Denis and Warnod, there were visible markers of Jewishness in the art produced by the Ballets Russes. Gabriel Astruc, the founder and manager of the Théâtre des Champs-Élysées where the Ballets Russes often performed, was often targeted for being a Jew. Astruc was also known for enthusiastically booking international troupes at his venue. In a headline article for *L'Action Française,* Léon Daudet viciously attacked Astruc's influence on Parisian culture, writing: "The Jew behind the Grand Saison de Paris is demolishing the Parisian season, as his species demolishes the French forest, completely … When Astruc is finished with Paris, he will do the same with Vienna or Berlin. This is the behaviour of the Jewish bank applied to the theatre."[46] Both the Russians and the Jews, therefore, were seen by some as the antithesis of the French and the West.

Other critics were more explicit in their attitudes towards Russians and dancing. French poet, critic, and essayist André Suarès believed that the Russians were more suited to dancing than the French due to their natures. Writing in *La Nouvelle Revue Française,* he declared dancing as the primal unity of body and soul, and indicated that it was for that reason that the Russians dancers were superior.[47] French poet, novelist, and politician Abel Bonnard wrote frankly, "Really, we no longer know what dancing is. We are not savage enough." He continued:

> As a community, we are too civilized, too polished, too prone to self-effacement. We have lost all knowledge of how to express feeling with the whole of our bodies: why, we are almost afraid to let it transpire in our features, or in the words we utter, so that all that remains is for it to seek refuge in our eye. Our very gestures have become impoverished, restricted, tight, and fall from us like branches from lopped trees. We all live in our heads. Our bodies, so to speak, have been abandoned and we no longer exist in them: they have become, as it were, impoverished and foreign to us, and have lost that palpitating sincerity which makes savages and the beasts of the wild so magnificent in our eyes. Thus it is only too comprehensible that that art which lives by reproducing man, sculpture, should be fading away at the same rate.[48]

Here we find an explicit articulation of cultural difference from the Russian "Other," something often used by critics as a way to reaffirm French identity.[49] Many critics at this time, especially right-wing writers like Bonnard, emphasized the "barbaric," "exotic," and "uncivilized" qualities of the Ballets Russes. However, as scholar Stephanie Lin explains, barbarism in the context of Russia was defined in specific terms in the mid-nineteenth and early twentieth century. Unlike the German "barbarism" that was often stereotyped as malevolent and brutal, Lin writes that "the barbaric qualities attributed to the Russians … refer not to a violent nature, but to one that is uncultivated, lacking education and reason, and therefore given to baser instincts."[50] In this respect, Bonnard believed that the Russians were superior dancers.

In his review, Bonnard draws upon a binary opposition of the mind and the body. This distinction between mind and body, between the intellectual and physical, and between the emotional and sensual have long informed Western thought. According to Bonnard, dancing rests on an absence of mental control, a reliance on intuitive movement and an embrace of irrationality. He asserts that the French are no longer able to dance because they have evolved into rational, intellectual, disciplined, and overly civilized people. These criteria of dance are the opposite of those used in art and music, which ideally required restraint, control, rationality, and the adherence to strict principles. The idea of dance as a primarily physical, irrational, intuitive practice corresponds with the ideas put forth by the rising field of anthropology in France at this time. A connection between dancing and primitivity was one that surfaced routinely in anthropological publications in which dance was identified as the earliest art of primitive societies.[51] In fact, this very idea would resonate in the modernism of Ballets Russes productions, particularly in the ballet and score of *Le sacre du printemps.* The link between dancing and primitivism problematized any exaltation of French ballet dancing. This explains why the working-class French dancers at the Opéra were deemed by Bonnard as mediocre: they were still civilized racially as French people, but degenerative to some degree. Thus the Russians were deemed better dancers by Bonnard due to the "primitive" nature of dance as a wordless, embodied art form. However, in dance, the body is, at once, artist, instrument, and art object. As such, contrary to Bonnard's beliefs, ballet is an artistic practice that entails a significant amount of discipline, rationality, creativity, control, balance, comportment, the strict adherence to codification, and significant self-reliance. Nonetheless, Bonnard's review reveals how some critics were committed to affirming differences between the Russians and the French. In the case of Bonnard, the Russian ballet was not superior due to its talented and virtuosic dancers and the intensity of their artistic training, but rather as a result of their primitive natures. Here we can see how some critics tried to create national and racial boundaries between the Ballets Russes and its French audiences.

Whether or not the Ballets Russes represented an "authetic" Russian culture or were "more suitable" for dancing, critics were intrigued with the company's success both in Paris and abroad. Many critics tried to determine what exactly made the Ballets Russes and its modern Russian style so appealing to the French public. In locating the sources of this success in Russian innovations, some forged a link between Russian identity and an improved form of ballet. In fact, we find critics crediting Russia (whether implicitly or explicitly) for the maintenance and revival of the art of ballet – an art form that, although it had originated on the French stage, had fallen into neglect in France. Russia ballet became a marker for artistic innovation, virtuosity, and modernity. As the reputation of the Ballets Russes grew in France and also internationally, critics began to inquire into the fallen state of French ballet, particularly at the Opéra.

Some critics argued that the Ballets Russes' success was due to the exceptional quality of its dancers. In doing so, they contributed to the promotion and valorization of Russian ballet and culture to the extent that "Russianness" now became a measure of quality for dancers and dancing: "Seriously, these Russian dancers have dazzled us. This publicity has exaggerated nothing, which, in the last fifteen days, celebrates their agility, praises their grace, extols their versatility; if anything, it has understated their merit – which proves the heights to which they rise … One is marvelled by the virtuousity of these incomparable dancers of the Imperial theatres of Moscow and of St Petersburg. Mmes Karalli, Karsavina, Baldina, Fedorova, Smirnova, Dobrolubova, MM. Morkine, Nijinsky, Boulgahow, Gregoriew, Pebrow, etc. are outrageously applauded upon their entrance."[52] In his article, this critic (signed "Paulino") noted that it was not merely the *étoiles* of the Russian Ballet that surpassed those at the Opéra, but additionally the discipline and stage arrangements of the Russian corps de ballet that were undeniably impressive. "Paulino" observed that specific Russian training in "group action" produced more diversity and freedom on the ballet stage. For example, he compared this Russian skill of coordinated and synchronized complex arrangements on stage to that of the French, which in its aim of balance between groups produced ultimately, in his opinion, a monotony of symmetrical arrangements.[53] He claimed that the Russian school was "crushingly" superior to that of the French, whose choreography had fallen into decadence. According to Paulino, the Russians preserved the choreographic beauty of classical ballet better than any other nation.[54] Specifically, the Russians maintained not only the royal connection but the interest of a cultured middle-class society that desired to maintain "in all their purity the better traditions of classical dance" that were introduced in the time of Catherine the Great to St Petersburg and Moscow.[55]

Critics frequently commented on the high quality of male dancing and choreography in Ballets Russes productions and compared them favourably to French ballet. In fact, they often argued that French ballet should borrow Russian qualities of choreography, particularly those involved in male ballet dancing: "The talent of the male dancers is again a distinctive sign that renders Russian choreography superior to ours, and one of the qualities which we should borrow from them. Thanks to the vigour, the agility, the virtuosity of these men, the ballet possesses the basic element of force that is lacking in ours. This element of force is naturally a decisive reason for diversity; our ballets, where one watches all but women, where the men only take a background and secondary role, have an eternal grace that degenerates into insipidity."[56] *Prince Igor* (1909), one of the Ballets Russes' first ballets presented in France, prompted much critical discussion on the troupe's use of men. A cast of twenty-five men at the opening of the ballet charged forward towards the audience producing a very powerful effect. Pierre Lalo commented: "This grace is revealed in the Slavic choreography by its very energetic sequences, which the steps of the archers, in the second act of *Prince Igor*, was a most striking example. It is the introduction of this element of collective force in ballet which appears to me to constitute the principal interest of the appearance of the Russian male dancers."[57] *Prince Igor* inspired a long captivation with the male dancers of the Ballets Russes on the part of the French press and public. Critics noted that Russian innovations in choreography for male dancers offered a new virtuosity, agility, and strength. In fact, the very "Russianness" of its dancers (or symbolic Russianness as many of the dancers were in fact Polish) was used to instill a new masculinity and virility in the male dancing body (explored further in chapters 6 and 7).

The association between Russian national identity and the quality of ballet dancing became so powerful that dancers in France (and later abroad) increasingly adopted Russian stage names for credibility. It was crucial for dancers to have Russian identities attached to them. John Drummond, in *Speaking of Diaghilev* (1997), best captures the essence of what ballet represented in the first decade of the twentieth century: "No one talked of 'ballet' in the early years of the century, it was always 'Russian ballet.' Teachers and dancers had to have Russian names, however grotesque the results for non-Russians; for example Hilda Munnings was Munningsova before she became Sokolova, and Nottingham-born Hilda Boot in the Pavlova company was Butsova. It was the power of the words 'Ballets Russes' that eventually gave the rump of the Diaghilev company another two decades of life."[58] As ballet historian Arnold Haskell notes, "Though the Diaghileff Ballet had its artistic headquarters in Paris and, when the supply from Russia was interrupted, was in constant need of dancers, not a single French dancer joined its ranks." However, there were numerous English recruits who took on Russian pseudonyms.[59] English dancers such as Alicia Markova (née Alice Marks), Lydia Sokolova (née Hilda Munnings), and Anna Bromova (née Annie Broomhead) all changed their names for professional purposes.

Former Ballets Russes *étoile* Lydia Sokolova remarked upon the importance of stage names and their national associations to a dancer's career and reputation. Diaghilev had personally changed her English name Hilda Munnings to Lydia Sokolova in honour of a former Russian dancer and her exquisite style. "Forget from now on that you have ever been anything but Russian," Diaghilev told Sokolova.[60] In her autobiography, Sokolova reminisces about when newcomer Anton Dolin (né Patrick Healey Kay) revealed his true name to the press: "He was young and inexperienced, and had not yet heard that there were some things one must never do in the Diaghilev ballet. He revealed that his real name was Patrick Healey Kay and even mentioned that I was English, too. When this appeared in print, Diaghilev was furious."[61] In the early years of the twentieth century, a Russian dancer represented an incredibly disciplined style of training as well as a professionalism never previously achieved by ballet dancers in France. Consequentially, having a Russian identity as a dancer gave one credibility, approval, and public attention. Upon meeting the king and queen of Spain, Diaghilev told Sokolova, "Hilda, don't mention your nationality. I have just told the King that all my artists are Russian."[62] This would change in the 1920s, when more and more French dancers kept their birth names and foreign-born dancers changed their names to French ones (for example, Janine Charat, Jean Babilée [né Gutmann], Yvette Chauviré, and Ninette de Valois [née Edris Stannus, founder of the Royal Ballet], David Lichine [né David Lichtenstein]).

Several other critics, however, were far more concerned with the Russian company's spectacular decor, costumes, and musical scores than the actual dancers and choreography. They argued that it was the fusion of arts that made the Ballets Russes great. These critics were most captivated by the harmonious relationship between all elements of its productions even though some were more partial to certain aspects than others. Thus critic Valerian Svetlov, drawing attention to the quality of painting, boldly concluded that "our painters have played an all-important part in the revolution of ballet … it is they who are the true authors of its renaissance, and it seems to me that both historic accuracy and mere justice demand that this fact should at last be admitted and loudly acclaimed."[63] Second only to his enthusiasm for the energetic dancing of its male dancers, Pierre Lalo was intrigued by the Ballets Russes' use of coloration within its ballets. "The second of two subjects [the first being the force of the male dancers] touching those which we may learn from the Russian performances is that of costume and decor. The costumes of the pieces … have a remarkable aspect, to which we have never seen in our own theatres and cannot compare. They form by their reunion of intensity – a force and a depth of extraordinary coloration … More than us, the Russians make use of bold and violent colours, vigorously opposing and contrasting each other … We employ only nuances as delicate as possible, degraded and melted with refinement."[64] Lalo's comments are a classic example of how critics compared the Ballets Russes to French ballet. According to Lalo, the Russian use of colour in their costumes and sets was totally different from that used in French ballet productions. The Russian principle of colour, in its power and boldness (energetic tones), he remarked, aimed "to suggest … not to pretend to imitate nature," but rather "to surround the drama and the characters with forms." This was achieved, in Lalo's view, by the choice of colours in the sets that were designed to play off one another and to react against the costumes. In doing so, Lalo argued, Russian decor and choreography were in perfect harmony with each other, their "energetic tones" creating "an harmonious unity."[65] Ultimately, he found that the harmony of decor, music, pantomime, and dance was extraordinary in the "new ballet" of the Ballets Russes' productions.[66]

Although Lalo drew attention to the collaborative nature of the new Russian style of ballet, he also noted the important and central role music played, writing that "in the Russian ballets, music is not secondary; it is the central part of the performance.[67] In other words, Lalo argued that it was the new importance placed on ballet music that made the ballet of the Ballets Russes so unique. In another article, Lalo wrote, "The music is here the principle and the centre of everything: it is the soul and essence of the performance, no longer an insignificant and neglected assessory."[68] Critics' emphasis on the music of ballet may reflect the fact that many reviewers of ballets were actually music critics, as in the case of Lalo. Such critics may have felt most comfortable discussing what they knew best or simply were enthralled that music could hold a more distinguished place in ballet. Eventually, specialists on dance criticized music critics for their overemphasis on the music rather than placing value on the dancing itself.

Thus far, we have seen the ways in which the French were enamoured or intrigued by the Ballets Russes. In some cases, one can argue that the Russian company attained a "fetish" status. However, not all critics were enthralled with the company. While some critics welcomed the innovations occurring on the ballet stage, others felt threatened by the success of such changes. For example, the innovations in ballet costume by the Ballets Russes compelled one critic to write an editorial entitled "Is This the End of the Tutu?" in *Comœdia.* This critic expressed his concern over the Ballets Russes' influence on French ballet, particularly at the Paris Opéra: "Mr Clustine, the Opera's new ballet master, proposes, among other reforms, to do away with, in so far as it could be done, the 'tutu' of our dancers. What an affair! Really, one could believe that all the Russians who come to Paris are revolutionaries!"[69] This critic was reacting to the Ballets Russes' exotic costumes such as tunics and sarafin pants on both female and male dancers, which were radically new costumes for the ballet stage. His article demonstrates a fear of the Ballets Russes' influence on the reforms occurring at the Paris Opéra ballet and, furthermore, its negative influence on traditional French ballet (and the French Romantic tutu). This anxiety was exacerbated by the appointment of Russian Ivan Clustine as ballet master of the Opéra in 1911. Critics expressed their weariness of having the Russian émigré, who had previously worked for the Bolshoi in Moscow, direct the Paris Opéra ballet and feared that the French company would become an imitation of the Ballets Russes. Clustine, in turn, defended himself in a subsequent article, insisting that "the Ballets Russes influence at the Opéra would be madness." He claimed that the two ballet aesethetics were entirely opposed and did not have "one point in common concerning their method of production." He assured the French public that it would be foolish to "change the context in which an oeuvre develop[ed]."[70] Thus this article about the potential loss of the tutu not only aggravated underlying fears about foreign influence on French art, but also elicited concerns about the preservation of French tradition in ballet at a time when French ballet had fallen into decline. The use of the tutu signified ballet's origins as a French art form. This critic is thus responding to the loss of Frenchness in modern ballet and, moreover, Russia's invasion of French artistic tradition.

Indeed, while the Ballets Russes was attractive for some, it provoked fear and anxiety about the foreign influence on French culture. Critic Victor Debay felt that the Russians were manipulating Parisian audiences. In his article "Les Ballets Russes" (1913) in *Le Courier Musical,* Debay asserted, "Foreigners consider Paris as a docile patient on whom all operations can be attempted."[71] Other critics expressed their hostility more directly. In 1914, music critic Louis Laloy, a fervent nationalist, cautioned: "The invasion of the barbarians is always to be feared … The barbarians of art are amongst us … They have been observing us for a long time and, at first, they laughed at our silly antics along with the masses, who were unaware that they were our front-line guards. Then they drew closer, gained in courage, saw the opportunity for fame that we had forgotten in the heat of battle; their covetousness was aroused, and *voilà,* they crept into the arena and now declare their turn to be artists."[72] Here we can see Laloy's anxieties about foreigners in France. Music critic Émile Vuillermoz also delineated his hostility, fear, and weariness over the Russian influence on French aesthetics. In an article from 1913, he opened, "Alone at last!" Our wild guests, after maddening, overwhelming and exasperating Paris, have now departed … we gaze at one another in bewilderment and weariness." He then captured the effect the Russians had on French culture, writing, "The guests were delightful, but they did some damage: here is a decapitated statue, a broken mirror, a stain in the silk, and here is a tear in the rug. The Russians have come our way, and now everything is in ruin and regret in the salons of the French aesthetic."[73] According to Vuillermoz, there were dire consequences to the exposure of Russian artistic innovations. We can see from such commentary that while the Ballets Russes fulfilled the Belle Époque's promise of pleasure and distraction, it also fuelled fears about degeneration and the cultural invasion of foreigners.

Russian émigré and dance specialist André Levinson was not at all seduced by the new and exotic ballet of the Ballets Russes. In fact, he made efforts to expose the company's fraudulent representation of Russia. Levinson pronounced the company's invention of a contrived

Russian identity and declared that he was not convinced of even *Firebird*'s authentic cultural depiction. While some critics were mesmerized by the new "Russian" spectacle of ballet, Levinson criticized the Ballets Russes for its falsification of authentic Russian folk art tradition: "Golovin's splendid production can justifiably be placed alongside Bakst's Oriental fantasies, but to regard *Firebird* as a contribution to the national mythology would be frivolous to say the least. It has nothing in common with real folk art and even the plot of the folk tale was presented in the scenario in an insipid, confused way. In the dances themselves there is almost no use of folk motifs."[74] In *Firebird,* Levinson could locate only slight traces of "true" Russian folk motifs within "Golovin's decors … of brown and green with gold," the "white chemises" of the captive princesses that "recall[ed] Polenova's paintings," and "Ivan Tsarevich's cafton and hat." In one Russian dance in the ballet *Le festin,* Levinson located "more Russian fluidity, laziness and sudden animation." Repeatedly, Levinson attempted to erode the fantasy of Russia that had made the Ballets Russes so seductively appealing to the French.

Furthermore, Levinson strongly opposed the choreographic innovations of Michel Fokine (who choreographed many of the Ballets Russes' ballets), calling him a "master rebel" who would cause "ballet's *suicide* on the public stage." He accused Fokine of "sacrific[ing] the forms of abstract mouvement for expression, pure dance for pantomime."[75] Instead, Levinson advocated a return to traditional "classical" ballet – the language and structure of choreographer and dancer Marius Petipa, who was responsible for the development of ballet in Russia in the mid- to late nineteenth century. In *Ballet Old and New* (1918), Levinson describes the works of Ballets Russes choreographers Michel Fokine and Vaslav Nijinsky as "aesthetic diversions" and "playthings of precocious snobbism and restless frivolity."[76] In other words, Levinson perceived the Ballets Russes as a superficial form of ballet. Levinson's hostility towards the Ballets Russes is grounded in his Symbolist leanings and his devotion to French choreographer Marius Petipa. His fierce defence of French "old ballet" and Petipa's "classical" ballet may also be indicative of his need to assimilate to his new country of residence. Like several other highly visible émigrés in the French intellectual world, Levinson also stressed his love for France, adoration of French culture, and loyalty to its traditions.

Levinson's observations were also part of a growing debate over ballet aesthetics at this time. As early as 1910, critic Robert Brussel noted the choreographic/aesthetic debate in his *Le Figaro* review of *Firebird*: "And if ever the displays of Russian art have carried a lesson, it's surely yesterday's performance that has generously provided it, not so much by the detail – moreover always sumptuous ... but by the principle that commands the spirit, and by the aesthetic debate of choreography that it raises." However, he continued, "It would be interesting to discuss the arguments; unfortunately, I am not able to do this here."[77] In adding a new vigour to debates concerning choreography, Levinson would lead the way in rallying the French to revitalize their own classical tradition.

While the return of ballet in France (via the Ballets Russes) brought about a focus on foreign talents, it also called the state of French ballet into question. In a *Le Figaro* article of 1910, French novelist and critic Marcel Prévost (1862–1941) presented what was for him the current predicament of ballet performance in France. His article opened enthusiastically, boasting that "the dance returns to us from the north, smart, sparkling, dripping with light and harmony ... Once again, well, here it is, the dance is one of the elements of the beauty and holiday of Paris ... Once again, the names of the ballerinas are on the lips of the crowd, and the names of ballets compete, to attract spectators and fill the houses, with the most famous titles of operas and plays." Seeming excited by the prospect of ballet's revival, he went on to observe: "What cheerfulness such a renaissance brings to the old fans of this charming art, at the same time childish and venerable ... One of them [a dilettante] was telling me yesterday, as we were leaving *Scheherazade*, about his enthusiasm ... he was leaving an opera house where the city's elite had cheered a ballet. After such a long eclipse (he cried, sweet tears in his eyelids), the dance will once again reign in Paris!"[78] Yet Prévost cautioned such enthusiastic fans not to be "too happy too soon." He reminded his readers that although the Ballets Russes' sojourn in Paris had been a "brillant success," it was the success of a foreign company during a short period of evenings. "Should we conclude that the ballet – after the Russian fashion – will fill, winter and spring, the enormous vessel erected by Garnier?" he asked. Prévost's answer was discouraging: "I would admit such possibility if only the French lifestyle of today permitted the formation and permanent keeping of a dance company like the one

St. Petersburg has sent us." He pessimistically concluded: "But such a company is not possible in Paris. It [the company] is not possible in a democratic country."[79] Even though the Ballets Russes was a success in Paris, Prévost implies here that it was impossible to create an equivalent company in republican France or, indeed, in any democratic nation. He argues this because he believed that the success of the Ballets Russes was linked to Russia's imperial tradition and that ballet by its very nature was an aristocratic art.[80]

According to Prévost, ballet served a specific function in an aristocratic government. The corps de ballet, he writes, was "a necessary accessory to a great Court of an aristocratic government" which depended on the prosperity and the glamour of the court for its existence.[81] In fact, he found the very idea of the corps de ballet inseparable from the idea of a court. "Chosen with great care and maintained in great luxury," he points out, the corps de ballet was always used to contribute to the magnificence of court entertainments and national celebrations. For a monarch, he explained, the corps de ballet served as a kind of "Royal Guard" of pleasure. He argued that a republican government and culture, in contrast, would not tolerate such a function with its "scrupulous maintaining of old customs and aristocratic moeurs" nor could it sustain ballet's splendour (the French ballet was not sufficiently funded) without the patronage of a court.[82] He proved his point by describing the situation at the Opéra, where, due to a lack of financial support, the ballet depended on private subscribers and, therefore, yielded to "the free and easy relation" between its ballet dancers and male subscribers. "How little our usual ballets compel the interest of real lovers of dancing!" he lamented. Prévost attributed this to the lack of discipline of French dancers, an inattentive public, and, in general, French ballet's descent into decadence. According to him, ballet could not serve as a democratic entertainment without falling into a decadent spectacle of the female body (for example, music hall ballet). Prévost would have been aware of the ballets that were being performed also in the music halls of Paris. His article is a good example of the concerns of bourgeois critics about the potential fall of ballet's status from a high art to a popular entertainment. In this respect, Prévost implies that France's very republicanism made the nation incapable and, perhaps, unworthy of true ballet.

Prévost's argument reveals a fundamental relationship between political culture and ballet for the French. Essentially, Prévost argued that it was impossible for France to have a strong national ballet troupe like that of Russia or as it had under the direction of Louis XIV during the ancien régime. According to him, ballet was an aristocratic entertainment that could not lend itself to democratic ideals. Prévost attributed part of the success and sensation of the Ballets Russes to its ability to transport French audiences into a foreign, aristocratic world and perhaps a nostalgic one. "And that which we applaud, that which seduces us in the spectacle of the Russian ballets," he writes, "is it not precisely the fact that for a few fifteen-minute periods we leave behind our habitual lifestyle, our republican way of life, even our country?" He explains: "Suddenly, at the sound of a passionate music, among the colours of uncommon violence, we become the citizens of a faraway land, governed in a fashion other than our own – a land where luxury is concentrated in the hands of a privileged group instead of being, like in Paris, dispersed here and there … a land where there is a monarch, a court, and courtiers. This sudden transposition enchants us."[83] Here Prévost suggests that it was not merely the Ballets Russes but the very politics associated with the art of ballet that transported Parisians to another place and time.

Thus Prévost's conclusion about the future of French ballet is especially grim: First, he points out that the pleasure offered by the Ballets Russes dancers was "exclusively a pleasure for the *happy few*" – meaning it drew in a selective, elite, and discriminative audience. The Russians, he explains, had come to Paris "expressly for [this group's] delight" where such audiences (admirers of dance) could "relish their archaic and subtle flavour." He concludes: "But the crowds that rush to the music halls will not follow us there … Old devotee, my friend, do not therefore shed pious tears of joy over the renaissance of your cherished art: this art is dead among us, utterly dead, and nothing will ever resuscitate it … Let us content ourselves with applauding it, and delighting when it is here. A courtly pleasure, a royal entertainment, let us reserve for the dance the welcome Paris reserves for queens."[84] Not only does Prévost declare ballet's demise in France, but he clearly does not perceive any potential for ballet to represent republican values.

Unlike Prévost, other critics demonstrated a willingness, if not openness, to resuscitate ballet in France. Camille Mauclair, in an article entitled "A Lesson of the Russian Season," highlighted ballet dancing's origins in French tradition rather than ballet's Russian manifestations. He declared that "dancing, too, has no less brought its surprises, but in a very different way ... On this occasion it has surprised us greatly to recognize, in Russian choreography, the principles of our ancient French choreography, absolutely forgotten today, but exported to Russia at the end of the eighteenth and the beginning of the nineteenth century by our own ballet masters."[85] He went on to locate such "French principles" in the dancing of the Ballets Russes stars. He wrote: "When it was said of Mlle Salle or of Camargo [eighteenth-century French dancers] that 'every step was an emotion,' it was as though Pavlova or Karsavina were already being spoken of; and the mimed dance of Nijinsky can alone restore to us some idea of what Vestris meant to our ancestors."[86] By implying that the Russians were merely realizing the visions of past French masters, Mauclair was essentially challenging the originality of the Russian ballet. In other words, he implied that Russian ballet was merely a refurbished version of traditional French ballet.

Mauclair's article then turned to the state of French ballet. He admitted the lack of French tradition found within France's own Paris Opéra ballet and its French dancers. "Where is there any indication of that measured, noble art in our corps de ballet, which hurls itself feverishly about in a fictitious Italian *furia*, in the livid illumination of a last judgment, and whose unbridled sensuality marks the limits of its capacity for expression?" he asked. Turning to the dancing of the Ballets Russes, he posed the following questions:

> Where can we find an equivalent to that Dance of the Bowmen, in *Prince Igor*, sustained by that masterpiece of Borodin's, and lovely as a Persian miniature come to life? Where can we find that dance of *L'Oiseau de Feu* [Firebird], in which Karsavina seems to defy the very laws of gravity, and is metamorphosed into a fairy? What theatre of ours has ever put on dancing equal to that of the bacchanal in *Cléopatre*, or the orgy of *Schéhérazade*, or beaten out a measure instinct with a melancholy, a fury, a languor so oriental and nostalgic as Rimsky-Korsakov's rhythms? Alas! how distant all this is from our *coryphées and corps de ballets*![87]

Here Mauclair acknowledges the same inadequacies and declined state of French ballet along with its corps de ballet as Prévost did. However, unlike Prévost, Mauclair believed that the French ballet could rise again. In fact, Mauclair fantasized about a reunion of French talents in the ballet scene, writing, "A Fokine inventing a ballet, to music by Debussy, and decorations by Maurice Denis, with a Karsavina on the stage, and a Messager to conduct, what a magnificent evening that would make … if it could ever be anything but a dream!" He then implores, "But who will remake, from top to bottom, our dancers and ballerinas? Who will deliver us from the ridicule of our own traditional ballet?"[88] Thus, as early as 1911, critics addressed not only the neglected state of ballet in France, but also the prospect of a renewed Paris Opéra Ballet (despite the pessimism of Marcel Prévost).

As we have seen, the Ballets Russes raised a variety of topics and anxieties among Parisian critics. By focusing on the Ballets Russes, critics found opportunity to discuss the state of ballet in France. Some critics, however, were not convinced that the Ballets Russes was unique in its talents. One critic claimed that the Ballets Russes' success had nothing to do with the dancers and dancing or with imperial tradition, but simply with the strong direction and management of the company. His article entitled "A New Ballet Master at the Opera" (1911) for *Comœdia* not only demonstrates how the Russian ballet encouraged comparison with the state of French ballet, but also reveals the growing inquiry into what exactly makes a great national ballet company: "One would not be able to deny that the question of the corps de ballet in our subsidized theatres has not for some time acquired considerable importance. The different Russian performances, whose incomparable brilliance has evoked among us a legitimate admiration, have raised inevitable comparisons. We have asked ourselves whether the elements at our disposal were not perhaps inferior to those of our friends and allies, and if the art of choreography, yesterday so highly honoured, is not in complete decadence in our beautiful France."[89] This critic (who signed as "L.P.") goes on to respond to the general pessimism (like that of Prévost) over French ballet, writing, "Pessimistic souls who have reached an affirmative conclusion have been perhaps a little too hasty in formulating their judgment." He argues fervently that the Russian originality and grace were no less to be found in the "first class principal dancers" of France who "possess[ed] equally remarkable qualities."[90] He questions whether such French dancers were well employed and competently directed.[91]

What this article reveals is that by 1911 critics were already turning their attention to French ballet and recognizing its future potential as a national art. This critic indicated that the problem with French ballet was not the quality of the dancers but rather the direction and management of the companies – here specifically at the Paris Opéra. In fact, noting the new efforts taken to revitalize the Opéra's corps de ballet, he explained that the Opéra looked to Russian innovation because Russia was able to preserve better "the beautiful traditions of art and living of eighteenth-century dance [which was French]."[92] This critic felt compelled to add that Ivan Clustine, the new ballet master of the Paris Opéra, although Russian, came from a French family: "None doubt that he will soon carry out what the management of the Opéra expects of him. Let us add that he is the member of an old French family which once migrated to Russia; a fact that makes him even more appealing."[93] By drawing attention to Clustine's French origins, this critic is implying that he is thus suitable to manage the Paris Opéra. L.P highlighted Clustine's French origins in order to appease worries about his Russian influence on the French tradition and perhaps to stress further ballet's own roots as a French art form.

Other critics were also determined to locate original French ballet tradition within the Ballets Russes' dancing. Pierre Lalo, in his 1909 article for *Le Temps*, proclaimed the Russian ballet to be an inheritor of French choreographic tradition and guardians of the ballet of the Sun King, Louis XIV. However, he insisted that the ballet of the Ballets Russes was not authentic French ballet. "Only the Russians deceive themselves when they think that their ballet brings back to life, in our eyes, the French ballet of the classical age," he asserts. "Indeed, it shows us an image of that ballet, but not a direct one; on the contrary, it is an image as seen through to mirrors that have sensibly transformed it." Lalo explained that the Russian ballet's diversity and complexity were rooted in the path ballet took in reaching Russia. According to Lalo, ballet originated in the French tradition of the classical style (under Louis XIV), travelled to Germany under the rococo style, and finally arrived in Russia, where it gained its Slavic flair.[94] He illustrates ballet's journey by comparing its development to that of the art production under Louis XV, which was translated into various forms across Europe: "Imagine an object of art from the time of Louis XV of which a copy is made in Dresden under the reign of

August III or a Sans-Souci under that of Frederick II, would together be reproduced in Saint-Petersburg during the epoch of Catherine the Great: you will have, more or less, the Russian ballet such as it is brought to us today; a curious mix of the original French art, a bit of German heaviness, and a bit of Moscovite barbarity."[95] Essentially, Lalo argued that the new ballet of the Ballets Russes, however novel and modern, still held its roots in the French ballet of the eighteenth and nineteenth centuries: the true, "pure" art of ballet was essentially French. This is a claim that was increasingly made by critics writing on ballet in France, and one that resonates within much of the political discourse at the time about a "true" national spirit of the French. While Lalo praises the Russians for their preservation of French traditional ballet and commends their accordance of great importance to the art, he also suggests that the art of ballet had been transformed and corrupted by German heaviness and Russian barbarism. This was not an unusual argument taken by the French in matters of art and culture. Russian art and culture was still appreciated by the French for its rawness, passion, mystery, and primitivism and thus served as escapism for the French. What we learn from reviews like those of Lalo is that as critics examined the Russian ballet, they took more interest in ballet as an art form and in developing their own conceptualization of what ballet should be or rather was.[96]

After commending the Russians for placing a great importance on the art of ballet, Lalo then draws attention to the neglected state of ballet in France. First, he notes the lack of French-born *étoiles* and attributes this situation to a poor, undisciplined French academy. Second, he argues that there were no more great French ballet musicians "who have a special talent in writing dance music" like that of Rameau in the eighteenth century. Third, he attributes the French ballet's neglect above all to the French public's disinterest and ignorance of the art form: "Finally, just as we have no school of dance or dance musicians, nor do we have the public, the enthusiasts, the experts in ballet. Should the National Academy of Music cease to present ballets, proscribe the ballet from it postings and performances, the public most assuredly would not protest. If anyone were to try to do the same thing in St Petersburg, there would be a revolution." Clearly, Lalo was aware of the dearth of true French connoisseurs of ballet and, within that select few, the absence of competent knowledge of ballet artistry. "None among us knows anything about choreography," he writes, "once we have said about a dancer that she is light on her feet, elegant, or charming, we have said everything; our knowledge and vocabulary are then exhausted." But the Russians, he argued, possessed the vocabulary and understanding of choreographic artistry:

> Listen to the Russians talk among themselves about ballet things: the most precise and diverse technical terms flow from their lips; they know all the steps by their names; they appreciate the difficulty with precision, they evaluate and compare, with the assistance of positive arguments, the talents of the dancers; they are experts, they are competent; the Frenchmen who listen to them admire in silence, without understanding a drop of what is being said. In short, they love ballet, they know about it; they have that in common with Théophile Gautier, Stéphane Mallarmé, and M. Degas: one could find oneself in worse company.[97]

Lalo's review not only reveals an awareness of the lack of understanding of and interest in French ballet among the French, but also offers an explanation as to why French critics tended to focus more on what was peripheral to the dancing – namely, decor, costumes, music.

What is telling about such discussions is that there remained a general confusion among critics over what to do with ballet and its tradition and how to adapt it into a modern republican art form. Some critics attempted to reclaim ballet by insisting that ballet's tradition was French not Russian (the Russians merely refurbished what was intrinsically French). Yet this offered no easy solution to the problem of reviving French ballet, as the French were faced with a complex historical legacy. Critics were thus confronted with the issue that the art form's "Frenchness" was one of another age – one of an absolute monarchy and court. While the response of our skeptical critic Marcel Prévost was simply that it was impossible to have an equivalent ballet troupe to the Ballets Russes in France, other hopeful critics struggled to reconcile French ballet with artistocratic ties. As we shall see, it is in the writings of André Levinson that we discover a possibility for a French national ballet. It would be in the 1920s that the problem of ballet's existence in France would be solved. The following pages begin the inquiry into how the recreation of a French ballet fared at the hands of critics following the end of the First World War when a series of new anxieties surfaced.

3

A Nation (Re)Turns to Ballet: The Quest to Redeem French Ballet

> The war has figuratively but powerfully dug a trench between yesterday's ideas and those of today … we have all been thrown outside ourselves by a tremendous shock.[1]
>
> – Camille Mauclair

The interwar period offers a different context in which to examine commentary on ballet. While surfacing as victors of the First World War, the French were devastated by its costs. The quote above captures well the sense of disruption, instability, and disarray that followed in the wake of the war. Feelings of cultural malaise, uncertainty, disillusionment, and weariness also arose in France as a result of the long brutal war. The French would deal with such anxieties in different ways. Some felt the need to reassert French national identity. In this respect, there was a heightened sense of national consciousness in the interwar period. Others, particularly women, turned to the offerings of modern life and embraced the changes brought with it. This, for some, exacerbated anxieties about gender roles. Some people channelled their feelings of disillusionment and despair into art, music, or literature. For example, Dadaism and surrealism sprang from a sense of absurdity of the war and the mental anguish generated by it. Others threw themselves into the many distractions, commercial enterprises, and pleasures that Paris had to offer. Many engaged in the new recreation and entertainment of sports, while others escaped into the vibrant nightlife of dancing. For those who felt that cultural life had been suspended as a result of the war (as the observation of Mauclair suggests), cultural reconstruction would lie at the heart of national renewal. The cultural project to revive French ballet played a part in the attempt to regenerate the nation after the war. As we will see, the discourse on ballet's national function and cultural value was part of a greater quest not only to define what was quintessentially "French," but also to rebuild national stability and cultural strength after the First World War.

The return of the Ballets Russes to Paris incited new types of commentary on ballet on the part of bourgeois critics and intellectuals and played a central role in the French project to reclaim ballet as inherently French. While later chapters examine the ways in which attitudes towards gender, sexuality, the body, health, dance, and modern aesthetic tastes shaped such commentary, the aim here is to reveal why the project of reviving ballet became so important to national identity in a period of recovery and profound change. By examining reviews of performances and commentary in the interwar years, we shall see how French ballet was able to re-emerge from behind the shadow of Russian ballet and how the French reclaimed ballet (or, rather, claimed modern ballet) as their own.

Exposure to the vibrant Ballets Russes played a decisive role in the project to revive French culture. Bourgeois critics and dance experts reconfigured ballet to serve French national interests. "Dance experts" emerged who played a central role in the quest to revive French ballet and to restore its status in national culture. Critics, and the dance experts who guided them, occupied themselves with a number of questions: could French ballet embrace the new nationalist and artistic possibilities exemplified by the Ballets Russes and reconcile its French roots with Russian artistic developments? Could French ballet function in a republican state when it was traditionally associated with a privileged imperial court and aristocracy? Could ballet, as an inherently French art, rise again to grandeur?

Early twentieth-century dance criticism in reputable Parisian journals and newspapers reveals the attempts by Parisian bourgeois critics and intellectuals to navigate these questions. What is clear is that this was no easy task. Critics struggled to renegotiate ballet as French. Many critics addressed one paradox: ballet held it origins in the French court, but France was now a democratic republic. Furthermore, and here in terms of gender politics, the Ballets Russes' "new" modern ballet returned the male dancer – a body that had been rebuked in France in the previous century – to the stage. In the interwar period, we find a dialogue among critics that focused on how to adapt new Russian developments in ballet to modern French political and cultural ideologies. Critics attempted to associate ballet less with Russia and more with French culture and nationhood. In doing so, they needed to reconcile French ballet's heritage and modern nationalism. The intrinsic question became: what was the relationship between ballet and politics in France?

FRENCH CULTURE AND THE BALLET: A BRIEF OVERVIEW

Commentary on ballet during the interwar years not only captured the anxieties and challenges faced by the French in this period, but was also deeply shaped by an ethos of nostalgia and memory. In order to fully understand the politically charged debates about ballet that surfaced in the early twentieth century and the French urgency to revive cultural life, it is important to recognize the close historic relationship between cultural affairs and French identity.[2] Beginning in the seventeenth century, the monarchy exercised considerable control over cultural production, in part via strict censorship. The Académie Française (1635), established by Louis XIII and his minister Cardinal Richelieu, exerted control over the French language – which was and continues to be seen as central to French national culture. Under Louis XIV, practically every aspect of cultural life was under the authority of the monarchy. A series of royal academies were eventually established for dance, music, architecture, painting, and sculpture. In fact, one of the first acts of Louis XIV as sovereign was to create the Académie Royale de Danse in March 1661.[3] Amid urgent state concerns, he issued his "Letters Patent of the King to Establish a Royal Academy of Dance in the City of Paris." This is indicative of the value placed on ballet as an important asset to the state and as a highly respected French art form. The Académie Royale de Danse served as a model for those that followed: Inscriptions et Belles Lettres (1663), Sciences (1666), Opéra (1669), and Architecture (1671).[4] Louis XIV's overall intention in establishing his academies was to centralize and to unify French culture under royal authority, to bring prestige to France and the monarchy, and to encourage emulation throughout Europe.

Dance was at the heart of French cultural life in this period. In 1669, the Académie Royale de Musique et de Danse (later known as the Paris Opéra) was founded with its corps de ballet provided from

Louis XIV's Académie Royale de Danse. All members at first were men, and female roles were performed by boys *en travesti.* A year later, under the direction of Jean-Baptiste Lully (1632–1687), opera and dance were transformed from court entertainments to professional arts. To a large extent, ballet moved out of the court ballroom and into the theatre.[5] In 1713, Louis XIV officially issued a decree, the *Règlement concernant l'Opéra* that made the Opéra a state institution with a permanent company of twenty dancers (ten men, ten women). He also created an official school of dance, the École Royale de Danse, which was open to boys and girls from poor families, aged nine to thirteen.

Ballet's centrality in French culture revealed itself during the French Enlightenment. As political life and private morals relaxed under Louis XV (r. 1715–74), a new style in art emerged, reflective of the new monarch's appetite for beauty and pleasure. This aesthetic style, labelled "rococo," was intimate, decorative, and often erotic.[6] A ready symbol of the ostentatious lifestyle of the aristocracy and nobility, rococo was attacked by Enlightenment figures as decadent and trivial. Denis Diderot criticized admirers of the rococo as strangers "to real taste, to the truth, to just ideas, and to the seriousness of art."[7] Enlightenment critiques of the rococo were more than purely aesthetic, but deeply entwined with the political, philosophical, and ideological challenges of the period.[8] Some Enlightenment philosophers, such as Montesquieu, Diderot, and Rousseau, feared that ballet had been corrupted by the influence of rococo and reduced to a decorative, sensual art form. Among other pressing political and social matters, they proposed a new type of dance that was capable of embodying ideas. Thus Enlightenment philosophers recognized ballet as an important art for the French. Inspired by the wave of French classicism in the late eighteenth century, Opéra choreographer Jean Georges Noverre adopted a dramatically expressive style of ballet, the *ballet d'action.*

The survival of ballet through the French Revolution is also useful to our understanding of its legacy and enduring cultural importance.[9] The Revolution successfully reconfigured ballet from serving the court and aristocracy to representing republican national values. In April 1790, Louis XVI ceded control over the Opéra to the Paris municipal government, the Commune of Paris, and it was held together by Pierre Gardel (1758–1840) throughout the French

Revolution.[10] After the declaration of the Republic in 1792, the Académie Royale de Musique was renamed the Opéra National, removing any reminiscences of its royal roots.[11] Gardel, among other artists at the time, signed a report promising to "completely abandon" the Opéra's corrupt aristocratic repertory and replace it within "decent" and "virtuous" republican productions.[12] However, once the radical period came to a halt in July 1794, "the Opera resumed its old repertory without missing a beat."[13]

Study of the French Revolution era is particularly useful because of the Revolution's attempt to "democratize" ballet and to use it to express republican rather than aristocratic values.[14] As the Revolution became more engaged in egalitarian rhetoric by the middle of 1792, the Opéra was made accessible to a broader audience by offering free performances for the sans-culottes and by making their subject matter cater to revolutionary deputies and soldiers.[15] Desperate to keep the Opéra open, Gardel staged mostly political productions. Ballets (still performed as part of opera) were set to new patriotic music and songs, particularly "La Marseillaise."[16] Just six days after the king's execution, Gardel presented the one-act patriotic ballet *Le triomphe de la république*, also set to patriotic songs.[17] As Judith Chazin-Bennahum notes in her book *Dance in the Shadow of the Guillotine* (1988), the ballet operated "as the servant of politics" – in this case, republicanism (republican virtue).[18] Now seen as yet another vehicle for expression (not unlike painting and music), the Opéra remained open even during the radical periods of the Revolution (with only a brief closing when the king was arrested in August 1792). Even the radical Jacques-René Hébert, publisher of the newspaper *Le Père Duchesne*, argued in favour of keeping the Opéra open. While the Opéra "has been the hotbed of the counterrevolution," he wrote, "it ought to be encouraged all the same because it supports a large number of families and nourishes arts of entertainment."[19]

Ballet at the Opéra thus managed to survive the great upheaval of the French Revolution, despite its aristocratic and court origins. While the Opéra was an exorbitant expense to the state, it was considered an important contributor to French culture. A Russian visitor in 1790 asserted that "the French say that whoever has been to Paris and has not seen the Opera is like someone who has been to Rome and has not seen the Pope. In truth, it is a completely magnificent thing, largely thanks to the splendor of the sets and the beauty of the ballets."[20] The political axiom "we must sustain this theatre, so admired by Foreigners, which draws them to France and which is the glory of the Nation" was repeated in the municipality's debates regarding the special privileging of the Opéra.[21] However, two developments surely helped to secure ballet's survival. First, ballet had already begun to distance itself from the court in the decades preceding the Revolution, literally removing itself from the court ballroom into the state theatre and no longer danced exclusively by the nobility. One tradition that remained was patronage. Dancers had to disassociate themselves from their former ties with aristocratic patrons, particularly during the Terror. However, the facade of luxury still played an important role in the Paris Opéra. In 1791, a deputy of the Revolutionary government remarked, "one could establish an axiom: no luxury and magnificence, no Opera."[22] Second, the *ballet d'action,* which combined pantomime (drama) with dance, had proven that ballet was a powerful vehicle through which to express ideas. In fact, an article from 1794 noted that the Opéra had contributed the most "to rais[ing] the public spirit by patriotic scenes."[23]

Although the Committee of Public Safety had extended several loans to the Opéra throughout the Radical Revolution, by 1799 the Opéra was on the brink of financial and administrative ruin. After the Revolution, the Opéra was no longer viable without substantial financial support which the municipalities were not equipped to offer. As first consul and later emperor, Napoleon Bonaparte recognized the Opéra as a vehicle with which to reinforce his power and grandeur. While the Opéra received state patronage, it fell under heavy censorship just as it had during the Revolution.[24] Ballet-operas were created to flatter Napoleon, who made it a point to appear regularly at the Opéra. James H. Johnson writes that "during his rule, Napoleon attended the Paris Opera twenty-six times, by far more visits per season than Louis XV, Louis XVI, or any other nineteenth-century head of state."[25] As we can see, cultural life was central to French identity, and ballet, as an art performed at the Opéra, played an important role in asserting French grandeur.

While ballet survived in France after the Revolution, its relationship to the state transformed when its subsidy from the French state diminished significantly under the July Monarchy (1830–48). Ballet (and the Opéra) became dependent on private support (for example, male subscribers) and thus fell victim to the "libertinism" of the haute bourgeoisie. Furthermore, by the 1890s, the lines between "high art" represented by the Opéra and the Opéra-Comique and the leading music halls became less rigid. As choreographers and composers moved between the Opéra-Comique and the Folies Bergère, ballet declined as an exclusive high art for the haute bourgeoisie.[26] For ballet devotees, it lost its capacity to represent the grandeur of the nation. It is in the interwar period that we find critics and intellectuals pronouncing the symbolic power that restoring French ballet could have on regenerating the nation, which meant in part being willing to subsidize the Opéra instead of relying on patronage. Ballet could serve as a needed cultural force through which to forge French cultural values and national belonging.[27]

CULTURAL CRISIS AND THE INTERWAR YEARS

It is important to address briefly the cultural climate to which the Ballets Russes returned and which commentary on ballet reflected. The First World War brought with it a new set of cultural anxieties. The war had taken a particularly heavy toll on France, affecting all aspects of social, political, and cultural life. After four years of warfare fought on French soil, the war had cost France much of its male youth. As historian Gordon Wright asserts, "No other warring nation had suffered such high proportionate manpower losses: of the eight million men mobilized, five million were killed or wounded."[28] In 1918, France was faced with an exhausted economy, chronic governmental instability, moral fatigue, population anxieties, and disenchantment. The sense of cultural malaise that lingered in the years that followed – elation from victory, yet despair for its painful costs – manifested itself in a quest for "normalcy" and stability.

In the postwar period, France attempted to recover from its misery and to dissipate feelings of confusion, anxiety, and doubt. Part of its endeavour was to delineate a coherent modern French identity. In this period, the French turned inwards and attempted to decipher and establish a unique (and hegemonic) national identity for itself. One way to do so was to revive the centuries-old association of Frenchness with a sense of high culture and cosmopolitanism. As historian Marc Ferro points out, high culture "became sterile during the war" and culture itself was "highjacked by war."[29] In other words, there was a decline in cultural production and intellectual activity, which was the result not only of departures to the front, but also of a war-centred consciousness. An article by veteran Pierre Drieu la Rochelle captures the instability of the postwar period: "This civilization no longer has clothes, no longer has churches, no longer has palaces, no longer has theatres, no longer has paintings, no longer has books, no longer has sexes."[30] Rochelle's statement is revealing in that it implies that all these aspects of life were of importance to the stability of the nation (fashion, religion, architecture, theatre, art, literature, and gender difference). Rochelle, who would later become a fascist, also represents the Far Right's need for cultural reconstruction for national regeneration.

As the nation struggled to recuperate after the First World War and to "return to order," concerns over gender boundaries became central to the increasing politicization of ideas involved in the search for a hegemonic French cultural identity. The war had necessitated a change in conventional gender roles when many women took up traditional male occupations. This crossing of gender boundaries raised concerns about the stabilization of the nation. Furthermore, it incited anxieties about men and their place in French society. The disfigured and shell-shocked condition of many returning soldiers and the loss of virility that often accompanied injury all deepened concerns about national decline. These postwar anxieties prompted a reconstruction of gender definitions in an attempt to reconcile old and new worlds. As Mary Louise Roberts has illuminated in *Civilization without Sexes* (1994), gender played a central role in postwar recovery. Through neonatalist discourse and other literary sources, Roberts reveals the role that propaganda played in negotiating traditional gender ideologies about sexual difference and how definitions of national and collective identities were inscribed with gender ideology.[31] Part of this process was a reaffirmation of gender difference and complementarity. Thus France's reconstruction appeared to hinge on the reinscription of conventional social roles for men and women.

In this atmosphere of cultural and gender instability, the performing arts (among other cultural institutions) turned to the exploration of modernism.[32] In doing so, they exacerbated widespread cultural anxieties about national stability, modern aesthetics, and gender roles. The Ballets Russes played a role in such artistic experimentation. The company showcased the male dancer, experimented with androgynous imagery, created new "pantomimic" and "anti-classical" ballets, and drew upon contemporary settings of modern life. It also reflected competing French notions of gender identity in many of its ballets. On the one hand, the Ballets Russes (along with the Paris Opéra ballet) continued to present traditional gender identities in its reinterpretations of classical ballets (e.g., *Le lac des cygnes* [*Swan Lake*], *Giselle, Les sylphides, Sylvia, Le mariage d'Aurore*). In doing so, it reinforced conventional ideas about gender not only through its storylines, but also through the promotion of the paraphernalia, such as toe shoes, tutus, leotards, tulle, and hair buns, that evoked ideal notions of femininity, grace, and sophistication. These ballets provided a world of fantasy, romance, nostalgia, and/or escape. However, the Ballets Russes also challenged gender roles in its avant-garde ballets (e.g., *L'après-midi d'un faune, Le sacre du printemps, Les biches, Jeux*). For example, in 1922, when Diaghilev revived *L'après-midi d'un faune*, he cast Nijinska in the role originally created by her brother.[33] The Ballets Russes broke traditional boundaries of gender within their works whether in dancers' postures, makeup, costumes, gestures, or choreography. In such ballets, female dancers were seldom dressed in tutus, but rather in tunics and harem pants, and choreography did not always require "feminine" pointe work, but rather bare feet or sandals. In 1924, *danseur* Anton Dolin startled French audiences by dancing on pointe in Nijinska's *Les fâcheux* and in Frederick Ashton's *The Dream*, an adaptation of Shakespeare in which the *danseur* portraying Bottom dances on pointe to create an illusion of hooves during his temporary transformation into an ass.[34] While the Ballets Russes drew upon alternate visions of gender identity, they did so by presenting them as the latest modern fashion.[35] In other words, they showcased them as a cultural commodity, a spectacle presented, no less, by a "foreign troupe."

Certainly, the Ballets Russes was not the only spectacle in Paris to experiment with modernism and gender identities. Music-hall performer "Barbette" (persona for the American Van der Clyde) was as much a cultural spectacle in the 1920s as the Ballets Russes. Van der Clyde became "Barbette" by wearing feminine attire and performing acrobatic routines first as a woman and then as a man.[36] The example of Barbette is significant in that Van der Clyde's identity, in the words of art historian Amy Lyford, "hing[ed] on a visual experience of the body as constituted by more than one sign for sex."[37] The Ballets Russes' androgynous imagery differed in that its bodies did not aim to entirely erase masculinity or femininity, but rather to present a modern vision of its fluidity. This deviation from traditional gender constructs on the ballet stage was different from other arts in that we find "borrowed characteristics" between the female and male dancers. Most important to understand about the Ballets Russes is that it framed the body as a powerful social and political tool of 1920s French culture. It offered a platform upon which new or competing representations of gender identity and the body could be expressed and disseminated in the mass press.[38]

Thus, in the interwar period, French cultural anxieties about the nation, modernism, and gender identity created an atmosphere conducive to artistic expression and experimentation. In turn, such artistic experimentation helped to restore Paris as the capital of modernity, by drawing in tourists, artists, writers, and intellectuals. Dadaism, surrealism, the "fantaisiste" of Cocteau and Giraudoux, the fox-trot "dansomanie," jazz modernism, Josephine Baker, the circus, the Ballets Russes, and the Ballet Suédois all served as spectacles to ease postwar anxieties.[39] In fact, throughout the 1920s, French society and culture turned to escapism within the world of arts and literature. As historian Alistair Horne points out, the unpleasantness of reality tempted the French "to bury themselves in all manner of imaginary pleasures and internal distractions."[40] In the words of historian Modris Ekstein, "The world became a figment of imagination rather than imagination being a figment of the world."[41]

After the war, the French were committed to maintaining Paris's reputation as a modern intellectual and artistic centre and to setting themselves apart from concurrent developments in Germany. However, the French were less enthusiastic about anything foreign and were more interested in finding and fostering French talents. As the cultural centre of the Western world, Paris became a place where foreigners came to be inspired, but not necessarily to offer inspiration to the French. The Ballets Russes, aware that Paris, as the "City of Light," remained an important city in which to succeed, returned to France after its wartime absence. However, it returned to a scene quite different than that of 1909. Why was the Ballets Russes welcomed back in France, under what circumstances was it able to survive there, and how did its presence affect French ballet at the Paris Opéra? Why did critics and intellectuals become so intent on defending French ballet in the interwar period? Moreover, what do these new attitudes towards ballet reveal about postwar culture?

THE BALLETS RUSSES RETURNS TO PARIS NOT SO RUSSIAN

The First World War had a tremendous impact on the Ballets Russes and the progress of ballet's revival in France. The war not only disrupted the Ballets Russes' productions, but it also halted discussions of reviving French ballet. In fact, many dance companies in France and abroad had fallen into abeyance during the war. After the June 1914 performances of *Midas* at the Paris Opéra, the Ballets Russes company was dismantled and Serge Diaghilev moved to Switzerland. The Paris Opéra was then closed until 1916. Diaghilev, however, managed to gradually reassemble his company at the Villa Bellerive, just outside Lausanne. Vulnerable financially (as wealthy Russian patrons had become scarce during the Russian Revolution) and artistically (with the dispersal of many of its original talented dancers), and with no permanent home, the Ballets Russes embarked on re-establishing itself – via a series of tours – as an international ballet troupe. At this time, the Ballets Russes began to move away from its original objectives of introducing exclusively Russian artistic talents and culture to the West. Léonide Massine, who joined as choreographer for the Ballets Russes after Fokine and Nijinsky left in 1914, presented his first ballet, *Le soleil de nuit* (*Midnight Sun,* 1915) in Geneva. Based on popular Russian folk legends concerning the yearly peasant rituals during northern Russia's "White Nights," it was one of the last ballets to use elements of Russian folklore as Fokine had done in *Firebird* and *Petrushka.*[42]

Despite its financial struggles, the Ballets Russes was able to tour the United States, Spain, Italy, and South America during the war years, and, in doing so, exported its modern conception of ballet. These extensive tours resulted in some local artistic collaborations and inspired an embrace of various national dances and customs within Ballets Russes' works. For example, accepting an invitation from King Alfonso XIII to perform at Madrid's Teatro Real, the Ballets Russes went on to other Spanish engagements in Seville, Granada, Cordoba, and Bilbao, which prolonged its survival.[43] Productions such as *Las meninas* (1916), which premiered in San Sebastian, Spain – the court's fashionable summer resort – captured the atmosphere of Diego Velázquez's famous painting while also honouring the traditions of the Spanish monarchy.[44] The Ballets Russes' six-and-a-half-month stay in Rome produced ballets inspired by Italian subjects and music, such as Carlo Goldoni's (1707–93) *Les femmes de bonne humeur* (*The Good Humoured Women*, 1917), which incorporated the commedia dell'arte's mix of mime, dance, and acrobatics, and the music of eighteenth-century Italian composer Domenico Scarlatti.[45]

Thus when Diaghilev returned to Paris in 1917, his ballet company, however "Russian" in reputation, now carried with it a new collaboration of international artistic talents rather than exclusively Russian ones. Diaghilev also continued to take up a variety of national themes in the Ballets Russes' ballets. Former Ballets Russes *étoile* Lydia Sokolova recorded in her diary that Diaghilev "had loved Italian pictures, French furniture, and German music almost as long as he had been reading Pushkin." She noted that "the new period which began in 1917, was a cosmopolitan one, for Massine's ballets were to take their subjects from several different countries, while they reflected artistically the diverse experiments of the school of Paris."[46] Increasingly, Diaghilev's artistic vision grew more cosmopolitan and less grounded in Russian themes and collaborations. Productions such as the cubist *Parade* (1917) and *La boutique fantasque* (1919) represent this new phase of the Ballets Russes that was now associated with international collaborations and contemporary themes rather than an agenda to expose Russian art to the West.[47] *Le tricorne* (*The Three-Cornered Hat*, 1919), for example, consisted entirely of Spanish collaborations and incorporated Spanish character dancing into its choreography.[48] Former Ballet Russes dancer and dance historian Serge Lifar remarked that although the Ballets Russes had perpetuated in some way Russian academic dance, it gradually ceased to be Ballets Russes and had become "European ballet."[49]

When the Ballets Russes returned to France, its international themes and modern innovations were well received. This proved that the art of ballet could not only recapture the imagination of the European public, but also continue to earn the respect of reputable artists of various disciplines and from various nations. Furthermore, the "internationalizaton" of the Ballets Russes had illuminated the potential for ballet to serve as a vehicle for any national identity and spirit. Aware of the growing nationalist spirit in interwar France, Diaghilev collaborated increasingly with contemporary French artists, composers, and designers, thereby offering them wide exposure and publicity. In doing so, the Ballets Russes played an important role in drawing talented French artists into ballet production. In particular, Diaghilev formed a close alliance with the French avant-garde, showcasing artistic styles such as cubism, surrealism and abstraction in his ballet productions. In addition, numerous works incorporated and honoured the original classical choreography of nineteenth-century French choreographer Marius Petipa, such as *Le mariage de la belle au bois dormant/Aurora's Wedding* (1922), *Le festin* (1925), *Le bal du lac des cygnes* (1925), and *Les contes de fées* (1925).

There were various reasons why the Ballets Russes managed to recapture Parisian audiences during the interwar years. Although Russophilia had diminished significantly in France, particularly after the Bolshevik Revolution and the new communist identity adopted by Russia, Diaghilev had cleverly transformed his troupe during the war years into a cosmopolitan and European enterprise. Diaghilev returned to a country that while victorious in war, was deeply traumatized by destruction, most of which occurred on its own soil. Parisians were in need of distractions to heal the wounds of four years of warfare. Like the other arts and entertainments that surfaced in the 1920s, the Ballets Russes helped fill the cultural void left in the wake of the war. The popularity of dance as a public social pastime exploded in the interwar years, particularly when American jazz, Argentine tango, the "Charleston," and other foreign dances all gained appeal among young adults, many from the middle classes. The new exposure to different forms of dancing lured audiences back to the modern ballet of the Ballets Russes. Furthermore, the blossoming of a physical culture movement inspired a new appreciation of the body, athleticism, and sports. All of these aspects created an optimal environment in which the Ballets Russes could flourish.

CRITICAL RECEPTION OF THE BALLETS RUSSES IN THE INTERWAR YEARS

Criticism of the period routinely noted the changing trends of the Ballets Russes. André Levinson's 1923 article, "Où en sont les 'Ballets russes'?" ("What has become of the Ballets Russes?"), for example, addressed the company's shift from a prewar embrace of Russian motifs to an increasing compatibility with contemporary French culture and tastes. While "Diaghilev remained voluntarily and proudly in total opposition to national tradition and outside of Russian ballet as gloriously surviving in his homeland," he prefaced, "he fought earnestly for what was the spiritual essence of Russian ballet adapted to his French prototype." Levinson asserted that "before the war, the term 'Ballets Russes' was plausible because Diaghilev had surrounded himself with the flower of two imperial operas and two schools."[50] He noted that, after the war, the Ballets Russes hired fewer Russians and that its ballets showed few signs of Russianness. Commenting in *Theatre Arts Monthly*, he explained how the war finally cut off Diaghilev entirely from Russia:

> In his troupe, soon reinforced, especially by Poles, refugees from the opera company of Warsaw, foreign elements predominated. Before long he had broken with the Russian decorators, the eclectic painters inspired by the icon and the folk imagery, and was making a medley of French rococo and archaic Greek. He associated easel painters with his productions, the illustrious creators of modern French art: Derain, Henri Matisse, and, above all, Pablo Picasso.[51]

"Today," he continued, "among 60 participants, one can only cite seven or eight dancers having served in the two Russian capitals." "Therefore," he concluded, "there is no need to call M. Erik Satie's *Parade* a Russian ballet."[52]

Parade is a good example of the Ballets Russes' artistic transformation. It premiered in 1917 with a scenario by French poet Jean Cocteau, music by eccentric French composer Erik Satie, score conducted by Swiss composer Ernest Ansermet, choreography by dancer Léonide Massine, and costumes and set designs by cubist painter Pablo Picasso. It was Cocteau's first scenario for ballet, Satie's first ballet score, Picasso's first collaboration with the Ballets Russes and debut in theatre design, and Massine's first commission in France as a choreographer. Like the shocking *Le sacre du printemps*, *Parade* was a radical departure from traditional ballet performance. Performed as a circus-like ballet, *Parade* was scorned by audiences but praised by critics for its innovative and transgressive aspects. The ballet drew upon motifs from French popular entertainment, such as ragtime, cabaret melodies, and fragmented rhythms (which outraged some classical composers); used extra-musical sounds (such as the typewriter, gunshots, sirens, and foghorns); and incorporated costumes made of wood, metal, cloth, and papier mâché (which limited dancers' movements). Evoking a modern atmosphere that was at once familiar and strange, and boldly mocking French society's high art and culture, *Parade* departed from the Ballets Russes' mythologized themes of folk Russia.[53]

In the early years of the 1920s, the Ballets Russes did manage to produce a few ballets that still drew upon Russian themes, albeit in an entirely different way. The war had greatly affected Diaghilev's vision of Russian national identity. The First World War brought with it the collapse of the Russian, German, Austro-Hungarian, and Ottoman empires, and after brutal civil war, Russia had come under communist control. Diaghilev never returned, nor did the Ballets Russes ever perform there. In fact, Diaghilev and his troupe came to represent to the Soviets the epitome of bourgeois decadence, and Diaghilev was "written out" of Soviet art histories until the 1960s.[54] Perhaps due to feelings of disorientation in exile, Diaghilev presented a series of nostalgic ballets in the early 1920s representing his lost imperial nation: *Chout* (*Le Bouffon* – a Russian legend in six scenes, May 1921); *The Sleeping Princess* (premiered in London, November 1921); and *Les noces* (*The Wedding*, 1923), which was his last "Russian" ballet.

The Ballets Russes' investment in modernism proved successful in the few ballets that continued to embrace Russian themes. *Les noces* received a positive reception from Parisian audiences, particularly those belonging to the elite Russian émigré community. The ballet demonstrates the Ballets Russes' ability to fuse Russian themes with popular French tastes – this time, with the avant-garde. The production was a collaboration of mostly Russian avant-garde artists, which included composer Igor Stravinsky, choreographer Bronislava Nijinska (Vaslav Nijinsky's sister), and designer Natalia Goncharova.[55] Using a Russian peasant wedding of the old regime as the subject of the ballet, Diaghilev's collaborators drew upon both Russian folk poetry and modern elements of primitivism, expressionism, abstraction, and futurism. Such elements were found in the musical score, choreography, and set and costume designs (which were kept simple and uniform).[56]

As with all of Diaghilev's productions, the prime objective of the ballet was to appeal to the widest possible audience (and to wealthy patrons!). The premiere of *Les noces* was a social event /charity gala that raised over 100,000 francs for several Russian expatriate organizations.[57] The patronage committee was led by Grand Duchess Marie, one of the most illustrious members of the Russian émigré community. While originally arranged to be performed at the Opéra in October-November 1919 or May-June 1920, *Les noces* was actually presented at the less prestigious Gaîté-Lyrique in June 1923.[58] Nonetheless, the production managed to attract a distinguished crowd. Drue Fergison notes that "in the audience sat the rich, famous, talented, and titled – a glittering cross-section of that international high society that made Paris a mecca during *les années folles.*"[59] Indeed, the audience was composed of the elite and cosmopolitan (artists, aristocrats, and even Romanovs). *Vogue* magazine noted that women in the audience wore "a profusion of diamonds and pearls on their décolletage" and diamonds in their hair.[60] The article also captured the type of audience that supported the Ballets Russes: wealthy women and rich foreigners. "Imagine: the Marquise de Ludres is to the right, high up in one of the first boxes, the Countess de Beaumont sits in a box across the way … a little further on, it's Gabrielle Chanel, all in white, glistening with pearls … Mme Sert, the Grand-Duchesse Marie, and the Countess de Chevigné and then and then … as at the Opéra, this evening it's Le Tout Paris and Le 'Tout Estranger.'"[61] This *Vogue* article reveals that the Ballets Russes still managed to attract the same fashionable elite who normally attended the Opéra. Thus, despite its fusion of the Russian past with the Soviet present, *Les noces* appears to have been well received. Serge Grigoriev, the Ballets Russes' *régisseur* (rehearsal director), noted that the ballet's success "was far greater than we had expected. It even reminded us of our triumphs of 1909 … Diaghilev was delighted with this ballet and its triumph."[62]

Responses to *Les noces* found critics still enraptured by the exoticism of the company. Some were overwhelmed with the motifs of violence and ritual in the ballet. Prominent critic and composer Émile Vuillermoz, writing in the large daily newspaper *Excelsior,* described the ballet as "a type of savage and barbaric exaltation" and that "the hallucinating cry of the castanets whipped at each blow."[63] Vuillermoz's review evoked nostalgia for the exotic and primitive elements that the Ballets Russes embodied before the war. Raymond Charpentier's review in *Comœdia* commended Diaghilev for being able to unite "primitive" and modern elements. He wrote: "[Diaghilev] profits from his virtuosity in attempting to unite even the irreconcilables:

the noise of music, the primitive and civiliz[ed], by the magic rhythm and the sovereign intervention of science."[64] Charpentier was picking up on the ballet's embrace of primitivism, mechanized movements, Russian exoticism, and cosmopolitanism. While Diaghilev and Stravinsky were more interested in capturing the solemnity of old Russian peasant rituals, Nijinska added elements of contemporary Soviet community and militarism. Nijinska once said her choreography drew upon her experiences in revolutionary Russia. She explained that her use of militarism in the ballet was to express "the air of Russia, a Russia throbbing with excitement and intense feeling. All the vivid images of the harsh realities of the Revolution were still part of me and filled my whole being."[65] In fact, militarism would have played a central role in the lives of many young Russian men during the early twentieth century, whether because of the Russian Revolution, the First World War, or the Russo-Japanese War.[66]

Other critics were more taken by the mechanistic elements of the ballet revealed in both the choreography and Stravinsky's score. In his review, French composer and critic Alexis Roland-Manuel referred to the Swiss conductor Ernest Ansermet as "the chief engineer" and "controller" and the instruments as "factory machines." Weary of the ability of machines to control human passions and actions, he remarked: "These actors of the everyday drama, borrowed from the popular imagination, appear to us here as simplified, living expressions of the relentless mechanism which rules the actions of man, including their loves."[67] Vuillermoz recalled the "metallic wailing of four skillfully mistreated pianos," "the mechanical, machine-like" gestures, and the "rhythmic puffing of this sonorous factory."[68] Both Roland-Manuel and Vuillermoz's reviews show the new apprehension of the machine age and the pace of technological development in the postwar world.

However, some critics were not so impressed by the ballet on both political and artistic levels. As in many Ballets Russes productions, the dancing in *Les noces* challenged classical ballet tradition in several ways. The choreography emphasized gesture over ballet technique (for example, in its salutes, marching, and repetitive poses) and incorporated folk dance and modern dance movements. Dancers executed mechanized movements with turned-in legs, awkward and stiff postures, uniformity, and symmetry. Nijinska once explained her reasons for leaving the dancers on pointe, writing that it "elongat[ed] the dancer's silhouettes and [made] them resemble the saints on Byzantine mosaics."[69] The male dancing incorporated militaristic salutes, uniform marching, and patriotic gestures (for example, the dancer's arm crossed over his heart). Gender difference was clearly defined in the choreography and gestures, and implied within the overall theme of the work. Moreover, the Russian folk dancing drew attention away from the principal performers and onto the corps de ballet. In fact, the two leading roles required little dancing – something very untraditional in classical ballet. In three very critical reviews, dance specialist André Levinson was most disturbed by the ballet's choreography, complaining of "automatized motions," the "mechanical reproduction of rhythms," dancers who looked like "soldiers at the rifle range," and collectivism (that is, the absorption of the individual into the collective drama).[70] The innovative choreography Levinson described as "Marxist" and "Bolshevik" for its group uniformity, stoicism, and overall austerity. He claimed that Nijinska had "passed through the collectivist reveries of the Soviets" and that the "entire Red army division [appeared] to be involved in the show."[71] He even called Nijinska a "pedantic and stubborn vampire." Levinson found the decor by Goncharova "excessive" and asserted that *Les noces* should have been limited to the score of Stravinsky in which he located a "heightened spiritual sense of being."[72] Levinson's hostility to militaristic motifs, particularly any associated with Soviet Russia, is not surprising as he was starkly opposed to communism.

Critics found the modernity of the Ballets Russes and its function as a platform for avant-garde experimentation most appealing (with the exception of Levinson). While some critics like Vuillermoz and Charpentier still found allure in the troupe's exotic themes, the spectacle of innovation, dramatic intensity, and high quality of music were all central factors in the ballet's successful reception in Paris. Levinson's biting response not only is indicative of his political leanings as staunchly anti-communist, but also captures the sense of loss, embitterment, and betrayal that many émigrés felt after the Russian Revolution. As a passionately anti-communist refugee from Russia, Levinson once recalled bitterly that Russian life was in ruins.[73]

The ballet *Les biches* (The House Party, 1924) elicited quite a different response from critics. As in *Les noces*, the Ballets Russes captured various aspects of the postwar world, this time culture in France. *Les biches* was everything *Les noces* was not. While *Les noces* explored the sombreness and uncertainty of postwar culture, *Les biches* embraced the gaiety, lightness, and frivolity of the Roaring Twenties in Paris. The ballet involved predominantly French collaborations, save the actual dancers, who were Russian, Polish, or English. The musical score was composed by French composer Francis Poulenc, the scenery and costumes designed by French artist Marie Laurencin, and the dancing choreographed by Russian Bronislava Nijinska. Poulenc's score, unlike that of Stravinsky in *Les noces*, was charming, light, and melodious; Nijinska's choreography contained subtle sexual transgressions (which had routinely attracted audiences to the Ballets Russes); and Marie Laurencin's designs were described as innocent and fresh.[74]

In *Les biches*, one can see how the Ballets Russes adapted to modern French tastes, pushed the boundaries of traditional ballet, and exploited gender stereotypes – a trend in the 1920s. The ballet embraced the theme of the stylish society world of the south of France in the postwar years. The ballet set was portrayed as "a lounge in an expensive ultra-modern villa" in the south of France.[75] The plot was loose, depicting twelve women attracted to three men, one man attracted to the youngest and most sexually ambiguous of the women, and an older, wealthy woman who attaches herself to the two remaining men, who repel her advances.[76] In many ways, the ballet echoed the frivolous and gay atmosphere of the "fête galante" paintings by French eighteenth-century painter Jean-Antoine Watteau. By leaving some characters sexually ambiguous, however, the ballet played on gender stereotypes, androgyny, and homosexuality, and was, essentially, a satire of 1920s sexual mores. For example, playing upon contemporary fears of the blurring of gender difference, the women were portrayed as predators and the men as prey, and the youngest of the women was presented in a similar manner to Victor Margaritte's "la garçonne" [a boyish woman]. As dance scholar Lynn Garafola describes, "[*Les*] *Biches* explored a host of taboo themes – narcissism, voyeurism, female sexual power, castration, sapphism – with a directness hitherto unparalleled on the ballet stage."[77] Francis Poulenc remarked: "*Les Biches* has no real plot, for the good reason that if it had it might have caused a scandal."[78] Jean Cocteau noted that "Madame Nijinska achieved greatness without intending to" and that "she was protected by the absence of theme and by the apparent lightness of the musical style."[79] Therefore, *Les biches* managed to embrace modern trends and social anxieties without going too far.

The ballet was received well. As one shareholder observed, "the ballet was a great success. H.R.H. [the Duke of Connaught] was enthusiastic. Nijinska was a marvel in it, the three men in it Leon, Zverev, Wilzak danced too beautifully."[80] Belgian pianist and musicologist Paul Collaer, who promoted modern music, called the ballet "a triumph" with "eight curtain-calls which is *rarissme* [exceedingly rare]." He described Nijinka's choreography as beautiful and "the very essence of dance," the preparation as "impeccable," the sets, the curtain, and the costumes as "a total success," and the music as "brilliant."[81] One critic remarked that "of all the ultra-modern ballets there is not one which I enjoy so much" and that "the dancing [was] brilliant in the extreme."[82] Critic Louis Laloy wrote that *Les biches* had "an air of elegance, a little abrupt and sportive, which was in the taste of our times." He continued: "These great artists [of the Ballets Russes] have found a music of a delicacy and freshness that is all French, a choreography also true, so very different and even opposite to that which it could inspire a wonderful drunken Stravinsky" [in that the ballet was so modern].[83] In fact, he went on to declare *Les biches* the new *Les sylphides* (notable in the nineteenth century for its idealized French femininity).[84] Nijinska herself remarked in the following years that "*Les Biches* [was] Taglioni's *Sylphide* and *Giselle* of our own epoch of dancing."[85] A series of similar ballets drawing upon French themes soon followed, such as *Les fâcheux* (after the comédie-ballet of Molière, January 1924), *La nuit sur le Mont Chauve* (April 1924), *Le train bleu* (June 1924), *Le festin* (February 1925), and *Les contes de fées* (February 1925).

Music critic Boris de Schloezer praised Diaghilev for drawing the public's attention to contemporary French art in the 1920s. "The adventurous life of Diaghilev, what a marvellous subject!" he boasted in an article. "This was not only the history of an extraordinary man, and in a certain sense a genius, but also that of an epoch of Parisian life." He noted that Diaghilev gained initial triumphs in Paris by exposing talented Russian artists such as Léon Bakst, Alexandre Benois, Igor Stravinsky, Tamara Karsavina, Vaslav Nijinsky, and Michel Fokine. "Diaghilev conquered Paris," he explained, "but he conquered it as a foreigner." He then remarked that Diaghilev would have remained as only an honoured guest in Paris had he not taken a different direction: "The stroke of genius was Diaghilev's turn to French art, surrounding himself with the young painters and the young musicians of Paris."[86] Schloezer claimed that without this transformation, without this "renaissance," Diaghilev's troupe would not have lasted in France. Schloezer noted that the Ballets Russes' *"grande époque"* was between 1919 and 1924 – a period when the company was collaborating with mostly French artists and composers.

The Ballets Russes, however, was not the only ballet troupe to incorporate modern themes and showcase French avant-garde artists. Also important was Rolf de Maré's Ballets Suédois led by choreographer Jean Borlin and consisting mostly of dancers from the Swedish and Royal Danish ballet companies.[87] Although the company only lasted from 1920 to 1925, it also collaborated with many top French talents such as poets Blaise Cendrars, Paul Claudel, and Jean Cocteau; composers such as George Auric, Arthur Honegger, Darius Milhaud, Francis Poulenc, and Erik Satie; and artists and designers such as Giorgio de Chirico, Fernand Léger, Francis Picabia, and Andrée Parr. In other words, it provided another opportunity for French artistic collaborations with the ballet (and introduced some competition for the Ballets Russes). The company also catered to Parisian tastes, often playing upon contemporary and whimsical themes, as in *Les mariés de la Tour Eiffel* (1921) – a satire on the bourgeoisie conceived by Jean Cocteau, which presented a wedding party on the top of the Eiffel Tower on Bastille Day. Cocteau had aimed to "rehabilitate the commonplace" and "the droll and homely aspects of the Parisian world."[88] Although its dancers were all classically trained, Borlin's choreography was avant-garde in nature and often embraced fantastical or abstract motifs. The company produced over twenty ballets in five years, and its works reflect the innovations occurring in stage design. Moreover, its performances received wide coverage in the papers and drew the attention of dance critics.

Although the Ballets Suédois spent a large amount of time touring, three of its ballets received particularly favourable reviews in Paris: *El Greco, Dervishes,* and *Les vierges folles.* One critic asserted: "Mr. Borlin has conquered Paris, just like M. Nijinsky did before the war." Another noted: "This performance places the Ballets Suédois next to, not behind the Ballets Russes."[89] André Levinson, however, was critical of the troupe's dancing abilities, writing that "whatever the contribution of its painters, musicians, and poets, the Ballets Suédois will never succeed in creating a work of art so long as its ballets are danced by the Ballets Suédois."[90]

The Ballets Russes' and Ballets Suédois' vibrant presence in the French capital, their French collaborations, and their modern flair confirmed that Paris was still the cultural centre of Europe. The spectacle of modern ballets like *Parade, Les biches*, and numerous others helped to ease postwar anxieties by offering something new and radically different. The visibility and successes of foreign troupes, like the Ballets Russes and Ballets Suédois, and their involvement in modern French artistic trends also prompted Parisian critics to think about France's own ballet company, the Paris Opéra ballet, and its place within modern French culture. Critics and intellectuals began to inquire why Paris's own ballet company was not achieving an equivalent acclaim. The ballet reviews published after the war reveal an increasing interest among critics in reviving French ballet, re-examining the nature of ballet, and inquiring into the state of dance reviewing. In fact, it is in this period that the "dance critic" surfaced in France. Thereafter, music critics shared terrain with the dance specialist, and in some cases had their dance columns usurped. Also in the postwar period, we find critics increasingly claiming specific characteristics of ballet as innately French. They did so by enunciating ballet's French origins. Thus the very presence of foreign ballet troupes in Paris recaptured the French public's enthusiasm for ballet production and inspired Parisian critics to claim ballet as inherently French and to promote French ballet.

MAKING BALLET FRENCH AGAIN

Three immediate factors encouraged the evolution of ballet's identity from Russian to French. The first factor was, as already outlined, Diaghilev's collaborations with French avant-garde artists. Diaghilev provided a new way for France to recognize its own artistic achievements by paying homage to contemporary French talents (for example, Erik Satie, Marie de Laurencin, and André Derain) and French themes. The second factor was the increasing efforts undertaken by critics, such as André Levinson, to capture the French public's interest in ballet, to highlight its origins in France, and to call for a revitalized national French ballet. The third factor was the series of reforms undertaken by new director Jacques Rouché at the Paris Opéra and the creation of "La Saison Française" (The French Season). Ultimately, a distinctly French national style evolved under Paris Opéra ballet director Serge Lifar in the 1930s.

Criticism that addressed ballet's future in France increasingly surfaced in bourgeois journals and newspapers such as *Le Temps*, *La Nouvelle Revue Française*, *Le Figaro*, *Comœdia*, and *La Revue Musicale*, some dedicating weekly columns to the topic of dance and many calling for a new national ballet and a French style. In the 1920s, we find reviews and articles entitled "La saison de ballets français à l'Opéra" (The French Ballet Season at the Opéra) (*Comœdia*, 7 June 1922); "Pour le ballet français" (For the French Ballet) (*Comœdia*, 5 March 1923); "Où en sont les 'Ballets russes'" (What Has Become of the Ballets Russes?) (*Comœdia*, part 1: 18 June 1923; part 2: 25 June 1923); and "Lectures chorégraphiques" (Choreographic Lectures) (*Comœdia*, 3 March 1924). Some critics expressed interest in the Paris Opéra ballet school's examinations and the training of its dancers – for example, "À l'Opéra: Avant les examens de la danse" (At the Opéra: Before the Dance Exams) (*Comœdia*, 22 July 1922). Such reviews demonstrate the attempts by critics to educate the public on classical ballet and to elevate its status in France. Intellectuals such as Jacques Rivière, Henri Prunières, and Russian émigré Boris de Schloezer devoted their energies to ballet and its music. Music critics struggled to negotiate ballet's place among the arts and attempted to relate ballet to traditional and contemporary currents in music and to nationalist sentiment.

Ironically, it was two Russian émigrés (André Levinson and Serge Lifar) who made relentless efforts to restore French ballet, to educate the public on the art of ballet, and to elevate ballet to its highest potential as an art form. Both contributed articles in multiple bourgeois journals, published books on dance, and gave lectures on ballet. More importantly, Levinson and Lifar both attempted and eventually succeeded in reconciling the two vying tensions of modern French ballet: first, French ballet's development in Russia and its subsequent transformation; and second, French ballet's heritage as an aristocratic art form. They both, through various means, found ways to refashion ballet for a modern democratic republic.

There are a number of possible reasons why Levinson and Lifar were so invested in the promotion of ballet in France. One must consider their particularly vulnerable and opportunistic positioning as Russian émigrés in this period. Levinson's previous activities as a professional journalist in Russia, his fluency in French, and specialization in dance, offered him a niche in which to find employment in Paris. With a vibrant Russian ballet troupe in Paris, Levinson's unique qualifications became sought after and he was soon regularly employed as a dance critic by several reputable Parisian newspapers. Levinson was truly passionate about dance, particularly nineteenth-century French classical ballet. While in Russia, he had already begun his defence of French classical dance and his criticism of the "new ballet" of Michel Fokine and the Ballets Russes. The Bolshevik Revolution, however, had destroyed his world, taking away his university position, publication opportunities, private library, and dignity. Like many members of the Russian intelligentsia, Levinson and his family fled the Soviet Union just in time. As a frequent visitor to Paris before the war, he was fluent in French and likely had both personal and professional contacts in the French publishing world. Disenchanted with his homeland and enamoured with Frenchness (in St Petersburg, he was a professor of French literature), Levinson took his family to Paris and established himself as a prominent figure in Parisian artistic and intellectual circles. Within a few years of his arrival, Levinson embarked again on his defence of French classical ballet and unrelentingly promoted the merits of the Paris Opéra ballet.

Serge Lifar, on the other hand, had come to Paris as a dancer of the Ballets Russes. Born in Kiev, Lifar had a comfortable childhood, growing up in a bourgeois household. His life took a dramatic turn, however, with the outbreak of war in 1914 and the Bolshevik Revolution in 1917. In his autobiography, *Ma Vie* (1965), Lifar expressed his shock at the violence and chaos of civil war. In the attempt to lure adolescents away from their bourgeois parents, the Red Army recruited Lifar, along with many other youths. Lifar's world, like that of Levinson, was torn apart. He saw private property abolished, houses declared state property, businesses closed, and friends killed. In 1920, when he was fifteen, Lifar found solace in dance when Bronislava Nijinska, who had established a dance school in Kiev, introduced him to ballet. In 1923, Lifar jumped at the chance to escape Bolshevik Kiev and joined the Ballets Russes, where he eventually replaced Nijinsky as its lead dancer. When Diaghilev died in 1929, Lifar's reputation enabled him to join the Paris Opéra ballet as its premier danseur and ballet master. An opportunist, Lifar managed to forge alliances with many French leading artists, writers, composers, and patrons, and became a prominent figure in the elite circles of Paris. While his anti-Bolshevism is clear, Lifar's other political commitments are unclear.

In fact, one can argue that his political commitments were in service to his primary commitment (as a dancer, choreographer, director, and theorist) to advancing the art of dance. In 1932, he was awarded the title of *professeur de danse* and began reforms of the Opéra's ballet school. As we will see, Lifar's contributions as artistic director of the Paris Opéra certainly played an important role in revitalizing French ballet. This book, however, is concerned more with Lifar as dance critic, theorist, and historian. The study focuses on Lifar in his capacity as a public intellectual by analyzing the ways in which his writings helped to reshape attitudes towards ballet and its dancers and reflected French cultural trends.

While the political leanings of Levinson and Lifar are interesting to consider in understanding their motivations for promoting ballet (Levinson was anti-Soviet and certainly not proto-fascist, and Lifar, as extremely opportunistic, was susceptible to the Left or Right), they did not aggressively assert their political views in their writings on ballet. It would be thus inaccurate to represent these émigrés as committed to specific political forms (republican or otherwise). It is clear that their primary commitment was to reshape public opinion about ballet and to redefine the art form to suit modern tastes in republican France. Therefore, it is important to clarify that critics (not only Russians Levinson and Lifar, but also French critics) promoted and attempted to remake "French" ballet by locating images that corresponded to republican values. As we will see, both served as effective vehicles for the transfer of foreign aesthetics, insisting that ballet was a "French art" and proposing the means to revitalize French ballet.

Many of André Levinson's articles reveal his extensive efforts to reclaim ballet as French, to reconcile French ballet's past and present, and to restore the reputation of French ballet production via the Paris Opéra ballet. In his article "Some Commonplaces of Dance II," for example, Levinson claimed that classical ballet was an essentially French art form despite the modern innovations by the Russian ballet. Referring to the productions of the Ballets Russes, he asked rhetorically, "but what are they, these [Russian] ballets, if not the supreme blossoming of French dance through Russian expression? It is France that coordinated and balanced the scattered elements of the common effort, in having completed and magnified the formula of it."[91] In another *Comœdia* article, Levinson reminded his readers that it was French dancer/choreographer Marius Petipa who went to

Russia, introduced French classical ballet, and reformed Russian ballet to a glorious state. Seeing that the art of ballet was declining miserably on his own soil, he explained, the "genius Petipa" left France and was adopted by the Russians.[92] Levinson presented Petipa as a hero of French classical ballet, which was the only pure and true style of ballet in his eyes. "While we can all agree essentially that dance is an art," Levinson once proclaimed, "dance is over and above all a French art."[93] Therefore, the triumph of the Russian seasons in Paris, Levinson argued, should not be seen as "an invasion," but rather as "a restitution" of what was initially French artistry.[94] The Russian reintroduction of ballet artistry in Paris merely reaffirmed its French heritage in that its dancers were classically trained (in the Petipa tradition) at the Imperial Theatre's ballet academy.

Levinson offers an example of how Parisian critics attempted to transform foreign images into distinctly "French" ones. By arguing that ballet was merely "preserved" in Russia and not developed there and that the Russian ballet was not an "invasion" but a "restitution" of nineteenth-century classical French ballet, Levinson is strongly asserting that ballet had not been subjected to foreign influences, that there was a "pure" classical ballet that was indisputably French. In fact, he claimed that a sign of ballet's authenticity as a French art form was reflected in the enduring use of the French language in ballet, regardless of the country in which it is practiced. "From St Petersburg to Naples, French is, moreover, the official language of the great choreographic art," Levinson pointed out in "Some Commonplaces on Dance II."[95] Quite striking is Levinson's referral to the French Enlightenment writer Antoine de Rivarol, whose discourses proclaimed the universality and aesthetic superiority of the French language and who predicted its lasting pre-eminence. According to Levinson, ballet realized the vision of Rivarol of the internationalization or, in Rivarol's words, "universalization" of the French language in that its codification remained in French as it spread across Europe. In this manner, as Levinson argued, ballet served as a vehicle for asserting the primacy of the French language, and the enduring use of the French language in ballet was another indication of ballet's indisputable "Frenchness." Moreover, Levinson implied that not only are French words used to describe the steps, but the steps themselves are French. In fact, he suggested that "[a] discourse on the universality of the French dance would be a good thing to do!"[96] Even the Ballets

Russes, which had strived to capture a sense of Russianness in its productions and publicity, still used French, the universal language of ballet, to articulate dance steps – many of which derived from French dance theoreticians. Articles such as these helped to erode the Russian identity of ballet. They not only drew the French bourgeoisie's attention to the origins of ballet, but also offered the French a new perspective into the future of ballet and the glory that the art could once again bring to France.

Yet the question was raised of how the French could honour an art form that, while earning them international grandeur and enduring recognition, originated under an absolute monarchy (one they had fought so hard to destroy). In other words, how could the French reconcile ballet's glorious heritage with modern nationalism? Levinson answered this by stating that ballet was a pure art that could be detached from politics and, therefore, did not have to be imperial. Levinson urged the French to turn to their own tradition and to present it in a new way – one that was distinctly French, but also compatible with modern times and a republican nation. Unlike critic Marcel Prévost, who vehemently believed that the French ballet could never represent republican life, Levinson argued that the French were fully capable of preparing ballet for themselves in a democratic republic. According to him, ballet was not only a medium through which to experience nostalgia of a time long past (as depicted by the cynical Prévost), but also a source through which to express modern trends, mentalities, aesthetic styles, and even contemporary national politics.

Levinson's article "For the French Ballet" (1923) reveals his enthusiasm for the creation of a renewed French style of ballet. However, he urged the French not to imitate the Russian ballet but to renew or reconstruct their own national style.[97] He insisted that a new French ballet could come out from behind the shadow of the Ballets Russes:

> It [the French ballet] must return to itself to recreate an art of French dance. For if a glorious example stimulates emulation, imitation degrades and kills ... No longer deform with genius, but develop and create forms. Express with clarity the essential matters of the soul. Seek not passionate extravagance but subtle meaning. Don't intoxicate with colour, construct. Translate by the graceful and exact play of lines its interior rhythm. Recover the complete and normal expression of the national spirit in its plastic form.

> Reform a discipline. Know it, restrict it. Next create, for France has, in its past, given dance its supreme expression and can now be called upon to launch its renaissance.[98]

Here Levinson suggests that French ballet could revive in modern form, embrace modern innovations in ballet productions (via the Russians), and still represent modern French political and cultural ideologies. Levinson made his case by pointing out that "even the legacy of French genius had not been isolated from outside influences." He cited the examples of Poussin's paintings of Italian peasants and Watteau's borrowings from the Flemish. He remarked that even Molière put himself in the school of Tiberio Fiorillo – "le fameux Scaramouche" – where he was introduced to the improvisation technique of the commedia dell'arte actor. Even the Russian ballet, he pointed out, with all its qualities, was really a mix of ethnic characteristics, including French classical tradition. In other words, Levinson addressed the traditional role of transnational artistic exchange in the establishment of national artistic styles. Therefore, he did not find it problematic for the French to adopt the well-received innovations of Russian ballet, such as the use of symphonic music in ballet. In fact, he suggested that some developments could be used as a tool to create a new French style of ballet.

That being said, Levinson urged the French to create this distinct modern style by grounding its technique in French classical ballet tradition, a tradition that he believed had been preserved at the Opéra. He also advised the Opéra to restore "classic ballet" (pure ballet in his opinion), an art form rooted in their own French heritage. This, he believed would not only restore the reputation of the Paris Opéra ballet, but also enhance the cultural pre-eminence of France. Levinson's efforts to revive the reputation of the Paris Opéra ballet can be seen in his positive reviews of its ballerinas. In his reviews, Levinson insisted that the Paris Opéra dancers, many of whom were French (e.g., Mlle Camille Bos, Mlle Huguette de Craponne, and M. Albert Aveline), were just as talented as great Russian and Italian dancers.[99] For example, he described Mlle Camille Bos as capable of achieving the same beauty in execution in her arabesque and *élévation* as the nineteenth-century Italian ballerina Marie Taglioni.[100] He also compared her virtuosity to the famous French ballerina Emma Livry (1842–1863).[101] This was quite a compliment, as Emma Livry managed to take away principal roles normally offered to Italian dancers at the Opéra. Here Levinson reconfirms the French heritage and glory by reminding the French that ballet was once great and could be so again with a new generation of talented French dancers. He insinuated that French dancers, in the manner of Livry, could rise above foreign dancers, in this case, the "Russian" dancers.

In his reviews, Levinson also consistently highlighted the Opéra dancers' classical training to prove that French classical tradition was still alive. For example, Levinson again compared another Paris Opéra dancer, Mlle Craponne, to Emma Livry, this time noting that Craponne replicated the same grace and *ballon* in her dancing.[102] A nineteenth-century reviewer had once elaborated on this quality of *ballon*, arguing that "Mlle. Livry had a *ballon* which has never been equaled – she bounds and leaps as no one else could do."[103] The execution of *ballon* by a dancer was understood as exhibiting great virtuosity and conceived here as a distinctly French trait. By comparing Mlle Craponne's *ballon* to that of Livry, Levinson was pointing out that the Opéra's dancers were still rigorously trained in French classical technique. Levinson's plea to the French was not only to develop their own modern style of ballet, but also to recognize the virtuosity and potential of their own dancers. Levinson's reviews helped to restore the reputation of the Paris Opéra ballet and its dancers and establish a professionalism and credibility in the art of dancing – more specifically, French dancing.[104] He and those few other experts on dance set new standards for ballet assessment by drawing attention to the dancing itself (that is, choreographic movement). Levinson was hailed by many prominent critics as the first true dance critic in France and as an "expert" at choreographic analysis. It is clear that his observations were highly valued by critics of the ballet.

Critics were not the only ones playing an integral role in reshaping public perceptions of the ballet. Two directors at the Opéra, Jacques Rouché and Serge Lifar, revitalized the Opéra by highlighting its relationship to French national culture. Rouché's reforms instigated much discussion of the potential for ballet to function once again as a key national cultural institution. While Rouché turned to thematic reforms and programs (for example, "La Saison de Ballets Français à l'Opéra" in 1922), Lifar went further by making extremely controversial changes at the Opéra and by creating a distinct French style of ballet. Their contributions to improving conditions at the Opéra were routinely chronicled and publicized in the press.

In 1914, Jacques Rouché was appointed director of the Paris Opéra.[105] However, because of the outbreak of war and the closing of the Opéra, his work really began after 1918. Rouché had a vision of restoring the Paris Opéra ballet as an institution of reputable quality. He made great efforts to turn France's eye onto its own artistic talents and to strengthen the credibility of the Paris Opéra's performances. However, Rouché faced many obstacles in his reconstruction work. As one critic observed in 1921, Rouché faced "unheard-of financial difficulties," "an insufficient subsidy," and "a disorganized theatre." This critic expressed his amazement that Rouché, with such limited financial resources, would be able to renew and regenerate *l'art lyrique français*: "The opera company was small, the choirs poorly disciplined, anarchy ruled in the dance, [and] the repertory was reduced to a strict minimum."[106]

Despite all these difficulties, Rouché managed to achieve several important accomplishments. In 1919, in collaboration with the Conseil Municipal, Rouché founded a primary school for young female dancers – dancers who would become future Paris Opéra dancers (at this time the average age of professional ballerinas was fourteen or fifteen, sometimes even twelve). We can see how this type of vocational training offered by the state increased the professionalism of the dancer. This reveals that the craft of dance was being taken more seriously by the state. Rouché also helped to organize the Paris Opéra library and museum – another stepping stone for the legitimacy of ballet as an art form. By establishing a museum and library, Rouché ensured the preservation of ballet history and of ballet production of France.[107] In doing so, he legitimized the heritage of French ballet and offered people new access to the understanding of dance. In addition, he extended the Opéra performance schedule to six performances a week and created new subscriptions of eight months (at this time, opera and ballet were still part of the same evening). Most likely, Rouché did this in order to bring in more financial support and to please subscribers, even though eventually he aimed to reduce their control over the Opéra. In 1922, Rouché announced "La Saison de Ballets Français à l'Opéra," in which ballets at the Opéra would present a repertoire of exclusively French choreography and French music. "La Saison Française" was to be a celebration of French tradition and a strategy to regain public enthusiasm for the Paris Opéra performances.

During Rouché's tenure as director, we find many articles investigating the activities at the Opéra and publicizing the changes that were being made to improve the quality of its performances. One of the most outspoken critics was André Rigaud. Rigaud was delighted with the reforms made by Jacques Rouché; his articles routinely commended Rouché's efforts at the Opéra, particularly those reforms made in its ballet company and school, the Académie Nationale de Musique et de Danse.[108] Rigaud's admiration for Rouché is best expressed in his *Comœdia* article of July 1923 in which he praised Rouché for his reforming efforts and for developing the first season of French ballets ("La Saison Française"). Rigaud pointed out that "the musical troupe and choirs were reorganized, order was somehow restored in the corps de ballet, the repertory was brought back to life, new works are observed by the day, they have made a serious effort to get out of the rut and to give to the Opéra a true artistic character." The contemporary Opéra now possessed "an elite company, remarkable choirs and a corps de ballet unique in this world; its repertory embraces all epochs and all genres, from the works of Rameau and Mozart to those of Maurice Ravel and Albert Roussel."[109] Rigaud explained that Rouché achieved this by welcoming young artists, by ensuring close collaborations among all artists, and by "renovating the art of decor and stage lighting [and] bringing all his attention to innovations in staging." Overall, he commended Rouché for finally incorporating contemporary artistic innovations in Paris Opéra productions.[110] "Under his enlightened leadership," Rigaud enthusiastically concluded, "the Opéra, which had begun to be despised, has gradually been reborn and will soon revive as in the happiest days of her past splendour."[111] Rigaud claimed that the Opéra's 1922–23 season was the most brilliant season of the Académie Nationale de Musique et de Danse.

Ultimately, the objective of "La Saison Française" was to celebrate and glorify French tradition in music, theatre, and dance. "La Saison Française" ran from October 1922 to August 1923 and its ballets were performed in venues ranging from the Paris Opéra and Théâtre des Arts to Versailles's Hall of Mirrors. Performances were staged by both the Paris Opéra ballet, with occasional guest premières danseuses, and the Ballets Russes. "La Saison Française" showcased works by French contemporary composers and ballets that represented French tradition and talents.[112] Many of the Paris Opéra ballet productions were performed when the Ballets Russes season had ended.

The participation of the Ballets Russes in "La Saison Française" was significant not only because the productions were French in theme but, more importantly, because the company was exposing and celebrating French artistic talents (both old and new) through ballet production. One review of *Matelots* described its musical score by composer George Auric as "without a doubt, the best work of [his] that possesses by its craft this invaluable quality of being essentially French."[113] Diaghilev's increasing French collaborations contributed to the re-establishment of ballet's identity as French through the exhibition of its contemporary artistic talents. However, it is important to note that while many of the musicians, librettists, and costume and set designers used by the Ballets Russes were French, not a single French dancer was hired. As dance scholar Lynn Garafola points out, in the ballets of the "La Saison Française," "the nationality of the composer had more to do with identifying a ballet as French than the nationality of either the dancers or choreographers."[114]

An abundance of articles responded to Rouché's "La Saison Française." Such a schedule was seen by critics as a bold challenge to *la saison russe* that had monopolized ballet in Paris for over a decade. André Levinson commended Rouché's hard work in challenging the former bureaucratic disarray at the Opéra and his courage to attack the Russian season that was then at the peak of its success.[115] In fact, many reviewers were overjoyed by "La Saison Française" and expressed great optimism and pride in the Paris Opéra ballet's participation. One reviewer extolled the season, praising "the effort on the part of the Opéra to place value on French choreography in inaugurating the first season of French ballets." He described the repertoire as "enriching itself, over the course of the season, in a great number of new works and works which have not been performed for a very long time."[116] André Rigaud hailed the Paris Opéra's ballet troupe for its virtuosity, discipline, and restored reputation: "The dance company and the choreographic repertoire of our National Academy of Music are valued by foreign troupes and repertories. One can even say that, at present, the corps de ballet of the Opéra is the best [*le premier]* in the world. Milan and Moscow once rivalled Paris. Today, Milan is requesting female dancers from France and the Soviets have driven away the aristocracy and those of the Mariinsky Theatre in Petrograd [St Petersburg] whose participants are now scattered around the world."[117] Responding to the second season of French ballets, Rigaud rhetorically asked, "We have Russian ballets, Swedish ballets, the Cambodian ballet, why doesn't Paris also have French ballets?" In fact, the Paris Opéra ballet's participation in "La Saison Française" inspired Rigaud to compare it to Paris's foreign ballet companies: "We never thought of comparing the company of Jean Borlin [Les Ballets Suédois] and that of M. Serge de Diaghilev to the Opéra ballet." He boasted: "Currently, the Opéra possesses an elite troupe, versatile and disciplined by regular and constant hard work. It is, therefore, capable of offering a season of ballets that will be danced flawlessly."[118] Rigaud's review reveals the sense of pride that was returning to the Paris Opéra ballet and to French ballet. Here we can see the wave of nationalism that moved through France in the interwar years and its penetration into cultural life and the arts.

André Levinson, however, found elements of hypocrisy in Rouché's "La Saison Française" for it was the Ballets Russes that in fact staged many of its productions. Levinson was particularly disappointed by the absence of the Paris Opéra ballet company and French classical tradition in the Festival of Versailles. In 1923, the Ballets Russes was invited by the French government to participate in the festival. After a restoration of the palace, the Ballets Russes performed in the famous Galerie des Glaces (Hall of Mirrors) on 30 June 1923. Ballets Russes régisseur Serge Grigoriev recalled that "the audience was of the most distinguished, including President Poincaré, the whole Cabinet, and most of the Diplomatic Corps."[119] Levinson criticized the "Saison Française" program for not using the French material, resources, vigour, talent and tradition at their disposal:

> The Opéra has fallen without a fight in front of foreign competitors. It didn't oppose the Swedes in May, nor the Russians in June … The participation of the French ballet at the Festival of Versailles was just as hidden. If only this repertoire had included works of Lully, or at least *Castor and Pollux* by Rameau [seventeenth- and eighteenth-century French composers]. Might have a reconstruction of *Ballet de la nuit* [Ballet of the Night] been improvised for the occasion?* Or could they not manage to dance *Cydalise*

> by [contemporary French composer] Mr Pierné at the site which inspired it? Of course, I must admit that the Russians have done very well and they extended themselves nobly for a great French cause. But the Opéra ballet gave up without a murmur to a privilege which is due to the successors of MM. Beauchamps, Lully, and Pécour … the idea of giving a French ballet season when there is no one to compare, borders on a joke.[120]

This article, entitled "Le paradoxe de Saison Française" (1923), embraced a powerfully laid-out argument on the disappointment, if not humiliation, of "La Saison Française." Levinson took the French ballet to task by criticizing the Opéra for not boldly running "La Saison Française" simultaneously during the Ballets Russes and Ballets Suédois summer seasons. He saw the Paris Opéra season of *ballets français* as superficial because it occurred once all the ballet troupes had left, so that there was nothing with which to compare performances. He argued that by waiting to run "La Saison Française" after the foreign companies' seasons had finished, the Paris Opéra ballet season had lost a great opportunity to challenge foreign troupes.[121] Levinson argued that "La Saison Française" could have been much more effective and achieved more by having confidence in its own tradition and by boldly facing its foreign competitors. He considered it a failure to present French-invested ballets such as *Cydalise et le chèvre-pied* at the Paris Opéra rather than at Versailles – the very place that inspired it.

Levinson was bewildered as to why, with all its French tradition, repertoire, and artistic talent, the Opéra's "La Saison Française" "surrendered itself unnecessarily." He went on to question the very organization and conception of "La Saison Française" and revealed a paradox of the Opéra ballet:

> What are the feelings that determine this strange attitude of the leaders of the National Academy? Modesty or indifference? That is the basis of their theatre policy? They have a staff whose choreographic culture is homogeneous and considerable with, as a base, classical dance. But is there any sincere desire, at the Opéra, for the victory of classical ballet? Do they realize that this tradition, which constitutes the main strength of the company … is entirely consistent with the meaning of all modern artistic effort?

> Of course, we cannot engage a battle and carry it out with the unspoken desire to be beaten. Such is, today, the paradox of the Opéra Ballet.[122]

Levinson was making two points: first, that the "Saison Française" failed to recognize an opportunity to rival the Russians directly; and second, that the French did not exploit their own talents and tradition. Levinson claimed that the directors thought that because the Opéra dancers were schooled in the classical tradition, they had to continue in the classical tradition; they had not realized that modern artistic trends were not opposed to the classical traditions. Could it be that the Russians represented a modern version of ballet and the French an antiquated classical one? Levinson seemed to be telling the French that just because they were holding on to the traditions of the classical ballet, it did not mean that they were inferior to the Russians or that they should slavishly try to imitate them.

Overall, Levinson saw enormous potential for the French ballet which had not yet been realized. He argued that this had been the result of a lack of strong leadership and an unwillingness to take risks at the Opéra. Although he supported Rouché and his national project to restore the Paris Opéra ballet to its former grandeur, he pointed out two obstacles that held the Paris Opéra back: first, the lack of a serious, complex, and stable conception of the art of ballet at the Opéra; and second, an absence of a directorial authority to put such a conception into place.[123] Levinson revealed his disappointment with Rouché's lack of temerity in "La Saison Française." He proposed that Rouché take the same risks he did at the Théâtres des Arts some ten years earlier when he presented his own performances during the Ballets Russes' peak era. Levinson noted that at the Théâtres des Arts, Rouché had boldly challenged the Russians even though it was the time of Karsavina, Nijinsky, and Pavlova. Levinson's critique of Rouché, rather than being an attack or rebuke, seems to have been more of a message to Rouché to risk again what he had risked in the past. He concluded, "It is not a question of conquest [i.e., waging war against an enemy, the Ballets Russes]. It is only of honouring the flag, of asserting a willingness, of issuing a program. Today, one has an army at one's disposal. But one has rolled up the flag."[124] In other words, the French had already surrendered although they had an army at their disposal.

Most interesting is that we find an outsider, a Russian, with a distinct and straightforward point of view on the potential of French ballet, attempting to renew French patriotic fervour. Levinson urged the Opéra and its directors to recognize and use fully their own traditions and talents and to reclaim the glory of ballet as theirs. In other words, Levinson had discovered a certain amount of doubt on the part of the French in the vitality of their cultural institutions. One could even extend Levinson's argument to a much broader context. His observation of the Opéra's "cultural malaise" can be seen as extending to the political arena. Levinson's outside status may have placed him in a privileged position to observe the malaise that afflicted France after the First World War. As Alistair Horne points out in his book *To Lose a Battle: France 1940* (1969), it is most often the outside observers who clearly see cultural malaise.[125] Levinson offered the French a "remedy" for this "malaise" by proposing the revitalization of its own Paris Opéra ballet and by attempting to reconceptualize French ballet as embodying grace, muscular strength, vitality, and virtuosity.

Another Russian émigré, Serge Lifar, also made great efforts both to educate the French public on the art of ballet and to resurrect a French national ballet of worth. As a former Ballets Russes dancer, choreographer, ballet director, dance historian, and dance critic, he published successful books on dance and contributed many articles to journals and newspapers. Soon after joining Diaghilev's Ballet Russes as a principal dancer in 1925, Lifar met Jacques Rouché, who was then director of the Paris Opéra. Rouché wanted to offer a new version of Beethoven's only ballet, *Les créatures de Prométhée*. Lifar was a replacement for Balanchine, who was supposed to undertake the choreography but fell ill. This began Lifar's long career at the Opéra and a his steadfast friendship with Rouché. At the Opéra, he was appointed ballet master in 1929 and later artistic director of the Paris Opéra Ballet (1930–58).

The type of directorial leadership Levinson had spoken of in regards to Jacques Rouché was fully embraced by Lifar. His most significant contribution to the new visualization of French ballet performance was in the structural changes he accomplished at the Opéra as well as his aesthetic reforms. These changes were no easy task as the Opéra had its own internal politics, many of which were wedded to antiquated tradition (for example, subscribers held a very influential role). Lifar thus was faced with the challenge of uniting old and new while attempting to revitalize and modernize the Paris Opéra ballet. Lifar's autobiography, *Ma Vie* (1965), recounts the laborious task he faced upon his appointment to direct the Paris Opéra in 1930. He recalled, "I was alone in face of the task to be accomplished, alone, that is, with nothing before me ... when I took over the direction of the National Opera Ballet, I found precisely nothing, no troupe, no audience, no living tradition, not even any realization of the situation or desire to remedy it."[126]

While Lifar's autobiography at times overdramatizes his role in the Opéra's revival, important reforms were implemented under his direction that surely helped to refashion the ballet at the Opéra. Lifar's most significant challenge was to reduce bureaucratic red tape. He recalled that, although a director, he had to work within a vast state organization where even the casting of a dancer could be the concern of a cabinet minister (perhaps still the workings of libertinism). Yet despite this, Lifar managed to foster individual talents and secure the integrity of the institution.

One of Lifar's first structural changes was to turn off the lighted chandeliers during the performance. This move was designed to direct the audience's attention to the ballet performance. In his autobiography, he explains how dance at the Paris Opéra was "regarded as an agreeable amusement, a display of effortless grace where pretty girls assumed poses and were accompanied by male dancers whose role was to show off the ladies."[127] Since the performances did not demand close attention from the audience, the tradition of keeping the chandelier lights on allowed the subscribers to socialize. Lifar explained, "In this way, people could recognize one another, the subscribers could exchange greetings and pay visits from box to box before going off to the sacrosanct *foyer de la danse* where old gentlemen met and made much of charming young women. And for a great number of people such opportunities as these constituted the most obvious reason for having ballet performances at all."[128] This leads us to another significant reform undertaken by Lifar, which was to deny the subscribers access to the infamous Foyer de la Danse. In the 1830s, the Foyer had been opened by the director of the Opéra as a "warm-up" room for the dancers and a space to "mingle" with male subscribers. The Foyer de la Danse was indeed "sacrosanct" in that it preserved a French tradition of libertinism. Within this drawing room/warm-up room at the Opéra, subscribers could converse with the dancers before and after the performances and even during intermissions.[129]

Another significant reform undertaken by Lifar was the introduction of programs consisting solely of dance, rather than presenting ballets as "poor relations of lyrical works." Lifar successfully convinced Rouché that such a new program would definitely establish the ballet, and, at the same time, the Opéra would gain a public of ballet lovers.[130] Lifar noted that out of 200 subscribers only six were in favour of evenings wholly devoted to ballet: "One of the six was Mapov who knew Russia and had been an admirer of the Imperial Ballet." Nonetheless, Rouché allowed Lifar the chance. Lifar recalls that the first evening of ballet performances was sold out and "the first was followed by others – always with the same result."[131] The success of ballet-only evenings reveals that ballet was being increasingly acknowledged as an art in its own right and that Lifar's new modernized aesthetic was gaining public interest.

Beyond administrative changes, Lifar was also determined to revive the artistry of ballet itself. In doing so, he faced the task of training his dancers in what would become a distinct and highly disciplined new French national style based on a uniting of French classical tradition with new modern visions (explored further in chapter 4). By reviving a classical ballet style, he honoured the celebrated French reformist choreographers Jean-Georges Noverre (1727–1810) and Marius Petipa (1818–1910). In fact, in 1938, critic Boris de Schloezer compared Lifar to Noverre – in the eyes of the French, a truly great honour for a Russian émigré. He also commended Lifar's undeniable pride in ballet's French heritage and was pleased that ballet was reconceived specifically as a French art form.[132] Incidently, Schloezer did not mention the Russian influence on ballet or even that Lifar was a Russian dancer.

Among more essential changes, Lifar demanded a new standard of artistic makeup in the Opéra's corps de ballet and forbade the wearing on stage of any jewellery that was not an integral part of the costumes or roles. He had real wigs made, and did away with elastic on dancing shoes and the wearing of "trunk-hose worn over tights."[133] He made all the male dancers shave off their moustaches and, with difficulty, made all the female dancers dance on the tips of their toes rather than on "demi-pointe."

Lifar succeeded above all in restoring the prestige of the French dancer. Under Diaghilev, French dancers were not recruited to join his company, and when Russian dancers were not available, he recruited dancers from England and Poland. At the Opéra, Lifar managed to establish a strong and prestigious corps de ballet and to create an increasing number of French *étoiles* – dancers who equalled and even surpassed the Russians. In doing so, he proved to the French public that it was never a lack of French talent that stood in the way of a great national company but rather poor management and direction (just as Levinson had argued).

Lifar strove for dancers (both male and female) to display their physical prowess yet execute their technique with grace.[134] Other changes included adding the rank of the male *étoile* – a rank previously held only by women. This move reflected Lifar's larger ambition to garner accolades for both female and male dancers. Scholars Georgianna Gore and Laurance Louppe capture such contributions of Lifar in *Europe Dancing* (2000): "Ballet, for reasons other than its historic traditions, was then truly, though not exclusively French … the Russian-born Serge Lifar, a former Diaghilev dancer, trained and imposed French artists to succeed the stars with Russian surnames such as Olga Spessivtseva and Nina Vyroubova. The new 'étoiles' were named Lycette Darsonval, Solange Schwarz, Yvette Chauviré."[135] In addition to Yvette Chauviré and Solange Schwarz, many other French names surfaced such as Suzanne Lorcia, Liane Dayde, Janine Charat, and male dancers Roland Petit, Albert Aveline, and Jean Babillée. Dancer Irène Lidova remarked later that "this new *élan* [fervour] hatched a generation of exceptional male dancers and remarkable French ballerinas."[136] Increasingly, French ballet dancers served as symbols of Frenchness for many, and publicity machines promoted them as representatives of Parisian cosmopolitanism.[137] After 1940, the Paris Opéra became more and more exclusively French. With the exception of some international *étoiles,* the corps de ballet was and remains today made up mostly of French-born dancers. Most importantly, French ballet achieved, once again, an international reputation of excellence.

However, Lifar's tenure at the Opéra and the changes he accomplished were feasible, in part, because of the political and cultural climate of the 1930s. Why did the French state decide finally to support the Paris Opéra financially? Why the sudden interest in supporting an eroded and neglected cultural institution? The 1930s marked a time of recuperation (from the First World War) yet also foreboding for France. It was a period of considerable economic depression and severe political instability. The year 1933 saw a deepening economic crisis and a rise in unemployment. The Depression exacerbated political tension within French society. While modernity was embraced in a multitude of ways to transform French society into a more unified form in the 1920s, the 1930s brought drastic divisions between the Left and Right. In fact, there was no strong lasting government after 1920. After the 1928 elections, a political shift to the Right occurred as Raymond Poincaré gained more power than the independent socialist Aristide Briand. In 1936, Léon Blum became France's first socialist prime minister only to have his government fall a year later. The rise of aggressive fascist regimes in Germany and France prompted the Radicals and Conservatives to form an alliance (the Popular Front) against the growing fascist movement in France. The Stavisky affair, a minor financial scandal perpetuated by a Russian-Jewish fraudster, revealed considerable corruption in the highest ranks of the government and even stirred rioting. All of these conditions fuelled rising fears that the French Republic was in danger.

In many ways, the political and cultural climate of the 1930s encouraged a nationalistic opportunity for the Paris Opéra and an interest in reviving the French art of ballet. The construction of a "True France" played a central role in cultural production in the 1930s.[138] The French (whether of the Right or Left) were increasingly desperate to affirm the French nation and to pronounce its spirit: the nationalist reaction spurred by the presence of the Ballets Russes in France reflected this growing nationalism earlier in the 1920s. Indeed, we discover a new level of commitment by the state to the visibility and prestige of the nation's cultural activities (we see this in the rampant enthusiasm for Jacques Rouché's "Saison Française"). For example, a series of major international exhibitions were held in France in the interwar period: the Exposition des Arts Décoratifs in 1925; the Exposition Coloniale (first in Marseille in 1922, later in Paris in 1931), and the Exposition Internationale des Arts et des Techniques dans la Vie Moderne (the Paris World's Fair) in 1937. All these expositions served to showcase France as a major European power and as culturally advanced.

The official nationalization of French theatres in 1939 is also symptomatic of this commitment to cultural activities. In the words of scholar Ruth Bereson, the state "openly assumed full responsibility as 'patron of the arts.'"[139] This is most evident in the formation of the Réunion des Théâtres Lyriques Nationaux, of which the Opéra became a part on 14 January 1939 and "thus placed itself firmly in the public sector."[140] The arts were seen as useful in serving the needs of the state. French nationalists also recognized the emblematic value of historical cultural institutions such as the Opéra, and the state made various efforts to realize certain visions of national cultural heritage. As historian Herman Lebovics points out, France was "resilient and flexible, able to grasp new trends onto old customs"; by the 1930s "cosmopolitanism and nationalism were proven compatible."[141] Thus, the merging of French classical ballet tradition with the modernism and cosmopolitanism of the Ballets Russes into a French national style would have been feasible in the eyes of the state.

Furthermore, the Russian monopoly on ballet in France had already diminished significantly by 1929. Serge Diaghilev died in late 1929 and the legendary Russian ballerina Anna Pavlova in early 1931. Although two new companies attempted to preserve the traditions and innovations of the original Ballets Russes – René Blum and Colonel de Basil's Ballets Russes de Monte Carlo (est. 1932) and Sergei Denham's Ballets Russes de Monte Carlo (est. 1938), these companies spent most of their time outside of France touring the globe. In addition, new ballet companies with strong national identities were founded in the 1930s and 1940s across Europe and the United States. Many of these national companies were founded by former Ballets Russes dancers, who drew upon their Russian training and exposure to modernism (for example, George Balanchine in the United States and Ninette de Valois in the United Kingdom). Furthermore, Paris-based private ballet companies began to surface in the 1930s and 40s, such as George Balanchine's Les Ballets 33 and Roland Petit's Les Ballets des Champs Élysées and Ballets de Paris, featuring a celebrated list of talented French star dancers.

In conclusion, we have seen how the presence of a foreign troupe in Paris during the interwar years served as a catalyst for commentary about ballet and French national identity. Discussions on ballet revealed French attitudes towards foreigners (particularly, Russians), new assertions of Frenchness, a heightened sense of nationalism, a renewed appreciation for the art of ballet, and a reaffirmation of France's heritage. In a postwar atmosphere of nostalgia and rapid change, critics and intellectuals (with the help of André Levinson) used ballet as a means through which to reconcile French cultural tradition with modern tastes. Increasingly, critics recognized French ballet as a site through which modern national identity and French grandeur could be asserted. This chapter introduced the efforts made by critics, most especially Levinson, to promote French ballet and to professionalize its dancers. Figures such as Jacques Rouché and Serge Lifar also contributed to the revitalization of French ballet after a public taste for ballet had been re-established in Paris.

Through a variety of efforts, the Paris Opéra once again became a temple to French art and the French spirit, and ballet was raised to the rank of a major art form that could fill an entire evening program at the Palais Garnier. It was in the development of a new modern and distinctly French dance aesthetic that the French could reassert a hegemonic French identity. Therefore, a French national style, which is maintained even today, was developed out of a long and complex process of reconciling ballet's French classical heritage with modern aesthetic objectives. As we will see in the following chapter, commentary on ballet would also engage in politically charged debates over ballet aesthetics as critics and dance experts pondered how to construct a distinctly "French" style.

4

Ballet and the Cultural Politics of Modern Aesthetics

May the 19th, 1909, was a great day in the history of the Russian Ballet of Serge Pavlovich Diaghilev; for it was on that day that it gave its first public performance. Thus began an enterprise that was destined to last twenty years: to create an enormous repertoire; to bring up several generations of wonderful dancers; *to raise the art of ballet to great heights*; and to diffuse it all over the world.[1]

– Serge Grigoriev

As we have seen, a new fervour for ballet was generated by the arrival of the Ballets Russes in Paris. In 1909, Serge Diaghilev and his premier choreographer Michel Fokine exhilarated French audiences with their representation of Russian culture and presentation of a new modern style of ballet. What came to Paris from Russia was not, strictly speaking, traditional Russian ballet but a Russian ballet in the grip of change, seeking and finding new modes of expression deliberately aimed at breaking with traditional concepts of dance. For the first time, ballet was revealed as a medium for the expression of modernism and, later, avant-gardism. This captivated French audiences, who were accustomed to an antiquated Romantic ballet. Ballet soon became a magnet for modern and avant-garde artists. Ballet acquired a new body of music (symphonic music) as well as a new relationship to music, decor, and mime that helped to produce a renewed sophistication. Furthermore, ballets were now performed independent of opera evenings. Ballet's audiences and benefactors changed, and its concept and function received serious reconsideration.[2] By the 1920s, the Ballets Russes had transformed the ballet into a meeting ground for a sophisticated, international elite and had brought recognition once again to ballet production.

As discussed in chapters 2 and 3, ballet criticism played a central role in shaping public opinion about the Ballets Russes and ballet in general. Commentary on ballet revealed, on the one hand, the allure of the Russian ballet and, on the other hand, French anxieties about foreign influences. Here, we examine the ways in which critics and intellectuals reconsidered ballet's worth as a high art form in the early twentieth century. Once again, the Ballets Russes played a central role in such discussions. The success of the Ballets Russes in attracting talented composers, artists, and designers to ballet production indicated to the French that ballet could serve as an important platform for artistic experimentation and innovation. In fact, the ballet stood at the forefront of modernist and avant-garde trends. In doing so, however, ballet's formal qualities lost their autonomy (the ability to stand on their own) and became subservient to other aspects of ballet production, such as music, decor, costumes, and narrative expression. How did critics respond to the new "modern" ballet of the Ballets Russes? What aspects of ballet production did they find particularly alluring, and why? In what ways did critics and intellectuals engage in discussion about ballet's nature as an art form and how did their lengthy discussions contribute to broader debates about modern aesthetics? Moreover, how did changes in aesthetic tastes relate to French culture in the early twentieth century?

Commentary on ballet became a powerful force in shaping the artistic climate of France in the early twentieth century. The Ballets Russes drove the discussion by presenting ballet as a collaborative art form that showcased the latest artistic trends. Critics and intellectuals responded to the "new ballet" of the Ballets Russes in various ways. Many critics were extremely enthusiastic about the company's new conception of ballet as a "fusion of arts." By giving music and design greater roles in ballet production, the Ballets Russes captured the attention of a variety of specialists, particularly music critics, who were enthralled by the new use of symphonic music in ballet. Thus the Ballets Russes' collaborative conception of ballet stimulated serious discussion of ballet after a long period of neglect. Ballet was now used as a platform upon which to critically discuss trends in modern aesthetics. In other words, critics could examine other components of ballet that did not concern the actual dancing. Before the 1920s, when there were no "dance experts" in France, the collaborative nature of ballet enabled critics to discuss their own speciality, whether music, drama, poetry, or design. Ballet's aesthetic worth was grounded in its ability to fuse other arts into it. However, in refocusing, the choreographic autonomy of ballet was sacrificed.

This chapter examines the aesthetic politics associated with ballet's ascendance as an art form. Ballet in France gained recognition only when it had "serious" music and art attached to it and, furthermore, when its dancing was performed by foreign bodies. Ballet commentary served to assert broader debates about modern French aesthetics, but, before the appearance of dance experts in the interwar period, curiously undervalued the corporeal aspect: the choreography and the technical virtuosity of the dancers. Nevertheless, the components of ballet that were exalted by critics reveal deep connections with attitudes and anxieties toward the body – as both instrument and art object.

FRENCH AESTHETICS, BALLET, AND THE POLITICS OF THE BODY

In order to understand early twentieth-century commentary on ballet aesthetics, it is essential to examine first the ways in which ballet has been valued as an art form in France and how its status was related to cultural attitudes towards corporeality. Ballet as an embodied art form – one in which the body/dancer is at once instrument, creator/artist, performer/practitioner, and art object – stimulated a variety of opinions about its nature and purpose. Historically, commentary on ballet was polarized by two vying concepts about the nature of ballet as an art: ballet's expressive versus formalist ("decorative") qualities. At times, the corporeal aspects of dancing elevated the art form, and, at other times, they devalued it. In other words, attitudes towards the body deeply shaped how ballet developed.

The earliest form of ballet in France, "ballet de cour" (court ballet), appeared in the sixteenth century and was a mixture of art, politics, and entertainment with the chief purpose of glorifying the state. Like Renaissance painting, early ballets at court were also used for diplomatic and propagandistic purposes. One example of a court ballet can be seen in the *Ballet des Polonais* (The Polish Ballet), commissioned by Catherine de' Medici and staged in 1573 to honour the Polish ambassadors who were visiting Paris on the occasion of the ascension of Henry of Anjou to the throne of Poland. It consisted of noble amateurs (sixteen women), not skilled professionals, performed in processional fashion, and, unlike medieval entertainments, had a secular rather than religious function. It is no coincidence that this ballet came a year after the bloody St Bartholomew's Day Massacre in 1572: the monarchy urgently needed to offer reassurance of peace and national reconciliation.[3] Court ballet's aesthetic function was to represent the aristocratic characteristics of grace, elegance, and decorum, rather than the physical display of strength and agility. The dancers' costumes were designed to reflect the latest aristocratic tastes, not the freedom of movement.[4] Thus ballet was not immediately understood as an art dependent on the skills of movement but rather as a court entertainment that could be infused with political and social meaning and could serve to express international diplomacy.

In 1581, the *Ballet comique de la reine* was created by Italian violinist, ballet master, and choreographer Balthasar de Beaujoyeulx (born Baldassare da Belgiojoso, ca. 1535–1587) and it has been often considered the "first ballet" in France. Commissioned by Henry III, king of France, as part of an array of festivities celebrating the marriage of the duc de Joyeuse to the queen's half-sister, it was quite a spectacle. The audience is said to have reached 10,000, and the performance lasted roughly six hours.[5] The *Ballet comique* incorporated, for the first time, the elements of music (both instrumental and vocal), spoken verses, costumes, and scenic effects (all receiving equal attention) and conveyed a single story line from Homer's *Odyssey: The Triumph of Virtue over Evil* (Jupiter over goddess Circe). Its aesthetic aim was to achieve a unity of the arts through a massive collaborative effort. Beaujoyeulx described the whole ballet as a well-proportioned body that pleases the eye (dancing), the ear (song and music), and the mind (poetry). Yet Beaujoyeulx insisted that the dancing be given the principle role: "I have, however, given the first place and honour to the dance."[6] He assigned the second and third place to music and poetry.[7] Ballet in general, however, remained unskilled, secular, and a means through which to assert the harmonious order of the realm.

The development of ballet skill and technique began in 1588. The treatise "orchésographie" written by French canon Jehan Tabourot (Thoinot Arbeau) provided the first specific definitions of the placing of the dancer's feet – "the five positions" of classical ballet – as well as establishing the idea of ballet turnout.[8] It also attempted to unite poetry, music, dance and design, but always presented a story – whether allegorical, historical, or legend. Expression, therefore, still played a more central role than technical virtuosity.[9] Gradually, additional demands upon the dancer's technical skills resulted in the increasing recruitment of professionals, that is commoners rather than nobles.[10] In doing so, court ballet became less exclusively aristocratic. Parts were assigned on the basis of ability rather than rank. Moreover, nobles and commoners interacted during these performances without regard for precedence. This development in the seventeenth century, which combined some technical skill with narrative expression, would form the basis of debates over ballet's aesthetic value in the eighteenth century.[11]

Ballet was not formally professionalized, however, until Louis XIV's rule. In 1661, Louis XIV founded the Académie Royale de Danse with the aim of improving dance instruction, establishing "technical principles" for the art and training of professional dancers to perform for him and his court.[12] Although Louis's intention had been to improve both social dancing and theatrical dancing in court ballet, inadvertently, his founding of the Académie Royale de Danse transformed ballet into an art of spectatorship rather than one of recreation, marking the end of the "ballet de court" as a court entertainment. The Académie Royale de Musique et de Danse (later known as the Opéra) was established in 1669 with a corps of male dancers. A year later, Jean-Baptiste Lully (musician, composer, and dancer) was given the task of directing the Académie. Increasingly, ballets were performed in the theatre rather than at court. As ballet became more professionalized, the king, who had been known as the most famous dancer of the seventeenth century, stopped dancing.[13] At this time, ballet transformed in two ways: first, as choreography became more demanding, many noblemen ceased to perform ballet on stage; and second, women took the stage. In May 1681, *Le triomphe de l'amour* was performed professionally at the Opéra with the lead girl's role played by a professional female dancer Mlle Lafontaine (1665–1738).[14] The development of professional ballet under Louis XIV, in the words of Sarah R. Cohen, "officially confirmed an assumption that had already been operating in the court for some time: the 'natural grace' of the aristocratic body could be taught to skillful commoners, who would perform as surrogates for their courtly counterparts."[15] In other words, ballet's attributes of "grace" and "noble virtuosity" became recognized as something that could be learned by anyone through practice: the bodily aspects of dance (for example, deportment or carriage) played a central role in late seventeenth-century French culture because of its ability to express aristocratic grace and noble virtuosity. Furthermore, dancers of Louis XIV's new academy replicated on the public stage the spectacle of the king and court, and an "appeal of the aristocratic body" became a "marketable aesthetic."[16] The professionalization of ballet made nobility itself a commercial product.[17] Here we can see how images of dancers began to be commodified.

When the Académie Royale de Musique et de Danse officially became a state institution in 1713, however, Lully's main objective was to develop French opera and make it distinct from Italian opera, which had established an impressive reputation in Europe. In doing so, Lully's direction of the Académie de Musique placed ballet on new ground (literally). A new style of ballet, "opera-ballet," was created by Pierre Beauchamps and composer André Campra (1660–1744), combining dancing with vocal music. With this transition, the Académie Royale de Danse was absorbed by the Académie de Musique and ballets became integrated into opera as entre'acts or "divertissements." This was a great setback for ballet's autonomy as an art form as it no longer had its own home. By the 1730s, ballets held a new position within operas as "divertissements," but dancing neither showcased technical virtuosity (athleticism) nor embodied any narrative function. Divertissements were composed of both singing and dancing elements, operatic aspects mixed with dance. With this change, ballet's function became more ambiguous and, despite their increasing technical proficiency, dancers were rarely called upon to use their expressive potential.[18]

Aesthetic debates over ballet's nature began to surface in the eighteenth century, a period when many aspects of French society were being reconsidered, challenged, and criticized. As dancers' development of ballet technique increasingly transformed ballet into a vehicle for virtuoso display, with dancers accomplishing multiple pirouettes (e.g., Anne Heinel) and complicated entrechats (e.g., Marie Camargo), questions arose over the direction ballet was taking; namely, should ballet continue to serve as a vehicle through with to assert political, social, and cultural values? In other words, was dance simply ornamental, technical, or plastic? In criticism of the opera-ballet, we find a highly politicized aesthetic debate among intellectuals over the aims of ballet (technical virtuosity [deemed decorative] or expressivity [the embodiment of an idea]).

The "decorative" use of ballet within opera triggered vigorous aesthetic debates among prominent Enlightenment philosophers over the function and nature of ballet as an art form. Some argued for the removal of dance from operas altogether. Enlightenment philosopher Jean-Jacques Rousseau, known for his contempt for the theatre, boldly asserted, "All dances that depict only themselves, and all ballet which is just dancing, should be banished from lyric theatre."[19] Many, like Rousseau, saw ballet as unnecessary "interruptions" in opera and their lack of narration boring (having no dramatic continuity). Others argued that ballet should be performed independently from opera. Encyclopedist Denis Diderot wrote in the supplement to his play *Le fils naturel* (1757), "The dance still awaits a man of genius; it is wretched everywhere because it is scarcely suspected that it is an imitative genre … a dance is a poem. This poem should therefore have its separate performance."[20] German literary critic Baron F.M. von Grimm, who moved to Paris in 1748, believed that ballet was dominating opera, writing that "if we read programs of the different operas, we can find a marvelous variety of fêtes and divertissements, but this variety [dancing] in its execution turns out to be the saddest uniformity. All fêtes are reduced to dancing for the sake of dancing." He continued: "Thus ballets in the French opera are nothing but an academy of dance … so many skillful dancers are used only for doing steps and tricks."[21] Others were also highly critical of the state of French ballet. French writer Toussaint Rémond de Saint-Mard in his *Réflexions sur l'opéra* (1743) observed: "There is in our ballets a certain uniformity which tires and bores me. Our dances are almost all designed one like the other, with no variety and no spirit." He asked, "Would it be so difficult to put more fire and invention into it?"[22]

The French Enlightenment's atmosphere of criticism, change, and reform did not limit itself to the fields of politics, religion, and education, but spread into the realm of the arts. In this period, we find extensive criticism of aesthetics, including those of dance. Commentary about the nature of dance can be found in canonical Enlightenment texts such as Denis Diderot and Jean d'Alembert's massive *Encyclopédie* (1751–77), Montesquieu's short article "Goût," and Rousseau's *Emile, or On Education* (1762). Even the French naturalist the Compte de Lacépède observed that dance "has reigned for such a long time at the theatre only for the pleasure of the eyes without going to the soul, and which perhaps did not deserve the name of art, since it did not represent nature."[23] Encyclopedist Étienne Bonnot de Condillac argued that "there are different kinds of dance … all are good provided they express something." He continued: "A dance that expresses grace and nobleness is good, but that which constitutes a kind of conversation or dialogue seems better."[24]

Recognizing ballet as an important art for the French, the philosophes attempted to articulate new standards for dance. Inspired by a revival of classicism, figures such as Diderot, Montesquieu, and Rousseau argued that all art should imitate nature and be guided by the ideals of the ancient Greeks and Romans. In the first chapter of his *Poetics,* for example, Aristotle argued that the function of dance was "to imitate character, emotion, and action by rhythmical movement."[25] In other words, dance functioned as something *outside of itself* and was used as "a substitute for words."[26] According to Aristotle, the dance ceased to be an art in itself to become a vehicle for dramatic expression. Aristotle declared that dance should interpret and imitate life. Reflecting this conception of dance, eighteenth-century theorist Abbé Jean-Baptiste Dubos (a politically active French author) noted, "The gestures of our dancers are usually attitudes and movements which serve only to charm, whereas the gestures of the antique dance were required to speak; they had to signify something."[27] Encyclopedist Cahusac was also inspired by the role of dance in ancient Greece and Rome in his treatise *La danse ancienne et moderne, ou traité historique sur la danse* (1754). In this treatise, he emphasized the importance of using pantomime or gesture and imitating nature in dance. He writes: "The different affections of the soul are … the origin of gestures, and the dance, which is made up of them, is consequently the art of executing them with grace and proportion relative to the affections they express."[28] The classical value attached to dance can be related to the way the Greeks viewed art more generally, as they seldom defined art or beauty as something distinct from knowledge, morality, religion, or life. Art (and beauty) never attained an autonomous cultural value. There was always a moral signification of perfection associated it. Therefore, one means through which to elevate eighteenth-century ballet was to reintroduce pantomime, which had played such an important role in Greek and Roman theatre.

Enlightenment thinkers' interpretations of dance as an expressive art form stem from the privileging of the mind over the body in Enlightenment thought. Their attacks of rococo art offer a good example of their hostility towards corporeality. The philosophes attacked the rococo style for being overly decorative, sensual, decadent, and corrupting. The popularity of court painter Antoine Watteau's *fêtes galantes*, or garden scenes, in which aristocratic young couples meet in amorous pursuits, suggests how well this new aesthetic matched the pleasure-seeking spirit of early eighteenth-century elite culture. It was this spirit (and the prioritizing of the senses over the intellect) that Enlightenment figures criticized. Yet gender politics were also involved in such criticisms. As art historians have shown, the rococo style was associated with femininity and elite women's influence over the modern French school. As one critic remarked, "Women are consulted too much … Since they have been guiding the arts, the arts have been degenerating."[29] Art historian Melissa Hyde notes that "the rococo was associated with an innately feminine smallness of mind and love of adornment and artificiality and also with an effeminized, arriviste aristocracy, both of which are markers of inferiority and the decline of French culture."[30] In other words, enlightenment thinkers feared that femininity was corrupting the arts.

The rococo style, with its excessive ornamentation and unnaturalness, came under attack not only in painting and music, but also in ballet. Some Enlightenment philosophers feared that the rococo aesthetic had reduced ballet further into a purely "decorative" art form, one that they argued lacked the capacity to signify ideas. There was a fear that ballet would degenerate into acrobatics. This is not surprising as this was a time when the body was increasingly associated with aristocratic corruption, frivolity, femininity, sexuality, and decadence, and the mind with ennobled ideas and masculinity. In other words, the intellectual/expressive took precedence over the corporeal. Enlightenment discussions of ballet reveal the relationship between masculinity and artistic status. As ballet became more decorative and reduced to bodily movement and corporeal beauty (thus feminized), it was seen as being in artistic decline. Because dance is an art form that relies upon bodily movement, dance theorists and choreographers had to navigate carefully between its corporeal and dramatic functions in order to meet the demands of the philosophes' tastes. The question now became how to make ballet more expressive and to maintain its masculinity (and thus legitimacy as an art) and status.

The Enlightenment's rhetoric of dance thus contributed to a new concept of dancing that emerged in the middle of the eighteenth century and that drew upon the inherent expressiveness of movement and classicism. Both dancers and choreographers sought to make ballet something more than technical display or mere political propaganda (as in court ballet). They envisioned a type of dance that could stand on its own and serve a similar narrative role as that of poetry or song. As a result, the *ballet d'action* style evolved: an opera in which dance replaced the sung or spoken word through its own rules of pantomime. Narrative was presented through movement (dramatic expression through movement) rather than traditionally through poetry or vocal music.

This new conception of dance as narrative or expressive was elaborated and refined by dancer-choreographer Jean-Georges Noverre in his *Lettres sur la danse et sur les ballets* (1760). In *Lettres*, Noverre presented ballet as an art that was designed to "copy nature faithfully and to delineate the emotions upon the stage."[31] Noverre insisted that ballet should represent action, character, and feeling. Influenced by earlier innovators of the *ballet-d'action*, Noverre emphasized ballet's potential for expressive and dramatic movement: "In the dancer, everything must depict, everything must speak, each gesture, each attitude, each port de bras must have a different expression."[32] Noverre complained that dancers cared too much about showing their technical skills and too little about the true purpose of ballet. This purpose, he argued, was to represent characters and express their feelings. "To be successful in theatrical representations," he once wrote, "the heart must be touched, the soul moved, and the imagination inflamed."[33] One way to achieve this was to urge ballet dancers to stop using masks, bulky costumes, and large wigs to illustrate or explain plot and character. He claimed that dancers could express such things using only their bodies and faces (that is, corporeal expression). In other words, he argued for a form of dramatic ballet that could portray a narrative entirely through movement.[34] "Let us destroy the masks and gain a soul, and we shall be the best dancers in the world," he declared.[35] By the last decades of the century, ballet was transformed from a merely decorative component of an opera into an art form that had established itself as a legitimate vehicle for dramatic expression. At this time, choreographers explored the variety of stories that could be portrayed through movement: mythological tales, classical tragedies, historical drama, love stories, and comedy.[36]

As we saw in chapter 3, ballet as an expressive art was used during the French Revolution for political purposes. Under the French Empire, ballet continued to develop technically and increasingly grew more independent from opera. No longer a mere accessory, ballet began to enjoy an independent existence by the early years of the nineteenth century. Ballet's development was then shaped by both Romantic sensibilities and the rise of the bourgeoisie. Ballet was reconceptualized within the themes of Romanticism: beauty, passion, nature, the supernatural, exoticism, and the power of love. The *ballet d'action* had ushered in the potential for ballet to stand on its own dramatically and, therefore, lent itself well to Romantic themes by making the story-ballet feasible. At first, narrative expression and dramatic action still played a more important role than technical display or footwork, particularly in the eyes of amateur critics. In 1807, critic Julien-Louis Geoffroy argued that "pantomime [was] the most beautiful and the most interesting part of dance because it uses only the noblest parts of the body. The legs and feet, which are so important in ordinary dance, are scarcely noticed in pantomime dance: here, it is the head, the face, and the arms that play the principal role."[37] However, Romantic visions and tastes encouraged the invention of a new type of ballet shoe, the pointe shoe, which enabled female dancers to appear lighter, more ethereal (less human), and more graceful.[38] This inspired a new type of dance movement revolving around pointe work and the female dancer, and, in turn, a newly designed costume, the tutu (falling at mid-calf).[39]

During the Romantic period, ballet movements lost the political meanings they had once embodied (such as those used by Catherine de' Medici to present diplomatic amicability) as they catered to narrative and decorative tastes. Increasingly, special technical innovations such as gas lighting, pointe shoes, new costumes with fitted bodices and buoyant skirts, and new music were all used to evoke an atmosphere of the ethereal, sensual, and exotic. The sylph in *La sylphide*, the willis in *Giselle*, the fairies in *The Sleeping Beauty*, and the Swan Queen in *Swan Lake* all embraced the theme of a tragic encounter between a mortal man and a supernatural female. Elements of the gothic appeared in set designs depicting castles, enchanted forests, haunted gravesites, and exotic settings. Furthermore, now it was the common man and/or woman who was glorified in ballet.

In turn, ballets became valued for their visual appropriation of bodies in space, their effective use of pantomime and new technical footwork, and their female dancers' display of elegance and beauty. In other words, the actual dancing became recognized as an important, if not central, component of ballet. This began the age in which the ballerina (usually foreign born) reigned upon the stage and dance became the domain of femininity. However, this did not necessarily entail an embrace of a "formalist" appreciation for ballet dancing. While the invention of the pointe shoe encouraged a new focus on and experimentation with choreography for women, the increasing privatization of the Opéra exploited the sexual commodification of its dancers and, therefore, catered to the tastes of an increasingly male audience (many of whom were subscribers). It is thus not surprising to find that choreography for men remained undeveloped and minimal.

However, a number of important discourses on ballet surfaced in the nineteenth century that aimed to further explore ballet's formal qualities and to establish technical rules. Where Noverre's books explained what ballet should be, those of Carlo Blasis (1797–1878) provided instruction on how to execute it.[40] Charles-Louis Didelot (1767–1837) and Jules Perrot (1810–92) were two prominent choreographers at the Opéra who greatly contributed to developments in ballet in terms of choreography and staging.[41] "Classical ballet" as we know it today, however, owes its conception to the choreography and theory of Marius Petipa (1818–1910). Petipa's choreography is notable for its high degree of inventiveness and variety; he made the emphasis upon form into a positive attribute, capable of capturing and holding an audience's interest. He valued technical virtuosity, stage arrangements of bodies, and the formal qualities of dance. His productions of works such as *Swan Lake* or *Sleeping Beauty* (both created by Petipa while in Russia) stressed formal values such as clarity, harmony, symmetry, and order. For example, a sense of order may be seen in the "pas de deux" formula in most of Petipa's works where the opening adagios are followed by individual solos for each lead dancer, whereupon the two dancers join again in a coda that is usually a display of technical abilities. In his choreography, academic ballet technique was paramount and its rules were rarely transgressed. Classical dancing was contrasted to character dances by the use of folk dance as a source of inspiration for steps and movements. This style of ballet followed Petipa when he left France in 1847 and moved to Russia, where it was preserved and developed further.[42] As we will see, dance critic André Levinson urged the French in the interwar period to re-embrace Petipa's classical ballet and to render it in a French modern style.

In France, critics responded to both the "romanticization" and "commercialization" of ballet in various ways. Some, like critic Théophile Gautier, writing on the Romantic ballet in Paris as early as 1830 and as late as 1870, recognized the potential for ballet to express poetic themes. He wrote in 1848: "Nothing resembles a dream more than a ballet ... One enjoys, while awake, the phenomenon that nocturnal fantasy traces on the canvas of sleep: an entire world of chimeras moves before you."[43] Gautier once described the famous Italian ballerina Marie Taglioni as a great poet and genius, and compared her talents to those of Lord Byron and Lamartine.[44] At the same time, he addressed the importance of beauty in ballet. According to Gautier, dance was "nothing more than the art of displaying beautiful shapes in graceful positions and to develop from them lines agreeable to the eye."[45]

However, as corporeal movement, particularly of female bodies, became the primary focus of ballet, the status of ballet as a high art declined. This was likely a result of the degraded status of the body in nineteenth-century French culture. The Christian notion of "sinful flesh" was reappropriated into the "rational" discourse of science by the French bourgeoisie.[46] French "rationalism" and science ushered in a prioritization of the mind over the body, measuring intellect as a mark of civilized society. In the proeess, the male body was less admired and lost its status as an unproblematic symbol of society. A consideration of the representation of the nude body in this period is helpful in understanding why ballet lost its status in this period when it rested more on its formal qualities. As Margaret Walters points out, the heroic and classical male body (male nude) faded out as a subject for painting and sculpture during the first half of the nineteenth century, and the female body (female nude) came "into her own ... when art [was] geared to the tastes and erotic fantasies of private consumers."[47] Thus corporeality and physical beauty became predominantly feminized. We find a similar phenomenon occurring on the ballet stage as the male dancing body was increasingly deemed problematic by critics. With Romanticism, the increasing numbers of women in ballet, the invention of the pointe shoe, and the privatization of the Opéra, the dancing body in ballet became associated with femininity, sensuality, and decadence. As audiences became almost entirely male, ballet became a feminine sphere in which no ideal man could exist.

It is, therefore, not surprising that critics Gautier and Jules Janin felt that male dancers did not fit within the dynamic and functions of ballet and that they disrupted its beauty and erotic potential. Gautier deemed certain movements inappropriate and emasculating for men. Janin argued further that the male dancer was unsuitable for ballet because of his temperament and physicality. He stated in 1832, "Under no circumstance do I recognize a man's right to dance in public" and, in 1840, he described the male dancer as "frightful," "ugly," with a "vacant gaze," "a creature made expressly to bear a rifle, saber, and uniform!"[48] By mid-century, the Romantic ballet had come to represent an otherworldly place, a place where gravity and reality were dissolved and where men of the real world did not belong. By the 1880s, male dancers were few and far between due to their unacceptable presence on the stage, and women had to perform male roles as "travesty dancers." This perpetuated further the eroticism of the female body on the dance stage. Further muddying their status, ballets were performed at both the respectable opera houses as high art and at music halls as popular entertainment.

Towards the end of the nineteenth century, several poets, fascinated by the art of movement, attempted to revive ballet's expressive qualities by envisioning it as an art form rich in interpretive potential. Both Stéphane Mallarmé (1842–1898) and his protégé Paul Valéry (1871–1945) attempted to create a philosophy of dance from a symbolist and literary perspective.[49] Mallarmé perceived dance exclusively as a non-verbal form of expression and communication. Relating dance to poetry, he envisioned dance as a form of writing, an *écriture corporelle* (corporeal writing), while he perceived writing as a form of dance.[50] The dancer (that is, female dancer), he observed, "suggests things which the written word could express only in several paragraphs."[51] Dance, like poetry, was also a signifying system and aesthetically autonomous.

Moreover, Mallarmé believed that dance served as a mediation between mind and body, with the dancer using her body (like a poet used a pen) as a vehicle or instrument to reveal an idea.[52] In this way, the dancer's corporeality became metaphor. According to Mallarmé, dance is not composed of vigorously trained bodies submitted to a codified choreographic discipline. Rather, dance is "a perpetual illusion which suggests but never states," and ballet is "a set of juxtaposed metaphors." In his essay "Ballets," Mallarmé claimed further that "the female dancer is not a woman who dances ... she is not a woman, but a metaphor ... she does not dance."[53] Mallarmé's views on female dancers reflect the dominant gender ideologies of the time that associated women's bodies with nature and male bodies with culture.[54] He once asserted that the female dancer as an artist was closest to nature and therefore able to portray animals better than actors.[55] He believed that women communicated directly through their bodies and operated by "instinct" rather than intellect or reason.[56] "The illiterate ballerina surrend[ers] herself to the effects of her profession," he explained; the dancer is an "unconscious revealer of truths."[57] In short, dance served as a metaphor for the intellect of the (male) observer and nothing more. In fact, the dancer is not even aware of her symbolic potential. The vocation and technical virtuosity of the dancer are ignored and she is denied any artistic autonomy, "intentionality," individuality, or intelligence.[58]

Philosopher-poets created a language of poetry not to serve the dancing itself or dancers, with whom they were not particularly concerned, but to express their own ideas. In other words, dance provided them with a useful metaphor through which they could illustrate philosophical and metaphysical viewpoints. Their examinations of dance are significant, however, in that they directed a different type of attention to dance by offering an intellectual and philosophical vision of it. The symbolist poets may have been attempting to sustain ballet as a high art form by pointing out its intellectual and spiritual qualities.[59] In other words, dance could elevate itself only if the body was perceived as metaphoric rather than corporeal. Symbolist poetry had a strong literary influence on the music, painting, and ballet of the early twentieth century. For example, Stéphane Mallarmé's poem about a daydreaming faun inspired Debussy to write a score and, later, Nijinsky to choreograph the ballet *L'après-midi d'un faune* (1912). Dance performance demonstrated itself as capable of embodying the same loftiness of feeling as poetry and painting.

From this portrait of ballet's development and the values that were attached to it, we can understand why technical virtuosity and corporeal beauty fell victim to the eroticization of dancers at the end of the nineteenth century. Criticism that catered to the tastes of its male audiences further fetishized female dancers' bodies on stage. Any formalist reading of dance was linked to eroticism due to its focus on the female body. Despite the frequent discussion of ballet in poetic discourse and the new articulation of its metaphoric potential, the status of ballet was steadily declining in France by the last decades of the century. As we will see, the Ballets Russes' success in France was due, in part, to the fact that it drew attention away from the dancing body by its greater reliance on music, decor, costume design, pantomime, and staging. Its "new ballet" was primarily a collaborative artistic enterprise in which the formal aspects of ballet lost their autonomy. This appealed to critics and particularly composers who were frustrated by the subordinate role of music in ballet. In fact, one music critic once remarked bluntly: "By means of an absurd illogic, have we not too often until now subordinated the thoughts of the composer to the stringent demands of the dancer? Humble servant of the most ludicrous choreographic conventions, had our dance music not fallen to a level a little too humiliating?" He concluded: "We would have bad manners to reproach them [the Ballets Russes] too bitterly for having broken a few of the bars of the prison in which we languish."[60] Thus the autonomy of choreography was sacrificed for ballet's rise in status.

THE BALLETS RUSSES' "TOTAL BALLET"

Writing as early as 1912, critic Valerian Svetlov declared that "the early Ballets Russes was not just a box office success, but a major event in the artistic life of Paris."[61] Indeed, Diaghilev's ballet had an extraordinary impact on music, design, theatre production, and high fashion. The period between 1909 and 1929 was a time of major innovation in the art of ballet and theatrical design mostly due to Diaghilev's non-traditional approach to ballet.[62] As a former art critic and the founder of a progressive Russian art magazine (*Mir Iskusstva*), Diaghilev's approach was based largely on a vision of modern exhibition. In this respect, he used ballet as a vehicle to showcase the latest artistic trends, whether in painting, music, or choreography. In doing so, traditional classical ballet was transformed into a dynamic modern art form. Diaghilev's Russian choreographer, Michel Fokine, rebelled from the classical tradition of French choreographer Marius Petipa and attempted to create a new form of ballet – a modern and dramatically expressive one. This modern style rested on the conception of ballet as a collaborative art form in which music, design, and drama would play a larger role.

Diaghilev's new conception of ballet came at a time of vibrant dialogues between the arts of music, painting, sculpture, ballet, theatre, and literature, and investigations into their influence upon one another. By the turn of the century, impressionism had profoundly shaped not only art, but also music and poetry. As Eugen Weber points out, "Redon called himself a symphonist painter; Gauguin spoke of harmonies of line and color which he called the music of painting; Cézanne painted an *Overture to Tannhäuser*; and Whistler … accept[ing] the suggestion that "Symphony in White" would be a better name for [*Young Women in White*] … henceforth composed symphonies, nocturnes, and variations, all possessing the evocative quality of the music he so much admired."[63] The Ballet Russes became the epitome of such artistic interchange and served as a platform upon which such relationships could flourish. Diaghilev gathered together some of the twentieth century's most cutting-edge international designers, choreographers, and composers, many of whom shared his ambitions to attach a modern aesthetic to ballet.[64] Many of these collaborators perceived ballet as a liberating new medium – one that could comprise many works of art of equal standing. Set design would no longer act as a mere appendage to ballet production, ballet music would be replaced by symphonic music, costume would be decorative ("illusionist"), and narrative and dramatic expression would direct the choreography.

The Ballets Russes would have a profound and lasting impact on dance, theatre, fashion, and the visual arts. In fact, the company's engagement with modernism through collaborative artistic expression became an extraordinary cultural force in France and beyond. It exposed audiences to the ideas behind artistic movements such as cubism, constructivism, and surrealism. As the Ballets Russes played a key role in transmitting the cultural preoccupations of the avant-garde to a broader public, it also strongly influenced those modern art movements.[65] Guillaume Apollinaire first coined the term "sur-realism" in a program note he had written for the Ballets Russes' production of *Parade* in 1917. He wrote that he could locate "a sort of sur-realism in which I see the point of departure for a series of manifestations of that New Spirit which promises to modify the arts and the conduct of life [*moeurs*] from top to bottom in a universal joyousness."[66] Works such as *Parade, Sacre du printemps,* and *L'après-midi d'un faune* were clear statements of modernism through their musical scores, decor, costumes and choreography. In fact, they were often referred to as "anti-ballets," which suggests that there existed an irreconcilability between modernism and ballet at the time. Diaghilev also presented ballets with contemporary settings – something novel and previously unexplored (e.g., *Jeux,* 1913; *Les biches,* 1924; *Le train bleu,* 1924). Ultimately, Diaghilev presented a modern potential for ballet, which, fortunately, appealed to French tastes. Furthermore, the Ballets Russes' successful presence in France drew other foreign dance companies, such as Rolf de Mare's Ballet Suédois, to base themselves in Paris and to become similarly a total manifestation of avant-garde art.[67]

The Ballets Russes' fresh engagement with modernism led to a modern style of choreography that was subordinated first to contemporary trends in music, and later to those of painting and decor (theatrical design). Such choreography (particularly that of Michel Fokine) came out of a reaction against the classical tradition. Critic Valerian Svetlov, reviewing the production of *Cléopâtre,* wrote that it was "an overturning of all the old standards, a negation of classical technique, of traditional canons." "Cléopâtre," he continued, "is a 'new factor,' a vitally interesting excursus into the realms of archaeological iconography and ethnographical dancing."[68] Interestingly, Svetlov described Fokine's style as having "twin poles of choreography" – meaning that his work both accepted and rejected the "classical" tradition of ballet.[69] On the whole, Fokine aimed at a new freedom of movement, similar to that of Isadora Duncan.[70] The Ballets Russes' specific deviations from the traditions of classic ballet included an abandonment of the strict "turned-out" classical technique; a new emphasis on group action from that of the solo "star" against a corps de ballet "backdrop"; a new focus on the male dancer or "ballerino" rather than the "ballerina"; radical changes in ballet costume such as the use of sarafan pants and tunics rather than traditional tutus and tulle skirts; and an emphasis on dramatic expression and gesture (pantomime) rather than choreographic autonomy. Such radical changes in ballet performance also broke boundaries of gender in ballet (to be explored further in chapter 6). In other words, all that was inherited from the French tradition (save the French classical training of the Russian dancers) appeared to be dismantled.

An equally significant change in ballet production implemented by the Ballets Russes was the introduction of symphonic music in ballet. The use of symphonic (and avant-garde) music, another innovation of Diaghilev, most certainly influenced the increase in ballet's artistic value in the eyes of the French. This new body of music brought with it serious consideration and value. Symphonic music held an esteemed position in France and the breakthroughs of French composers such as Berlioz, Lalo, Debussy, Ravel, Auric, Poulenc, and Satie took their place within nationalist ideology and musical discourse. The fact that these composers decided to collaborate with the ballet (that is, the Ballets Russes) most certainly indicated to Parisians that the art of ballet held some artistic prestige. Rather than ballet dictating its accompanying music, ballet scores became less dependent on choreography and delivered dramatic expression of their own – some could even stand on their own (for example, Stravinsky's *Firebird*, 1910). This is what appealed the most to modern composers.[71] Stravinsky's *The Rite of Spring* (1913), for example, demanded that dancers execute a primitive style of dance, dispense with pointe shoes and classical technique, and adapt their movements to unprecedented rhythms. It was also a symphonic piece of music that could stand on its own. In other words, such scores did not even require the dancers to evoke an emotional response. Eventually, music critics as well as choreographers became preoccupied with locating the value of music in ballet.

The work of Léonide Massine, who replaced Michel Fokine as chief choreographer at the Ballets Russes in 1914, offers a good example of the new role music played in ballet production. The incorporation of symphonic music was at the centre of Massine's choreographic vision. Like Fokine, he adhered to an overall correspondence between decor, costume, music, pantomime, and choreography, but he highlighted further the musical component in his ballets. In fact, he engulfed himself in the task of creating a "correct ballet interpretation of a symphonic work."[72] Rather than using pantomime as the central means of expression, his aim was to delineate a correlation between "balletic" form and "musical form" in order to express the inner essence of a symphony. However, as he recollected, he was aware that his work "ought not to be simply an abstract interpretation of visual form." In other words, Massine did not want his ballets to emphasize the autonomy of corporeal form – the ability of corporeal movement to embody its own meanings (line, form, harmony, balance). Instead, he used corporeal movement as a tool through which to expresses musical qualities.[73] Here we can see how the artistry of classical ballet became subservient to other arts (in this case the music) and choreography lost its ability to stand on its own.

In his two ballets, *Les présages* (1933) and *Choreartium* (1933), Massine realized his vision. Based on Tchaikovsky's Fifth Symphony, *Les présages* (The Portents) was extremely bold in uniting the symphonic music of Tchaikovsky (a highly respectable work) with ballet. The work can also be seen as an early path towards abstraction in ballet (i.e., towards a choreography that has no reference to plot, theme, or era). *Choreartium*, set to Brahms's Fourth Symphony, further exemplified Massine's experimentation and exploitation of the relationship between ballet and symphonic music (the former subservient to the latter). In the work, he desired to achieve a more abstract choreographic interpretation. As one reviewer from the *Sunday Times* commented, "In a truly extraordinary way, Massine has given us a transvaluation into choreographic values of a hundred musical features of the symphony; the ballet works itself out consistently ... as a design reproducing in the subtlest way the design of music ... the more musical we are, and the better we know Brahms, the more pleasure we derive from *Choreartium*." He went on to explain: "Strictly speaking, no one art is translatable into another, not even poetry into music. The most we can get are convincing parallelisms between the two; and the fact that some parallelisms are much more difficult than others, and have consequently not been attempted hitherto, is no reason for denying a choreographic genius like Massine the right to attempt them."[74] Massine is described as a "choreographic genius" who managed to successfully employ "the many things in music that can be paralleled in choreography."[75] It is evident from this review that although critics were beginning to value choreographic innovations, musical expression in ballet took precedence over choreographic expression. This is not surprising as many critics reviewing the Ballets

Russes productions were music critics who would have been pleased to see music used in such an important way in ballet. This review is a good example of why music critics were particularly fascinated by the Ballets Russes.

Not only did the Ballets Russes inspire a public interest in modern ballet production, but it also encouraged legitimate criticism of ballet production by its ability to fuse modern innovations of a variety of arts. Indeed, the Ballets Russes encouraged dialogue on the art of dance by offering those outside the field the ability to discuss ballet production in terms of its revolutionary music, costume, and decor. In fact, one observer writing in *Vogue* in 1926 remarked that "to make an intelligent criticism of the ballet you need to have some knowledge not only of dancing, but of contemporary developments in other arts, music, painting and even literature."[76] Diaghilev's vision of ballet as a collaborative art form enabled critics to discuss the ballet in a more extensive fashion. Having little technical knowledge of choreography or dance aesthetics, critics had the opportunity to discuss ballet in the context of their own expertise: whether contemporary music, literature/drama, or painting/set design. In other words, Diaghilev's Ballet Russes offered other interesting components beyond choreography – components that were deemed worthy of discussion. As we will see, such changes in critiquing ballet production encouraged more discussion and debate over ballet's position and its value as an art.[77]

The idea of a "fusion of arts," however, was not unique to France. In the early years of the twentieth century, Richard Wagner's theories of the *Gesamtkunstwerk* – a fusion of all the arts resulting in a "total art" – initiated a search for a unity of arts across Europe. Diaghilev's *Mir iskusstva* (World of Art) group in St Petersburg had developed this concept further in its manifesto *Complicated Questions* (1898–99), another good example of the internationalization of aesthetics.[78] Eventually, Diaghilev realized his own vision of a "fusion of arts" through the ballet production. In doing so, Diaghilev transformed ballet dancing into a "total" theatrical form, comprising music, design, and dramatic expression. In theory, decor, music, costume, and choreography were to be assembled in a harmonic unity. Diaghilev and Fokine's "synthesism" aimed at total emotional expression through every component of ballet production. Fokine, for example, insisted that the music express the emotional content of the work, the "pantomime" accurately describe the period in which the ballet took place, and the costuming adhere to the plot. He saw the dancer as a dramatic artist, writing that "the whole body should dance, not just the feet."[79] Ultimately, Fokine offered a new vision of choreographic drama, but at the expense of ballet's choreographic autonomy. As we will see, critics praised the Ballets Russes for its dramatic and poetic expressions, its decor and costume designs, and most frequently, its music, but hardly ever for its choreography.[80]

CRITICAL RESPONSES TO THE RUSSIAN "NEW BALLET"

> Nothing like it had ever been seen. Suddenly, unexpectedly, a new, marvelous and totally unknown world was revealed: a world, whose existence not one of these Parisian spectators had even suspected and which so intoxicated, so overwhelmed them that for a time all else was blotted out completely. A sort of psychosis, a mass delirium, seemed to sweep over the spectators which the Press re-echoed the following and many a succeeding day.[81]
>
> – Serge Lifar

Critics responded to the conception of ballet as a "fusion of arts" in different ways. Some critics applauded the Ballets Russes' modern form of ballet and its "fusion" of choreography, set design, music, and dramatic expression. Guillaume Apollinaire, in his program notes to *Parade* (1917), described its collaborators (Picasso, Satie, Massine, Cocteau) as having realized notions of modernity for the first time in a new and complete form of art.[82] Music critic Pierre Lalo, writing in *Le Temps,* admired the way music, decor, and dance harmonized together in *Les sylphides, Spectre de la rose, Prince Igor,* and *Schéhérazade.* Lalo described *Prince Igor* as "the most comprehensive performance and the best we have yet been shown in the Russian seasons … [in that] the music, decor, and dancing are in the most full and most profound harmony."[83] In his review of *Sacre du printemps* in August 1913, Henri Ghéon addressed the inseparability and harmony between the choreography and the music in the ballet: "I very much admire the *Rite of Spring* not only for its new and direct music, but also the choreography, which is inseparable from it."[84] Ghéon also commended the Ballets Russes' union of pure dance with mime and argued that it offered a chance to elevate the art of ballet: "The ballet also becomes drama. As soon as it is no longer a simple divertissement, it imperiously calls to the aid of pure dance, the sublime art of mime which had never been separated … How the new career that has opened itself to the ballet has gained more breadth, more possible variety, and more heights!"[85] Yet another critic, Robert Brussel, remarked that in its productions, "all the arts contribute: the painter, the musician, the choreographer, each of them is also suggestive of a single poetry."[86]

Ballet as a "fusion of arts" enabled critics to discuss the Ballets Russes in several ways. In offering a range of artistic components to critique, a variety of specialists could engage in ballet commentary. Some critics pointed out the poetic aspects of the Ballets Russes' collaborative approach and its emphasis on subject matter. Critic Robert Brussel noted the Ballets Russes' novelty in incorporating modern poetics within its ballets. In his review of the Ballets Russes' *Firebird,* he wrote, "the poem is the matter of a lyrical drama, very rich and complex, [and] a very rare development in a ballet."[87] Critic Henri Ghéon declared Michel Fokine a true poet. He asserted that "a master choreographer of this value is a type of poet; he only knows how to speak in his time."[88] Similarly, literary critic Jacques Rivière referred to the ballet composer as poet, remarking that in *Sacre du printemps,* like *Petrushka,* Stravinsky took on multiple roles. "Stravinsky," he wrote, "is certainly collaborating not only as a musician but also as a poet. He participated in the invention of the subject matter … We must not overlook the importance of Roerich," he continued, "long concerned with a prehistoric kind of mysticism and the way that it is found in more than one design of the choreography."[89] Music critic Boris Schloezer described Diaghilev's aesthetic approach as taking "the most diverse aspects." "There is an aesthetic of tragedy like that of Flaubert, for example," he wrote. "The doctrine of the Ballets Russes, and that of Diaghilev … views art solely as a source of pleasure."[90] Music critic Victor Debay was so captivated by the emotional expression and dedication of the Ballets Russes dancers that he once declared, "They work together in action, they love their job, express their art, and devote themselves their whole body and all their heart."[91] Likewise, art critic and poet Jean-Louis Vaudoyer wrote that it was "the love and the sincerity" of the company that "render[ed] [it] so convincing.[92] As we can see in such commentary, both the dancing and dancers' technical skills were neglected by critics.

Abel Bonnard's observations also drew value away from the formal aspects of ballet dancing (that is, technical virtuosity). In a review of the Ballets Russes, he expressed his enthusiasm for its dancers' "miming" as well as his dissatisfaction with the formal aspects of dancing, or in his words "drear gymnastics" that he saw embraced by the Paris Opéra dancers.

> How great must be one's joy at recapturing through this dancing, all the bewildering modalities of the human body and its richness of gesture, for no longer do we find ourselves merely gazing at those drear gymnastics, so characteristic of our ballerinas. Here, once more, in the vivacity of this miming, we see feeling expressed, not merely upon the narrow stage of the features, but as a living force from the crown of the head to the toes, and so molding the material it inspires that, for an instant, the whole body is joy or sadness to the very tips of the fingers; a clear hieroglyph of rage, hatred or desire.[93]

Here the dancer's body is seen primarily as a vehicle for dramatic expression rather than athleticism and technical virtuosity. Louis Laloy also pointed out the opposition between the naturalness of the Ballets Russes dancers (who were "less bound to the "torture of *pointes*") and the "mechanical," "artificial," "stiff," and "false" expressions of the Paris Opéra dancers.[94] Referring to Russian dancers, Lalo wrote that "their better cultivated spirit allow[ed] them to enter into a role just like dramatic performers."[95] Laloy, like Bonnard, attempted to locate clear differences between the Russian and French dancing body, regardless of the fact that the Ballets Russes dancers were technically trained in St Petersburg under the French style of Marius Petipa. Here we can see dominant attitudes towards dance's formal qualities. Clearly, dramatic expression was deemed by many critics (here amateur ones) more a sign of a talented dancer than technical virtuosity. Was dancing still perceived as the most primitive tool of expression and gesture viewed as a noble attribute (that is, mind over matter)? Did Bonnard imply that the French dancers at the Opéra were inferior because their training was grounded in French classical technique? Or did French critics simply avoid the examination of the dance itself because of their lack of understanding of choreography?[96]

Jean Cocteau was another key figure in the transitional period when ballet became "modern." Cocteau was fascinated with the new modern form of ballet presented by Diaghilev's Ballets Russes and played a decisive part in its development through his collaborations with the company (as well as with other ballet companies).[97] Through his work with the ballet, Cocteau contributed to the breaking up of classical aesthetics to extend the possibilities of modern ballet. He thus supported the idea of ballet as a "fusion of arts," writing that "the music, choreography, scenery, costumes, lighting form the paper on which the dancers write the signs as noble as Chinese calligraphy." Regarding the vital function of design in ballet, he asserted that "the costumes of a ballet should be inseparable from the dancers like the spots of a fawn or bird feathers."[98] Envisioning ballet as a collaborative art form, Cocteau showed little interest in locating any potential expressive autonomy in choreography. In fact, he argued, "it should never be forgotten that Diaghileff's approach to ballet was through music – the weakness of present-day ballet is largely due to approaches through choreography and decor – or, both, accompanied by a devastating ignorance of the key art of music."[99] According to Cocteau, music played the most important role in ballet and strengthened the credibility of the art form.

The Ballets Russes' introduction of the use of symphonic music in ballet production prompted a new body of critics to become seriously engaged in reviewing ballet. This musical innovation indicated to the French a new and growing investment of modern music in ballet. Not surprisingly, we find an increasing amount of ballet criticism in the music columns of major bourgeois newspapers and journals between 1909 and 1938. Robert Brussel's review of the Ballets Russes' *Firebird* in *Le Figaro* offers a good example of how music critics reviewed ballet before dance expert André Levinson arrived in Paris. Brussel's review focused almost exclusively on Stravinsky's score and the way in which the music complemented the dramatic expression of the ballet. "The music of Mr Stravinsky addresses this beautiful story in an absolutely new way," he began. Brussel believed that Stravinsky's score was innovative and went on to describe it as "choreographic": "This young composer, student of Rimsky [Korsakov], and gifted in an incredible way, has written a score which, not in an instant, ceases to provide this feeling of the work, and which, in being free of all traditional constraints, is nevertheless choreographic to the highest degree. But choreographic in an unforeseen and unsuspected way; the score permits developments, processions, gesture, and a renewed form of '*pas d'action*.'" Here Brussel asserts that Stravinsky's score is "choreographic to the highest degree." However, Brussel's use of the term "choreographic" is somewhat misleading. "Choreographic" here referred to the score's compatibility with gesture and pantomimic expression rather that its correspondence or adaptability to the actual dance steps. In the words of Brussel, it "permits developments, processions, gesture, and a renewed form of '*pas d'action*.'" The *pas d'action* was a scene in a ballet that captured the story or drama by means of mime and pantomime. He made an analogy between the role of symphonic music in ballet and the lyrical arts (for example, opera): the score "is to ballet what the symphony of the orchestra should be to lyrical drama; it ignores following the conventional way of cut pieces, the adagios, the *scherzi* of virtuosity; it evokes, it suggests, it supports mimetic drama, it is only picturesque in part, it elevates itself in places of emotion, it possesses expressive virtues very rare up until in ballet: it's a work that supports the interest by itself."[100] Brussel implies that Stravinsky's music can stand on its own and that it does not merely complement the ballet's expressive elements but directs it. Brussel's review is insightful in several ways; it reveals, first, critics' primary concern with music and the role it plays in collaborative works in the performing arts; second, music critics were, consciously or not, contributing to the revival of ballet by praising its new musical components; and finally, the way in which critics virtually ignored any aesthetic critique of the actual dance steps and did not recognize the choreographic strengths of ballet.

Others expressed their reservations about the collaborations occurring within this new modern ballet. For example, Jean Cocteau expressed his wariness of applying symphonic music to ballet production. His reasons for this rested on his views of the bourgeois institution of theatre itself. Perceiving the theatre as corrupt due to the frivolity and idleness of its haute-bourgeois audience, Cocteau feared that the theatre would corrupt even "a Stravinsky." Regarding Wagner as having been corrupted by the theatre, Cocteau believed that Stravinsky found "himself involved in it by circumstances … even though he composes in spite of the theatre, the theatre has none the less infected him with its microbes … This [ballet] music comes from the bowels; an octopus from which you must flee or else it will devour you. It is the fault of the theatre … the café-concert is often pure; the theatre is always corrupt."[101] This statement by Cocteau is somewhat hypocritical in relation to his later observations of the Ballets Russes in which he praised ballet as a wordless art with vast possibilities for dramatic expression similar to that of silent film. Nevertheless, his remarks on the new relationship between music and ballet reveal that ballet's position and constitution as a theatrical art form remained precarious. Is it ballet that is corrupting Stravinsky's music or its status as a high art form for the haute-bourgeoisie? Cocteau's observations are ambivalent.

The positive accounts of the Ballets Russes' "fusion of arts" aesthetic were not shared by one of the important critics of dance of the day – André Levinson. Levinson presented an altogether different picture of the Ballets Russes at the time. He stood alone in his opinion, representing an interesting source of information in his positions as both critic and ballet historian. In his collection of essays *Ballet Old and New* (1918) Levinson described the Ballets Russes' presentation of ballet as a spectacle and entertainment rather than a genuine art form. He argued that the "Russian ballet … lacked not only a theoretical foundation, but any ideology at all."[102] His writings reflect his dissatisfaction with ballet being transformed into a collaborative art form in which music and decor seemed to dominate. In *Schéhérazade,* for example, Levinson recalled seeing neither dramatic movement nor dance, writing that there was "'in the ballet sense of the word,' as our critics would put it … no dancing at all."[103] Levinson forcefully criticized the "fusion of arts" concept of the Ballets Russes. "The new ballet," he asserted, "pretentious but poor in content, naturally seeks support in the other arts. Having improved its form and tradition, having shifted its center of gravity from dance to pantomime, the new ballet has tried to borrow its missing significance from painting and music." As a result, he explained, the Ballets Russes' productions "were a dazzling and noisy victory for Russian stage design" and their music was "no longer compatible to choreography."[104] In other words, the music directed the choreography rather than the choreography informing the music. Levinson pointed out the consequences of turning to avant-garde art and symphonic music to give a "value and substance" to ballet and suggested that, in doing so, it eliminated the choreographic autonomy of the production. This is a rare example of a critic evaluating the bodily movements of ballet (that is, classical ballet technique) rather than the decor, music, or costuming. In fact, he admitted that just a year before "when my article was published, the battle against the dominance of the picturesque over the dynamic essence of choreography was still a dangerous heresy for an author's reputation."[105] Levinson's observations reveal the boldness involved in putting forth an argument for the autonomy of choreography in 1918.

Furthermore, Levinson pronounced the Ballets Russes to be the "new ballet" which had lost a "unity of dramatic action and classical dance" and which he found pursued "literal realism through eroticism" rather than the idealism of "classic" ballet. In his review of *Schéhérazade*, for example, he accused Fokine of the "pseudo-dramatization of ballet" and criticized the choreographer's eroticism as too explicit. "[Fokine] strives deliberately toward some type of realism," he observed. "The gestures and mime of erotic experience are presented so concretely that there is almost no room for the audience's sexual imagination, and the artistic value of the conception is destroyed."[106] According to Levinson, the ballet's explicit eroticism took away from the more subtle sensuality of the "Orientalist" subject matter. In Diaghilev's "new ballet," he locates a loss of symbolic gesture and stylized movement, both, in his opinion, fundamental to the art of dance. Levinson then elaborated on the metaphysical nature of classical dance and criticized the Ballets Russes for its "frivolous" application of it:

> "The movements from which Pavlova's art is composed are as beautiful as style in a sculpture, as rhythm in a building. They are revelations of hidden beauty. They are something symbolic – a logical testimony to the perfection of the universe." I cite these words with emotion, so well do they correspond to that apperception of the metaphysical nature of classical dance, the visible herald from the world of ideas, which has stirred and exalted me for many long years. How could we exchange these secret voices, which sound distinctly in ballet's mute symbolism, for the aesthetic diversions of the new ballet masters, for the playthings of precocious snobbism and restless frivolity?[107]

Levinson went on to note that "the self-imposed limits of dance schemes, the significance of body discipline, [and] elevating spontaneity to the level of expressivity" were the essence of classic ballet. He closed this essay suggesting that "perhaps faith in a foreigner's opinion will help the ever 'advanced' and susceptible to lure our audience into valuing not the Russian ballet's tinseled decor and exotic trappings, but the golden essence of the art."[108] This "golden essence" to which Levinson refers is essentially the French classical ballet aesthetic of Marius Petipa.

Levinson's criticism of the Ballets Russes is an example of the early arguments for a dance-for-dance's-sake concept of ballet. In his ballet commentary, Levinson's arguments for ballet's autonomy were along the same lines as those of modern art and music. In fact, by embracing an interdependence of arts, the "new ballet" of the Ballets Russes deviated from the path that other arts were taking in the early twentieth century towards "pure art." In the late nineteenth century, new visions of aesthetics emerged that replaced a utilitarian and moral view of art with a philosophy that valued art as an end in itself. An art-for-art's-sake ideology had taken hold that boldly asserted the value of formalism. This shift stimulated much debate over contemporary aesthetics.

In France, the phrase "l'art pour l'art" first appeared in print in 1833. The concept was introduced earlier in the writings of Madame de Stael (*De l'Allemagne,* 1813) and in Victor Cousin's philosophical lectures at the Sorbonne (*Du vrai, du beau, du bien,* 1816–18). Poet and dramatic critic Théophile Gautier became a prominent advocate of art for art's sake, capturing the concept in his preface to *Mademoiselle de Maupin* (1835): "Nothing that is beautiful is indispensible to life ... Nothing is truly beautiful unless it is useless; everything useful is ugly, because it expresses a need, and the needs of mankind are ignoble and disgusting ... the most useful place of a house is the latrine."[109] In other words, art is separate from and owes nothing to society. It is a distinct world that should not be judged by the standards of morality and utility. In the two treatises of Albert Cassagne (*La théorie de l'art pour l'art en France,* 1906) and Paul Strapfer (*Questions esthétiques et religieuses; la question de l'art pour l'art; un philosophie religieux du 19. siècle,* 1906) – which advocated for the autonomy of art – Charles Baudelaire, Edmond and Jules Goncourt, and the Parnassian poets were all cited as being part of Gautier's movement. Édouard Manet was also linked to an art-for-art's-sake ideology. In defence of Manet's formalism, Émile Zola wrote in the *Revue du XIXe. siècle* in 1867:

"[Manet] does not know how to sing or to philosophize; he knows how to paint, and that is all."[110] Other classicizing painters of the mid- to late nineteenth century, such as Paul Baudry, William Bouguereau, and Jean-Léon Gerome, exhibited tendencies towards an art-for-art's-sake stance in that they opposed realism and attempted to cultivate a "pure art" style. That the art-for-art's-sake ideology began as a French phenomenon is significant, as we will see in the following chapter, as Parisian critics and dance experts embraced this concept in developing a distinctly French national style.

The famous case of *Ruskin v. Whistler* in England captures the vying interpretations of the function of aesthetics in Europe at this time. The writings of Gautier and Baudelaire had a profound influence on the American painter James Abbott Whistler when he arrived in Paris in 1855 to study at the L'École Impériale et Spéciale de Dessin. Whistler abandoned realism and embraced the French avant-garde theory of *l'art pour l'art.* In 1877, upon visiting the recently opened Grosvenor Gallery in London, John Ruskin (critic, artist, and professor of art) came across some paintings by Whistler. He found them so offensive – in particular the *Nocturne in Black and Gold: The Falling Rocket* (ca. 1874) – that he complained publicly in his journal *Fors Clavigera* (1871–74) that Whistler was a "coxcomb" with the "Cockney impudence" to "ask two hundred guineas for flinging a pot of paint in the public's face."[111] Eager for cash and publicity, Whistler parlayed the insult into a national media event by suing Ruskin for libel.[112] The celebrated trial of November 1878 concluded with the jury finding Ruskin guilty and awarding Whistler contemptuous damages of one farthing without costs. The outcome of this case serves as an indication that understandings of modern aesthetics were changing towards the end of the century.[113]

Essentially, Whistler defended an art-for-art's-sake philosophy, arguing that art should be valued in and for itself. He believed that painting should be valued not for its subject matter or its ability to convey morals and ideas, but for its rendering of line, colour, and composition. He entitled his works "nocturnes," "arrangements," and "harmonies" to indicate an artistic interest alone, divesting the picture of any outside anecdotal interest that might have been otherwise attached to it. As a result, Whistler's nocturnes were often completed in a day or two, appearing more as sketches than as the "finished works" expected by Ruskin. Whistler argued that the monetary value of his canvases depended not on the number of hours that went into their production but the lifetime of experience and skill he brought to the act of painting. Whistler held that only artists could grasp the value of art, and he was convinced that aesthetic judgment was a matter of opinion rather than science. In his view, a critic, necessarily partial and impressionistic, had no business damaging the reputation and livelihood of a dedicated painter. In contrast, Ruskin argued that art contained and conveyed ideas as a type of "visual treatise." He believed that the value of an artwork (aesthetic and monetary) rested in its successful rendering of ideas and its "finished product." This ideological stance involved a deep reliance on the critic and, at some level, an authority and legitimacy of the profession of the critic.

Linda Merrill, in *A Pot of Paint: Aesthetics on Trial in Whistler v. Ruskin* (1992), has explained the way in which the clash between Ruskin and Whistler was symptomatic of the shift from Victorian to modernist art. She argues that the obstacle for Whistler was that the term "abstract" had not yet entered the aesthetic lexicon.[114] Most interesting is Merrill's gender analysis of the vying ideologies of art. She points out how Whistler's works were seen as lacking "masculine" firmness and morality (Ruskin's ideals) and thereby were cast as feminine and frivolous. In other words, works of art that appealed to the mind were considered masculine, while those that appealed to the bodily senses (here visual formal qualities) were deemed feminine. Merrill's study is useful for contextualizing the changing visions of ballet within such aesthetic shifts. Her examination of the transition between Victorian "representationality" and the introduction of abstract modernism helps us to consider better the shifting value of dance from narrative expression to abstract "pure" form. It sheds light on why critics and intellectuals did not recognize the formal aspects of dancing (that is, technical virtuosity) in the early years of the twentieth century. The corporeal aspect of ballet was linked not only to the pleasure of the senses, but also to the body, which was increasingly degraded and feminized over the course of the nineteenth century. However, as we will see in the following chapters, the blossoming of physical culture in the interwar years would open an opportunity to reassess ballet as a corporeal art form.

New, modernist aesthetics continued to flourish in France. Impressionism, post-impressionism, and expressionism all attempted to emphasize the painterly qualities and unique sensory experience of the artist. French symbolist poets argued for a pure poetry, one that was removed from the ugliness, hypocrisy, and rapacity of nineteenth-century industrialized society. In contrast to this materialist, utilitarian, and practical view of the world, symbolist poetry emphasized an ideal world beyond the material, and sought an ideal language to express that world.[115] The ultimate exponent of what was considered *poésie pure* (pure poetry) was Stéphane Mallarmé (1842–1898). For him, the poet's task was to purify language. This purified and difficult language would try to express the inexpressible, the absent, the symbol, and, moreover, to transcend referential meaning. Thus symbolism was concerned with formal elements of language for the purpose of transcending form itself.[116] Levinson's "classic" idealism of ballet would rest, to an extent, on a similar symbolist notion of form. While he did not advocate an abandonment of representation in ballet nor desire a purely abstract ballet, he suggested a type of formalism that could still signify a higher meaning.

We can also see a similar trend in the world of modern music. By the middle of the nineteenth century, the cult of the composer as genius, cultural icon, or artistic prophet had become generally accepted in European musical culture. These years saw the expansion of the symphony orchestra, from the thirty or forty players of the previous age to almost a hundred or more. In fact, it is in this period that audiences, critics, and composers placed symphonic (orchestral) music above all other genres of the time. The new conservatories and schools for the training of instrumental musicians led composers to demand an incredible amount of technical virtuosity from every instrumentalist in the execution of their scores. Composers pursued even more colour and emotion in their music while shedding the constraining discipline of classical forms. As a result, by the end of the century, a heated debate emerged over whether music aesthetics and criticism were best handled by composers and musicians or by professional critics (a similar debate found within the visual arts).

In the early twentieth century, composers pushed for more autonomy in music by insisting that music be liberated from its metaphoric function and valued for its formal qualities. "Why not love [music] for its own sake?" Stravinsky recalled in 1935. "Why not love it as one loves a picture, for the sake of the beautiful painting, the beautiful design, the beautiful composition? Why not admit that music has an intrinsic value … music needs no help."[117] One music critic observed in 1929: "Contemporary music, hostile alike to Wagner and Debussy, drives straight at a disassociation of the arts, at 'pure music' … at a music that seeks salvation in itself alone." He described this trend in various arts: "Pure poetry, pure painting, pure music – so many cells wherein each art, isolated, pursues its conquest of the Absolute. In each cell the art-work represents an end in itself. Poetry eliminates discourse. Painting eliminates the subject. Music eliminates expression."[118] While André Coeuroy expressed his disapproval by trying to point out that "pure music" was merely a phase and temporary rebellion, his statement reveals the growing trend towards a pure-art ideology. Thus aesthetic autonomy found its place within the world of music just as it had in painting when a music-for-music's-sake ideology took hold. As we will see in chapter 5, similar assertions of "pure art" were made in the context of dance.

THE UNIVERSALITY OF BALLET

In addition to the Ballets Russes' embrace of a "fusion of arts" or "total" ballet concept, critics addressed further aesthetic issues in their reviews. The "interactive nature" or "universality" of the Ballets Russes' modern aesthetic of ballet was also a common theme touched upon by its contemporary observers. As outlined in chapter 2, the originality of Diaghilev's Ballets Russes had demonstrated to France and the world that ballet could be used as a site of international artistic exchange as well as a vessel of national identity and spirit. Diaghilev's productions integrated authentic source materials with extraordinary artistic imagination. Levinson's frequent yet sarcastic reference to the "National Series," the ballets *Le festin* and *Firebird,* revealed Fokine's "scope of creative possibilities within the realm of Russian national subjects."[119] Diaghilev was able to extend his "creative possibilities" to embrace a variety of national themes in his ballets from Russian to Spanish to French, and so forth.

Several critics responded to this shift by praising the universal nature of ballet: its ability to carry national (and even political) themes and to serve as a forum in which to expose international artistic trends. In fact, Diaghilev was often labelled an "ambassadeur de l'art" due to his ability to use ballet as a site for various national artistic expressions.[120] Some critics connected Diaghilev's internationalization of ballet with his own personal international adaptability.

Jacques Rivière professed that, after 1914, Diaghilev and his troupe had made a clean break from their Russian origins:

> It has been a long while since Mr. Diaghilev's company left Russia; since 1914, the company lost all connection with its homeland and began to travel around the world. However, it seems that the war and the Russian Revolution increased its separation from its homeland and permanently cut it from its base ... Mr Diaghilev did not cowardly resign to his solitude, he has instead tried to gather around him collaborators and support: he has forged alliances with artists from the countries in which he has travelled; he also skilfully assimilated himself to the extent that a foreigner is able ... In his latest creations, in particular, the French, Spanish, and even Italian elements have gained considerable importance.[121]

Critic Boris Schloezer noted Diaghilev's ability to transcend (but not denounce) his Russian nationality to become Parisian and European. He wrote in *La Nouvelle Review Française* that with "the war, the revolution, the fall of the czarist regime to which he held so many ties, it would seem, to break the career of Diaghilev; but the Russian, without renouncing his nationality, had turned himself into a Parisian, into a European."[122] However, he concluded that "never was Diaghilev less Russian than when he became Parisian and put on the ballet *Parade*." According to critics, Diaghilev's own internationalism shaped the nature of his ballets. Serge Lifar, in his autobiography, noted Diaghilev's desire to make a significant contribution to European ballet and his ambition to create "a new European ballet that by its importance would prevail greatly over all the national and local arts, as great as they might be."[123] Schloezer declared that Diaghilev's "universality" was just as important as that in the literary works of Dostoevsky.[124] This indicates that the new aspect of universality in Diaghilev's modern ballet was not only being highlighted by critics, but also placed within the context of other genres.

The idea of the universality of dance, however, was not a new concept for the French. In fact, it was a subject frequently addressed by poets. Many symbolist poets, such as Stéphane Mallarmé and Paul Valéry, were captivated by dance as a wordless art form not bound to the constraints of poetry and prose in terms of language. Many saw dance as an ultimate art of symbolism that could extend itself to reach a wide spectrum of people and nations. Mallarmé once wrote that the dance "becomes for the spectator with imagination the mysterious and holy interpretation of universal life and of our inmost being."[125] Valéry went further, arguing "to my mind the dance is not merely an exercise, an entertainment, an ornamental art, or sometimes a social activity; it is a serious matter and in certain of its aspects most venerable."[126] He continued: "It is a fundamental art, as is suggested if not demonstrated by its universality." Jean Cocteau observed, "the ballet represents, more and more, an international language, in which each one expresses itself with the singularity of its own style."[127] Such visions suggest that ballet, as a versatile art form, could transcend national boundaries and express any national spirit. While the growing recognition of ballet's adaptability would serve well the French attempt to reconcile its ballet tradition with modern republican ideals and aesthetic tastes, it also posed a threat to France's claim over ballet as an inherently French art form. Furthermore, the notion of ballet as an international expressive language diminished the significance of French as its technical language.

Nonetheless, the Ballets Russes' innovative stylistic and thematic components revealed to France that the art of ballet could be used as a tool not only to embrace modern aesthetics, but also to represent national culture.[128] In other words, it brought forth the potential for ballet to carry national artistic identity and thus disclosed all manner of nationalist possibilities for France. If the French were to re-embrace ballet as a national art form, how was a national ballet aesthetic to be forged? What conception of ballet would be most suitable for a French republic? What aesthetic qualities were deemed French, and how could they be applied to ballet? The construction of a French modern ballet aesthetic would find itself entangled within broader debates in modern aesthetics, particularly those about music since many reviews of ballet in the early twentieth century were written by music critics.

As we have seen, the arrival of the Ballets Russes in Paris greatly influenced ballet criticism by broadening its aesthetic discussion to that of music, decor, mime, and poetry. With the appearance of the "dance specialist" in the interwar years, critics and intellectuals focused more attention on dance aesthetics and on restoring French ballet. The new appreciation for technical virtuosity and the formal and athletic aspects of ballet arose due to a number of factors (explored further in chapters 6 and 7). The period after the First World War saw a blossoming of physical culture. Various definitions of modern masculinity and femininity surfaced, reshaping attitudes toward the body, athleticism, health, beauty, and professionalism (particularly, for women in the performing arts). The wide popularity of dance in the interwar years reflects these cultural shifts. As more varieties of dance performance appeared in the 1920s and 1930s, ballet (and dance, in general) would receive unprecedented attention. In fact, dance aesthetics became a cultural force in the 1920s when Paris became *the* dance capital of Europe. International dance troupes made a point of performing in Paris theatres, and several foreign companies even based themselves in Paris, such as Rolf de Maré's Swedish ballet troupe, the Ballets Suédois.[129]

In the 1920s, a specialized press on dance began to surface, such as *La Danse* (1921), *La Tribune de la Danse* (1923), *Revue International de Musique et de Danse* (1926), and *Arts et Mouvement*, although some of these magazines acted more like bulletins than anything else. Increasingly, writers went to great lengths to educate the public on the art of choreography, to review new books on modern ballet, and to locate a distinctly French style of ballet. For example, Antonine Meunier, who wrote *La danse classique* (1932), and, later, Pierre Michaut, who wrote *Le ballet contemporain* (1950), both contributed a much-needed dance history (through text and photographs) as well as detailed explanations of the technical aspects of classic ballet. Meunier's book includes a detailed description of the "école française," a dictionary of dance terms, information on sténochorégraphie, and ninety-four illustrations. Music critic Henry Prunières, in his review of Meunier's book, praised the 150-page work as an important dictionary of dance, with a new and clear method of explanation. Prunières stated that it offered a great service not only for professionals of dance, but also for amateurs. He expressed his confidence that the work would contribute greatly "to dissolve the obscurity which surrounds this noble art."[130] Michaut's 386-page study included 129 illustrations and covered the period between 1920 and 1950.

The collection of articles dedicated to dance and choreography that appeared in *La Revue Musicale* in March 1938 also illustrates the new appreciation for ballet in France. The issue was entitled "Le ballet contemporain" (Contemporary Ballet) and consisted of articles on various topics concerning modern ballet: "Souvenir de Diaghilev" (In Memory of Diaghilev) by Pierre Michaut; "La danse et la musique" (Dance and Music) by Serge Lifar; "Pour ou contre une chorégraphie autonome" (For or Against an Autonomous Choreography) by André Boll; "Poésie de la danse" (Poetry of Dance) by Roger Lannes; "Le décor de ballet" (Ballet Decor) by André Boll; "Avenir du ballet" (Future of Ballet) by Fernand Divoire; and "Questions chorégraphiques" (Choreographic Questions) by Julie Sazonova. The fact that these articles appeared in *La Revue Musicale* and constituted the entire monthly issue demonstrates that, by 1938, the autonomy of choreography was worthy of discussion within a respectable French music journal.

5

In Search of a National Style

In France, the influence of the Ballets Russes and its new conception of ballet as a "total art" inspired many artistic and intellectual figures to reconsider the artistic potential of ballet production. The new role of symphonic music in ballet helped to restore ballet's credibility but, in doing so, displaced ballet's overall function. In the early twentieth century, critics began to inquire into the nature of ballet, to redefine ballet's aesthetic role, and to link it to French identity. These critics, however, tried to define ballet and trace its developments and potential at a time when the concept was being tested, stretched, and expanded to new and, at times, unorthodox places. Ballet remained on experimental ground in the early twentieth century and was constantly redefined to fit modern tastes. Both dancers and non-dancers (critics, artists, poets, and composers) articulated modern ballet in their own way – whether it was to broaden the genre, to revitalize its vocabulary, or to use it as a tool to break down prevailing norms. The Ballets Russes served as an ideal vehicle through which such experimentation was made possible.

While the Ballets Russes infused ballet with modernism, their productions prompted much debate among critics over the aesthetic nature of ballet. The critics' conceptions of modern ballet can be broken down into two aesthetics: the Ballets Russes' "total" ballet and one that grounded itself in ballet technique and French tradition (for example, choreographic autonomy). These two seemingly vying definitions of ballet surfaced in commentary published in Parisian bourgeois newspapers. As we saw in the preceding chapter, some individuals emphasized the value of those aspects peripheral to dancing, such as the music, decor, or poetic and dramatic expression. Others – such as André Levinson and Serge Lifar, who understood ballet's technical language and could interpret choreography – drew attention to ballet's formal qualities and the beauty of bodily movement, particularly in the interwar years, which witnessed the rise of physical culture and brought forth new attitudes toward corporeal beauty and athletic skill.

As nationalist sentiment grew in France, critics and intellectuals expressed their weariness of foreign influences on French art and culture. These anxieties escalated in the cultural climate of the postwar period when France was in desperate need to reassert its cultural and artistic pre-eminence and to pronounce French identity. Ironically, the key player in establishing this identity was Russian émigré and dance expert André Levinson. Levinson insisted that ballet was a distinctly French art form that embedded Frenchness in its formal aspects (that is, classical technique). His writings elucidated how ballet could serve in the French project for national renewal. Both Levinson and Serge Lifar were instrumental to the French reconception of ballet and the eventual establishment of a national aesthetic style. Ultimately, their modernist reinterpretation of ballet as grounded in technique or formal qualities was redefined as a quintessentially "French art" and thus rendered one of the highest forms of republican political expression for the haute bourgeoisie. In other words, through the enunciation of ballet's nature as an autonomous art form that rested on dancing, the French were able to move away from the modern aesthetic put forth by the Ballets Russes and construct an alternative vision that was capable of representing Frenchness. This was possible due to the Paris Opéra ballet's eventual embrace of neoclassicism, a traditional style that embodied French republican sentiments but also appealed to modern tastes. In other words, the French managed to reconcile their past with their present by embracing a "dance for dance's sake" ideology that brought technical virtuosity (and thus Frenchness) to the forefront of analysis of ballet.

As we have seen in previous chapters, the two vying interpretations of ballet as dramatically expressive versus formal ("decorative") were not new ones. Enlightenment thinkers raised similar arguments in the eighteenth century. In early twentieth-century France, the two main proponents of these apparently opposing conceptions were choreographer Michel Fokine and critic/dance historian André Levinson. Fokine was instrumental to the Ballets Russes, creating a "new ballet" that was modern and primarily expressive. As a choreographer and theorist, he wanted to diversify ballet and explore its correspondence with music, decor, and costume design. Moving away from a focus on the formal aspects of dance (technique), he reintroduced the centrality of gesture and pantomime in ballet. Levinson, on the other hand, believed that the value of dance lay in its physical properties as "l'art plastique" and insisted on the centrality of form or ballet technique. He demonstrated this through an examination of the aesthetic nature of "old ballet" ("classic" ballet). Levinson's ultimate aim was to free modern ballet (as presented via the Ballets Russes) from its dependency on decor and music (something that future Opéra ballet director Serge Lifar also desired). Levinson was regarded as a dance specialist, and his writings were enormously useful to those critics writing on ballet in respectable bourgeois papers at this time. Many critics embraced and recycled many of his ideas about dance in their reviews. Thus we find two contrasting conceptions of the definition, structure, and purpose of modern ballet even among those who had similar national backgrounds, political leanings, and class status.[1] The debate was so distinct and enduring that, in 1938, an article was published in *La Revue Musicale* entitled, "Pour ou contre une chorégraphie autonome" (For or Against an Autonomous Choreography). It is within the context of this controversy that a concept of modern French ballet emerged and eventually manifested itself in a modernized, autonomous, and much-valorized Paris Opéra ballet.

As commentary on ballet increasingly captured cultural anxieties about the corrupting influence of the Ballets Russes on French art, it also revealed a desire to preserve French ballet and to create a national style distinct from the Ballets Russes. Thus critics' visions for a modern national style begin with the criticism of the Ballets Russes but was also made possible by it. The very reduction of choreographic autonomy imposed by the Ballets Russes had stimulated inquiries into the true nature of dance and investigations into what were inherently French characteristics of ballet. As we will see, opinions about how to reconceptualize French ballet were deeply connected to broader politics in the arts in France concerning nationalism, modernism, and tradition. The implementation of a different modern ballet aesthetic (one based on choreographic autonomy and corporeal expression) self-consciously played a role in the rhetoric of the regeneration of a nation.

FOKINE'S "NEW BALLET"

In order to understand how critics and intellectuals articulated a distinct French style of ballet, it is important to present the aesthetic put forth by Ballets Russes choreographer Michel Fokine, who played a central role in the conception of the company. Fokine's new vision of ballet stimulated a rich dialogue in the press over the nature of ballet and provoked fears about the foreign influence on not only ballet, but also music, design, and decor. His innovations, however, must be understood as part of a larger enterprise of Diaghilev's Ballets Russes and its greater ambition to appeal to the tastes of Paris's haute-bourgeois audiences. As we will see, Fokine's "new ballet" emphasized dramatic unity, poetic expression, exoticism, and transgression.[2]

In his review, dance critic and historian Valerian Svetlov described Fokine's ballet *Egyptian Nights* (1908) as a "violation of every tradition of the good old times ... a rejection of 'turned-out' classical technique ... [a] violation of the ballet 'canon.'"[3] Indeed, Fokine argued against classical ballet's conformity to tradition, such as its dependence upon a highly stylized and "artificial" form of mime that he found was meaningless to most of the audience, and its limited traditional costume – the ballerina's standard costume of tutu and pointe shoes. Although he did not advocate the complete abandonment of academic ballet technique, which he considered the only form of training that could equip a dancer with the necessary strength and versatility, he believed that the choreographer should be able to dispense with it if the ballet's theme so required. He considered pointe work inappropriate to many themes and replaced it with his own conceptions of various period and national dance forms.[4] *Le festin*, *Daphne and Chloé*, *Schéhérazade*, *Le spectre de la rose*, and *Narcisse* are all examples of Fokine's new style. In *Daphne and Chloé* (1914), for example, the women wore light tunics and sandals instead of pointe shoes and were, at times, barefoot.

Fokine viewed dance as the ultimate means of expression. In an article entitled "The New Russian Ballet: Conventions in Dancing. M. Fokine's Principles and Aims" (1914), Fokine wrote, "All arts help us to sense and to feel the world surrounding us, to reveal its meaning, its beauty ... But the dance, in addition thereto, helps us, to understand ourselves more thoroughly ... In every rhythmic movement we find the order and method in our own body."[5] Lincoln Kirstein, who studied under Fokine, described the choreographer's principle: "To have studied under Fokine is to have experienced an unforgettable illumination into the source of gesture, the definition of style, the creation of theatrical effect. His exercises are not dry, back-breaking labour. When he indicates a reaching motion of the arms, he says, 'Reach as if you are touching' … he discovers for his pupils the basic idea behind motion."[6] Fokine's ballets catered to the expression of psychological and metaphysical notions without words. Similar to the symbolist poets, Fokine looked on the body of the dancer as serving more as an instrument of an idea than a manifestation of ideal beauty of line, form, and rhythm. Fokine envisioned ballet as the poetry of movement and preoccupied himself with the poetic correspondence between music, colour, and movement. He once stated that "dance was poetry without words."[7]

Fokine demanded that ballet be first and foremost expressive. He attempted to distinguish the principles of his "new ballet" from other forms of dance performance circulating at the time in Europe. In "The New Russian Ballet," Fokine presented five rules of his new ballet. The first was that subject matter should dictate choreography. He aimed "to create a new form corresponding to the subject the most expressive form possible for the representation of the period and the character of the nation represented." The second rule was that dancing and mimetic gestures had to convey meaning only if they served as an expression of the dramatic action and were "connected with the scheme of the whole ballet." The third stated that such mimetic gestures be expressed with the whole body rather than just the toes and hands. The fourth rule endowed expressiveness to ensemble and corps de ballet dancing. In other words, group dancing would no longer be ornamental but sentimental. Lastly, rule five outlined the new modern ballet structure as a collaborative art form:

> [The new ballet] is the alliance of dancing with other arts. The new ballet, refusing to be the slave either of music or of scenic decoration, and recognizing the alliance of the arts only on the condition of complete equality, allows perfect freedom both to the scenic artist and to the musician. In contradiction to the older ballet it does not demand "ballet music" of the composer as an accompaniment to dancing; it accepts music of every kind, provided only that it is

> good and expressive. It does not demand of the scenic artist that he should array the ballerinas in short skirts and pink slippers. It does not impose any specific "ballet" conditions on the composer or the decorative artist, but gives complete liberty to their creative powers.[8]

Fokine often remarked that he found the rules of old ballet too restrictive. He wrote that "to free the dancers of the future ballet from unnecessary rules, limiting his talents, constitutes the aim of the new movement ... Man is limitless in his versatility and he endlessly changes his plastic language ... therefore he should not be limited in his expressions or confined to one formula." It is interesting that Fokine ultimately formulated rules on the new ballet after insisting upon the importance of allowing an open range for the development of ballet. He wrote, "No single form of dance must be accepted once and for all. The best form is the one which most fully expresses the content and naturally corresponds to the given problem." Fokine may have felt compelled to set new rules of ballet in order to distinguish his own dance aesthetic from the "free dance" of Isadora Duncan.[9] It is also apparent that Fokine resolutely attempted to distinguish "his ballet" from German modern dance, which he found problematic.[10]

Fokine's dance aesthetic was based on a principle that "the purpose of each movement in the ballet should be expression." According to Fokine, ballet's expressiveness should be at all times truthful. Fokine was referring to two aspects of "truthful expression": national identity and natural human movement. On nationalism in dance, Fokine writes, "If the music is in the mood of Spanish national melodies and rhythms, then the dance must interpret the similar national characteristics. Climatic conditions and historical factors have created different national temperaments and in different dances, naturally resulting in specific form peculiar only to this country." In the case of Spain, he writes, "the rhythmical tapping of the heel, the restrained, sensuous curve of the entire body's line, the serpentine movement of the arms is more natural, in this case, than 'natural' movement of barefoot dancing."[11] Fokine believed that his ballet was truthful in that it attempted to capture the authenticity of style and gesture of a particular place and time. He recalled, "When I composed an ancient Greek ballet, I studied the artists of ancient Greece; when I produced 'Le Coq d'Or,' I studied the old Russian chap-books and broadsides;

and when I produced 'Schéhérazade,' 'Cléopatre,' 'le Spectre de la Rose' and the Polovtsian dances in 'Prince Igor,' in each case I made use of different materials appropriate to the ballet in hand."[12]

The second aspect of truthful expression lay in Fokine's perception that dance expressiveness should manifest itself through natural human movement. He believed that traditional ballet "discarded the natural human body ... [and] devised descriptive and symbolic movements which described nothing and did not symbolize anything." He wrote, "The ballet has repudiated expressive gestures and subsequently the dance became inexpressive, acrobatic, mechanical, and void. In order to restore to the dance its spiritual content, it is necessary to base it on gestures, and, in turn, to build gestures on the laws of natural expressiveness."[13] In other words, modern ballet had to rest on more than form.

Thus we can see how Fokine's "new ballet" developed out of a desire to modernize ballet but to distinguish it from modern dance. This vision entailed a move away from classical ballet technique and production (grounded in the work of French choreographer Marius Petipa). Fokine also revealed the ways in which ballet could "truthfully" express national identity and tradition. In offering both these functions, he expanded the possibilities of ballet production and sparked a new allure for ballet in France.

Critics had mixed reactions to the choreography of Fokine and the Ballets Russes' vision of ballet as a "total art." Some responded favourably to Fokine's choreography and the new modern conceptions of ballet production. In a review of the Ballets Russes' *Firebird* (1910), the ballet was hailed as "an entirely new direction for the art of dancing"; another review stated that it was "destined to surprise, captivate, and transport."[14] The dramatic critic Robert Brussel described Fokine as one of the most unique artists in the world and the direction of his choreography as encompassing a poetic and dramatic unity.[15]

Others expressed their reservations, particularly those critics who feared the Russian influence on French composers. In his *Le Temps* article from 1912, for example, Lalo criticized the Ballets Russes' production of *L'après-midi d'un faune* (1912) for its lack of unity and harmony, its discord and decadence, and its Russian "barbarie." In fact, he interpreted the audience's applause as a "bad sign" that "revealed the degeneration of the French spirit." He remarked: "The

Russians … have contributed to the decline of our taste by their ignorance and carelessness of unity and harmony, by their love of sumptuous and flashy entertainment." Lalo perceived the Russian ballet as not only aesthetically flawed, but also corrupting. He described the Ballets Russes as "real barbarism, under the false appearance of a delicate art. That's what the Russian shows are, despite their research and refinement: the mark of the Barbarian is on them."[16] In his review, Lalo implied that the Russian ballet had corrupted the "delicate art" of French classical dance and suggested that "Frenchness" in ballet rested in its harmony, unity, and balance (although Lalo does not clearly distinguish the source from which such qualities should originate). Lalo's concluding remark, "the stigma of the barbarian is common to them all," reveals a common attitude on the part of French critics towards Russian culture and its assumed lack of civilization. Lalo was writing in the pages of *Le Temps*, one of Paris's most important and most respected papers. It was politically moderate and catered to a republican bourgeois readership.

Lalo was equally worried of the collaboration of French composers in the Ballets Russes' productions. In pointing out the disharmony between French music and Russian choreography, he wrote that in *L'après-midi d'un faune*, there was a contradiction between the "slavish archaism and hardcast rigidity of the choreography and the flexible flow of Debussy's prelude or Mallarmé's poem – both so alien and distant in their attempt to interpret antiquity."[17] In other words, Russian ballet was not compatible with French music. He concluded his review with an equally critical opinion of the Ballets Russes' *Daphne and Chloé* (1914), in which he found the choreography confusing and less characteristic, the music lacking rhythm, and the decor "unintelligible." In this Ballets Russes production, dancers wore light tunics and sandals (sometimes they were barefoot) instead of the traditional French tutu and pointe shoes. Even though both ballet scores were written by French composers, Claude Debussy (then the hero of French tradition) and Maurice Ravel respectively, Lalo did not find the French compositions adding any French nationalist spirit to the productions.

What we see happening in the realm of ballet criticism is an engagement in the internal politics of French music and its desire to remain "pure." By the mid-nineteenth century, there were two centres of musical activity: Germany and France. Apart from the work of Hector Berlioz, who is considered to be the only native French Romantic composer, Paris became an active meeting place and home to many foreign musicians, such as Frédéric Chopin, Franz Liszt, and Richard Wagner. Many of these composers became fascinated by cultural minorities and studied their folk songs and tales to depict nationalist sentiment in their works.[18]

However, while a French avant-garde was developing in literature and the visual arts in the mid-nineteenth century, French music remained underdeveloped and strongly influenced by German aesthetics. In fact, German music became widely accepted in France during this period. Franz Liszt (1811–1886) and Richard Wagner (1811–1883), for example, attempted to synthesize German Romantic ideals in their music and to express the beauty of nature and deep emotional states. While incorporating both literary and formal elements as necessary parts of music, they experimented increasingly with harmonic and orchestral arrangements. For Liszt, music represented a means for the total expression of nature and feeling. In order to convey this, he invented entirely new musical forms.[19] Richard Wagner likewise attempted to create a "total art" in music where the harmony was inseparable from the orchestration, the music inseparable from the poetry. He successfully fused these various elements into an integrated whole. As we have seen, this idea of a "fusion of arts" (*Gesamtkunstwerk*) was later embraced by Serge Diaghilev and Michel Fokine in the Ballets Russes. The innovations of these foreign composers played a central role in shaping French music (and opera).

The Franco-Prussian War marks a decisive shift in the direction of modern music in France. The French defeat at the hands of the Germans stimulated a wide search on the part of music critics and composers to delineate French qualities in music and to develop a style compatible to modern culture. France's turn to nationalist music was led by Camille Saint-Saëns (1883–1921) and Romain Bussine, who, in 1871, founded the Société Nationale de Musique. Its goal was the "de-Wagnerization" of French music and the codification of authentic French musical concepts. This involved a refutation of anything remotely attributable to German musical concepts. The legacy of Richard Wagner's *Gesamtkunstwerk* was artfully condemned by Saint-Saëns. His book *Germanophilie* (1910) represents a type of cultural puritanism that was circulating at the time.[20]

Composer Claude Debussy (1862–1918) played a vital role in the search for a distinctly French voice in music. Debussy was largely responsible for bridging the gap between nineteenth-century Romanticism and the twentieth-century modern period.[21] His compositions reflected not only French musical traditions, but also the creation of an aesthetic sensibility now identified as "modernist."[22] His *Prélude à l'après-midi d'un faune* (1894), inspired by Mallarmé's poem, and the three *Nocturnes* (1900) established him as one of France's greatest composers. Like the symbolist poets, who developed a language that could subtly evoke emotion, imagery, and associations, Debussy cultivated a hypersensitive tonal palette that transcended nineteenth-century musical rhetoric.[23]

The de-Germanization of music in France encouraged a rediscovery of all that was musically French. This manifested itself in a variety of ways within French music. Similar to the Ballets Russes, one approach embraced by many Breton composers around 1910 was a turn to folk motifs. Inspired by the "Russian Five" (Balakirev, Rimsky-Korsakov, Borodin, Cui, and Mussorgsky), whose works incited nationalist fervour in Russia, they hoped that folk-music-inspired compositions would be as successful in France. For example, having received academically French training, Paul Ladmirault (1877–1944) turned to Breton folk motifs to celebrate nationalist spirit and, as a result, attained great admiration from established composers such as Gabriel Fauré and Maurice Ravel.[24] Acclaimed musicologist and journalist Louis Vuillemin (1879–1929) bequeathed a legacy of works celebrating Brittany's history and culture.[25] However, this turn to the regional "folk" would be suppressed after the First World War when national hegemony was considered of the utmost importance.[26]

While the use of folk motifs played a significant role in the representation of national identity in the early productions of the Ballets Russes and in Breton music, French traditionalists had an altogether different perspective regarding modern nationalist expression.[27] Claude Debussy, for example, was decidedly against the use of folk motifs to express nationalist ideology.[28] He complained once in a letter about the use of folk music. "In my opinion," he wrote, "one should never touch this music … Your young musicians might with advantages turn to it for inspiration – not by copying it, but trying to transpose its freedom, its evocative power, its sadness and its rhythms." He continued, "The advice given by Wagner has been very bad for the music of a great many countries. One should only use the folk music of one's country as a basis, never as a style of writing …

Cherish it as passionately as you like, but do not dress it up in academic robes or make it wear gold spectacles! It's only because of my love for music – and not only for French music – is boundless that I'm always sorry to see its riches wasted, and its true significance – I might say its national significance – distorted."[29] Debussy's words reflect the French rebuke of German Romantic music that was common at the time. As music historian Rollo Myers explains, France's musical tradition was deeply bound to the idea of "civilized living and thinking."[30] French composer Albert Roussel (1869–1937) best captured this sense when he wrote, "The cult of spiritual values is the foundation of any society that claims to be civilized, and music, among the arts, is the most responsive and the most elevated expression of these values."[31] Furthermore, French music had always been valued for its intellectual and imaginative rather than emotional qualities. Myers asserts that "all French art shows the same preoccupation with form and technique, the same attention to polish and detail, to balance and clarity above all." Qualities such as "balance," "clarity," "form," and "technique" were all deemed French. These manifested themselves in either in the composer's "musical material" (the inspiration from folk motifs and national themes – Ladmirault) or "manner of presentation" (embedded in their musical language, style, and "mental and psychological makeup" – Fauré and Debussy).[32] This is significant because we see the potential for nationalism to be found within the formal elements of a composer's style not just within themes. Revitalization of French ballet followed a similar trajectory by moving away from the "new ballet" of Fokine and by locating "Frenchness" within the formal elements of ballet.[33]

With this brief overview of the development of French national music, we can understand Lalo's desire to "protect" French composer Claude Debussy and his French style. He was not pleased that French composers were collaborating with the Russian company and feared the direction their music would take. This is not surprising as Lalo was strongly nationalist, anti-Wagner, and invested in the project to cultivate national music in France. Lalo's *Le Temps* review of 1912 echoed a widespread effort to rid French art of foreign influence and to restore pure French tradition at the time. Some critics as well as artists and musicians thought this could be achieved through an embrace of the tradition of French classicism, not the "decadent" direction of modern art taken by the impressionists, cubists, and art nouveau craftsmen at the turn of the century. A sixteen-page political cartoon from *La Baïonnette* (18 April 1918) captures this tension within the art world by presenting the seduction of France (Marianne) by the avant-garde, here in the context of the Ballets Russes: "Look how [Marianne] is swept off her feet in a fantastic vertigo: frenetic dances, crazy dresses, odalisque culottes, sultan's turbans – her head turned round, with green hair – enough to make you think she's lost her rudder. With indulgent smiles, she watches as people are tricked by the ridiculous work of the cubists, cu-cubists, 'art nouveau' furniture made by insane cabinetmakers. She wants to see, again and again, the barbarian ballets danced, with conglomerations of decor painted with broom-sized brushstrokes."[34] This anti-modernist reaction led to the official banning of Wagner's music on the French stage between 1915 and 1919 (a similar ban occurred during the Franco-Prussian War).

After the First World War, the Ballets Russes' "fusion of arts" became gradually less appealing as the French grew concerned over the influence of Wagner's conceptions and the potential loss of ballet's Frenchness. As Myers points out, "there was a strong reaction against the whole idea of a fusion of arts, and the pendulum of fashion swung emphatically in the opposite direction." A new principle emerged among artists to keep their arts distinct and separate from each other. "The tendency now," he writes, "was to stress the differences rather than the points of resemblance between them; and 'pure' music, 'pure poetry' and 'pure painting' were the new aesthetic slogans."[35] In the interwar period, there was an attempt to assemble an outstanding collection of musical works that could reveal a recovered France. It became important to establish a continuance of tradition yet to offer a modern edge.

It is in the revival of neoclassicism that the aesthetic autonomy of music or "pure music" was asserted.[36] Neoclassicism made its way in music via Igor Stravinsky.[37] In 1920, Stravinsky composed *Pulcinella,* a ballet written for Serge Diaghilev and based on compositions ascribed to Giovanni Pergolesi. It is considered a landmark work in twentieth-century neoclassicism in music. Neoclassicism embraced the classical ideals of clarity, balance, and line as well as simplicity in form. It opened many avenues for composers and became an essential ingredient in the rise of modernism in music.[38] Many neoclassical works took their inspiration from Greco-Roman classical subject matter (e.g., Stravinsky's *Apollon musagète* and *Oedipus Rex*, Satie's *Socrate*). Another identifying feature of this neoclassical revival was the purely musical aspects of a work. Neoclassical composers felt that music needed to be liberated from its metaphoric function and valued for its formal qualities. This "purification" or autonomy of music came to offer a new means through which to represent national identity. We find similar assertions of "pure art" being made within the context of ballet in the interwar period.

FRENCH IDENTITY THROUGH AESTHETIC AUTONOMY

At the turn of the nineteenth century, French symbolist poets articulated their own aesthetics of ballet by attempting to locate philosophical expression in dance movement (albeit in a different manner than that of Fokine). According to Stéphane Mallarmé, ballet was the visualization of a metaphysical world, and poetry was its ideal language. In the aspiration to transcend form, he regarded each step as a "metaphor," "symbolic," and "a poem freed of all the apparatus of writing."[39] In fact, he boldly asserted: "The theatre is a higher spirit … the ballet is the supreme theatrical form of poetry." Mallarmé implied that ballet movement has poetic value (rather than just pantomime), yet he never went quite so far as to locate it within the choreographic beauty or the formal elements of ballet technique. Mallarmé envisioned the dancer as an ideal being who could transcend human nature and who could become the "element she incarnates."[40] He perceived the dancer as a symbol, never an artist or creator. Thus her virtuosity was to be found in the purity of her expression not her technical (i.e., physical) abilities.

Paul Valéry, like Mallarmé, also described dance as the "visual embodiment of the Idea" or "the pure act of metamorphosis." In *L'âme et la danse* (1921), he envisioned dance as a revelation of spiritual truth. "For the dance," he wrote, "is an art derived from life itself, since it is nothing more or less than the action of the whole human body; but an action transposed into a world, into a kind of *space-time*, which is no longer quite the same as that of everyday life."[41] In his study *Philosophie de la danse* (1936), he offered a philosophical and abstract idea of dance that presented the metaphysical potential of ballet. Valéry saw dance as the most abstract of all the arts and as an art form in its own right: he once wrote that "the richness of a work of art consists in the number of meanings or values it can assume, while still remaining itself."[42] Although Valéry claimed dance as an autonomous art, he did so in the sense of its potential as a vehicle for expression. In fact, he once asserted that "a formula for pure dance should include nothing to suggest that it has an end."[43] Moreover, he was not concerned with understanding the technical nature of the dancers' movements or their artistry as such. It was the wordless nature of dance to which symbolists were so attracted.

Valéry's valorization of the ballet (whatever the form) presented the art of ballet in a new light and with a new potential. By locating poetic and intellectual value in dance, he deemed dance as aesthetically credible. In his *Aesthetics,* he asserted that dance was a serious and venerable art form and claimed that dance "is a fundamental art, as is suggested if not demonstrated by its universality, its immemorial antiquity, the solemn uses to which it has been put, the ideas and reflections it has engendered at all times."[44] André Levinson often heralded Mallarmé and Valéry as heroes who endeavoured to restore ballet's status as a legitimate and noble art form. However, as we will see, it was Levinson who demonstrated how the formal qualities of ballet could express poetic themes.[45]

Many poets became interested in ballet for its potential to represent ideas non-verbally. Mallarmé, Valéry, Wilde, d'Annunzio, Claudel, Anouilh, and Cocteau all were eager to place ballet within a symbolist and poetic genre.[46] During Cocteau's lifelong association with ballet, he went to great lengths to address the artistic value of dance. Cocteau deliberately turned to dance as the medium in which, in a number of instances, he was able to express his visions better than in words.[47] He was intrigued with the wordless aspect of modern ballet, particularly with its dramatic potential. The use of pantomime in ballet was for him the ultimate tool for expression. In fact, later in his career, he asserted that the "end of pure film came when 'talking' was added to film." Cocteau believed that ballet was capable of "furnish[ing] psychological insight into man" and "describ[ing] social conditions."[48] While Cocteau recognized the ballet as a credible artistic form, he valued dance for its ability to represent something outside of its formal qualities. He saw dance as a means through which to fully visualize the poetry of everyday life.

Both the symbolist and Fokine interpretations of ballet as poetic endured throughout the early twentieth century. In 1938, *La Revue*

Musicale devoted an entire article, entitled "Poésie de la danse" (Poetry of the Dance), to the poetics of ballet. The contributor, Roger Lannes, raised some provocative questions and pointed out the complex nature of the dancer as both creator (artist) and creation (art object). He began with a series of analogies between the creative act of the poet and that of the dancer. He wrote, "If there are, as Jean Le Louet believes, two poetries: that of Rimbaud who dedicated himself to revolt and that of Mallarmé and Rainer Maria Rilke who reserved themselves to Solitude, the dance appears to me to depend on these two wills, or better, of these two instincts." He went on to explain that the poet uses the poem as a means of knowledge more than a means of expression in that the poetic creation permits one to advance towards an internal knowledge. Therefore, poetry involves the attainment of self-knowledge. He implied that this process is more difficult for dancers because their bodies are their material, noting that while the painter, the sculptor, and the composer all work with materials outside of themselves, the dancer is alone with his/herself. The dancer is both creator and creation and, as such, struggles more than the poet in the act of creative expression. In this way, the dancer experiences both intensive revolt and solitude. Lannes wrote, "From second to second, he extracts from his body a different body, he abolishes that which he just was in order to attain that which he is going to be." Lannes commented specifically on the work of Lifar. "Forgive me," he asserted, "to have thought it necessary to intervene in order to make known publicly what the poets and poetry of today owe to dance and to the fabulous power of one Serge Lifar."[49]

The language of Lannes's article reveals a growing sophistication in dance discourse by the 1930s, when we find less of the sarcasm of earlier ballet reviews and more consideration of dance as a serious art form. Articles such as this, which compared poetry and dance, contributed to the elevation of ballet's status in that poetry was one of the most revered art forms in France (as ballet had once been before its decline). Lannes's article was originally a paper delivered at a conference that was part of the Exposition International de Paris in October 1937.

While critics recognized Fokine's new pantomimic style of ballet as an excellent source for the expression of feeling, they avoided any choreographic criticism. Although many critics drew attention to the quality of poetic grace in ballet production, they seldom allocated it to the execution of choreography. For example, critic Robert Brussel, like the poet Mallarmé, located poetics and grace within the metaphoric body of the dancers, not in the form, elevation, and line of the dancing body. "Karsavina's beauty," he once wrote of the Ballets Russes' prima ballerina, "is perfect, incomparable: substance itself seems bewildered at being the adorable veil of so much grace … with such exquisite slowness her neck delicately droops. And when the dark, dark eyes open in the dead whiteness of her face, how delicious is the vision of poetry and grace she evokes."[50] While the idea of grace (as opposite to effort) surfaced frequently in ballet criticism in the early twentieth century, it holds ambiguous implications. The traditional idea of classical ballet movement as espoused in the Romantic era was that it was a manifestation of grace and muscular energy perfected so that there was an absence of visible effort or of "bruit": the idea of grace as being the opposite (antithesis) of effort. However, Brussel, like the symbolists, located grace in terms of the pantomimic, poetic, and metaphoric expression of the dancer, not in the formal qualities of dancing.

Few critics before André Levinson attempted to locate the intrinsic beauty of choreography. One exception can be found in an article of 1912 in which critic and editor Jacques Rivière made an extraordinary discovery. In his landmark article "Des Ballets Russes et de Fokine" (Of the Ballets Russes and of Fokine), Rivière asserted, "Many people have not yet understood what there is to admire in the Russian ballet; it is the dancing." He went on to announce that critics have all been looking at the wrong things: "One has spoken at random of colour, barbarism, orientalism, one has praised the music of Stravinsky … one has declared that Bakst is a great genius. But one has not been resigned to admire that which these performances have most unique, that which they render different not in quality but in nature of all that has been given to us in seeing here."[51] In other words, the actual dancing. Rivière then drew attention to the art of bodily movement: "I understand better now what moves me so deeply in the dance: nothing plastic, no attitude, but to see a human being *penché* [tilt over on one leg], *tendu* [stretch or extend leg], prepare to leap: and suddenly he advances himself, he runs, he turns, he raises his arms, he obediently exerts himself frantically to the obscure rhythms of his life that overwhelms."[52] Here we see an attempt on the part of a respectable critic to highlight classical dance technique rather than the decor, costumes, music, or even gesture (although he does so with difficulty without the formal vocabulary of ballet technique). Moreover, such an observation comes from a nationalist figure writing in an outwardly nationalist periodical, *La Nouvelle Revue Française.* By emphasizing formal qualities of ballet dancing, Rivière may have been – however, implicitly – drawing attention to the Frenchness of classical ballet technique, particularly in using the French ballet technical terms *penché* and *tendu.* One question at hand (and one that was seldom addressed) was when does dance stop being an end in itself and become a means to an end? Only one critic of note approached this issue: André Levinson.

It is in the writings of André Levinson, and later the laborious efforts of Serge Lifar that we see how the idea of dance as a pure art (choreographic autonomy) could establish a distinctly French modern ballet. In France, there were no "experts" on dance before André Levinson arrived in Paris in 1921. Levinson (here in his position as dance historian) best articulates how writers of dance had regarded ballet:

> No one has ever tried to portray the intrinsic beauty of the dance step, its innate quality, its esthetic reason for being. This beauty is referred to the smile of the dancer, to the picturesque quality of his costume, to the general atmosphere surrounding him, to the synchronizing of his bodily rhythm with the beat of the music or again to the emotional appeal of the dramatic libretto of the ballet: but never is it shown to lie in the contours of the movement itself, in the constructive values of an attitude or in the thrilling dynamics of a leap in the air. All the other arts are foisted on the dance as instructors.[53]

Levinson was correct in his observation that most criticism of ballet centred on all that was peripheral to the dancing. This is because most critics in France did not have a critical language with which to analyze the choreographic elements of ballet. Not having any training in ballet, they often focused on what they knew best – the decor, costumes, or music.

One memorialist spoke of Levinson as having "founded a genre" while another remarked that he had "created choreographic criticism."[54] Indeed, Levinson may have been the first professional dance critic in that he offered the first real analytical examination of the choreographic element of ballet. "Our ordinary methods of analysis are of very little use in dealing with this art, which is primarily a discipline of movement," he wrote. "The dancer in motion is a harmony of living forms, masses and outlines, whose relations to each other are continually varied by that 'motion which causes lines to flow.'"[55] In light of this, he dedicated himself to educating the public on the art of choreography.[56] His article "Lectures chorégraphiques" reveals an impressive attempt to inform readers on the art of dance choreography, its developments, and even its debates.[57] Levinson not only presented the formal aspects of dancing, but also provided a bold critical language and purpose to use it. He explained: "The art of dance is so peculiarly inarticulate that it has never possessed a proper aesthetic philosophy. Choreographic thought – and here we fall straight way into the use of an improper and misleading term – has always been condemned to expression through paraphrases – high-sounding but inaccurate." He continued, "We approach the dance by aid of analogous hypotheses and the habits of thought employed in our consideration of other arts, with the inevitable result that we substitute the obvious facts of a static art for the elusive dynamics of the dance."[58]

Levinson described dance as an autonomous art that appealed to the beauty of human movement. In his essay "The Spirit of Classic Dance," he presented laws of "classic" dance.[59] "The technique of a dancer is not like the mechanical workings of a disjointed doll; it is physical effort constantly informed by beauty." He continued: "This technique is no supplementary reinforcement to his art, nor is it a mere device, designed to gain easy applause, like (according to Stendhal) the art of the versifier. It is the very soul of the dance; it *is* the dance, itself."[60] Levinson perceived ballet technique as constituting the soul of "classic" ballet; essentially, verticality, turnout, and pointe work. He served as an interpreter of the aesthetics of classicism in dance by bringing discussion of these aspects to the forefront.

Most fascinating are the analogies through which Levinson described classic dance. Levinson perceived the formal beauty of "pure dance" along the lines of architecture: "In so far as it is possible to compare movement with immobility," he wrote, "we find many points of analogy between architecture and ballet … Like architecture, the ballet is an emanation of geometrical and spatial conceptions ... One of the fundamentals of the ballet dance is equilibrium, the search for absolute balance."[61] Here we can see Levinson's analyses of the formal aspects of dance: "[The ballet] reduces its splendid and vibrant instrument – the human body – to its tectonic not plastic elements. For the plastic volume is autonomous, limited by the form. The framework of the dance is like the draft of a temple formed by lines – lines which are often ideally prolonged in space. This is why classic choreography can disregard certain plastic particularities of the human body which would break its unity of line." Levinson also related the technique of "classic" ballet – particularly that of turnout (the outward rotation of the hips and legs) as a human victory over nature. In other words, he proclaimed that the classical dancer appeared to ignore all natural laws: "The body of the dancer is freed from the usual limitations upon human motion. Instead of being restricted to a simple backward and forward motion – the only directions in which the human body, operating normally, can move with ease and grace – this turning outward of the legs permits free motion in any direction without the loss of equilibrium; forward, backwards, sideways, obliquely or rotating ... The dancer then is a body moving in space according to any desired rhythm."[62] He argued that "classic" ballet transformed the dancer into an object of perfection, much like a machine, by disciplining the body to serve an ideal function. He asserted, "The accomplished dancer is an artificial being, an instrument of precision, and he is forced to undergo rigorous daily exercise to avoid lapsing into his original purely human state."[63] Levinson went on to compare the lines and forms of classic dance to those of a modern airplane:

> His whole being becomes imbued with that same unity, that same conformity with its ultimate aim, that constitutes the arresting beauty of a finished airplane, where every detail, as well as the general effect, expresses one supreme object – that of speed. But where the airplane is conceived in a utilitarian sense – the idea of beauty happening to superimpose itself upon it – the constant transfiguration ... of the classic dancer from the ordinary to the ideal is the result of a disinterested will for perfection, an unquestionable thirst to surpass himself. Thus it is that an exalted aim transforms his mechanical efforts into an aesthetic phenomenon.

> You may ask whether I am suggesting that the dancer is a machine? But most certainly! – a machine for manufacturing beauty – if it is in any way possible to conceive a machine that in itself is a living, breathing thing, susceptible of the most exquisite emotions.[64]

It is fascinating to find Levinson attaching a modern aesthetic of beauty to classic dance: here the connection between classical ballet and the modern technology of the twentieth century. He could have been indicating that classical dance is indeed compatible to modern times and not an antiquated aesthetic. Levinson, for the first time, focused complete attention on the dancing body itself. According to him, ballet needed to be understood as resting on the mechanics of movement and human physics. Moreover, he did not distinguish genders within corporeal beauty in declaring the dancing body a machine.

Most significantly, Levinson was the first to propose that ideas could manifest themselves within choreographic form. In 1922, he stated: "It is easy to describe the technique, the gymnastics of the ballet dance, but who would think of establishing for each movement a corresponding psychological idea?" He put forth his idea of choreographic autonomy of expression, writing that "the ballet dance ... is not determined by any exterior motive. It includes its own law, its own logic, and any departure from that logic, pertaining to a body moving in space with the aim of creating beauty by *organized dynamism*, is perfectly apparent to the spectator."[65] Ultimately, Levinson demonstrated how dance in its purely formal aspects was capable of embodying spiritual human truths. Such poetics in dance aesthetics can be seen in Levinson's formal description of the classic turnout and the way in which it widened the space around the dancer, "pushing back the invisible walls of that cylinder of air in the center of which the dancer moves ... multiplying to an infinite degree the direction of the movement as well as its various conformations. It surrounds the vertical of the body's equilibrium by a vortex of curves, segments of circles, arcs; it projects the body of the dancer into magnificent parabolas, curves it into a living spiral; it creates a whole world of animated forms that awake in us a throng of active sensations, that our usual mode of life has atrophied."[66] Levinson's description of "classic" ballet may be seen to echo a type of symbolist escapism. He located the idealism and otherworldliness of the dancer in his or her technical virtuosity.

Levinson, who was also a dance historian, articulated the two functions of dance that were vying for supremacy well before the twentieth century. He described these as "movement and story, abstract form and pure expression, execution and pantomime (gesture)." In other words, dance as movement or dance as imitator. He remarked that "down to this day the balance between these two tendencies remains unstable."[67] This raises the question of what actually divides pantomime from choreographic gesture. It is Levinson who provides the best description in relation to antique dance:

> The technique of ballet creates a system of artificial movement, whose smallest details are foreordained, prescribing the amplitude of the various movements within definite limits, subject to its inherent logic and acting upon the "plane" of pure forms, without paying attention to the specific emotions of pantomime. Its mechanical and decorative canons are inalterable; it has evolved through two centuries of uninterrupted tradition. The antique dance does not present such homogeneity, the intrinsic law of dance is less evident. The Greek dance formed, above all, the gymnastic and rhythmic basis of the pantomime. The ballet, on the contrary, is pure dance and its spiritual content is expressed through the interplay of balanced lines and masses.[68]

Levinson is presenting an aesthetic debate that had circulated for some time in the art world. Art critic Clement Greenberg captured the new modern approach to painting that manifested itself at the turn of the twentieth century: "Realistic, illusionist art had dissembled the medium, using art to conceal art," while "modernism used art to call attention to art." He continues to explain that "the limitations that constitute the medium of painting – flat surface, the shape of the support, the properties of pigment – were treated by the Old Masters as negative factors that could be acknowledged only implicitly or indirectly" and that "modernist painting had come to regard these same limitations as positive factors that are to be acknowledged openly.[69] Painting became valued for its plastic or painterly qualities rather than its representative and illusionary three-dimensional space. Modernism revealed that the painterly tools of art were the fundamental substance of the artwork. The tensions between representational (i.e., expressing something beyond itself) and formal qualities also existed within modern ballet aesthetics.

Fokine, in contrast, believed that he was arguing for the right of creation in ballet. He argued that it was the subject matter that dictated the choreography (the correspondence of style of dancing and gestures with style of periods represented). In other words, he argued that dance was dictated by something outside of itself. Fokine did not consider that formal elements of the dance could attain symbolic and expressive qualities. He viewed the formal aspects of dance as void and as having no value in and of itself. He defined dance as natural expressiveness and human movement and argued that without gesture or symbolism dance would become mechanical and empty. Furthermore, he found classical traditional poses illogical and even ugly. Regarding classical ballet's "turned-out" technique, he wrote: "If we assume that each pose must be the reflection of our inner self, that each pose should convey a motion, and that each motion must contain meaning, it will be clearly apparent that movement of the legs to the sides are illogical, inexpressive and ugly."[70] He even declared that "the expressionless human body is either a corpse or a doll." Fokine attempted to relate his aesthetic of dance expression to that of landscape painting: "In landscape painting we search for the soul of the artist who created them, we do not accept a landscape painting that expresses nothing. How can we tolerate an expressionless human? Wherever there is a living body … there also should be spiritualization."[71] Of course, the real question in this aesthetic debate is whether a landscape painting can express nothing. In ballet, Fokine did not think that spiritual truths could manifest themselves within classical choreography: "What is a leg protruding to the side supposed to represent? It is not the beginning or the end of a movement, nor is it in the stage of its progress. Instead of expressing a movement, the entire body seems to search for balance, trying to find this balance despite the lifted leg. What kind of gesture is that?"[72] As the prophet of "Dance is Expression," Fokine believed that the formal aspects of dance played a secondary role. He once remarked, "The Dance is poetry without words … The Dance is *music* of bodily movement … The Dance is animated sculpture," indicating that dance was always the representation of something else.[73] André Levinson and Serge Lifar would have stated, "The Dance is the Dance."

Levinson's and Lifar's vision of ballet, as "Dance for Dance's Sake," was the exact opposite of Fokine's. They perceived ballet's "unnaturalness" as something that made it beautiful. They also located an inner life within ballet's formal elements, which dictated its expression and meaning. Levinson criticized Fokine for his failure to consider the choreographic autonomy of expression.[74] He based his criticism on a distinction between gesture of the theatre and choreographic artistry. Fokine, however, while pronouncing ballet's purpose as fundamentally expressive, believed fervently that movement and music were inseparable.[75] Lifar criticized Fokine's ballet aesthetic, writing that the "literary theme, settings, and music of Fokine's ballets, although affording the whole a great power of attraction, are also its weakness. According to him, Fokine has stifled dancing and reduced it to a state of slavery."[76] Both Levinson and Lifar proceeded to free dance by first dismantling its dependency on music. Lifar, in his *Manifeste du chorégraphie* (1935), proclaimed his new modern aesthetic of ballet in which dance was independent of music: "The first principle of the new ballet – independent of the other arts its sisters – is the ballet-dance; the ballet must be before anything else danceable and borrow its rhythms from nowhere but find them in its own divine essence." He enunciated that "any ballet whether musical or not *must arise* from its own origin *and not from music*."[77] Levinson also insisted that "classical dance, despite the way it bends so easily with the musical element, has an autonomous existence. It has no need to derive psychological or dynamic impulses from music. It draws directly from the same source that nourishes music as well: the human spirit."[78]

To answer Fokine's inquiry, "How can we tolerate an expressionless human? Wherever there is a body … there also should be spirituality," Levinson and Lifar stressed the capability of corporeal movement to embody spiritual expression. In this regard, it is interesting to compare the revolutionary ideas of painter and fellow Russian Wassily Kandinsky with those of Levinson and Lifar (insofar as we can compare a static art form and an art of movement). In a catalogue from a Guggenheim exhibition in 1911, critic Hilla Rebay outlined Kandinsky's revolutionary approach to painting:

> There is no representation of objects, nor any meaning of subjects in these paintings of free invention called non-objective art. They represent a unique world of their own, as creations with a lawful organization of colors, variation of forms, and rhythm of motif. These combinations when invented by a genius can bring the same joy, relaxation, elevation and animation of spiritual life as

> music … painting, like music, has nothing to do with reproduction of nature, nor interpretation of intellectual meanings … Non-objectivity has beauty and spirit combined … Non-objective art need not be understood or judged. It must be felt and it will influence those who have eyes for the loveliness of forms and colors.[79]

Whether Levinson and Lifar were heading towards a non-objective concept of dance is unlikely. However, the principles they put forth in their writings undoubtedly opened the door for later generations of choreographers. By stripping away dance's dependency on music and decor and by locating the beauty of the art within choreographic form and dance movement, they each, in their own way, echoed Kandinsky's vision that form could possess not only beauty, but also spirit. Levinson and, later, Lifar located spiritual truths in form and line, in elevation and balance in a similar way as Kandinsky found beauty and meaning within form, matter, and colour.

Although Diaghilev, Fokine, Levinson, and Lifar came from a similar Russian artistic and intellectual environment, they each embraced different perspectives on modern ballet aesthetics. In juxtaposing their dance writings, it is important to emphasize that they occupied different roles in the cultural milieu. Levinson, not being a choreographer or director, held a privileged position as a critic who had the ability to lay down the laws of ballet and establish a new "credo" without being dependent on an audience for his survival. His reputation as an intellectual gave his discussion of the ballet credibility. On the other end of the spectrum, Diaghilev as director/entrepreneur was certainly more interested and invested in what would attract audiences than taking up a cause for the art of dance – he left that up to his choreographer Fokine. It does appear that all figures seemed to fear that ballet might fall from its status as a high art form and be lost among all the other forms of dance that were on display in Paris in 1920s – thus their need to distinguish its aesthetic through principles (and even rules). These other dance forms included acrobatic dancers at the music halls, jazz dancing, German modern dance, the "free dance" of Loïe Fuller and Isadora Duncan, and tango dancing. Nevertheless, the financial success and extensive exposure of Diaghilev's company helped to elevate ballet's credibility as an art. Diaghilev/Fokine and Levinson/Lifar offered two ways of promoting ballet among the arts and increasing public awareness and understanding of ballet. Together, the Ballets Russes and the dance discourse that it generated greatly affected the way ballet was shaped and perceived across Europe, North America, and Australia. The popularity of the Ballets Russes, the efforts made by critics to promote and redefine ballet, and the new appreciation for dance forms and abstract art all paved the way for Serge Lifar to revitalize France's own Paris Opéra ballet. This leads us to ask how the French could embrace a modern style of ballet.

Levinson addressed this question by offering the French the possibility of reconciling ballet's past political and cultural associations with modern visions. In his criticism, Levinson attempted to convince the French (specifically Jacques Rouché, director of the Opéra in the 1920s) that they had nothing to be ashamed of as far as their "classic" dance tradition was concerned. He argued that it was possible to reconcile new and old styles of ballet – modernism with classical traditions. Levinson suggested that the French embrace a modern style of ballet, but one different from that of the Ballets Russes. In other words, he attempted to define a new type of modern ballet based on old and new components – a style which the French could claim as their own. Levinson's plea may have been an attempt to elevate French morale at the time by declaring that certain seeds of modernism existed in France, that there was nothing to envy in the Ballets Russes, and that it was unnecessary to emulate a foreign troupe.

Levinson was weary of the direction in which ballet was turning and felt that classical ballet technique and its aesthetic were deteriorating at the expense of innovation and novelty. He demonstrated this by juxtaposing Diaghilev's modern ballet with French "classic ballet." Levinson criticized Diaghilev for compromising the art of ballet by presenting it as a collaborative art form and, more so, as a spectacle. He accused Diaghilev of introducing elements extraneous to ballet in order to attract and please an audience. In fact, he went so far as to accuse Diaghilev as "selling out" dance. Levinson observed that by the 1920s, the Russian ballet of the Ballets Russes had become reduced to "a humble servant of the other arts which had united to dominate it" and that "in short, the Ballets Russes [was] no longer a light, but a reflection."[80] He complained frequently that he could hardly find any dancing at all within the Diaghilev productions. In regards to *Firebird*, he claimed that "the merits of this ballet lay completely outside the realm of choreography."[81] Likewise, Levinson criticized the Ballets Russes' production of *Petrushka* as degenerating all elements of the dance itself. "Petroushka," he wrote, "is not and does not pretend to be a ballet. The dance is at no time treated as an end in itself, but used rather as a means of psychological expression."[82] However, he assured his readers that French "classic ballet" would prevail: "Two formidable armies are leagued against the ballet – those who do not see and prefer to touch, to hear, to feel, and those who 'could' not if they would. But the classic ballet, strong in its tradition in accordance with the spirit of order and discipline which animates the elite of today, will triumph over this conspiracy of the blind and the paralytic, which I shall never cease to denounce."[83] Levinson powerfully attacked the productions of the Ballets Russes for their subordination of dance in its attempt to achieve artistic synthesis. In fact, he confronted the idea of a fusion of arts head on:

> If the history of art is the history of the gradual differentiation of the individual arts, then the dream of the primeval unity (brought to unprecedented heights through the endeavors of Richard Wagner, though not accomplished by him) is mainly an ailment of the contemporary theatre. In my view (and not only mine), such fusion, the creation of *Gesamtkunstwerk* which combines into a single endeavor the highest potentials of all the arts is only possible at a rudimentary stage in their development ... Experience has shown that striving for a synthetic coordination of the arts inevitably leads to the predominance of one and the subordination of the rest. The only surprising thing is that the characteristic feature of the new ballet is the subordination of the main element – dance – to pantomime, and to scenic design with Fokine and to music with Prince Volkonsky.[84]

Levinson implied that the French could embrace a new and more developed version of modern ballet aesthetics of their own while still honouring their own French tradition.

Levinson's argument rested on the claim that classical dance (originating in France) was not antithetical to modernism. "Opponents of classical dance technique," he wrote, "pretend to consider it an academic code, imposed on the dance arbitrarily by pedants and long since obsolete."[85] He insisted that the classical tradition of the Opéra ballet was compatible with modern artistic efforts. In his attempt to place classical ballet within a modern context, Levinson was resolute that dance held an autonomous status. He argued that ballet could be avant-garde and traditional, but insisted that it was the dance that needed to stand on its own.

The approach to dance criticism taken by critic and nationalist Louis Laloy is a good example of how Levinson's contemporaries were influenced by his writings and expertise. Reviewing in the 1920s, Laloy, who would have read Levinson's works on dance, increasingly made references to the art of movement in ballet. "At the Opéra the art of dancing may be termed as classical," he wrote. "It seeks beauty in perfect proportions, exact symmetry, with pure curves and well-defined figures, divesting the body of all sensual suggestion to the point of seeming to overcome the very laws of gravity, thus forming the ideal expression of a geometry dealing with time as well as space with the stage as the three dimensions and music as the measure of time."[86] In Laloy's article, we find a new consciousness of the body in time and space: time played out in the music, and space through bodily movement (choreography).[87]

Throughout his writings, Levinson passionately fought for the restoration of classical dance in France. He went to great lengths to teach the public how to understand movement of the body. Most impressive, however, is the fervour with which he directed the French to recognize the nationalist and expressive potential of their own art. Unfortunately, Levinson died in 1933 and never had the chance to see the revitalized Paris Opéra of Serge Lifar nor the founding of the first choreographic institute, the École Supérieure de la Danse in 1947. Although many dance scholars claim that he never fully developed his dance theory, one may argue that he established principles from which Serge Lifar (among others) drew. Interestingly, the last volume that Levinson ever wrote was a lengthy study of Serge Lifar.

With the development of a French national style the artistic legitimacy of ballet attained political significance. After Diaghilev's death in 1929, ballet entered a precarious yet fertile period due to the incredible growth in public enthusiasm for ballet. As the Ballets Russes disbanded, other troupes were formed in various cities, many employing the modern innovations of Diaghilev but some branching off in other directions. Like Ivan Clustine, interim director of the Opéra ballet from 1911 to 1914, another Russian émigré was given the task of directing the Opéra ballet: Serge Lifar. Lifar's legacy rests on his wide-ranging role as director, choreographer, dance historian, dance critic, and dancer. As dance historian, he endeavoured to educate the public on the artistry of ballet. As director of the Paris Opéra ballet, he managed to accomplish bureaucratic changes. Finally, as theorist and choreographer, he reformed "classic" ballet and instilled a new vitality to French ballet. By reworking the classic ballet of French ballet masters (such as Petipa) within the renaissance of dance that was transpiring in Paris at that time, Lifar cultivated a new taste for ballet, created an enduring French style, and redeemed the Paris Opéra ballet as an institution of French grandeur.[88]

In his capacity as dance historian and critic, Lifar provided the public with much-needed insight into the artistry of ballet, including its formal vocabulary, technicalities, and artistic function. He declared: "I should like to make theatre audiences familiar with the vocabulary of my art, its terminology and the analysis of its steps. Perhaps they will then realize all the importance of the dance and regard it with a more understanding and intelligent admiration."[89] His treatise-like book *Lifar on Classical Ballet* (1951) details the formal positions of French ballet, the names and descriptions of all its movements, and pointe work technique – all demonstrated through a series of sketches. The work is considered today one of the classics of ballet literature. The distinct French style of classical ballet that Lifar established at the Académie Nationale has endured for decades as have his choreographic works. In June 1942, Lifar proposed to the minister of national education, Abel Bonnard, the idea of establishing the first school of choreography in France. In highlighting that ballet had regained its status in Europe after decades in decline, he claimed that the Opéra ballet was in a vulnerable position. He asserted that is was crucial to found such a school to ensure that Paris remained the dance capital of the world. Furthermore, he argued that, as a "fully" naturalized Frenchman and the only *choréauteur* (choreographic specialist) in Paris, he would be the ideal candidate to direct such a school despite his foreign birth.[90] The École Supérieure de la Danse was founded in 1947 and inaugurated by Lifar. This was a dream come true for Lifar and a powerful symbol of ballet's triumph in France.

As we have seen, Serge Lifar managed to reform the Opéra in a variety of ways, especially bureaucratically and ideologically. Indeed he set a new standard for dance in France and, in doing so, was able to transform ballet dancing at the Opéra into a serious vocation. Because of Lifar, ballet would be presented for the first time at the Opéra as an independent program. Furthermore, the national ballet academy and ballet company would both reside within the Palais Garnier (Paris Opera House). While Lifar sought to implement many reforms at the Opéra, he was also very much aware of the potential already available at the Opéra and of the French tradition on which he could build. He recalled his surprise at finding among the dancers at the Opéra "a complete technical culture [technical virtuosity], extensive even in *la batterie* [the beating of the legs in the air] and *l'élévation* [the height of the dancer's leg or jump] – that Russian ballerinas generally neglect" and "a tendency towards a sort of unification of feminine dance and masculine dance."[91] He remarked in his autobiography that he discovered much talent at the Opéra, including dancers Olga Spessivtzeva and Suzanne Lorcia and young rising dancers Yvette Chauviré (age thirteen) and Mia Slavenska (age fourteen).[92]

Next, Lifar endeavoured to reform the art of ballet itself within the walls of the Opéra. However, this was not an easy task. In 1930, upon accepting his position as ballet director, Lifar attempted to organize an homage to Diaghilev's memory (in the tradition of the Ballets Russes in *Bacchus and Ariane)*, but he was ultimately unsuccessful in doing so. In his autobiography, *Ma Vie*, Lifar expressed vividly his difficulty in choosing a new direction for dance and his struggle to reconcile old classical ballet with new, modern creations:

> The critics had influenced me and rightly so, I realized perfectly well that if my ballets met with success they owed it to the dancer and not to the choreographer. My choreographic conceptions did not touch the audience enough. I had been brought up in the principles and ideology of the Ballets Russes and I began to see that this ideology, although not necessarily false, was, from many points of view, weak and above all never completely solved the problem. What, then, was to be done? Go back frankly to the good old classical ballet? But surely that would mean giving up all thought of new creations. I was at a cross-roads … old subscribers were demanding that I should leave the Opera "so as to prevent me from dealing a death-blow to the French ballet."[93]

The idea of presenting revivals of classical ballets came about due to the difficult economic conditions at the Opéra. After Jacques Rouché, manager of the Opéra, revealed to Lifar that he would have a tight budget for new ballets, Lifar cut the "modern" ballets except for those of Prokofiev and replaced them with modern revivals of classic ballets. He wrote: "Two solutions came into my mind: the purely classical, that is to say the great masterpieces of the repertory, or, again, the 'modern,' personal, daring, provocative ... I had not yet hit upon the third solution, the best, the only practical one ... I ... put aside all creations and proposed the revival of four remarkable ballets, four ethereal ballets – *Suite de Danses* by Khlustine, *Le Spectre de la Rose* by Fokine, *Giselle* and finally a Divertissement taken from *La Belle de Bois Dormant* by Petipa."[94] The revival series was a great success and symbolized the union of old and new. Lifar recorded that the success of *Giselle* made ballet history. He wrote, "Spessivtzeva's interpretation of the part of *Giselle* was, in my opinion, the absolute perfection of choreographic art." *Giselle* had revealed to him "spiritual liberation through the Dance," and "a new horizon, a fresh path" that he was to follow for later creations. "Diaghilevism," he writes, "had been left behind," and a new classicism would benefit by "experiences undergone and lessons learned."[95] One well-known critic asserted proudly, "France gave Petipa to Russia, and now Russia has given Lifar to France."[96]

Ultimately, Lifar realized that he had to reconcile his experience working under Diaghilev with new modern visions of French ballet. Eventually, he found he had no choice but to abandon Diaghilevism altogether. He wrote, "Diaghilevism kept as it was could no longer really nourish the Dance, and Expressionism could do that still less. I realised that a great aesthetic battle was engaged against this latter, not for my personal reasons or those of the Paris Opera, but for the Dance itself, for its future, for its history, it was essential to fight against Expressionism, which was no doubt rich enough in theatrical qualities, but which, because of the easy solutions that assailed it, was fatal for the essence of choreography."[97] Lifar believed that Diaghilevism was "fatal" to classical choreography because it reduced choreography to a subordinate position to music. He remarked in his book *La danse* (also appearing, in part, as an article in *La Revue Musical* in 1938) that he "desir[ed] to liberate dance from the gilded cage where music had for a long time held it captive."[98] In noting

Lifar's determination to be the saviour of French dance, biographers stress his commitment to prove that dance could be divorced from music.[99]

Lifar was successful in implementing a style based on a reconciliation of classical and modern approaches to ballet. He found a way to commemorate classical ballet tradition (eighteenth- and early nineteenth-century French ballet) through its reinterpretation as a modern, autonomous art form. This reinterpretation allowed the French to celebrate both tradition and innovation. Tradition was celebrated by honouring classic ballet's origins in France, specifically, Vestris's and Noverre's reforms; and innovation by adopting the technical and expressive developments of Petipa and, later, Fokine. Thus Lifar combined the strict technical vocabulary of French academic tradition with a modified version of the experimental style to which he was exposed as a member of the Ballets Russes. However, he stressed that classical ballet was truly French not Russian. "Classical dance is not and was never 'Ballets Russes,'" he adamantly claimed. "Classical [ballet] was born in France, it developed in Italy, and was only *conserved* in Russia."[100]

Lifar developed a modern classical ballet that was grounded in a neoclassical style and in the idea of dance as autonomous. In doing so, he created a long-lasting association between neoclassicism, Frenchness, and technical virtuosity (all of which held gendered associations). He stated in his autobiography, "I have embarked upon a reform of movement and of dance technique that one calls neoclassical."[101] Lifar's ballet *Icare* (Icarus) served as a platform upon which to explore a modern neoclassical style. In *Icare*, Lifar managed to capture dramatic and poetic expression through formal aesthetics and to legitimize dance's autonomy as an art form.

> It was in Greece I realised that the Dance, Man's flight, should convey in plastic form his highest aspirations and that it should suffice to imitate them, to magnify them, that is to say that the Dance must become once more what it was essentially and originally, an independent art, perhaps the first of all the arts. To illustrate these truths what better theme could be found than that of Icarus, if the classical mode of expression could be rediscovered and if it were adapted to celebrate the efforts made by the Icaruses of our days and of always, to know and to discover.[102]

Lifar's new French style was rooted not only in neoclassicism, but also in choreographic aesthetics that united old and new ballet. For example, according to Lifar, his ballet *Créatures de Promethée* encompassed the tendencies of Diaghilev in the dramatic role of Prometheus and the French academic tradition of using a large corps de ballet. Later in his career, he described the differences between Russian (then Soviet) and French ballet style: the former was modernism informed by realism, folklore, and sport, and the latter expressed through symbols and by the style and emotional language of steps and lines.[103] Here we can see that different national cultures were embracing modernism in ballet along distinct lines.

Lifar's *Manifeste du chorégraphie* (1935) offers the clearest delineation of Lifar's theoretical conception of French ballet.[104] Lifar recalled: "I wanted to express ideas on my art, the Dance, which went beyond the anecdotal. I was sure that the future of the Dance lay in the direction of the neoclassicism that I was engaged in revealing. I wanted to proclaim this loudly and distinctly."[105] Lifar's *Manifeste* put forth the radical argument that ballet needed to be freed from its dependency on music. "My object, while proclaiming a new aesthetic, was to defend the independence of the Dance from music," he wrote. He outlined his principle: "My principle was defined in a very simple formula. Rhythm forms the link between music and dancing, but everything that is rhythmical is not necessarily danceable. We cannot with our bodies express just any kind of musical measure. But on to rhythm music can be grafted. It is therefore up to the musician to submit. He must compose in collaboration with the choreographer. Thus the work produced in common must gain in homogeneity." He concluded: "In a word, I proclaimed in my *Manifeste* that for a ballet, the Dance must have the first word and the last."[106] One reviewer opened his article in *La Revue Musicale* by stating that Lifar's *Manifeste du chorégraphie* was the "cry of revolt of a choreographer against the tyranny of the musician."[107]

In his *Manifeste*, Lifar asserted that the legitimacy of ballet rested on being "freed from all musical accompaniment." He based his argument on the revolutionary claim that rhythm was inseparable from the dance and, in fact, originated in its own divine essence.[108] He explained the process by which dance was able to manifest its own bodily rhythm independent from music, articulating that "the thematic of sound must henceforth yield to a corporal thematic gesture and movement which will give rise to an imaginary melody."[109] Thus he proclaimed that "musical rhythm derives from dancing rhythm" (*le rythme musical est né du rythme dansant*) – the exact opposite of Fokine's principles of dance. Additionally, he contended that rhythmic dance existed in a variety of cultures, including Bohemian tambourine dances, Spanish castanet dancing, czardas dancing, and Russian popular dance.[110] In other words, Lifar emphasized that even within national and folk dancing, there existed a natural and autonomous dance rhythm.

Lifar demonstrated this capacity of dance to be independent from music in his ballet *Icare* (1935). *Icare* was particularly original in that it was produced first without music – that is, the score came after its creation. The melody would manifest itself first within corporeal movements. Arthur Honneger then composed a score that comprised an ensemble of percussion instruments. In his article entitled "For or Against Choreographic Autonomy," published in *La Revue Musicale*, art critic André Boll recalled his own experience of *Icare*, writing that Lifar was a "liberated dancer" who "conceiv[ed] a choreography of real interest, with two or three moments of physical beauty." He described the music as "purely rhythmic" and a "music of organized sounds" created "skillfully by Szyfer."[111] According to Lifar, the ballet received six curtain calls, an unprecedented event in the history of the Opéra. He reported that "from the very next day discussions began in the artistic world which had been aroused by an intuition that a capital aesthetic revolution had taken place." In fact, the newspaper *Comœdia* responded by publishing an article entitled "Can Ballet Exist without Music?" Clearly, Lifar had startled both dance and music figures in suggesting that music should be composed after the choreography, and this article sparked a lively debate among them. Lifar recalled that a "number of very eminent persons gave their opinions – which were often rather wide off the mark." He noted that the matter was discussed by art patrons, especially Marie-Louise Bousquet. Bousquet as well as Anna de Noailles were both major patrons of the ballet. Each ran renowned salons that attracted the intellectual, literary, and artistic elite of the day as well as promising young artists.[112] Eventually, Lifar went on to give lectures on the subject of dance and music at the Sorbonne. He later published an article entitled "La danse et la musique" in *La Revue Musicale* in March 1938.

However, it was also on a technical level that Lifar needed to liberate the dance and to reform ballet at the Paris Opéra. "In the name of Dance I had won a victory," he remarked. "Now I had to consolidate its effects in a practical manner. And this meant facing up to the old problem: how to obtain recognition, in effect, of the Dance's autonomy as an art."[113] Lifar began by introducing evenings at the Opéra devoted solely to the ballet. He had hoped that it would establish the ballet as an autonomous art and at the same time give the Opéra a public of ballet lovers.[114] Lifar admits that he then "had to deal with the Dance itself; that is to say [I] had to train male and female dancers who would be able henceforth to display not only their physical efforts and their technique but also grace."[115] He recalled that dancers Suzanne Lorcia and Serge Peretti were the first dancers who permitted him to apply his choreographic reforms at the Académie Nationale de Musique et de Danse.[116] Lifar argued that inner rhythm or musicality must exist within the dancer and that it was not the music that the dancer followed, but rather "the rhythm that has been communicated to him by the dance." He noted that dancers Anna Pavlova and Olga Spessivteva possessed an extraordinary musicality, but one which "was, so to speak, not musical, but danceable" (*dansante*). He explained this by claiming that "the dancer always lands a little earlier than the music." He pronounced his strict laws of dance – laws that would become the epitome of modern French ballet technique. He wrote, "The dance is not a theme, but a symphony; it complies with special and very strict laws; it has its subtonic chords, its major and its minor, its modulation and its orchestration; briefly, its theory, which has not yet been formulated, but which we are convinced will be formulated some day."[117] Lifar created special studies for the adage (the instruction on partnering) – now a signature element of Paris Opéra ballet training. He also introduced Tchaikovsky into the Opéra repertory. Lifar recalled that the French musicians at the Opéra objected to Tchaikovsky because he was Russian and claimed that "they had their Massenet and that he was good enough for them."[118] This reveals the French fear that Russian music (even Tchaikovsky, who was seen as less "Russian") would corrupt French ballet.

Lifar perceived dance as the most expressive, most communicative, most accessible, and most universal of all the arts.[119] Ultimately, Lifar managed to charge formal qualities of dance with the power of expression. His neoclassical style put pure dance into place and created a new, modern French technique of dancing (figures 5.1 and 5.2). Most fascinating is the extraordinary range of his choreographic works that went from intensely expressive to nearly abstract (*Istar, Aeneas, Les créatures de Promethée*). Lifar wrote later in 1965: "Today, French ballet serves as the guardian of traditions, but has never been afraid of innovations and now proves it once again by the choice of its repertory, where *Giselle* is paired with *Icare*."[120] In redefining ballet as an autonomous and versatile modern art form, Lifar also reinvented the position and function of the choreographer – which he retitled as "*le choréauteur*." He often expressed the challenges in dealing with dance as an art form due to the ephemeral nature of the art. He complained once that "it was impossible to convey dance's emotional tenor, philosophy, and metaphysics" because of the "lack of suitable means of notation, inadequacies of cinematography, etc … No other art, indeed, demands such an epitome of knowledge."[121] He contrasted this with the eighteenth-century saying "as stupid as a dancer," which referred to the idea that a choreographer lacked any culture.[122]

Lifar's laborious efforts to raise the standards of dancing at the Opéra ballet had paid off by 1940, when his new French ballets received unprecedented acclaim among critics and Opéra audiences. In their reviews, critics praised Lifar's efforts to enhance the prestige of France via the Opéra ballet. The centenary performances of *Giselle* in 1932 and *Sylvia* in 1941 (both restaged by Lifar) were both used to commemorate the fiftieth anniversary of the death of the celebrated French composer Léo Delibes, who had originally composed the music for *Coppélia* in 1870 and *Sylvia* in 1876.[123] This nationalist homage to the French ballet composer and to ballets produced in the early years of the Third Republic elicited accolades from the press. Lifar's new ballet, *Le chevalier et la demoiselle,* also resulted in favourable reviews. A few years later, a writer from *La Chronique de Paris* observed that by then there was less attraction to the "religion of choreographic liberty" of Isadora Duncan and more fascination for the expressive potential of technical skill.[124] In 1941, French composer Arthur Hoérée declared, "Few theatres from around the world can pride themselves on a choreographic repertoire this vast and varied, on a school of dance so well trained and so rich in major works." He continued: "In this passing of the torch, one has to admit that Serge

Lifar has carried the flame entrusted to him higher and further than any other, at a more pressing rate and with the fervour of a priest."[125] From statements such as these, we can clearly see that by 1940 Lifar had restored French grandeur to the Paris Opéra ballet and successfully cultivated an appreciation for ballet's choreographic autonomy and technical skill.

In addition to reviving classical ballet at the Opéra and staging over fifty ballets for the company, Lifar desired to cultivate a more informed and discriminative ballet audience for the Opéra ballet company. In his capacity as dance theorist and ballet historian, he made extraordinary efforts to educate the public on ballet. In 1935, he published his *Manifeste du chorégraphie.* In 1938, he published two books on ballet, *La danse: Les grand courants de la danse académique,* and *Ballet: Traditional to Modern.* In the 1940s, more studies on ballet were published in France, including *Serge Diaghilev, His Life, His Works, His Legend* (London, 1940), *Serge Lifar à l'Opéra* (1943), and *Pensées sur la danse* (1946), and, in the 1950s, works such as *Lifar on Classical Dance* (1951), *Traité de chorégraphie* (1952), *Le livre de la danse* (1954); *Les trois Grâces du XX siècle: Légends et vérité* (1957), and *Au service de la danse: À la recherché d'une science: Chorélogie* (1958). In the 1960s, he wrote *La danse: La danse académique et l'art chorégraphique* (1965), and *Histoire du ballet* (1966). He published his autobiography *Ma Vie* in 1965 (trans. 1970). His writings on ballet contributed to the survival of ballet, attracted a new generation of ballet enthusiasts, and fostered a new type of admiration for the art.

In the preceding pages, we have traced the ways in which ballet made its way back into the French artistic scene. By embracing a modernist reinterpretation of ballet as pure form, the French were able to redefine ballet as quintessentially French and as an emblem of republican political expression. The next two chapters examine how attitudes towards the body in ballet changed so that a conception of French ballet as grounded in its formal aspects (such as technical skill and the beauty of form and line) became possible. Within the debates over ballet's function and status as an art, anxieties surfaced about gender boundaries and the use of the body (male and female) as the central mode of expressivity. As we will see, ballet served as a platform upon which to renegotiate gender norms, artistic professionalism, and attitudes towards corporeality.

Figure 5.1 Published in a 1947 photography collection featuring ballet dancers by French photographer Serge Lido, this image captures the modern neoclassical style of French ballet that Lifar developed and officially enshrined at the Paris Opéra ballet and the formalist principles that Levinson promoted in his criticism. Dancers: Ludmilla Tcherina and Edmond Audran.

Figure 5.2 From the 1947 Lido collection, dancers Colette Marchand and Serge Perrault in *Plain-chant*, choreographed by Serge Lifar for the Paris Opéra ballet in 1943 and inspired by the Jean Cocteau poem of the same name.

6

The Return of the Male Dancer

I was to dance opposite Jean Babilée [Paris Opera dancer], the greatest dancer since Nijinsky and before Nureyev and Baryshnikov.

– Leslie Caron, Paris 2005[1]

With the help of Russian émigrés André Levinson and Serge Lifar, the French reclaimed ballet as their own through the transfiguration of an aesthetic, focusing on technical virtuosity and corporeal form and fusing tradition with innovation. This modern aesthetic of ballet was embraced by the French as the defining feature of its national ballet company, the Paris Opéra ballet. However, the quest to create a national style of ballet and to elevate its reputation in France entailed a renegotiation of gender and the body in ballet. As we will see, changing notions concerning gender identity and the body, particularly during the interwar years, helped to reshape perceptions about ballet and its dancers, and created an appreciation for corporeal beauty and technical skill. By examining ballet commentary in respectable bourgeois journals, we can see how gender and body politics played an integral role in elevating the status of ballet and transforming it into a vessel for the display of French cultural pre-eminence.

Once again, the Ballets Russes played a key role in renegotiating the body in ballet performance and reworking its gender dynamics. The company's innovations in ballet production changed the way ballet dancers were presented, and these images were disseminated through new strategies of ballet marketing. The enormous publicity for the Ballets Russes undertaken by Gabriel Astruc promoted particular images of and notions about ballet dancers as well as the profession itself. Karsavina, Nijinsky, Rubinstein, Massine, and Lifar all became symbols of glamour and excited public adoration. Their names and photographs were featured daily in social columns, the press, and glamour magazines not only in France but across the globe as they gained international stardom (not unlike theatre actors). Their personalities inspired photographers, filmmakers, and early documentarians as well as authors of teenage fiction. Stars such as Anna Pavlova, Tamara Karsavina, and Vaslav Nijinsky acquired fame and wealth in the early twentieth century. Thus the profession of the ballet dancer now offered the potential for economic independence, artistic/creative expression, an education, international travel, community, and even stardom.[2]

The Ballets Russes' alternative representations of ballet and ballet dancers stimulated much discussion among critics and intellectuals over men and women's roles in ballet as well as about the nature of ballet. One key innovation of the Ballets Russes was the central role that men played in its productions. Rather than occupying the stage as mere accessories to female dancers (as Parisian audiences expected), the Ballets Russes' male dancers took on dynamic, autonomous, and important roles in ballet production. As French composer and critic Émile Vuillemoz remarked, "Masculine dance was brought to our eyes, alive and exalted."[3] Principal dancer and choreographer Vaslav Nijinsky enraptured Parisian audiences and gained a heroic and cult-like status.[4] Moreover, his technical virtuosity and extraordinary talents of dramatic expression raised the standards of male dancing in ballet.

Why were audiences and critics so taken with the male dancers of the Ballets Russes? To what extent was this re-emergence of the male body onto the ballet stage a disruptive cultural force in early twentieth-century France? In other words, what was the cultural climate that allowed for the acceptance of and even reverence for its male dancers? While the Ballets Russes' new focus on male dancing incited much praise and admiration among critics, it is important to remember that it was a foreign troupe and thus displayed "foreign" male bodies on stage. How did the French negotiate the role of their French male dancers on the national ballet stage? How did the male dancer rise from being a mere support for the female ballerina to a dancer in his own right? Undeniably, the reinforcement of masculine norms played an important part in natonal identity. To what extent did critics refashion the images of the male dancer in their attempt to re-establish ballet as a legitimate modern art form in France that could personify French grandeur? As we will see, the male dancer was re-embraced by French society for a variety of reasons including: critical discussion on male ballet dancing by artists, writers, music, and dance critics; the Ballets Russes and the new images of male dancers it brought forth; new attitudes towards masculinity, masculine beauty, and athleticism in French culture; the formation of exclusively male dance classes at the Opéra; and the development of "masculine" technical movements (the gendering of choreography).[5]

When the Ballets Russes arrived in Paris, notions about masculinity and femininity were unstable and the source of much anxiety in France. The defeat of the French by Germany in the Franco-Prussian War had prompted concerns about French masculinity and manliness while the feminist movement provoked fears of depopulation and immorality. Both simulated fears of national degeneration. Discourse in major bourgeois newspapers served as a key site in which to express French attitudes toward male dancers, masculinity, and male corporeality. The rhetoric connected ballet and French ideologies by exploring the ways that ballet reflected, reinforced, and/or challenged French cultural values and norms. In other words, critical responses to male ballet dancers were shaped by the shifting notions of Frenchness, gender, and bodies on display that were occurring in early twentieth-century France. As we will see, after the arrival of the Ballets Russes in 1909, critics attempted to revive the reputation of male dancers and to adorn them with a new vitality, athleticism, and purpose. By analyzing the professionalization of the male dancer, we can then attempt to explain why and how critics reconceptualized the female dancer.

DANCE, MASCULINITY, CORPOREALITY

It is important to consider first the historic role of men in ballet, the attributes that were attached to them, and why male dancers lost their legitimacy on the French national stage. The conception of male dancers evolved with shifts in French values concerning, masculinity, dance, display, and corporeality. Under Louis XIV, the arts, particularly dancing, played a central role in elite French society. Louis XIV asserted: "The Art of Dance has always been ... one of the most advantageous and useful to our nobility ... not only in the times of war in our armies, but also in times of peace in the entertainment of our ballets."[6] Here Louis XIV refers to the usefulness of dance as an exercise to stengthen the body, create coordination, and build stamina for battle. For example, military drills entailed a great deal of "choreography" and required soldiers to move together as one body much like a corp de ballet. In fact, fencing and dancing masters were often the same person. Louis XIV's statement captured the link between masculinity, nobility, and physical fortitude in seventeenth-century France. Military men were predominately noblemen whose masculinity was defined as "tall because of a good diet," "strong from military exercise and riding on horseback," and "trimmed by dance."[7] The aristocratic male body was one that was physically distinguishable through training in these two disciplines: military exercise and dance. Noblemen learned to "coordinate their movements with one another to serve collective ends." As Chandra Mukerji reveals, books on military strategy and dance "showed readers how to fight or dance *together.* The dancers or soldiers were not supposed to be just trained individuals, but formed members of a group that could act as a political force, whether showing grace in a public ballet or prowess in battle."[8] Mukerji reveals that books of the period rendered the formations of dances and military strategies in similar ways by "order[ing] the bodies of aristocratic men into politically meaningful forms" that signified their place in court and military life.[9] In other words, there existed an aristocratic model of bodily discipline, and those who excelled in forms of discipline, such as military training and court dancing, were socially rewarded.

It is not surprising then to find that Louis XIV as a "warrior king" was also an accomplished dancer.[10] In 1655, Louis XIV danced his first solo, "Le génie de la danse" (The Spirit of the Dance), in the *Ballet des plaisirs,* a ballet choreographed by Pierre Beauchamps and performed before the court. Louis XIV's dancing was described by observers as "unique," "ravissant," and "parfait" in regards not only to his noble carriage, but also to his grace and technique. In this period, a language of ballet developed to judge the quality of ballet dancing and to measure nobility itself. A specific rhetoric of dance emerged: terms such as "grâce," "ravissant," "élan," "ballon," and "volonté." The use of these terms endured, acquiring new associations and symbolic meanings throughout the years. In fact, they remain as markers of professionalism and virtuosity today. In the seventeenth century, the attribute of "grace" referred specifically to the "noble grace" of aristocratic men. Young men flocked to dancing masters to perfect their stylized ballet footwork, learn popular social dances, and study deportment. Reportedly, there were over two hundred dancing schools in Paris aimed at training young noblemen to dance gracefully.[11] This indicates that knowing how to dance well was vital to a nobleman's success at court. The way in which one carried oneself or, put more simply, one's posture or deportment in dancing became one of the key signifiers of noble status. In the privileged world of the French court, power was signified not only in one's entitlements to entertainment, but also in the ability to produce entertainments.[12] Court ballet functioned to glorify the state (and thus Louis XIV) and to entertain and define the French elite. In court ballet, the male body on display served as an indication of the power, privilege, and pleasure of elite men.

However, traditional notions of dance and social status soon shifted when it came to ballet dancing.[13] In 1661, six years after performing his first ballet solo, Louis XIV established the first of his many academies, the Académie Royale de Danse, whose function was to perfect ballet dancing and to offer public performances on the Paris Opéra stage. The Académie initially consisted only of men. At this time, "natural grace" changed from being the exclusive possession of the aristocracy into something that could be taught to male commoners. As scholar Sarah Cohen notes, the ballet master and commoner Pierre Beauchamps stood in for King Louis XIV himself in the ballet *Plaisirs de l'île enchantée* (1664) and "he and many of his colleagues were already performing the *danse noble* with a virtuosity unmatched by any members of the court."[14] The dancers trained at the Académie Royale de Danse were able to replicate the grace of the king and the spectacle of the court on the public stage and, in doing so, "carried ... the appeal of the aristocratic body, whose 'natural grace' now appeared all the more alluring through the virtuosity of its performers."[15] This is significant for several reasons. First, we can locate an early notion of the "professional body" through the skilful embodiment of "grace" by trained dancers; grace thereafter became the measure of a dancer's virtuosity. Second, we find the attribute of "grace" being related not only to class (i.e., aristocratic virtue), but also to gender (i.e., masculinity). For example, the minimal footwork established in the school of Louis XIV was considered masculine even when a few women joined the ballet in the late eighteenth century. Lastly, the ability of trained commoners to replicate the aristocratic virtue of grace signified broader shifts in eighteenth-century society concerning privilege and rank. As Cohen point out, this was a time when nobility was increasingly developing into "a commercial product" and "a marketable aesthetic."[16] Literally, wealthy members of the bourgeosie (i.e., commoners of the Third Estate) purchased titles and thus became members of the Second Estate.

The institutionalization of ballet and its move from the court into the theatre transformed the significance of the body in ballet dancing as dancers were no longer members of the nobility. The execution of bodily grace changed in function from one that intrinsically defined noble status to one that represented a version of it. The dancing male body lost its social function as an exhibition of noble identity and physical distinction. Instead, it became a signifier of the aristocratic body. However, during the eighteenth century, the aristocracy became increasingly attacked for its lack of virtue (i.e., as decadent, frivolous, corrupting, and effeminate). The decorative display of bodies in ballet dancing also came under attack. As we have seen, Enlightenment figures were less impressed with technical skill and more interested in ballet's potential for dramatic expression. Rousseau boldly asserted that "all ballet that is just dancing should be banished from lyric theatre" because it imitated nothing.[17] In other words, the ballet dancing body's association with the "corrupt" aristocracy became problematic and needed to be reconfigured if ballet was to survive. The reforms of dancer and choreographer Jean-Georges Noverre echo Rousseau's assertion. In 1760, he urged his fellow dancers to abandon *entrechats*, *cabrioles*, and complicated steps (e.g., *tours de force*), which he considered to be meaningless and mere displays of technical virtuosity.[18] Noverre's "ballet d'action" emphasized plot structure, dramatic expression, pantomime, and natural movements.[19]

Attempts to heighten moral standards that seemed corrupted by the decadence of the ancien régime surfaced in discourse on aesthetics. In painting, new ideals of masculinity were articulated through neoclassicism. In opposition to the whimsical rococo style, neoclassicism embraced the classical motifs and the values of order, civic virtue, balance, and harmony.[20] Rather than depicting playful scenes of aristocratic leisure and amorous pursuits, neoclassical subjects turned to classical and Roman content and form to pronounce heroism, civic loyalty, patriotic sacrifice, courage, and later brotherhood.[21] The male body, modelled after the classical body, came to signify all these things. Male bodies were depicted in heroic terms within a narrative context, rendered in ideal classical forms, and showcased publicly as an emblem of civic virtue and patriotism. Yet, a hegemonic masculinity rarely existed. As art history studies have revealed, at least two varieties of masculinity existed in the late eighteenth century. Studies of high art of the 1790s have identified feminized images of male beauty, intended for the male viewer, at the same moment when a virile and fraternal version of nationalism was being forged. Thomas Crow, for example, has pointed out how late eighteenth-century artists were "asked to not only envisage military and civic virtue in traditionally masculine terms, but were compelled to imagine the entire spectrum of desirable human qualities, from battlefield heroics to eroticized corporeal beauty as male."[22]

These new images of male corporeality were manifested not only in art and sculpture, but also in theatre and opera/ballet. The reading of corporeality in ballet shifted from one that rested on the formal execution of steps and its socio-political signification to one that was primarily expressive and capable of capturing a variety of metaphorical meanings. French ballet not only survived but was revered internationally for its pre-eminence. Two male Opéra dancers, Gaétan Vestris (1729–1808) and his son Auguste (1760–1842), became well known for their virtuosity and profound expressivity. Taking on classical and heroic roles, Gaétan Vestris was heralded as "L'Apollon" and "Le dieu de la danse" (God of the Dance). Auguste Vestris also gained international renown for his talents: his first appearance in London in 1780 was enthusiastically welcomed. British politician and writer Horace Walpole wrote in a letter in December 1780: "The theatre was brimful in expectation of Vestris. At the end of the second act he appeared; but with so much grace, agility, and strength, that the whole audience fell into convulsions of applause; the men thundered; the ladies, forgetting their delicacy and weakness, clapped with such vehemence, that seventeen broke their arms, sixty-nine sprained their wrists, and three cried Bravo! bravissimo! so rashly, that they have not been able to utter so much as *no* since, any more than both Houses of Parliament."[23] However exaggerated Walpole's account may be, it is clear that Vestris represented the "exquisite perfection" that made France known internationally for its ballet and its virtuosic male ballet dancers.[24]

Men's presence on the ballet stage became increasingly problematic over the course of the nineteenth century when technical skill in ballet was emphasized and developed further. In France, the modernization of ideas about the body had eroded older notions in Greek and humanist thought that idealized the body. Masculinity was increasingly associated with the mind, the intellect, and civilized society, and disassociated from the body. Physical fitness and physical education were discouraged as "unthinking activities" and intellectual pursuits were encouraged. Auguste Vestris's "athletic virtuosity" was criticized by Noverre, who wrote, "Young people proclaim [him] a miracle; people of sense and taste are content to sigh with disappointment." French critic Julien-Louis Geoffroy wrote in 1804 that Vestris's athleticism had "lower[ed] the art" and degenerated it into "circus acrobatics."[25] Critics abroad noted that Vestris had "unluckily directed [his] attention to an inferior branch of the art, the rapid execution of steps" and had not attempted to possess "something sentimental that appeal[ed] to the mind as well as the eye."[26] Once a signifier of heroism and civic virtue, the male body lost its value over the course of the nineteenth century as corporeality became almost exclusively associated with femininity and decadence. In fact, in the early nineteenth century, the image of the male nude began to disappear from painting and sculpture. The male body no longer had a public presence and no longer represented neoclassical elements of civic order, heroism, masculinity, and nobility.[27] As art historian Margaret Walters points out, before the nineteenth century "the male nude [had] carried a much wider range of meanings, political, religious, and moral, than the female … the male nude is typically public: he strides through the city squares, guards public buildings, is worshipped in the church. He personifies communal pride and aspiration." Walters explains that "few artists brought a new romantic energy to the classic male nude" in the Romantic era and, when they did, it was in the image of "the defeated rebel, the victim, the outcast."[28] Modern attitudes about the body and gender brought about a situation in which it seemed "unnatural" to look at the male body and "problematic" for men to enjoy looking at men dancing.

As Judith Surkis points out, during the July Monarchy, popular imagery implicitly "targeted … men's corporeality as a powerful symbol of political illegitimacy." The attack on men's corporeality was linked to the corruption of the monarchy and the "illegitimacy of the law."[29] Men could not be reduced to the corporeal body, and, when they were, it was more often as an object of scorn. For example, King Louis-Philippe was routinely satirized through the depiction of his body as "deformed," "hybrid," "impotent," and "monstrous" (not unlike Louis XVI during the French Revolution).[30] Surkis also illustrates the ways in which public dancing under the July Monarchy was regulated and strict boundaries were set for men. "Vigorous dances were out of line with the moves sanctioned by 'the law,'" she writes. Not only did male corporeality and dance movement lose their virtuous classical associations, but they also lost their capacity for public display. After 1848, Surkis writes, "men's bodies needed to become publicly invisible and in a sense, private."[31]

In this condition, the male dancer was no longer desired as he was no longer perceived as capable of embodying classical heroic form or of meeting the new tastes of ballet audiences, which became increasingly male. By the mid-nineteenth century, ballet had become unique as an art in that it was a profession in which men were degraded. Romanticism did not allow for a "real" male upon the dance stage, but did permit the female who epitomized mystery, metaphor, investigation.[32] In the nineteenth century, the ballet became an ideal feminine space in which the body of the ballerina (ideologically and figuratively) came to represent "poetry, loss, grief, beauty, desire, eroticism."[33] It is at this time that we find "grace" attached to a highly feminized, ethereal notion of beauty represented by the dancer on pointe. "Grace" became the domain of women.

As a result of this shift in body politics on the ballet stage, the topic of the male dancer was a common subject for critics in the nineteenth century. Some revealed their contempt for the male dancer and went to great lengths to demonstrate how ballet was more suited for females. Writing in the later part of the nineteenth century, French novelist, poet, and celebrated champion of ballet Théophile Gautier was infamous for his contempt for the male dancer. According to Gautier, the male dancer's athleticism made him "abominable." "Nothing is indeed more abominable," he wrote, "than a man displaying his red neck, his thick muscular arms, and legs with calves like a parish beadle's, while his whole heavy virile frame shudders with his leaps and pirouettes."[34] The implication here is not only that the male dancer did not fit within the Romantic aesthetic, but that he symbolized moral degeneracy and the "rude power of the working classes."[35] Gautier asserted that "for us the male dancer is something monstrous and indecent of which we cannot conceive." We even find images portraying the male ballet dancer as half-human, half-monster (fig. 6.1). Several others agreed with Gautier that ballet was more suited for women and male dancing was repugnant. Renowned critic Jules Janin, who was an important ballet reviewer in the 1840s, wrote that "the grand danseur appears to us so sad and so heavy! He is so unhappy and so self-satisfied! He responds to nothing, he represents nothing, he is nothing." Janin continued:

> Speak to us of a pretty dancing girl who displays the grace of her features and the elegance of her figure, who reveals so fleetingly all the treasures of her beauty. Thank God, I understand that perfectly, I know what this lovely creature wishes us, and I would willingly follow her wherever she wishes in the sweet land of love. But a man, a frightful man, as ugly as you and I ... that this fellow should dance as a woman does – impossible! ... That this bewhiskered individual who is the pillar of the community, an elector, a municipal councilor, a man whose business it is to make and above all unmake laws, should come before us in a tunic of sky-blue satin, his head covered with a hat with a waving plume amorously caressing his cheek, a frightful *danseuse* of the male sex, come to pirouette in the best place while the pretty ballet girls stand respectfully at a distance – this was surely impossible and intolerable, and we have done well to remove such great artists from our pleasures ... Today the dancing man is no longer tolerated except as a useful accessory.[36]

In such writings, we can see how the male dancer in ballet was perceived not only as dangerously effeminate and clumsy, but also as contaminating and disruptive. Men or rather masculine identity belonged in a different public realm. By the end of the nineteenth century, men all but disappeared from the ballet stage and were replaced by female travesty dancers, women who danced male roles. Audiences became almost exclusively male and ballet descended into severe decline. Furthermore, a "stigma of emasculation" was attached to men who chose to make a career of ballet. Ballets Russes

Figure 6.1 "The most displeasing aspect of a female dancer is that she sometimes brings along a male dancer." This caricature illustrates the new prejudices against the male dancer that developed in the nineteenth century. The male dancer is satirized by being given a grotesque face and is portrayed as trying to upstage the ballerina: the male figure is on pointe with the woman acting as a support.

collaborator Alexandre Benois as a Russian observer noted in his diary, "By the end of the 19th-century, the sect of balletomanes and 'le tout Paris' in general regarded male dancing as something degrading."[37] How did the male dancer rise again in France?

THE BALLETS RUSSES AND THE MALE DANCER

The first Ballets Russes performance in Paris on 19 May 1909 consisted of a program of three very different styles of ballet. In addition to the one-act *Le pavillion d'Armide* (an homage to seventeenth-century Versailles culture) and *Le festin* (a mélange of various classical ballets), Diaghilev presented *Prince Igor* (also called *Polovtsian Dances*), a ballet divertissement from Borodin's opera of the same name. *Le pavillion d'Armide* and *Le festin* were both recognizable as traditional classical ballets, but *Prince Igor* offered something very different. In this production (among others), the Ballets Russes presented the male dancer in a new way, now as a muscular, athletic, and "virile" male. It also highlighted ensembles of male dancers rather than the traditional corps of female dancers.

One of the first Ballets Russes productions presented to the Parisian public, the ballet instigated much critical discussion over the role of men in modern ballet. Music critic Pierre Lalo, writing in *Le Temps,* recalled the novelty of the performance and praised the Russian ballet for its development of choreography for men. "The talents of the male dancers are once again one of the distinctive signs that render Russian choreography superior to ours, and one of the qualities that we should borrow from them," he began.

> Thanks to this vigour, this agility, this virtuosity of the men, the ballet possesses here [in Russia] an element of strength lacking among us. This element of strength is naturally a necessary result of diversity; our ballets, where one sees only women, where men hold only a hidden and secondary role, have an eternal grace that degenerates into shadow. This grace is revealed in the Slavic choreography through more energetic episodes, which in the steps of the archers, in the second act of *Prince Igor,* are the most striking example. It is this introduction of the collective element of strength in ballet that seems to me to constitute the principal interest in the appearance of Russian male dancers.[38]

In fact, as Lalo observed, *Prince Igor*'s opening scene confronted the audience with a powerful, dramatic, and transgressive vision: a row of Russian male dancers (armed with arches) marching and leaping vigorously towards the front edge of the stage. Significantly, Lalo asserts that the strength of the male dancers made this ballet a success.

Similarly, critic André Rigaud was impressed by the early productions of the Ballets Russes that showcased the talents of its imperial-trained male dancers. In his review of *Prince Igor*, he went so far as to declare that "the dances of *Prince Igor* ha[d] created a type of revelation."[39] Rigaud was not alone in his excitement. The poet and influential patron of the arts Anna de Noailles, who also attended the first performance, remarked that "it was as if Creation, being stopped on the seventh day, now all of the sudden resumed … I understood I was witnessing a miracle." She continued: "No one thought that in the realm of art, there might be something utterly new under the sun, when, in instant splendour, there appeared the phenomenon of the Ballets Russes."[40] The Ballets Russes unveiled to France a new potential for the art of ballet, and the reintroduction of the male dancer was at the centre of its novelty. Its productions consistently presented the male body as an expressive instrument both dramatically and musically.

The Ballet Russes and its choreographers incorporated the *danseur* as a central component to ballet production by creating, once again, roles specifically for male star dancers, choreography designed according to the strengths of such dancers, and even music composed that embraced the personal mood of the dancer. As a virtuosic dancer and innovative choreographer, Vaslav Nijinsky played a major role in the productions of the Ballets Russes: one could argue that he managed to attain a heroic stature. He was once labelled the "Vestris of the North."[41] Other male dancers who played a central role in the Ballets Russes after Nijinsky included Leonide Massine, Anton Dolin, and Serge Lifar. As Lynn Garafola asserts, Lifar "was groomed by Diaghilev for stardom, launched on a path that asserted not only his preeminence within the company as an individual, but also the preeminent role within its repertory of a new kind of hero."[42]

Certainly, the Parisian exaltation of anything Russian at the turn of the century played a role in the enthusiastic reception of the Ballets Russes and its male dancers. A Russian identity offered a virility and masculinity acceptable on the French stage (as was the case for the Ballets Russes' many Polish dancers). However, Diaghilev's company orchestrated a variety of male images upon the ballet stage. It presented male dancers as not only powerful, athletic, virtuosic, and strong, but also sensuous, erotic, and even androgynous – for example in *Le spectre de la rose* (1910), *L'aprés-midi d'un faune* (1912), *La chatte* (1927), *Apollon musagète* (1928), and *Prodigal Son* (1929).[43] Diaghilev's launching of male dance figures created a performative space in which both female and male dancers were eroticized and aestheticized. In doing so, the Ballets Russes set out to demonstrate that men could also create beautiful, graceful, provocative, and even poetic movements in ballet. Critics were divided as to whether the Ballets Russes' new imagery presented male sexuality or androgynous sexuality. Images of the classical male body were reproduced in several ballets, and interpretations were left open in regards to sexuality. *Narcisse* (1911), for example, presented male imagery of classical Greece that was acceptable to heterosexual audiences due to their classical context. But *Narcisse* also was thought to represent self-indulgence, aesthetic androgyny, male homosexuality, and the transgression of social norms. Consequently, the character Narcisse is punished for his self-/male adoration.

While the Ballets Russes presented many innovations in ballet production and direction, its creators were playing upon existing androgynous forms and erotic imagery circulating in France among elite, eccentric circles. Ephebic masculinity was not a new image in French visual culture. In the eighteenth and nineteenth centuries, artists rendered this type of masculinity within French neoclassical contexts. At the turn of the twentieth century, androgyny became increasingly linked with modernity. For example, gender ambiguity became acceptable in high cultural circles within the context of theatre. Sarah Bernhardt played cross-dressed roles as Hamlet in Paris in 1899, as Cyrano in 1909, and as Judas in 1910. At the turn of the century, illustrator Aubrey Beardsley reconceptualized images of knights as slender, effeminate youths. His caricatures portrayed women not as passive but as free-thinking, sexually complex, and even dominating figures. Imagery of the dandy and androgyne circulated among the elite. In offering similar or competing representations of gender identity to audiences, the Ballets Russes played a crucial role in stimulating discussion of gender dynamics in ballet and, particularly, the place of men in ballet.

The wide-ranging responses to the Ballets Russes' androgynous imagery (particularly in the body of Vaslav Nijinsky) reveal how the male body became a site of social debate and controversy. In 1911, one critic remarked that "the most sensual charm of Nijinsky's dance is due, in effect, to the paradoxical mixture of a totally androgynous dance, where femininity, that is grace, is united with the most singular masculine acrobatics."[44] Here the critic interpreted the male dancer as signifying both the feminine (defined here as grace) and the masculine (defined here as acrobatics). It is in the reception of *L'après-midi d'un faune* (1912), however, that we discover most vividly the ways in which audiences and critics responded to the Ballets Russes' presentation of its male dancers.

L'après-midi d'un faune, performed at the Théâtre du Châtelet on 29 May 1912, presented the story of a faun (half-man, half-animal) who falls in love with a nymph. Its accompanying music was the impressionist score by Debussy, its costumes were designed by Russian artist Léon Bakst, and its dancing was choreographed by Nijinsky. The choreography, however, elicited a strikingly different response among audiences than its music and decor. Nijinsky had attempted to replicate the profiles of dancing figures on ancient vase painting. In doing so, he disregarded the five positions of classical ballet, infrequently used classical "turnout (the outward turn of the legs from the hips), and included twisted and contorted forms and movements unlike anything else seen on the dance stage.

The ballet clearly displayed sexual overtones. The faun is tempted by several nymphs (clothed in semi-transparent gowns). The nymphs run away and leave a scarf behind. The faun lays the scarf on the ground, faces downwards, and satisfies himself. Although it lasted only about ten minutes, the ballet "electrified" audiences.[45] Grigoriev, ballet master of the Ballets Russes at the time, recalled that at the end of the première, "one half of the audience broke in frantic applause, and the other into equally frantic protests."[46] Hissing and booing were drowned out, however, by shouts of delight. In light of this, Diaghilev ordered an encore of the entire piece.

Whether the audiences and critics were scandalized by the piece's choreography throughout or merely by the final scene in which the faun masturbates, the Ballets Russes became the talk of the town. A biting response came from *Le Figaro*'s editor Gaston Calmette, who professed to be shocked by the ballet. Substituting his own article for what would have been a review by *Le Figaro* critic Robert Brussel, an avid supporter of the Ballets Russes, Calmette attacked the piece for its "animal realism" and for its "lecherous faun, whose movements [were] filthy and bestial in their eroticism, and whose gestures [were] as crude as they [were] indecent." He launched an attack on the piece as art: "I am ... certain that any of our readers who were present yesterday at the Châtelet will join with me in protesting against the extraordinary exhibition which they had the audacity to serve up to us in the guise of a serious work, decked out with all the refinements of art and imagination ... Anyone who mentions the words 'art' and 'imagination' in the same breath as this production must be laughing at us."[47] While he described Nijinsky's choreography as "loathsome miming," Calmette did, however, acknowledge Nijinksy as an "amazing artist." Fittingly, Calmette's front-page article was entitled, "Un faux pas" (A Mistake or, literally, A Wrong Step). The review fuelled a flood of defences of the ballet, beginning with a letter from Diaghilev himself, which included supporting statements from prominent artists and intellectuals. The Diaghilev-Calmette exchange led to a request on the part of the police to change the last gestures of the ballet and culminated with Diaghilev's reluctant modification of it in subsequent performances.[48] Ironically, Calmette's article served as advantageous publicity for the program, drawing even more spectators to the Châtelet. While this exchange of letters increased the public's interest in the production, it also diminished the shock value felt on the opening night.

Most newspapers, however, published favourable reviews of the ballet. Balletomanes, like English dance critic Cyril Beaumont who attended the performance, interpreted the last gesture as erotic symbolism and commented on the merits of its subtlety.[49] Many reviews avoided discussing the sexual tones of the ballet altogether. Music critic Pierre Lalo, writing in *Le Temps,* argued that there was nothing in *L'après-midi d'un faune* that was morally offensive. He implored, "Is there any offense against taste and against art? That is another affair and that is the only question here." Lalo expressed his bewilderment that the same audiences of the cabarets and café-concerts would be shocked by the subtle gestures in the Ballets Russes' *Faune.* Lalo makes an important point here regarding the audience and its tastes. Clearly, there remained a distinct boundary between ballet as a high art and dance as a popular entertainment. Audiences did not expect the same erotic display on the ballet stage as that found in other popular theatricals existing in Paris at the time. Moving on from the issue of Nijinsky's "gesture," Lalo devoted the rest of his article to a review of the ballet's decor, music, and choreography. In particular, he concentrated on the relationship between the ballet's music and choreography and defended it against criticism that thought it incongruent.[50] The leading daily newspaper on theatrical events, *Comœdia*, presented a three-column article by its editor, Gaston de Pawlowski, praising the performance, along with photographs of the dancers and Bakst's decor, quotes from Mallarmé's poem, and two favourable articles by Louis Vuillemin and Louis Schneider.[51] Vuillemin's article focused on the complementarity of the ballet's music and choreography rather than its presentation of male sexuality. He stated that he had "never enjoyed so much a perfect union of pantomime and music."[52] Schneider, likewise, drew attention to the relationship between music and choreography in the work. He asserted that Nijinsky's choreography had drawn upon Debussy's score with "absolute sincerity" and that it had obtained an "intimate" and "perfect fusion," and "a direct cohesion" between music and bodily movements.[53]

Auguste Rodin's article in *Le Matin* also offered steadfast praise. Rodin stated that Nijinsky had "never been so remarkable as in his latest role."[54] Rather than focusing on the faun's final sexual gesture, Rodin highlighted the artistic merits of the choreography and the personal style that Nijinksy brought to male ballet dancing. As a sculptor who was fascinated by classicism, lyricism, and the beauty, rhythm, and movement of the body, Rodin drew much inspiration from modern developments in ballet technique and expression, particularly in regards to the male form. Thus, in his article, he drew attention to the beauty of line and form in Nijinsky's dance movements, writing that "Nijinsky possesse[d] the distinct advantage of physical perfection, harmony of proportions, and a most extraordinary power to bend his body so as to interpret the most diverse sentiments." He described Nijinsky as "marvelous" in the ballet *L'après-midi d'un faune.* Nijinsky performed "no jumps, no bounds, nothing but attitudes and gestures of a half-conscious creature. He stretches himself and retreats, with movement: now slow, now jerky, nervous, angular, his eyes spy, his arms extend, his hands open and close, his head turns away and turns back … His whole body expresses what his mind dictates." Rodin, in his own work, had moved away from the rigid realism (and idealism) of classical sculpture in favour of rougher, more masculine, less conventional statues. His figures were often left "incomplete," revealing only what he deemed as the most expressive part of the body. In his "modern classicism," expressive corporeality and the natural beauty of the human form were central. Rodin concluded his *Le Matin* article by stating that Nijinsky "possess[ed] the beauty of the antique frescoes and statues" and that he was "the ideal model for whom every painter and sculptor ha[d] longed." He declared: "I wish that every artist who truly loves his art, might see this perfect personification of the ideals of beauty of the old Greeks." Rodin's observations are significant in that we find the male dancing form rather than that of the female serving once again as the inspiration for art (here in sculpture). Interestingly, Lalo's rhetorical question "Is there any offence against art?" resonates throughout Rodin's article. Rodin's *Le Matin* article was reprinted in *Le Figaro* the day after Calmette's moralizing review.

Reviews like those of Beaumont, Lalo, Rodin, Vuillemin, and Schneider reveal the way in which critics attempted to reconceptualize ballet and to legitimize its artistry. Schneider's failure to elaborate on what he meant by "more intimate" is a clear example of this. Whether explicitly or implicity, critics were de-eroticizing the ballet environment by focusing their reviews not on the eroticism and crudeness of the Ballets Russes productions, but rather on their artistry, novelty, and the dancers' virtuosity. This is particularly interesting since other entertainments, such as the cabaret, music hall, and café-concert, were becoming more popular at this time. It appears as if critics were attempting to distance the ballet from these other venues by highlighting its artistic merits.

Diaghilev's Ballets Russes and the positive reception it attracted played a crucial role in the public acceptance of the male dancer. Beginning in 1909, we find repeated attempts to restore the reputation of the male ballet dancer on the part of intellectuals and critics, who linked the return of the male dancer to the revival of ballet as an art form. In other words, they suggested that the legitimacy of men's presence on the ballet stage would bring about a legitimation of the art form itself. Artists, intellectuals, and music critics, including Auguste Rodin, Valentine Gross Hugo, Pierre Lalo, Henri Ghéon, Jacques Rivière, and Jean Cocteau, promoted the new visibility and virtuosity of male dancing as revealed by the Ballets Russes. As early as 1909, French artist Valentine Gross Hugo noted Nijinsky's talent, writing that Nijinsky exhibited a noble grace and had a virtuosity she described as "splendid."[55] Henri Ghéon's experience of the Ballets Russes prompted him not only to draw attention to the beauty of masculine movement in their productions but to insist upon the importance of the male dancer in ballet more broadly. In his article for *La Nouvelle Revue Française,* Ghéon described Nijinsky as restoring a virile and noble beauty that had been lost since the great eighteenth-century dancer Vestris: "He [Nijinsky] has resuscitated before our dazzled eyes, this marvellous and chimeric being extinct since Vestris, the '*danseur.*'" He remarked that Nijinsky, through his virile and noble beauty, was "the most striking indication of the rise of ballet" thus far.[56] Ghéon's review of Nijinsky is significant for two reasons; first, it reveals that noble grace was once again linked to masculine virtuosity, and, second, it demonstrates that critics perceived the virtuosity of male dancers as central to the revival of ballet.[57]

Other commentators on ballet were similarly captivated by Valsav Nijinsky and the personal style that he brought to male ballet dancing. Both Auguste Rodin and Jean Cocteau went to great lengths to defend the male dancer's masculinity and capabilities, often using the example of Nijinsky. In an article in *Comœdia* from 1910, Cocteau responded to complaints that Nijinsky was not masculine enough: "I have heard him reproached for not being male enough. Nijinsky is not effeminate." Cocteau asserted that Nijinsky possessed "a unique god-like air about him, coming from who knows where, and without weighing itself upon the troupe." According to Cocteau, Nijinsky evoked a unique and mysterious identity that was not necessarily feminine. Commenting on Nijinsky's performance in the ballet *Giselle,* Cocteau wrote: "He produces the effect of a half-wonder [and] one has the impression that a nearly impossible event has happened." Cocteau recalled an "unquestionable mystery" that emanated from Nijinsky which immediately enveloped the public the first time he appeared on the stage of the Châtelet theatre.[58] Cocteau concluded by observing that there was "an amalgam of admiration, of respect, and of amazement (astonishment)" that surrounded Nijinsky.[59] In his ability to appeal to audiences' emotions, Nijinsky was seen as embodying "pathos" on the ballet stage.[60] Such praise reveals how critics contributed to the redemption of male ballet dancers and conferred a celebrity status upon them.

Some critics argued that Nijinsky was vital to the success of the Ballets Russes in Paris. Critic Jacques Rivière declared that Nijinsky, not prima ballerina Tamara Karsavina, was the source of inspiration for Diaghilev's Ballets Russes troupe. "The Ballets Russes, it's Nijinsky," he began. "He alone animates the entire enterprise … he has been the inspiration, in the literal sense." "It was Nijinsky," he continued, "who forced the others to not be content with mediocrity … now that he has retired, all has flattened; Karsavina, without him, is only a pleasant dancer; she has not renewed, on her own, this spirit, this accent, this pathos that we have come to know of him."[61] Rivière was bold in claiming that the virtuosity of prima ballerina Tamara Karsavina rested upon the talents of her male partner, Nijinsky, given the elevated status of the prima ballerina in the previous century. Essentially, Rivière suggested that a female dancer needed the male dancer to really shine. In an earlier article, he elaborated also on Michel Fokine's talents, describing him as a "true genius" and as "a man who felt his body to the depth of this soul."[62]

Undoubtedly, the Ballets Russes altered traditional perceptions of ballet in France by bringing the male dancer to centre stage. Talented dancers such as Vaslav Nijinsky, Michel Fokine, Léonide Massine, Adolphe Bolm, Albert Aveline, Anton Dolin, Serge Lifar, and David Lichine attracted new interest in the artistry of the male dancer as they each gained public adoration and prestige. In a *Le Figaro* article of 1910, critic Robert Brussel described Fokine as a "great artist" and a "mime of a rare power," Boulgakow (Ballets Russes dancer) as having "significant talent," and Nijinsky as producing "always elegance" and "prodigious elevation."[63] Critic Henri Ghéon claimed that Nijinsky "justifi[ed] the place of young men in ballet."[64] In fact, Nijinsky's name became recognized (and is still recognized) as the supreme expression of the art of ballet, thus showing how the importance of the female dancer had been supplanted by the early twentieth century.

The reintroduction of male dancers on the French stage (via the Ballets Russes) and the success that accompanied it led some writers to reflect on the sorry state of French ballet and the fate of its male dancers. Henri Ghéon, for example, attempted to locate the source of the decline of the male dancer in his article of 1910. In explaining why male dancers in French ballet had become effeminate, he drew a connection between the values attached to ballet and the state of its male dancers. "In the degenerate ballet," he observed, "the exclusive reign of the woman has reasons, we don't deny it, less aesthetic than sensual."[65] According to Ghéon, the sensual demands placed on French ballet had left little room for male artistry or even masculine themes as feminine sensuality (i.e., eroticism) became more important than artistic/technical virtuosity. Ghéon explained that this emasculated the male dancer and turned him into a "hybrid being" and a "foreign form" in ballet production. Ghéon went so far as to proclaim that this made him, when his face was hidden, "only distinguishable from the women by the exaggeration of his musculature." The *danseur* thus became "a sort of acrobat and female athlete." This led him to ponder over the renewal of French ballet. He concluded with an appeal to the Russians: "Archers of Prince Igor renew this seedy atmosphere! Give way to heroism in the grace that gives us a Nijinsky! It is high time that the ballet makes itself more masculine."[66] Ghéon suggests, first, that the more ballet is appreciated for its plastic rather than sensual forms, the less feminized it will become and the more valued; and second, that the French ballet should emulate the Russian ballet by restoring heroic grace and masculinity to the ballet stage. But why did audiences respond so well to the art of Nijinsky? Why was he applauded for his grace and skills? Why were audiences so enthusiastic about the return of the male dancer on the ballet stage? How could the French value their own male dancers on the Paris Opéra stage? In other words, how did attitudes towards the male body change?

Criticism of ballet and its dancers reflected French anxieties about masculinity, modernity, and the body. The fact that observers of the ballet either applauded the male dancer or continued to rebuke his presence on the stage reveals the vying tensions over the boundaries of "suitable" male and female behaviour (and feminine and masculine ideals) in early twentieth-century France. The overwhelming acceptance of the Ballets Russes, the recognition of the virtuosity of its male dancers, and the eventual acceptance of the French male dancer can thus be contextualized within the broader cultural shifts in French masculinity that occurred at the turn of the century. Within this context, it is important to differentiate French perceptions of the Russian (foreign) body from the French (national) body. The Russian foreign body took on a more virile, primitive meaning for the French. The "Russian" dancers of the Ballets Russes were deemed acceptable due to their perceived abundance of masculinity. It was important enough that many of the Polish dancers in the company adopted Russian names to ensure their virility on stage.

FRENCH MASCULINITY, CULTURE, AND THE BODY

By examining such ballet commentary, we can see how the male dancer served as a vessel through which to assert contemporary ideas about masculinity and the body. In order to understand the tactics of the Ballets Russes and the significance of the commentary that they incited, it is important to contextualize both within the broader crisis of gender identity occurring in France in the early twentieth century, particularly after the First World War. Over the course of the nineteenth century, ideal masculinity lost its heroic classical associations of the previous century. Masculinity became linked with intellect (the mind) rather than physical prowess (the body). As we have seen, this cultural shift had a detrimental effect on men in ballet. The repudiation of male ballet dancing was grounded in a broader reshaping of the way "respectable" men presented themselves. For example, men's fashion transformed from the more detail-oriented and decorative clothing of the late eighteenth century, which drew attention to the male body (e.g., feathered hats, knee breeches, full coats, wigs, stockings, bright colours, and buckled shoes), to the more modest, muted, utilitarian garb of the nineteenth century (e.g., the derby hat, dark frock coat, covered legs, and simple cravat, as we see portrayed in the Paris landscapes of the impressionists). In the former, the male body was accentuated and intended for display, and in the latter, clothing drew attention away from the body (although it still served as a visual marker of status). As Christopher Breward notes, in the nineteenth century, "men gave up their right to all the brighter, gayer, more elaborate, and more varied forms of ornamentation, leaving these entirely to the use of women, and thereby making their own tailoring the most austere and ascetic of the arts." In doing so, Breward argues, "man abandoned his claim to be considered beautiful. He henceforth aimed at being only useful."[67]

Towards the end of the nineteenth century, however, traditional ideologies of masculinity and manhood became destabilized. The French defeat in the Franco-Prussian war was a huge blow for the French, particularly because it had been a war provoked by them. Military defeat held various implications that fuelled anxieties about national security, diplomatic isolation, governmental politics, racial degeneration, depopulation, health, and, moreover, masculinity. The corporeal body became the site for the examination of the (present and future) state of the nation. As Robert A. Nye points out, medical and scientific discourse turned "as never before [to] the bodies and masculine qualities of men."[68] In 1872, physician and demographer Jacques Bertillon's advice to a father on how to choose a son-in-law for his daughter suggested that he look for "'doubtful traits of virility,' a high or broken voice, sparse beard, effeminate or ambiguous physique" as warning signs.[69] Here we can see a turn to the body to define manliness and the value placed on virility and bodily strength (i.e., physique).

Indeed, the military defeat of the French had stirred up anxieties about the physical state of its men. In its wake, gymnastic societies flourished in the hopes that vigorous physical training would help prepare the French for any future war. A physical culture movement surfaced in the 1880s that promoted health, hygiene, athleticism, and sports (both recreational and competitive) and that linked the French body to national regeneration. As prominent hygienist/physician Dr Philippe Tissié once asserted, "physical education is the great key to our physical, intellectual, and moral regeneration."[70] In 1880, the republican government revealed its commitment to physical culture by passing a law that made gymnastic training compulsory in all public boys' schools. Educator Pierre de Coubertin once asserted that French secondary schools "had become too scholastic while pupils of private schools were 'narrow-chested, round-shouldered aesthetes.'" Coubertin, who wrote many speeches and papers on the physical and moral benefits of exercise, embraced a sense of classicism (the idea of Olympism) and advocated for a strong physical culture that "supplemented on the one hand by nobility, what is so aptly called 'fair play,' and on the other hand by aesthetics, that is the cultivation of what is beautiful and graceful."[71] In other words, he argued for a healthy physical culture (e.g., sportsmanship) and an aesthetic and artistic representation of sport. It was in this union of "muscle and spirit," he observed, that the development of modern life and society rested. Courbertin's observations are important in showing the link between sport and art in physical culture as we often find critics and intellectuals using interchangeable language to describe both activities in the early twentieth century.

Not only was sport linked to the physical and moral regeneration of the French race, but it was also used to encourage patriotism and leisure.[72] Initiated by Coubertin, the Olympic Games were re-established and held in Paris in 1896. The Olympic Games are a good example of how sports culture (newly institutionalized and commercialized) placed the (male) body at the centre of public consumption and national pride. Coubertin's vision of the mutual enrichment of sport and art manifested itself in the establishment of five art competitions as part of the Olympic program, featuring architecture, painting, sculpture, music, and literature. The purpose was to attract artists to physical culture. Such changing ideals prompted a reconsideration of how the male body should appear. As George Mosse points out, male beauty was "confounded with strength and the developing of one's muscles."[73] It is at this time that a masculine neoclassical ideal re-emerged within discourse, visual imagery, and the performing arts. Mosse locates conceptions of manliness in the male body within visual images of male heroism and verbal descriptions of men in action. In this respect, corporeal beauty was no longer necessarily feminine beauty. The increasing number of columns allotted to sports in journals such as *Le Figaro* and *Le Temps* and the growing number of sport- and health-related magazines such as *L'Auto* (est. 1903) and *La Culture Physique* (est. 1904) also attests to the popular interests in athleticism and masculinity. Imagery from such journals revealed a new heroic masculinity through which the male body could, once again, be displayed and even exalted.[74] Thus tastes for neoclassicism and its classical heroism renewed an aesthetic celebration of the male form.

A clear example of the way in which attitudes towards the corporeality of men changed can be seen in the rhetoric of the 1890s surrounding the Dreyfus affair. As historian Christopher Forth has shown, the rhetoric and images used during the Dreyfus affair reflected French anxieties about masculinity and modernity, and facilitated ongoing debates about the state of French manhood through the First World War.[75] Forth draws special attention to how the Dreyfus affair engaged with changing ideals of the male body. He points out that the Dreyfusards had "hoped to transcend the problematic gender implications of their professions by asserting the virile nature of their bodies and deeds." However, he notes that "the substantive *intellectuel* was by 1914 still being counterposed in popular usage to *manuel*, thus distancing Dreyfusards from the virtues of muscular force and action that were increasingly lauded throughout French culture."[76] Physical culture had encouraged a new age of body consciousness among Frenchmen by emphasizing the muscular body as the ground of manhood. The ideal, healthy male body was one that exhibited muscularity, strength, and precision. The youthful athlete became a more compelling manly ideal than the bookish and sedentary intellectual.[77] In other words, physical strength, athletic prowess, and the virile nature of men's bodies (the "Herculean force") all became more desirable attributes than intellect. The physical culture movement usurped previous masculine ideals of intellectualism and, in doing so, "mounted the period's most explicit gender critique of men who privileged mind over muscles."[78]

In the early twentieth century, we find increasing connections between athleticism, sports, art, and republican ideology. Modern nationalism pushed a classical heroism to the centre of republicanism. Republicans used the physical culture movement as a means through which to promote "unity, equality, emulation, and preparation for national defense" and to encourage discipline, health, and hygiene.[79] The interwar years, however, witnessed a deepening crisis of masculinity and another wave of promotion of physical culture, particularly muscularity and sports. Apart from losing roughly 10 per cent of the active male population and 40 per cent of expected births, France witnessed masses of soldiers returning home maimed physically and psychologically. Those men who experienced "shell shock" were viewed as having failed the test of manhood. As the construction of manhood was linked to the construction of nationhood, the French worried about their future.[80] France's greatest fear was German rearmament and strength. Physical culturists, nationalists, and eugenicists expressed their anxieties about France's physical inferiority. As Joan Tumblety notes, "the figure of the disabled war veteran was omnipresent – in the Armistice parades, in the popular press, and on the street corners of French towns ... men and women continued to die from tuberculosis in very high numbers ... [and] the long-lived phenomenon of *denatalité* was exacerbated by the war."[81]

With deepening fervour, physical culture was heavily promoted as a solution to what appeared as national weakness. Blossoming in the 1920s as a transnational phenomenon, the physical culture movement promoted images of masculinity and femininity within a new context of the physical body, athleticism and exercise, hygiene, and the general health of the nation. Some figures promoted the health of the individual or the improvement of "racial breeding," while others stressed the vitality of the nation or emphasized the need to strengthen the armed forces. Ideologies of masculinity, however, are never stable or homogeneous. As Tumblety writes, "whatever the strength of patriarchy and masculine privilege in this era, masculinity was characterized as unstable – a test that men could fail and a set of physical and moral qualities that needed to be entrained or policed." In other words, ideal masculinity entailed discipline and commitment. In the interwar years, there remained competing definitions of the ideal man in France. As Mosse shows, alternative ideals of manhood existed, such as the socialist ideal of masculinity, which promoted "a more peaceful masculinity dependent on solidarity rather than struggle."[82] Postwar novels also attempted to recover a sense of masculinity lost by the war, some through imaginative portrayals of soldiers (what Mosse calls "Warriors"). Nevertheless, the mass press and physical culturists were "fixated" by the appearance of the body. Tumblety points out how both "articulat[ed] this through a striking visual register and by attending to such topics as fashion, beauty, and health, as well as the celebration of the sporting hero."[83] As we will see, the topic of dance also played a role in the quest for physical and national regeneration in France.

The growing popular awareness and acceptance of the human body as capable of grace and beauty, regardless of sex, made the French public conscious of the beauty of all movement, whether in sports or the performing arts – at the professional or amateur level. For example, grace became an important measure of talent in competitive sports. In the 1920s, tennis champions René Lacoste and Suzanne Leglen became the epitome of grace on the court, and cyclists in the Tour de France were systematically described as having skill, elegance, and grace. In fact, as Christopher S. Thompson writes, in cycling "physical elegance was closely correlated with moral rectitude: the ungraceful was disgraceful."[84] Increasingly, qualities of grace and elegance were regularly used to measure talent not only in sports but in male ballet dancing.

What we see happening in the early twentieth century is the development of new ways to view the body and the new meanings attached to it. The blossoming of physical culture in France contributed not only to ballet's renewed popularity and legitimacy as an autonomous art form, but also to different perceptions of the male dancer. New imagery of the male body and the link between athleticism and masculinity both opened an acceptable space for the male dancer. The interconnections of athleticism, masculinity, and nationhood that were forming at the turn of the century prepared Parisian audiences for the reception of the Ballets Russes' male dancers. The Ballets Russes had entered the Parisian scene after the embrace of physical culture and managed to continue successfully during the movement's peak in the 1920s. The central role of male dancers in the Ballets Russes and the vigorous choreography created specifically for them enabled the French to accept (at least to an extent) the display of the male body on the ballet stage as they appealed to new ideas concerning masculinity. However, it is important to remember that, at the turn of the century, ballet was regarded as a degenerative art form. The acceptance of the Ballet's Russes' male dancers was feasible, in part, because they were foreign bodies on the French stage. In this way, the male body was not a direct threat to the health of the nation. As an ally of France (via the Franco-Russian entente), Russia and its strong, athletic, and virile men did not elicit the same anxieties as those that surfaced over the emergence of German physical culture. It is, therefore, not surprising that the Ballets Russes, with its new type of male ballet dancer (one that was virile, athletic, and poetic), was so well received by the French. It did, however, stimulate inquiries into the state of French ballet dancers at the Opéra.

The quest to redeem the masculinity of French male dancers held political and national significance. In the interwar period, both the Right and Left were deeply committed to restoring a sense of manhood to French men. As historian Mark Meyers has shown, the fascist Right's obsession with hyper-manliness made them a target for parody by Far Left republicans who attempted to mark them, alternatively, as effeminate, particularly during the 1930s.[85] Left-wing Henri Pollès, for example, remarked once that fascist men "flatter the crowd as a woman who flatters a man she wants to seduce ... Like women, they reserve their decisions and then reveal themselves to be brusque, devastating, and unpredictable."[86] By attempting to feminize fascist men, republicans could promote republican maniliness. Both the Right and the Left would have been greatly invested in the masculinization of the French male dancer at the Opéra in this period, particularly because ballet was still deemed a high art in France. The male dancer thus became a platform upon which to delineate new images of manhood in France, to restore boundaries of femininity and masculinity on stage, and to promote new images of the male dancer that aligned with the overall health of the nation. As male physical fitness and muscular beauty became equated with the health and morality of the nation, the French male dancer's physical presence on the ballet stage seemed less problematic as long as he represented the republican ideals of masculinity that rested on athleticism, grace, and vitality. Critics thus emphasized athleticism and virtuosity in male ballet dancing, and the visual display of male dancers proliferated in newspapers, posters, and photographs as athletic (fig. 6.2). These new images of men in ballet, like in sports, contributed to the overall shift in French society's attitudes towards male bodies on display, and, on some level, one can argue helped to transform the relationship between men and their bodies in various ways.

CRITICS AND THE REFASHIONING OF THE MALE DANCER

By raising issues about gender, the body, and ballet in their reviews of the Ballets Russes, critics contributed significantly to the reshaping of cultural perceptions of ballet and its dancers (even though their opinions were diverse and contrasting). They did so by reconceptualizing notions of gender and bodies on display. In this way, dance criticism provides a valuable source of insight into the politics of gender and the body in modern France. Both critics' and choreographers' portrayals of ballet stars greatly affected the reputation of ballet in France and helped eventually to legitimate its occupation at the Paris Opéra – criticism being the most widely circulated source of ballet "education" for the theatregoing public. The new values placed on the male athlete and the new masculinities that accompanied it contributed to the acceptance and eventual adoration of the French male dancer.

In the early twentieth century, figures such as André Levinson, André Rigaud, Jacques Rivière, and Serge Lifar committed themselves to reviving the status of the male dancer and educating the public on his potential for choreographic beauty and athleticism. As we have seen, remarkably, many critical essays and reviews on ballet in the

Figure 6.2 Lifar dancing the title role in his ballet *Icare* produced at the Opéra in 1935.

early years of twentieth century supported the return of the male dancer to the ballet stage. In the interwar period, both Levinson and Lifar dedicated sections of their published works specifically to the new presence of the male dancer. As Diaghilev's Ballets Russes presented the *danseur,* Levinson and others took time to prepare, explain, and legitimate his presence on the ballet stage. As choreography became more understood and valued by critics, dancers were assessed on the basis of their strength, agility, precision, and formal qualities.

In their reviews, critics increasingly highlighted male dancers' technical skills, poetic expression, grace, and athleticism. Before André Levinson, however, French critics of ballet relied on an underdeveloped critical language that had emerged in the eighteenth century. Once again, critics undertook the task of reappropriating key attributes such as *grâce, élan* (movement without effort), and *volonté* (discipline). After the introduction of the Ballet Russes, we find critics attributing the qualities of *grâce, élan,* and *volonté* not only to female dancers, but also to male dancers as essential qualities of virtuosity and professionalism. This is significant for several reasons: first, it demonstrates that critics were taking a serious interest in male dancing; and second, it reveals that critics were developing a new standard by which to judge male dancing. In his defence of the male dancer, Henri Ghéon discussed the role of gender in ballet and the possibility for masculine grace. "The woman has too much grace by vocation and culture not to have made the dance her own domain … I believe there is a place by her side for a masculine grace," he asserted, "and one that is not effeminate, but that saves, on the contrary, the femininity of the ballerina herself."[87]

André Levinson took the time in many of his articles to define "grace" and to clarify other qualities of virtuosity in ballet. Many of his reviews and articles emphasized the importance of grace in the execution of choreography by both male and female ballet dancers. He, and those critics who emulated him, measured virtuosity (male and female) by the idea of balancing strength and gracefulness (i.e., grace and muscular energy perfected so that there was an absence of visible effort or of *bruit*). Here Levinson draws upon the formal qualities of nineteenth-century "classic dance," which defined grace in this way. For example, Nijinsky (via Fokine's choreography) was hailed for his extraordinary agility and elevation through jumps (fig. 6.3). According to critics, he possessed the ability to channel his powerful strength into an illusion of effortlessness. "Remember Nijinsky's phenomenal jumps!" Levinson wrote of the Ballets Russes' star. "Without obvious preparation, without the deep squat of a plié, he would suddenly and lightly soar, as if hovering for an instant in the air, and then come down almost noiselessly." He describes Nijinsky's jumps as a "miracle of strength, harmony, self-control and music," where "the material impulse, the contraction of the muscles, is hidden by the art" and "elemental male strength is tamed by the effortless, matchless grace of an ephebe."[88] Here Levinson contends that male ballet dancing requires both masculine strength and ephebic grace.

Nijinsky was considered the epitome of grace and virtuosity among critics and set a new standard for male ballet dancing in France. Jacques Rivière's review from *La Nouvelle Revue Française* offers a good example of how critics were assessing male ballet dancing by the 1920s and how Nijinsky became the standard by which to compare

Figure 6.3 Photograph of Vaslav Nijinsky in costume for the "Danse Siamoise" in *Les orientales* performed in Paris in 1910.

other male dancers. In this review, Rivière compared the dancing of Léonide Massine (Nijinsky's eventual replacement in the Ballets Russes) to that of Nijinsky, declaring that Nijinsky's absence was a great loss. His discussion of Massine's performance affirmed Nijinsky as a true genius who exemplified "grâce," "élan," "élégance," "bonne volonté," and "the extraordinary power of radiance."[89] Massine appeared skilful, yet too "strict and thin," and lacked Nijinsky's quality of "emanation." According to Rivière, Massine lacked "grâce" and "bonne volonté" within his "complicated gymnastics."[90]

Dancer and dance critic Julie Sazonova, in her reviews of *Giselle* and *L'oiseau bleu,* described dancer Serge Lifar as executing the highest elegance, precision, and grace. In 1936, she wrote that "Lifar as one knows him, possesses to the highest degree the gift of expressive dance and he expresses in the love duo in the first act [of *Giselle*] a profound tenderness without ever sacrificing the dance to pantomime." She continued: "Lifar delights us by the elegant finesse of his *battements brisés-volés* of the Blue Bird, by the precision and the grace of his pirouettes in the variation of the prince … Lifar executed … his *cabrioles* with a supreme mastery, in floating in the air with an ease that was astounding."[91] As a former dancer, Sazonova wrote reviews that were unique, offering a distinct language (ballet terminology) in which to assess ballet dancing. In doing so, she offered a model of dance assessment for men that other critics could emulate. By applying the characteristic of grace to both female and male dancers and, eventually, to the execution of the dance steps themselves, critics and dancers alike were revolutionizing dance criticism. In doing so, they redefined virtuosity in ballet and universalized its vocabulary across gender lines. These reviews are a good example of how the gendering of characteristics can be reconfigured by the tastes of an age.

Critics also drew explicit parallels between dance and sports, and highlighted the beauty of masculine form in both. As early as 1910, critic Henri Ghéon addressed the notion of classical beauty and lamented the failure of contemporary French culture to appreciate the male body as an ideal form in dance. "Certainly, we have forgotten how to admire the masculine body," he begins, "but, is it not a sign of barbarism? And is it possible to admit that the principal source of joy for the plastic arts by the Greek people for us remains permanently dried up?" He related the beauty of masculine movement in ballet to the beauty of masculine form within sports. He writes, "I distinguish a great beauty in boxing, in spite of its bloody ends, in tennis, in all the sports that put male forms in action … it is important for us not to remain so unresponsive … I do not see … that the free play of dance is deprived in principle of such resources."[92]

Other critics specifically addressed the similar role that grace and strength played in sports and dancing. In doing so, they drew attention to the enormous amount of discipline and training that was involved in ballet dancing. For example, in several of his articles, André Levinson emphasized the training of male dancers and drew upon the similarities between athletic training in sports and the athletic training of dancers: "Look at sports. A record is established which breaks all predictions. It seems to be beyond human forces, it seems fortuitous, supernatural. A year later, it is an average. The accommodation of the muscles and the nerves has occurred. It is the same in the art of dance. It is likely to progress. What was a prodigious success of Vestris … is required today of a student."[93] Levinson suggests here that ballet dancing progressed in a similar manner as did sports due to similar demands for perfection. In his *Comœdia* article of 1922, Levinson expressed his appreciation for the work of ballet instructor M. Ricaux at the Paris Opéra. He commended Ricaux, who was an instructor of boys, as a man of great talent for his ability to improve male ballet dancing by instilling a new vigour into it. He asserted that the resuscitation of French ballet lay also with the artistic development of the male dancer. "Who knows if … these lines will not be the first page of a Renaissance of French dance?" he boasted. He outlined the "technical basis" of this kind of resurrection, which he deemed as being "the art of the male dancer."[94] Clearly, Levinson envisioned a new modern style of classical ballet for France that relied upon a revitalization of the artistry of male dancing. In fact, Levinson argues that one reason for the demise of the French male dancer was the use of (female) travesty dancers in France. In Russia, where classical ballet still flourished, he explained, travesty dancers were seldom used and were perceived only as rare necessities due to efforts to preserve the traditional role of the male dancer. In other words, Levinson suggests that the Russians recognized the important role of the male dancer in ballet and were aware of the dire consequences of his removal. Here, once again, we see a link between the role of the male dancer and the status of ballet.

André Rigaud's article, which appeared on the front page of *Comœdia* in 1922, also highlighted men's dance classes at the Opéra academy and the important role of the male dancer in ballet. Its caption read, "La classe de danse des hommes à l'Opéra" (The Dance Class of Men at the Opéra) under the heading "Renaissance d'un art" (Renaissance of an Art). Rigaud began by asking, "One always speaks of female dancers! If we could talk a little about male dancers?" "A ballet interpreted only by female dancers would, no doubt, be a thing very elegant," he writes, "but it would become inevitably monotonous." He noted that the role played by men in modern ballet had become more important through the development of choreography for men.[95] Rigaud described the vigorous training of male dancers and the process by which they were able to achieve the *agilité* and *virtuosité* so admired by the public:

> M. Gustave Ricaux strikes the ground with his stick: the lesson begins: The students, beginners who have been at the Opera House for the last six months, and the "old timers" who entered the ballet more than twenty years ago, are arranged in a circle around the room, one hand on the bar … the piano begins … and that is that, in one movement, all left feet begin dancing. A half-turn! All the right feet are now moving themselves in tempo. The rhythm of the music has changed and, with it, the movements of the dancers adjust. They continue in this manner for twenty minutes executing the basic elements of choregraphy: *dégagés, pliés, battements, développés*, etc. … These are the "ranges" of the dancer, the daily limbering exercises which allow him to retain his agility and his virtuosity and to accomplish the choreographic prowess that we admire.[96]

Rigaud described the manner in which the instructor corrected each male dancer as he executed specific ballet steps such as *jetés, battements, coupés, brisés, entrechats-cinq, pirouettes,* and so forth. In other words, he emphasized the precision, intensity, and discipline involved in ballet dancing. He commended Ricaux for incorporating not merely traditional but also modern music in his classes, which thus exposed his dancers to the new rhythms of modern music. Rigaud concluded his article by enunciating, once again, the incredible amount of sustained training that went into male ballet dancing: "The lesson is completed. There is a rush to lunch, after which they will repeat another class in the afternoon and will dance in the evening. And the next day, it all resumes. Ah! It is a tough profession that of a dancer, it demands endless work, a sustained drive, and the spectactor who admires an evening of elegant *cabrioles* and jumps in the air that appear effortless, is unaware of the labour involved in achieving such elegance and lightness."[97] Rigaud's article is a good example of how critics attempted to restore the profession of ballet by revealing dancers as hard-working, disciplined, athletic, and driven artists.

Certainly, choreographers played a vital role in altering perceptions of male dancers. Choreography became more demanding technically and required more strength and atheticism from men. In fact, we find athletic masculinity increasingly being promoted by choreographers in France, who implemented "French male qualities" into their choreography such as leaps and beats (especially taken up by Serge Lifar). "Beats," such as *grande batterie,* are movements in which the dancer jumps in the air and crosses his or her legs, beating the calves against one another (fig. 6.4). The accomplishment of multiple beats in the air served as one particular marker of virtuosic male dancers. While they emphasized masculinity of strength, directness, and weight, choreographers also demonstrated that men could be graceful and fluid and that they could exhibit technical virtuosity and passionate expression. Inevitably, as choreography gained its autonomy in ballet, the technical virtuosity of both male and female dancers developed further.[98] Such developments ultimately fostered the social and cultural appreciation for the male dancer and helped to secure his artistic place in the ballet world.

Massine's ballet *Choreartium* (1930) offers an interesting example of the way in which male and female bodies were reconceptualized in ballet, particularly in the 1930s. The ballet presented both female and male dancers as occupying equal ground upon the dance stage. In his ballet, Massine used the strong psychological correspondence between the choreography and music to employ themes, to portray characters, and to express distinct emotions. The work represented an exploration of rhythmical movements in space through the deployment of dancers as markers for musical qualities. In other words, Massine reduced dancers' bodies to forms that expressed musical tonalities. In his biography Massine wrote: "I decided to do the choreography of the ballet, which I entitled 'Choreartium,' according to the instrumentation of the score, using women dancers to accentuate

Figure 6.4 This image of Lifar as Icarus offers a good illustration of male "beats."

the delicate phrases, while the men interpreted the heavier, more robust passages. The music, with its rich orchestration and its many contrasts, lent itself admirably to this kind of interplay between masculine and feminine movements."[99] In *Choreartium*, dancers mimicked gendered tonalities in music. Massine accomplished this by visualizing a series of movements and groupings with varying asymmetrical masculine and feminine forms. In doing so, he dispensed with classic male and female partnering and, instead, "balanced the interplay" between male and female dancers, whose bodies symbolized specific notes and tonalities.[100] The ballet delineated gender difference by juxtaposing masculine and feminine movements. Massine defined masculinity as "robust and heavy" and femininity as "delicate." The energetic "masculine" technique of the male dancer in the ballet made an especially strong impression on audiences and revitalized the role of the male dancer by presenting him as athletic and strong (e.g., *tour en l'air*). In turn, it reinforced traditional feminine ideas about ballet dancing by presenting female movement as delicate and refined. Here we can see how choreographic developments in ballet reinforced ideologies of gender that rested in opposition.

As director of the Opéra ballet, Serge Lifar made many efforts to legitimize the position of the male dancer in his capacities as dancer, critic, historian, director, and choreographer. He expanded choreography for men and introduced dance solos for men in both original and revival works. In these works, his new vision of the virtuosity of the male dancer corresponded with new attitudes towards the muscular, healthy body that were circulating at the time. Thus, Lifar instilled in the male dancer a new vitality and athleticism, but one that did not erode his poetic presence (as Levinson also suggested).

In his capacity as dance critic and choreographer, Lifar also succeeded in creating a "modern" concept of ballet – one that universalized balletic qualities. In his book, *Lifar on Classical Ballet* (1951) he expanded the usage of early nineteenth-century ballet qualities, ones that had been previously reserved for female dancers. Defining *élévation* as "the flight of the soul" and "not a technique, but a state of mind," and *ballon* as "the take-off of the body" (rather than as ethereal femininity), Lifar reconceptualized important balletic qualities. This new usage of traditional balletic terms is significant for two reasons. First, Lifar, in his enunciation of the difference between *élévation* and *ballon*, makes no distinction between their appropriation to gender (although we will see later that Lifar's application or execution of such qualities are different for women and men). Second, Lifar locates the source of these qualities within the dancing itself. Such qualities do not originate in accompanying poetry, pantomime, music, or metaphor as perceived by the symbolists poets Mallarmé and Valéry or others who argued that dance was dependent on music. Lifar's vision entailed something different.

In *Lifar on Classical Ballet,* Lifar outlined the application of *élévation* and *ballon* in ballet dancing using the examples of *Prince Igor* and his own ballet *Icarus.* "A dancer may have *ballon* without necessarily possessing *élévation,* and vice versa," he began. *Ballon* could be found in the Polovtsian dances of *Prince Igor,* where it was required in the "vigorous jumps and sudden savage bounds" of the choreography. *Ballon* here was not an ethereal, feminine attribute (as in nineteenth-century Romantic ballet) but rather a "purely earthbound conception of the dance." The character dances, Lifar explained, "develop close to the ground, and the dancer, firmly upright on the earth that bears him, furnishes by his leaping a striking illustration of the laws of attraction … he bounds, the better to fall; jumps but does not fly." In *Icarus,* Lifar located *élévation* "from beginning to end." Here the hero's movements "fly upwards as if he were no longer subject to the laws of gravity. He rests on the ground, the better to leap." Lifar explained: "His element is space in which he will soon soar with wide-spread wings. If he happens to come into contact with the earth, it is only to draw fresh strength from it, to fly still higher."[101] Thus we find traditional terms of ballet renegotiated in modern ballet and applied strictly to choreographic movement. Moreover, *élévation* and *ballon* are understood as gender-neutral qualities of ballet dancing (technique). In other words, there is a shift in attention from the personas of the dancer (and their sex) to the ballet dancing itself (the execution of the choreography): classical ballet vocabulary used to judge ballet dancing was reconceptualized for the modern man and woman.

Serge Lifar's revitalization of the Ballet de l'Opéra also entailed a reconfiguration of the dance roles of the female and male dancer. Lifar placed great value on both female and male dancing, in some ballets appointing the central role to the *danseuse* while in others to the *danseur.* For example, in 1935, Lifar created *Icare,* one of his signature ballets in which he danced the leading role and, in 1941, created *Istar* for the young dancer Yvette Chauviré.[102] Lifar envisioned male and female dancing as each requiring a distinct artistry. Similar to Théophile Gautier, who believed resolutely in the gendering of choreography in the nineteenth century, Lifar, in his reformation of choreography, offered the *danseuse* and *danseur* their own specific virtuosity. For example, Lifar writes in *Lifar on Classical Ballet*: "The soul of the dance is in elevation, but elevation is not the same in man as in woman: the former hails his victory by a haughty conquest of space in which he bounds and briskly shoots upwards to the skies; the latter follows him in his flight, but without ever forgetting those terrestrial roots, the pointes, the *danseuse*'s style of elevation."[103] Lifar's gendering of choreography delineated both aesthetic and ideological boundaries for male and female dancing. Here Lifar distinguishes not just choreography, but actual qualities of dancing – *élévation* and *ballon* hold distinct functions for men and women.

It was in the application of such qualities that gender ideology was most visibly present. Lifar once remarked that such "boundaries" rested upon laws of nature. For example, Lifar envisioned jumps as intended only for men: "Is not this the law of nature?" he asked.[104] Lifar established an ornate French national style where jumps were clearly the domain of men and pointe work was the domain of women. Lifar thus reinforced gender difference in ballet in his vision and eventual standardization of French ballet technique. By appropriating distinct and, at times, opposing styles in ballet dancing, Lifar offered not only an autonomous place for both male and female dancer but distinct (and gendered) realms of expertise. One might argue that gender in ballet was restabilized according to early twentieth-century ideals of gender opposition (although male dancers remain stigmatized to a degree as effeminate).

As director of the Paris Opéra ballet, Serge Lifar made great efforts to transform the ballet into a more serious and technically proficient art institution. He inspired many changes at the Opéra that forged a new and revitalized appreciation for French ballet. We have already seen several ways in which his transformative measures extended to both ideological and bureaucratic levels. We also saw how he developed a modern national aesthetic for ballet in France, one that was grounded in dance choreography and a neoclassical style. In fact, the neoclassical style of ballet remains the trademark of French ballet today. Furthermore, like André Levinson, Lifar saw the return of the male dancer as a vital factor in the revival of French ballet. Lifar's reformation of the Paris Opéra ballet along with his neoclassical style managed to restore the idea of the male dancing body as beautiful and as heroic. In fact, this "néo-classique" style embraced the idea of the body as beautiful, whether male or female. Ultimately, he legitimated both the female and male dancer in ballet so that their presence was accepted and their individual artistries appreciated.

As we have seen, commentary on ballet served as a vehicle through which to assert contemporary notions about masculinity, male corporeality, and the beauty of male form. In the effort to regenerate the nation, criticism in major bourgeois journals emphasized "normative" masculine traits of male dancers in order to make French ballet compatible with a republican France. The problematic nature of male ballet dancing was resolved (at least theoretically) by linking male bodies to the new masculine virtues of athleticism, strength, and virility that were associated with republicanism and the general health of the nation. For this reason, intellectuals and dance experts all avoided explicit discussions of male homosexuality in ballet in their reviews as sexual deviance was seen as infectious to the national and social body. In doing so, men in ballet could be acceptable on the French stage and thus legitimatize ballet as a quintessential art for the haute bourgeoisie.[105] Even the Ballets Russes, with its transgressive imagery, still presented heterosexual relationships in its productions (although allusions to homosexuality might be read). Critical responses to the Ballets Russes reflected the company's fluctuation between reflecting conventional gender ideologies and refashioning competing ideologies of gender that circulated in France, and abroad, after the First World War. Serge Lifar, while adorning the male dancer with a new centrality and athleticism in ballet, also presented ballets that reinforced conventional notions of gender complementarity and difference. Nonetheless, we can see how ballet became a space in which ideologies of gender were defined in new terms. This placed the male dancer's masculinity on new, although still unstable, ground. Thus a gender analysis of ballet offers a better understanding of the process by which the male dancer was reintegrated into ballet in France. Furthermore, the fact that new ideals of masculinity found a place in discussions of ballet reveals the way in which ballet functioned as cultural force in the early twentieth century.

While early productions of the Ballets Russes drove many critics to claim that the revival of the male dancer was essential to the success of ballet in France, it took nearly two decades before the French came to terms with having their own French male dancers revered at the Opéra. As we have seen, this shift was rooted partly in a neoclassical revival in the 1920s and 1930s as well as an athletic space in which to assert heroic male form. In proposing and implementing neoclassicism in ballet, André Levinson and Serge Lifar provided an aesthetic opportunity for the return of the male dancer and the acceptability of male corporeal beauty on the stage. They were able to do so by reconfiguring traditional gender dynamics in ballet production. The revival of neoclassicism and a new abstract representation of the body opened a space for the renegotiation of both the male and female dancer upon the ballet stage, and for the increased professionalism of the art of ballet. Ultimately, the return of the male dancer and the professionalization of the female dancer enabled a modernization of ballet choreography and production. By the 1940s, a series of rising male stars captured the Parisian public's attention. These included David Lichine, Roland Petit, André Eglevsky, Maurice Béjart, and Jean Babilée.[106] Trained at the Opéra ballet school under the direction of Lifar, Babilée captured the French classicism articulated within the writings of Levinson and Lifar. He was revered for his technical virtuosity, expressivity, musicality, grace, *ballon*, athletic prowess (he was most famous for his soaring leaps), dynamism, and vitality.

While Diaghilev's Ballets Russes and Serge Lifar's reforms at the Opéra were vital to paving the way for male dancers and developments in choreography for men, it would take years for the public to recover its delight in a masculine style of performance, such as that of Nijinsky. Even though the current director of the Conservatoire de Danse de l'Opéra recalled that the 1950s saw the largest enrolment of boys at the Paris Opéra School, it was not until the 1960s and 1970s that dancers such as Rudolph Nureyev and Mikhail Baryshnikov received the same devotion from the public as did Nijinsky: "The extraordinary talents of Baryshnikov, Villela, Nureyev … and their numerous guest appearances with companies around the world, have drawn attention – even adoration – to their art. A danseur like Baryshnikov inspires the devotion of the public, management and choreographers alike, and the name of either Nureyev or Baryshnikov guarantees a sold-out house; it is primarily for these dancers that new works are being created."[107] In the '70s and '80s, Nureyev and Baryshnikov ensured sold-out performances at the Metropolitan Opera House in New York City and each earned six-digit salaries. Furthermore, they attracted boys to ballet, inspired more education on dance whether through film or television, and evoked a poetic masculinity in the works they inspired.

7

The Rise of the Professional Female Dancer

Lifar's reign at the Opera ensured that ballet held a place of importance there, and his company included ballerinas of international renown like Yvette Chauviré, Lycette Darsonval, Liane Daydé, and Nina Vyroupova.[1]

– *European Review* (1970)

Over the course of the early twentieth century, ideal notions of male and female identity were continually reinvented. The "crisis of masculinity" that followed the Franco-Prussian War (and was exacerbated after the First World War) was accompanied by a "crisis of femininity." Questions arose over the identity of republican women, the relationship between women and the state, women's health, women's economic independence, and women's presence in the public sphere.[2] By the interwar period, shifting attitudes towards women's work, health, artistic expression, professionalism, and corporeality gave rise to new conceptions of femininity. For example, the embrace of physical culture refashioned respectable femininity as new attitudes towards athleticism developed and physical health was linked to national strength. How did shifts in perceptions of gender identity and corporeality affect the status of the female dancer in France? To what extent was the status of the professional female dancer shaped by contemporary tensions over femininity, achievement, and athleticism? What was the relationship between the status of ballet and attitudes towards the female body? Why did the stigma of dancers' sexual availability erode in the early twentieth century?

Ballet was used as a means to express ideas about femininity, female corporeality, and female artistry. As critics tried to justify the new role and value of the male dancer on the ballet stage, they also attempted to reconceptualize the female dancer. Early twentieth-century critics played an important role in shaping a new reputation and professional credibility for women in ballet, which, in turn, contributed to ballet's revival. Reviews of female dancers focused less on their eroticism as "public" working-class women and more on their technical virtuosity as professional artists. By pointing out the extensive discipline, athleticism, grace, and technical virtuosity of female dancers, critics and intellectuals adorned the female dancer with new republican values, many of which were shaped by the physical culture movement.

In order to understand critics' efforts to elevate the profession of the female dancer in France, it is important to consider the cultural climate of the late nineteenth and early twentieth centuries. At the fin de siècle, there existed competing ideologies of femininity. Fears of depopulation and degeneration encouraged a reinforcement of traditional images of womanhood that rested on marriage, motherhood, and morality. The feminist movement, however, argued for women's economic independence, suffrage, access to education, marriage reform, property and child custody rights, and sexual liberation. Thus the turn of the century was a period of gender instability and cultural anxiety. The weakening influence of the Catholic Church also stirred anxieties over the moral health of the nation. The secularization of schools in the last decades of the nineteenth century meant new moral instruction to its pupils. Replacing the traditional Catholic curriculum, educators aimed to regenerate the nation through a cultivation of both the mind and the body. In the 1880s, laws were passed that incorporated mandatory physical fitness in the curriculum of both boys' and girls' education. While in the 1830s cultural convictions dictated that "acrobatics deformed girls' bodies and endangered their reproductive organs," hygienists began to recommend that girls go to dance classes to strengthen them, to give them "grace," to correct deformities, and to improve coordination.[3] Under the Third Republic, ideal masculinity entailed a *reintroduction* of male corporeality that rested on classical male beauty, athletic prowess, and heroism (one that had disappeared in the nineteenth century), while ideal femininity involved a *renegotiation* of female corporeality as women's associations with the body (Woman = Body) never eroded. As Londa Schiebinger notes, female and male bodies each had "a distinct telos – physical and intellectual strength for the man, motherhood for the woman."[4] The emphasis on physical fitness in women aimed at the achievement of health (especially reproductive health) and beauty (also a marker of moral goodness).[5]

Modern ideas about working women and their bodies were propagated in various ways at the turn of the century. Degeneration theory incited fears of physical and moral decay in France, using the aristocracy and working poor as examples. However, working-class women's bodies were also eroticized in a way that catered to modern tastes and trends. In painting, for example, images of such women were used to capture a modern "realist" aesthetic style. The enduring association of working-class women with sexual availability was exploited in the art of modernist artists such as Manet, Degas, and Renoir. Degas's portrayal of bathers and dancers is a good example of the fetishization of working-class women's bodies in this period. The negative reception of Degas's sculpture *Little Dancer Aged Fourteen,* exhibited in 1881, is not surprising as the statuette's realism revealed the dancer's athleticism and strength rather than her erotic appeal. Repulsed by the rendering of the statue as excessively muscular, critics deemed the dancer-figure as deformed, primordial, bestial, and degenerate.[6] By imprinting muscularity, fatigue, and thinness onto the statuette, Degas de-eroticized the dancer's body and deprived it of any poetic value. Similarly, in dramatic theatre, new demands on critics to reveal the personal lives of actresses prompted the fear that the erotic appeal of theatre women would diminish.[7] As Lenard Berlanstein notes, "a theatre that was not sexually charged would have been unfamiliar, undesirable and even un-French in the late nineteenth century." It was this eroticism that made theatre "French theatre."[8] Once the erotic appeal of women's bodies was stripped away, the traditional function of French art and theatre was challenged.

As we can see, female corporeality and working women's bodies were infused with political, social, and cultural meanings. Over the course of the twentieth century, attitudes towards female corporeality transformed as French bodies (both male and female) became increasingly equated with the health and strength of the nation, albeit on different terms. Moreover, notions about women's bodily display in public changed significantly. Critics and intellectuals who desired to elevate ballet's status in France had to navigate the politics of the female body and find a way to highlight dancers' athleticism and technical virtuosity while maintaining clear boundaries of femininity. One way to do so was to envision the female dancing body as capable of embodying both athletic skill and poetic expression. In doing so, they attempted to de-eroticize female corporeal beauty in ballet and to redefine ballet's function.

This chapter reveals how ballet spawned discussions about femininity, women's artistic achievement, and female corporeality. The chapter begins with an examination of the changing meanings attached to the female dancer in the eighteenth and nineteenth centuries. During the course of the nineteenth century, women's roles in ballet were deeply shaped by Romanticism, the rise of the bourgeoisie, and commodity culture. Next, the chapter illustrates the ways in which the Ballets Russes presented female dancers in its works and in its publicity, and analyzes how ballet commentary responded to such representations. Critics' portrayals of female dancers reflected and shaped contemporary attitudes towards women's roles, women's bodies, and ideals of femininity. An analysis of reviews of female dancers reveals also the new relation of women, achievements, and athleticism in postwar culture. As we will see, dance criticism serves as a unique lens through which to examine how shifts in gender ideology affected modern notions of female performers in France. In the cultural climate of the interwar period, Serge Lifar as director of the Paris Opéra ballet, managed to revitalize ballet training and choreography for women, de-eroticize the ballet environment at the Opéra, and bestow republican ideals of modern femininity upon the Opéra's dancers.

WOMEN AND FRENCH BALLET

When the Paris Opéra was founded in 1671, its corps de ballet (drawn from Louis XIV's Académie Royale de Danse) was all male. By 1681, however, a few women appeared on the Opéra stage, such as Mlle La Fontaine (1665–1738) – known as the "Queen of Dance" – Marie-Thérèse de Subligny (1666–1736), and Françoise Prévost (1680–1741).[9] Ballet technique in its undeveloped form, however, remained masculine. In 1726, Marie Camargo (1710–1770) was the first woman to manage an "entrechat quatre" – a dance step (athletic jump) until then performed only by men (she achieved this by shortening the length of her skirt). Voltaire was so taken by her skill that he declared that she "was the first to dance like a man."[10] Most likely Voltaire was referring to Camargo's elaborate footwork, which at the time was the domain of male technical style. Another critic, writing in *Mercure de France,* also noted Camargo's virtuosity: "Mlle Camargo danced with all the liveliness and intelligence that could possibly be expected from a young person aged fifteen ... Her cabrioles and entrechats were effortless, although she has still many perfections to acquire before she can venture comparison with her illustrious teacher. She is considered to be one of the most brilliant dancers to be seen, in particular for her sensitive ear for music, her airiness, and her strength."[11] In 1734, female dancer Marie Sallé was also praised for her dancing skills.[12] Voltaire complimented Sallé for having the most eloquent expression, gesture, and step. In comparing the talents of both Camargo and Sallé, Voltaire wrote, "Ah Camargo, how brilliant you are! But, great gods, how ravishing too is Sallé. Your steps are so light, hers so smooth! She is incomparable, yet you have something new. You leap like the Nymphs, but she dances like the Graces."[13] Here we see female dancers in the eighteenth century valorized for their strength, grace, expressivity, musicality, intelligence, and technical proficiency – all criteria by which ballet dancers are judged today. Ballet dancing, however, was not yet a feminine domain. During the second half of the eighteenth century, the Paris Opéra was dominated by male dancers such as the Italian-French virtuoso Gaétan Vestris and his son Auguste Vestris, famed for his jumps and leaps. However, women such as the German-born Anne Heinel, the first female dancer to do double pirouettes, also were gaining in technical proficiency and admiration.

With the Romantic revolution and the innovation of pointe work, women secured their place in ballet. Narrative themes, costumes, and technique all centred around the female dancer. In this period, the prima ballerina (usually foreign-born) reigned upon the stage. International ballerinas Marie Taglioni, Fanny Cerrito (Elssler), Carlotta Grisi, and Lucile Grahn showcased their technical abilities, gracefulness, and charm in Paris and abroad. *La sylphide* (1832), in which Marie Taglioni danced the lead role, is traditionally noted as the first Romantic ballet and the first to use the newly invented block pointe shoe instead of the traditional high heel or darned shoes. The narrative centred on a supernatural creature who is loved and inadvertently destroyed by a mortal man. To create an effect of lightness and the ethereal, the choreographer Filippo Taglioni (Marie's father) explored the technical use of the pointe shoe. *La sylphide* popularized the use of the white tutu as it did Romantic themes, developments in ballet technique, stage decor, and lighting.[14] In fact, as dance historian Selma Cohen notes, the ballet had an immediate effect on popular culture with "Parisian women dress[ing] their hair 'à la Sylphide' and 'Taglionism' bec[oming] a verb."[15] Here we can see a clear example of how the arts are often shaped by foreigners. The concept of the pointe shoe was introduced by an Italian!

Evoking a sense of the ethereal and exotic, female ballet dancers became the epitome of femininity, beauty, and sensuality. A society columnist for *L'Illustration* asked in 1844, "How did the dancer Fanny Elssler 'take Paris'? She smiled with her siren lips and her white teeth; she moved her arms, legs, her head, all her body with the grace of a true daughter of Eve. Her waist, filled with damnation, issued a dare."[16] One dancer of the Second Empire remarked bluntly, "What's the use of doing yourself so much harm, when you can please just as well with much less effort? If you haven't a good figure, you must use your talent, but if you are pretty and well formed, that makes up for everything."[17] As these statements reveal, talent became less important than looks. Dancers, however, existed in a highly stratified internal structure. While the première danseuse came to represent grace and authority on stage, where her personified chastity eroticized her (a moral agency that was grounded on accessibility rather than attainability), the ballet girl or corps de ballet were characterized as unmarried, approachable, erotic beings. Regardless of rank, the stigma of working-class origins and sexual impropriety branded the female dancer from the 1830s well into the twentieth century.

Women's reputations as ballet dancers were powerfully affected by a long tradition of aristocratic libertinism that was exacerbated in the 1830s when the Opéra fell under private management and was no longer entirely subsidized by the state. The Paris Opéra's increasing dependence on male subscribers resulted in their influence over its opera managers and the governing board of which they were now members. Catering to the demand for performers' interactions with subscribers between acts and after the shows, the new manager Louis Véron opened the Foyer de la Danse as a space in which dancers could both rehearse and mingle with male "admirers" (fig. 7.1). Thereafter, these men could freely roam the corridors, rehearsal studios, and dressing rooms of the Opéra.[18] Their influence also carried over to the Opéra productions themselves. Ballet divertissements

Figure 7.1 Salle Le Peletier of the old Paris Opéra. The lower portion of this 1841 lithograph identifies the female Opéra dancers and their male "sponsors" by name.

were placed in the second acts of operas to allow the Jockey Club's ballet subscribers the opportunity to dine with their ballet dancers/mistresses before the performances. Having a dancer as a mistress indicated the status of the haute-bourgeois man as well as the aristocratic man. The female dancer's place in French society was thus paradoxical: she was necessary to the haute bourgeoisie but also a threat to its moral order. The Paris performance of Wagner's *Tannhäuser* on 13 March 1861 caused an uproar when Wagner, who staged the production, placed the ballet divertissement in the first act of the opera. Furious at this change, members of the Jockey Club disrupted the performance by whistling in unison throughout it. Consequentially, Wagner withdrew his work in disgust.[19]

Theatre criticism responded to this shift in ballet's function and value by catering to the erotic responses of male audiences. Reviews of ballerinas in the nineteenth century tended to focus on the dancer's dramatic expression (pantomime), poetic presence, and physical beauty. Critic Julien-Louis Geoffroy believed that pantomime was the most important, beautiful, and interesting part of ballet because "it use[d] only the noblest parts of the body," which he deemed as the head, face, and arms rather than the legs and feet.[20] According to Geoffroy, narrative expression and dramatic action played a more important role than technical display or footwork. Théophile Gautier, the most outspoken figure on the subject of ballet during the mid- to late nineteenth century, declared that "it must not be forgotten that the first quality a dancer should possess is that of beauty; she has no excuse for not being beautiful and she can be reprimanded for her plainness."[21] Gautier based much of his dance criticism on the shaping of a dancer's body from her forehead, nose, and head to her legs, arms, and bosom. While he praised Italian ballerina Marie Taglioni as "one of the greatest poets of her time," calling her "a genius in the same measure as Lord Byron or Lamartine,"[22] he also claimed that ballet consisted of "dance, poses, and rhythmical movement, and why not admit it, the physical voluptuousness and beauty of woman."[23]

Critic Jules Janin, who was an important ballet reviewer in the 1840s, remarked that "one of ballet's attractions was the dancer's revealing costumes." He confessed that he favoured those ballets with themes that "permitted the nymphs to be lightly dressed."[24] Many reviews of this period commented on the figures and minimal costume coverage of the female (most foreign-born) ballerinas.[25] The increasing eroticization of the female dancer is clear in Janin's review of Italian newcomer Fanny Cerrito in 1847. He begins: "She bounds like a gazelle and dances like the verdant hills; she is lively, alert, passionate, everything she could be … Imagine Mlle Taglioni transformed into a full-breasted woman, with beautiful well-connected limbs – legs, arms, hips – and no wings on her strong and proud shoulders."[26] The greater emphasis on the virtuosity of the female dancer (with the advent of the pointe shoe in the early 1830s) and erotic appeal of the corps de ballet was accompanied by a progressive shortening of the tutu to better reveal the legs and legwork. In the 1830s, the hem of the tutu was at mid-calf and by the 1860s at the knee. By the 1890s, the tutu extended only to mid-thigh.[27] This raises the question of whether there existed a distinction between ballet as an aesthetic experience and ballet as an erotic spectacle. Thus, as ballet technique developed, the dancer needed her costume to be less restrictive to accommodate dance movements. However, in doing so, she displayed more of her body to the public. The very visibility of her body degraded her vocation and transformed the function of her movements into an erotic display of the female body.

After the collapse of the Second Empire, the social function of the Opéra continued to be shaped by the rise of the bourgeoisie and commodity culture. Under the Third Republic, the Opéra remained an elite institution for the haute bourgeoisie and was deemed a luxury that equalled, if not rivalled, that of the imperial theatres in Europe. Instead of abandoning aristocratic practices, the haute bourgeoisie merely reconfigured them. In the libertinism of the Third Republic, keeping a female performer as a mistress was less debased as a courtly practice but continued to serve as a measure of a gentleman's status and wealth. As Lenard Berlanstein notes, "Fashionable writers of the nineteenth-century presumed that they were perpetuating authentic eighteenth-century practices when they insisted that the correct form of elite libertinism was a quest for reputation and prestige." Berlanstein points out that the purpose of a mistress changed from being mere sexual gratification to a marker of one's status and wealth:

> The ultimate purpose of keeping a woman, they said, was not to enjoy intimacy with her but rather to have Le Monde know that she was under your protection and displayed your wealth … As in the First Republic, politicians of the Third replicated the libertine behavior of the former monarchical courtiers. The journalist Pierre Giffard identified senators and deputies as the most common types who kept young dancers at the Opera … Edmond de Goncourt cited the case of the Paris municipal councilman Alphonse Humbert who … took a player at the Comédie-francaise as a lover because, said Goncourt, "the actress at the Comédie is the favored mistress, imposed on all men who have arrived in political life."[28]

Thus aristocratic libertinism was reappropriated as a sign of republican bourgeois masculinity in the late nineteenth century. In other words, ideal French masculinity was linked to the sexual objectification of the performing woman. The journal *La Vie Parisienne* announced that female dancers were the "cream of the demimonde," and that to have one as a mistress was "the supreme test of epicurean habits."[29]

Beginning in the late 1860s, membership in the infamous Jockey Club became less select than it had been in the 1830s. As a result, ballet audiences at the Opéra were less discriminating. Ballet music was deemed mediocre, as were sets, decor, costumes, and choreography. Increasingly, ballet was taken less seriously as an art, and the virtuosity of its performers, who were now predominantly female, received less attention in reviews than their smiles.[30] French journalist and writer Alfred Delvau wrote frankly in 1867: "One is more deliciously stirred by the sight of the ballet corps than by the great arias of the tenor in vogue or reigning donna. They are so eloquent, these little dancers – even those who are not dancing – with their rose jerseys and their gauze skirts! Eloquence of the flesh, certainly!"[31] As ballet historian Arnold Haskell points out, "The French dancer had lost her vocation. Ballet was a short cut to a private income and was not to be thought of as a career for *une jeune fille bien élevée*" (a young girl of good standing).[32] By the 1890s, men all but disappeared from the ballet stage and were replaced by female travesty dancers. Consequently, ballet attracted a predominantly male audience. One critic described the female dancer in the late 1890s: "As soon as she [a dancer] enters the Opéra her destiny as a whore is sealed; there she will be a high-class whore."[33] He was not exaggerating: the economic conditions at the Paris Opéra made occasional prostitution a necessity for many of its female dancers. The financial and sexual exploitation of female dancers played a central role in the way ballet was valued as an art in the early years of the Third Republic.

Towards the end of the century, the symbolist poets attempted to redeem ballet as a lofty art form and to adorn the female dancer with poetic qualities. In the process, they reduced the dancer's body to a metaphorical idea. In their desire to transcend form in their poetry, they also sought to transcend form in bodily movement. By highlighting the dancer's metaphoric qualities and by promoting ballet as the ultimate manifestation of pure poetic form, symbolists offered an alternative understanding of the function of female corporeality in the art. Paul Valéry was one poet who attempted to do this. He opened his *Philosophy of the Dance* writing "Let me begin at once by telling you without preamble that to my mind the dance is not merely an exercise, an entertainment, an ornamental art, or sometimes a social activity; it is a serious matter and in certain aspects most venerable."[34] He continued: "For the dance is an art derived from life, itself, since it is nothing less than the action of the whole human body; but an action transposed into a world, into a space-time, which is no longer quite the same as that of everyday life."[35] Dance was like recited poetry, Valéry argued, in that it was immediate, had its own laws, and created a state of mind. According to Valéry, dance was a metaphysical world of movement.[36] According to this vision, ballet's value rested on its ability to convey poetic expression.

According to the symbolists, the dancer was a manifestation of poetic metaphor. She was exalted for her ability to transcend her body in order to reveal an idea on stage. Valéry pointed out that the female dancer was "a thing without a body" and "a little heap of limbs and scarves." Poet Stéphane Mallarmé described the dancer as "an unconscious revealer of truths,"[37] going so far as to claim that the dancer was "a set of juxtaposed metaphors" who "does not dance."[38] According to the symbolists, the dancer must transcend the activity of dancing (technical virtuosity) in order to attain poetic value. The virtuosity of her ballet technique was less important. Ballet as a poetic form was understood primarily as an expressive art form (the dancer "does not dance" and, according to some, does not even have a body) and as a feminine art form (only women were thought capable of embodying poetic metaphor and beauty on stage).

It is useful to consider the status of women in ballet within the broader changes occurring in the theatre world at the end of the nineteenth century in France. As Lenard Berlanstein notes, theatre "was supposed" to carry a strong erotic appeal and was "intended to be more meaningful to male than female spectators" in the nineteenth century.[39] By the 1880s and 1890s, however, women's new activities as consumers played a role in reshaping French theatre. At this time, theatre catered to its female audiences by showcasing the latest fashions, hairstyles, and feminine trends in a way that was more explicitly commercialized. As Berlanstein notes, the "obstacles to legitimatizing the influence of the stage on fashion weakened dramatically once the Third Republic was established."[40] The new attention given to actresses' personal lives and off-stage activities in magazines and mass-circulation dailies de-eroticized the theatre environment by demystifying their identities into "ordinariness" and thus enabled bourgeois women to identify with them.[41] Celebrity actresses and prima ballerinas became the models of femininity and taste. A 1911 article entitled "Madame Is Served: Our Actresses at Meals" captured the cultural power of the celebrity performer. The author described the actresses' dining habits, whether they ate alone or with their pets. The piece noted that the actresses "ate only fruit and tea or water, for 'they are constrained to gastronomical privation by love of their art."' The article concluded with a reminder to its female readers that "everyone was dieting at the time."[42] Here we can see the ways in which the press mediated between the French public and ideas about female performers.

As Berlanstein's study reveals, there was a greater toleration of women who were "ambitious, achieving, and public" by the end of the nineteenth century.[43] (Louis) Octave Uzanne was one contemporary who believed that the erotic culture of the stage was diminishing in France and that theatre had become "more moral and bourgeois" at the turn of the century. In his book *The Modern Parisienne* (1912), he noted a fellow journalist's remark that "actresses and dancers are now very respectable." He concurred, writing, "Many actresses now affect respectability, marry and live like good bourgeoises, and are excellent mothers."[44] By juxtaposing theatre women against the other categories of women in Paris, particularly prostitutes, Uzanne's book encouraged a de-eroticization of theatre and an appreciation for actresses' artistry and decency. Regarding the dancers at the Opéra, he readily noted their hard work, discipline, and demanding physical training. He asserted that one could no longer find the *petit-rats* scurrying around the Opéra but instead the dedicated, career-driven performers: "This miniature corps de ballet soon learn to love its art, and discipline and punctuality are (who would believe it!) perfect." Here Uzanne challenges traditional notions of dancers as immoral, lazy, degraded working-class women, and instead adorns them with republican virtues of marriage, motherhood, honest labour, discipline, punctuality, and skilled craftsmanship. However, he also described the dancer as lacking any intellectual capabilities: "The modern dancer is graceful and attractive, dedicated from her earliest years to physical training; she has very ordinary intelligence, and rarely possesses any intellectual qualities. Her art is applied to the body only, not to the mind, and as the development of her muscles has engrossed all the waking hours of her youth, she has never had the time for instruction, or for feeding her little bird's brain."[45] Although Uzanne's commentary brands the female dancer as minimally intelligent, it does provide insight into the ways in which female performers were recast at the turn of the century. Uzanne made a point to include the technical language of dance steps in his discussion of dancers to emphasize ballet as a skilled craft, writing that the dancers' "principle studies consist in learning how to accomplish *Assemblés, jetés … ballons, pirouettes, pointes … grand fouettes, élévations* and other exercises." He discussed in detail the routine of the ballet lesson, which also emphasized the dancer's artistry and skill.[46]

Clearly, there existed an underlying tension between the sexual availability of young dancers and the public regard for the artistry of ballet in the late nineteenth century. Berlanstein writes: "Knowledgeable about ballet, [the paternalist type] competently doled out praise and criticism of the performances … According to *La Vie Parisienne,* paternalists did not forget that, whatever else dancers did, their art and career were important. One Monsieur, according to this journal, told his mistress right after intercourse, 'Remember, you perform tonight.'"[47] While this is an indication that ballet's integrity as a French high art had not entirely eroded, it also reveals the precarious position of ballet dancers as working women. They were, at once, members of the working poor and artists of a high art form. The study of rhetoric about performing women thus offers a view of French attitudes toward women's involvement in the public sphere, working-class identity, women as interpreters of art, and the way in which working-class women played a role in defining bourgeois male identity (via libertinism). In other words, it reveals the meanings attached to women performers and how they were integrated into French culture.

The status of theatre women at the turn of the century changed along with attitudes towards women and the public sphere. Public women seemed less frightening as "women were less stigmatized for consuming, enjoying commercial leisure, and pursuing individual destinies."[48] Increasingly, the republican order could not maintain the separation of public and private spheres. Women's ambition, achievement, and autonomy were tolerated as long as they did not neglect their domestic responsibility. Berlanstein argues that such shifts enabled the Third Republic to confer its "official approval on actresses" by bestowing a new republican feminine identity upon them. The result was the increasing moralization of the theatre and, furthermore, the allocation of honours given to theatre women.[49]

Women in the performing arts were nevertheless controversial, and an examination of their status thus offers an important window onto cultural attitudes towards all women in France. As Berlanstein points out, "By being unconventional or ambitious, theatre women embodied fears about the direction women were taking in the late nineteenth century."[50] French theatre women were deemed both "exceptionally prominent" and "peculiarly proscribed."[51] They were represented as either sympathetic figures or subversive and corrupt deviants. Similarly, ballet dancers were stigmatized as erotic but also capable of embodying grace, elegance, and sophistication. This paradoxical position of theatre women created much discussion of their place in French society and anxieties over the extent to which their public visibility threatened all women. While advocates attempted to remove barriers to actresses' acceptance, some moral reformers pushed to reduce actresses' visibility. In this way, actresses served as "barometers of the acceptance of women in the public sphere."[52] The late nineteenth-century theatre, therefore, became a site for the construction of modern female identities.

While theatre and ballet are similar in that they both held deep associations with French heritage and aristocratic culture, ballet was incorporated in a variety of other contexts in which to consider women in the performing arts in this period.[53] The French were able to reimagine actresses in a way that was at this time impossible for ballet dancers. At the end of the nineteenth century, the popularity of theatre was at its peak in France and, like music and art, was recognized for its ability to promote republican values. However, while theatre depended on dramatic expression through the use of voice and text, ballet dancing was grounded in corporeal expression (whether through pantomime/gesture or ballet technique). The study of ballet and its dancers thus requires the examination of cultural attitudes towards not only women working in the public sphere, but also public dancing, female corporeality, and athleticism.

Even though tastes for physical culture were surfacing at the end of the nineteenth century, most ballet discourse at this time did not attempt to "professionalize" dancers by revering their athletic abilities and technical virtuosity. Even into the early years of the twentieth century, there was little acceptance of technical form (athletic prowess) as the defining feature of ballet. In 1907, the critic André Mangeot criticized Opéra principal dancer Carlotta Zambelli for her sterile, artificial French technical style and for her inability to produce beautiful gestures.[54] To prove his point, he invited the ballerina to pose for a series of photographs to demonstrate the lack of beauty in her postures. Refusing to do so, Zambelli answered that her style was fluid and couldn't be recorded in static photography – at this time, photography was not yet capable of capturing "action" movements.[55] This interaction captures the tension between the amateur critic and the artistic technician. In his article, Mangeot reiterated the enduring aesthetic debate in ballet: should dance serve as a representation of dramatic expression or stand on its formal qualities? Mangeot asked, "Is dance, as artists have always wished it, BEAUTY EMBODIED IN GESTURE, or as dance professionals and the great majority of the public image, AGILITY EMBODIED IN MOVEMENT?" His conclusion was that if dance was the latter, it "ceased to be an art."[56] He described ballet technique as constituting "unnatural movements" and as "a battle against nature." According to Mangeot, beauty was supposed "to capture nature." He observed that the emphasis on technique at the Opéra produced *danseuses* with overdeveloped calves that appeared as "deformities" that led to "ugliness." As a result, he noted, "it is a sad fact that the choreographic exercises we see at the Opéra *are not dance*." Mangeot's review is a good example of how some critics resisted placing value on the formal qualities of dance (i.e., technical virtuosity) and insisted on investing ballet with something outside of the actual dancing. Indeed, the feminization of ballet as a social and artistic practice and the increasing emphasis on technique both degraded ballet as an art.

Reviews like that of Mangeot serve as an indication that physical culture had not yet accepted women's athletic prowess, their skills as professionals, and their authority as art experts. While there was a distinct correlation between hygiene, physical health, and feminine beauty in the early years of the twentieth century, women's physical activity could also "excite concerns about degeneration, masculinization, and social disruption."[57] In fact, athleticism in women, while increasingly acknowledged as healthy, was also associated with feminism and deviance (e.g., bicycle riding and boxing). At the turn of the century, there existed both a resistance to and incitement towards accepting the female body as strong, athletic, professional, versatile, and public. Observers' hesitations or discomfort with conceiving dance as a pure art form whose foundation lay in technical skill stemmed from broader anxieties about the body (often linked to femininity) attaining such an abstract and autonomous artistic value.[58] The enthusiasm for the Ballets Russes' new conception of ballet as reliant on its poetic, musical, painterly, costume, and set design components reflects French tastes for modern developments in dramatic expression, music, and design. In other words, the Ballets Russes was successful because it did not seek to locate artistry solely in the body and, more precisely, in the female body.

By the turn of the century, ballet in France had transformed into an all-female, eroticized spectacle for primarily male audiences. The ballet became predominantly associated with eroticism and the fetishizing of the female body, particularly after the incorporation of travesty dancers. In this state, it was impossible for republican ideals of masculinity and femininity to be reflected on the ballet stage. This leads us to ask to what extent the de-eroticization of theatre women affected the ballet and its performers. How and to what degree did the art of ballet manage to distance itself from its associations with sexual promiscuity in the first half of the twentieth century? How did a "modernization" of ballet (via the Ballets Russes) affect the ideologies surrounding ballet dancers? Furthermore, what happened when theatre and ballet became meaningful to both male and female spectators?

REFASHIONING THE FEMALE DANCER

When the Ballets Russes arrive in Paris in 1909, attitudes toward theatre women were already changing, and theatre was increasingly becoming meaningful to both men and women. The Russian company's first season of ballets swept away Parisian audiences with their colourfulness, dynamism, virtuosic dancers, quality music, and exoticism. Like theatre, the Ballets Russes attracted both men and women. In fact, a number of illustrious female patrons enthusiastically attended its performances. The Ballets Russes' presentation of ballet as a "total art" appealed to artists, musicians, literary figures, and fashion designers. As a result of this shift in patronage and the manifestation of ballet as a "total art," ballet audiences became more hetereogenous and discriminating, and ballet no longer served as an erotic spectacle for exclusively male audiences. Epitomizing modernity and later avant-gardism, the company came to symbolize the latest trends in fashion, particularly for women. As Mary E. Davis writes, "After the troupe's initial Paris performance in 1909 nearly every major couture house in the city offered clients clothing that resonated in some way to the visions conjured on the ballet stage under Sergei Diaghilev's direction ... haute couture met high culture on new ground."[59] The Ballets Russes costume designers – many of whom were Parisian – drew upon existing Parisian tastes to create outstanding innovations in fashion design. Shortly after its arrival, Davis notes, "The Ballets Russes became fully attuned to Parisian fashion, responding to tastes and trends, and adapting the latest styles for its artistic presentations."[60] As these tastes extended to a wider constituency of women, the company, "mediated and inspired by fashion, quickly became a part of everyday life for many in the French capital."[61] As we can see, the ballet became a cultural force though which Parisian modern style could be forged. Similar to theatre in the 1880s and 1890s, the ballet and its stars became sites through which to assert varying notions of modern femininity.

The Ballets Russes' innovations in choreography played an important role in drawing audiences to ballet, particularly theatre audiences. Fokine's "new ballet" prioritized dramatic expression and pantomime over classical ballet technique. Ballet became admired for its dramatic elements and theatricality.[62] In his *Memoirs*, Fokine reflected on the appeal of his "new ballet," boasting that it had rapidly taken over other expressive theatrical forms in France, particularly opera. The appeal of Fokine's dramatic ballet is not surprising as the popularity of French theatre was flourishing in the early years of the twentieth century. In other words, there was already a taste for dramatic expression in France when the Ballets Russes arrived. As choreography developed substantially for both female and male dancers, gender difference was reconfigured within ballet. Ballet became about gender oppositions but on new aesthetic terms. Partnered dance, dance solos, a unisex corps de ballet all captured laws of opposition to one extent or another. While the Ballets Russes experimented with gender identity, it merely reconfigured gender difference rather than eliminating it.

The innovations of the Ballets Russes, and the new ballet audiences that it attracted, played a significant role in the redemption of the female dancer in France. While the Ballets Russes productions presented the male dancer in a new way, they also revitalized the role of the female dancer. The company did so by presenting varying and sometimes competing images of female dancers in its ballets. For example, in its early years, the Ballets Russes presented both traditional and transgressive images of femininity in its ballets – something not new to French theatre. Traditional images of femininity were found in ballets such as *La pavilion d'Armide* (1909), *La sylphide* (1909), *Giselle* (1910), and *Swan Lake* (1911) – all of which presented the female dancer in a way that was familiar. More transgressive images of femininity surfaced in ballets such as *Cléopâtre* (1909), in which the ballerina played a seductress; *Schéhérazade* (1910), in which the ballerina played a less central role, wore harem pants, and danced barefoot; and *Petrushka* (1911), in which the ballerina became a parody. In presenting both classical and modern works, Diaghilev offered contrasting images of female dancers and femininity. By expanding their roles, the Ballets Russes showcased the versatility of its female dancers – something that critics continually praised.

From its debut, critics responded favourably to the dancers of the Ballets Russes for their grace, talents, discipline, and versatility. For example, critic Robert Brussel, writing in *Le Figaro* in 1910, attributed Tamara Karsavina's Parisian success to her natural grace and immeasurable talent. He wrote: "It is due to her, in large part, that the honours of the season returned; she did more than shine there, she captivated and moved the audience by her natural grace and immeasurable intimate art. Mme Karsavina, who is and who will always be one of the glories of the Russian ballet, forms with her person, her attitude, her being, and her talent, a quite rare ensemble, despite everything in the choreography."[63] Brussel located three types of grace that Karsavina possessed, all of which centred on her artistry: "the grace of form, the grace of attitude, the grace of movement; she excels in the dance on the ground as well as in the air." He commented on both her expressive and technical virtuosity: "The Russian dancers have, in general, a remarkable *port de bras*: that of Mme Karsavina is the most sensitive and the most expressive that can be imagined. Her dance, the technique of which becomes day after day more precious, is made of a very determined and nevertheless subtle, ineffable charm; it is this admirable artist who, once again, has determined in large part the great success of the Russian season."[64] Brussel's review of Karsavina's performance reveals the new way in which female dancers were discussed at the turn of the century. Brussel emphasized and understood Karsavina's skills on both the dramatic and technical levels. He not only located grace and talent within the Russian female dancer's technique, but also used ballet terminology. In fact, he observed that her ballet technique was improving day by day. The expression "un art personnel" was mentioned several times in Brussel's article and referred to the idea that each principal dancer should have her own individual artistic style. Brussel credited Karsavina for the success of the ballet company. This suggests that there was a link between the status of ballet and the ways its female dancers were assessed. Reviews like those of Brussel helped to usher in a new regard for the female dancer in France by offering a new type of ballet criticism.

As was the case with Romantic ballerinas Fanny Cerrito, Marie Taglioni, Carlotta Grisi, and Lucille Grahn of the early nineteenth century, female dancers once again attained a global celebrity status; their distinctive styles became popularized, dictating what was feminine in fashion. In fact, we find notions of glamour and celebrity attached to many of the prominent women dancing in Paris at the turn of the twentieth century. Isadora Duncan, Loïe Fuller, Anna Pavlova, Tamara Karsavina, Ida Rubinstein, Carlotta Zambelli, Bronislava Nijinska, and Alicia Markova all became the muses of new cosmopolitan images of femininity circulating in newspapers, films, and advertisements.[65] However, it is important to note that most of the celebrities mentioned above were foreign-born. It is only in the 1930s and 1940s that we find French ballet dancers hailed and adored: Yvette Chauviré and Janine Charat, for example. This could be an indication of the heightened sense of nationalism before and during the Second World War.

In the interwar years, as France was working to reinstate traditional gender ideologies, the Ballets Russes experimented more explicitly with alternative female imagery in ballet (e.g., *Le train bleu*, 1924, and *Les biches* (*The House Party*), 1924). Bronislava Nijinska's choreography for *Les biches*, for example, replicated the image of the "garçonne" (boyish woman) and displayed its women as energetic, wilful, sportive, and sexually playful.[66] As Lynn Garafola notes, the female characters "transgressed gender boundaries" and "behav[ed] like men."[67] The understanding of ballet based on the notion of the dancer as feminine, composed, delicate, light, and ethereal was replaced by images of the dancer as athletic, energetic, strong, and

Figure 7.2 *Le train bleu*, 1924. Note the sportive costumes and non-balletic poses of the cast. Costumes by Coco Chanel.

self-assured. In her memoir, Ballets Russes dancer Lydia Sokolova recalled being described as "a most unfeminine woman, though there was nothing particularly masculine about her character. Thin, but immensely strong, she had iron muscles in her arms and legs, and her highly developed calf muscles resembled Vaslav's [Nijinsky's]; she had the same way of jumping and pausing in the air."[68] Thus images of the female dancer as having a taut, strong, athletic, muscular body began to emerge. New concepts circulated of the dancer as hard-working and training for long hours in the practice studio similar to an athlete, as did an emphasis on the execution of dancing in regards to elevation, vigour, agility, virtuosity, and power.

As we have seen, dance critic André Levinson played a significant role in reshaping perceptions of ballet and ballet dancers. He did so by drawing attention to dancers' technical strength and physical training. Levinson, and those who emulated him, asserted that dancers were professional artists in their own right by highlighting them as "technicians" and "impressionarios." He understood that ideal classic ballet entailed rigorous and intensive training. "The constant transfiguration … of the classic dancer from the ordinary to the ideal," he wrote, "is the result of a disinterested will for perfection, an inextinguishable thirst to surpass [her/]himself. Thus it is that an exalted aim transforms [the dancer's] mechanical efforts into an aesthetic phenomenon."[69] Here Levinson argues that the aesthetic value of ballet lies in the formal (technical) qualities of the dancing body that are perfected over the course of a dancer's career.

Repeatedly, Levinson emphasized the discipline and training of ballet dancers and de-eroticized the ballet. According to Levinson, technical virtuosity was essential to a dancer's identity and performance and, in turn, would bring credibility back to the art form. Therefore, Levinson preoccupied himself with the operations at the École de Danse de l'Opéra. In a *Comœdia* article from 1922, he described his visit to the Opéra dance school. He opened by stating that while one would expect an environment similar to that of a Degas drawing of nudity and extreme deprivation, one discovers quite a different atmosphere. "It's going to be noon," he notes, "one has worked since ten-thirty … one rehearses during the afternoon and will dance in the evening … Here is the existence that one likes to call frivolous and flighty [*évaporée*]. Considering this labour and perfection, one cannot be but moved. So truly the work enobles, it's the most noble of crafts."[70] Here Levinson portrays ballet as a skilled craft. The dancer is seen not as a promiscuous working woman but as a disciplined artistic technician. Levinson describes in detail the technical routines of the class and the rigour of the meticulous training that the students underwent. "All these young people who execute a habitual series of exercises at the 'barre' – *battement, ronds de jambe, pliés* – practise the classical language for ten or twelve years. All have already obtained personal success."[71] Levinson's description of the ballet classes at the Opéra dispelled public assumptions of dancers as immoral, indolent, bored, and mundane and revealed more accurately their dedication, hard work, and artistic virtuosity. By emphasizing the intensive training, mastery, and discipline required of the artistic practice of ballet, Levinson attempted to professionalize the art form and to restore the artistic legitimacy of the female dancer. Moreover, Levinson portrayed the female dancer as capable of embodying republican virtues of honourable labour and hard work.

By the 1920s, we find increasing attempts by critics to describe choreographic form, technical virtuosity, and the individual expressive styles of dancers. Critic Antoine Banes, writing in *Le Figaro* in 1920, highlighted Karsavina's "marvelous pointes" in regards to her mastery of the intricate pointework in the choreography of the ballet *Pulcinella* (1920).[72] His review serves as a good example of how critics avoided discussing the erotic potential of dancers' bodies and focused instead on the quality of the dancing. As choreography became more understood and valued by critics, they increasingly located qualities such as strength, agility, precision, and form within women's dancing. In a review of the Ballets Russes' *Les biches*, Louis Laloy described Bronislava Nijinska as a master of ballet who exhibited elegance, balance, athleticism, and technical brilliance. "It is Mme Nijinska, ballet mistress of tremendous resourcefulness, who knew how to take advantage in this manner of all the classical moves, passages on *pointes, pirouettes, entrechats, tours* and *enlèvements*," he writes. In *Les biches*, Laloy located an abstract style of dance that he described as "the air of a slightly rough [*brusquée*] and sportive elegance, which is the taste of our times … This great artist has found for a music of completely French delicacy and freshness, a choreography different and even opposed to that which could have inspired the magnificent drunkenness of a Stravinsky."[73] Laloy went on to call *Les biches* the "*Sylphides* of our times." Both *La sylphide* (1832) and *Les sylphides* (1909) had signified the epitome of nineteenth-century romantic femininity, whereas *Les biches* was a playful look at the social mores, etiquette, stereotypes, and transgressive relationships of the 1920s. Laloy's review implied that modern femininity could embrace elegance and athleticism, grace, and strength. His observations were artistically accurate, as former Ballets Russes star Alicia Markova once described Nijinska's dancing as exhibiting "terrific strength and, yet ... softness."[74]

In his praise for the creative styles of individual dancers, Levinson recognized "the individuality of the female dancer ... in the scope and nuances of '*l'expression plastique*,'" or formal qualities. Levinson wrote of Karsavina, "But that which distinguishes Karsavina, it's the supreme grace of these *ports de bras* which is the preparation for the *pirouette*, a necessary mechanism to turn, a thing of beauty."[75] Here we find *grâce* being allocated to the execution of ballet technique rather than to the embodiment of an idea. In other words, grace refers to the actual dancing, not merely the mood of the dancer: the female dancer actively partakes in her poetic expression through her technical skill. In the Ballets Russes production of *Cléopâtre*, for example, Levinson offered a formal analysis of the female dancing:

> [In] the variation of *Cléopâtre* ... after a rapid *pas de bourrée*, the dancer does a *degagé* in the great second position and while her arms cause the body to move in a rotating fashion, the supporting leg, by the effort of a kick, detaches from the ground and pointe base, rises. Thus, in this jumping while turning step, the acting leg envelops in a vast circle from the vertical ascension of the body, which turns while rising. By executing three times the grandiose and light movement which I just described, the dancer reclimbs backwards to the inclined plateau – and she descends it diagonally, by a series of *pirouettes* and *temps battus*, admirable and complex, according to the heavily emphasized rhythm of the accompaniment ... We will praise again the spirit and the opulence of these *temps sautés* and this so rare quality: the *ballon* ... Shall we reproach the dancer for the most beautiful thing in the world: her youth? No! But we insist of her work that sculptures form and make precise the lines; and then we will see her bloom.[76]

Levinson articulated ballet movements and their beauty in execution through a distinct critical vocabulary. Moreover, he was able to describe the female dancer's movements and body without eroticizing it. Thus as dance became understood and valued as a pure art form of movement and the dancing body as its instrument, the fetishization of the female body played a less prominent role. The question arises: can a woman have a body without being the body? In other words, can the female body on stage be divorced from the objectification and marginalization of the body as "Woman"? The notion of authentic movement and the appropriation of a "pure art" ideology can be seen as a "gateway" to such a transformation.[77]

Levinson was one of the first critics in the Parisian scene to understand ballet as a pure art form that could be appreciated for its formal qualities – moving forms, lines, and elevations. He observed: "We have too long been blind to the beauty and richness of the static and dynamic forms in 'classical ballet.' We were too busy and excited with all that is peripheral to dance itself: the costumes, the miming, this or that treatment of the subject, the beautiful image." Regarding the formal qualities of dance, he asserted, "The actual combination of masses and lines seemed secondary and less interesting to us. Classical ballet seemed monotonous, obsolete; it seemed that we knew it inside out ... We never looked at dance as dance, and never had any conception of the aesthetic value of its complex construction."[78] According to Levinson, the dancing body could be perceived in purely formal or "static" terms. He defined the dancing body as a complex construction of the "combination of masses and lines." By reducing the body to masses, lines, and forms, Levinson is de-eroticizing and (one can argue) de-sexualizing the dancing body. Thus legs, arms, thighs, torsos all become forms through which to express beauty, harmony, vitality, or poetic meaning. In doing so, Levinson gives the female body a different type of attention.

In fact, Levinson went so far as to dehumanize the dancer by comparing her to a machine and even an airplane. In his critique of Paris Opéra dancer Carlotta Zambelli, Levinson wrote: "In order to make a *danseuse* out of a gracious child, it is necessary to begin by dehumanizing her." He continued: "Her muscles fully comply with the requirements of the desired movement. Her legs turn out to amplify the resources of balance. Her torso becomes a solid form. Its members act more as a function of an overall movement. Her silhouettes are abstract and symmetrical lines."[79] Thus the dancer's body is transformed to serve a particular function, in this case, the harmonious unity of forms, lines, and movements. Levinson claimed that the *danseuse* was, in fact, "an artificial being" and "fake." As an unnatural form or, in Levinson's own words, "an instrument of precision and daily work," the dancer escapes from returning to her pre-dancing "human form." Levinson then compared the form and function of the dancer to those of an airplane. Just as the entire construction of an airplane is designed for the supreme goal of speed (with the concept of beauty superimposed), Levinson argued that the dancer aims to construct a similar unity for the goal of balance and beauty. He boasted, "Would the dancer therefore be a machine? Ah yes! A machine to manufacture beauty."[80] The formal analysis of ballet dancing may have reshaped opinions about female dancers by eroding the perception of them as promiscuous working-class women (i.e., their pre-dancing human form) and their potential for eroticization.

As critics like Levinson made great efforts to teach the public about the art of ballet and to expose the incredible discipline and training involved, they also drew special attention to the talented dancers of the Paris Opéra. Although they were enthralled with the talents of the Ballets Russes' women, they became increasingly concerned with the state of the Opéra dancers. Levinson, among others, attempted to restore credibility to the Paris Opéra ballet through his positive reviews of ballerinas there. In his reviews, he placed the Opéra dancers, many of whom were French, on equal footing with great Russian and Italian dancers.[81] Levinson's review of the Opéra's première danseuse Camille Bos did just this. Levinson claimed that Mlle Bos's phenomenal *arabesque* and *élévation* were comparable to "the many Russians, and the one Italian, the legendary Taglioni."[82] He compared the perfect proportions of Bos to those of nineteenth-century *étoile* Emma Livry, who was well-known for her romantic roles (*La sylphide*, Offenbach's *Le papillon*). Emma Livry (1842–1863) was a French ballerina who started to take the title roles previously offered almost exclusively to Italian ballet dancers. The infamous Italian ballerina Marie Taglioni was so impressed with Livry that she adopted her as her protégée. Such a reference was thus an enormous compliment to any young dancer.

In his article "Mlle de Craponne, première danseuse" (1923), Levinson described another Opéra French dancer as occupying a place truly her own at the Opéra, writing that "the talent of Mlle Craponne charms by the balance of her faculties, by the harmonious development of her total personality."[83] Once again, Levinson attributed Livry's unique style to a rising French star. In this article, Levinson described Craponne's dancing as embracing *ballon* – a quality that Livry and the great Italian Romantic ballerinas had mastered: "For she possesses this extremely rare gift of *ballon* that alone confers at times of elevation a genuine beauty. It's not a matter, having jumped very high, to sink to the bottom in a great thud on the floor shaken by a dead weight. This graceful tension of all the being that makes the body glide and the open arms slow down and absorb the fall, this elasticity of the *coup de pied* and the legs that enable the dancer to rebound after touching the earth, is one of the many merits of Mlle Craponne. This hidden spring is essential to the salutatory momentum of the ballerina."[84] By locating *ballon* and grace in Craponne's dancing, Levinson made references to French classical ballet tradition (here within the Romantic tradition). Positive reviews of Paris Opéra dancers such as those by Levinson contributed to the increased reputation of the Opéra ballet by transforming perceptions of female ballet dancers and dancing.

Levinson's review of Opéra dancer Mlle Bos also serves as a good example of how critics attempted to de-eroticize the female dancing body. In his review, he located the beauty of human form not just in the choreography, but also in the proportions of the dancer's body. Most astonishing is that he managed to do so without sexualizing the body. "Mlle Bos," he writes, "is perfectly proportioned. But for her to attain in the *arabesque* and *élévation* the same prodigious results that we have noted for the others, the correspondence between the length of the torso and those of the legs must be modified; this short torso and her elongated legs are necessary to be a dragonfly, a swan, or a grasshopper." Levinson explained that to become a great artist in ballet one must attain a complete "unité plastique" (unity of form)."[85] This critic has chosen to describe the female dancer's body in aesthetic (i.e., formal) rather than erotic terms. As Levinson points out, the female dancer is foremost an artistic form capable of producing harmonious lines and shapes. All these qualities – "unity of form," "harmony of lines," "proportion" – were also associated with neoclassicism in France. Essentially, Levinson is bestowing neoclassical values (often associated with republicanism) upon the French female dancer.

Reviews like those of Levinson encouraged critics to locate artistic value in corporeal movement and technical virtuosity. They offered

Parisian critics a critical language with which to discuss ballet and its dancers. Levinson urged the French to appreciate the talent of their own dancers at the Opéra and enunciated the glorious French tradition that had been preserved there. However, other cultural forces transpiring in France were instrumental in altering perceptions of female ballet dancers. Why were new images of ballet dancers (via the Ballets Russes) so successful on the French stage? Why did critical discussion of ballet dancers shift from the whimsical reviews of the nineteenth century that catered to the erotic demands of male subscribers to the serious reviews that highlighted dancers' technical virtuosity, elegance, versatility, and athletic strength? In other words, how did female dancers come to represent professional artistry more than erotic display? In order to answer these questions, it is crucial to consider the landscape of postwar culture. As we will see, critics attempted to renegotiate the place and value of the female dancer at a time when traditional gender identities were being challenged and the stigma of women working in the public sphere was eroding.

WOMEN AND INTERWAR CULTURE

As French culture in the 1920s presented images of the new postwar man, the figure of the modern woman also took an increasingly central position. During the First World War, women had usurped male territories quite literally by working in factories and offices. While men felt emasculated by the nature of trench warfare, their physical and mental wounds, and their inability to end the war quickly, women witnessed unprecedented freedom in working in public-sphere jobs previously reserved for men.[86] They were thus able to gain economic independence and to experience a sense of professionalism and accomplishment. As Mary Louise Roberts outlines, boundaries between masculine and feminine became increasingly blurred during and after the First World War.[87] For some women, their lifestyles earned them the title of "la garçonne." This prompted fears among those who yearned for a return to order and "normalcy" after the war. New gender confusion led to a marked increase in public debate concerning female identity and women's proper role. In the postwar years, notions of femininity were redefined in various ways, some of which were labelled as progressive while others were deemed as shocking. In the 1920s, fashion styles changed dramatically; women cut their hair short, wore pants, smoked cigarettes, drove cars, fenced, and even boxed.[88] Career-minded women represented a threat not only to the social order of separate spheres, but also to motherhood, traditional femininity, and even the strength of the nation (via pronatalism). Anxieties arose over the growing visibility of independent, single, childless women. As Roberts has shown, literature, journalism, and natalist propaganda of the period encouraged women not only to marry but to bear lots of children. Thus figures such as dancer Ida Rubinstein (exemplary of bisexually active celebrities) and bachelorettes such as designer Gabrielle (Coco) Chanel represented modern challenges to traditional notions of femininity by their independence, success, sexuality, artistic innovations, and overall lifestyles. They offered alternative visions of female identity for women in the interwar years. So did the many foreign images of modern women, particularly international celebrities such as Greta Garbo and Marlene Dietrich.

Within the world of dance, women were increasingly working not just as interpreters (i.e., dancers), but also as creators (i.e., directors, choreographers, scene and costume designers). Anna Pavlova founded her own ballet company in 1910, Bronislava Nijinska established her Théâtre Chorégraphique in 1925, Marie Rambert formed her company in 1926, and Ida Rubinstein's Les Ballets Ida Rubinstein was created in 1928. As ballet (and dance, in general) became more legitimized as an artistic and expressive form, female dancers were recognized as authorities on the art of dance. Women increasingly participated in dialogues concerning dance as former dancers and "experts" in their field; as instructors, choreographers, and directors; as serious and competent critics; and even as judges for dance competitions (e.g., Irene Lidova, Julie Spinova, P.W. Manchester, Julie Sazonova, and Tamara Karsavina). Ballet offered women not only another medium for artistic expression, but also new opportunities to engage in critical response, to reveal their intellectual potential, and to contribute to cultural discourse.[89] In their capacity as critics, women played an important role in the elevation of ballet's status. Once again, we find women usurping male territory, here within the landscape of the performing arts where they were supposed to merely execute not invent.

The difficulty of reconciling femininity and achievement affected not just women in ballet but women engaged in a variety of fields.

Women's new active role in sports is another example of the reconfiguration of women's presence in the public sphere. Women athletes increasingly gained prestige and celebrity status after the First World War. French tennis champion Suzanne Lenglen is a good example of women's progressive achievements at the time. Lenglen, who was an Olympic champion in 1920 and by 1925 a multiple winner at Wimbledon, gained international celebrity similar to that of ballerina Anna Pavlova years earlier. Her success and that of other female athletes at the time reveal not only the new French enthusiasm for sports but an acceptance of women as professionals and athletes.[90] It also indicates that some form of respectability could be attached to the public display of women's bodies in this period. However, women's sporting bodies were presented in such a way that did not make them overtly erotic or masculine and unattractive. Lenglen's athletic body remained "feminized" through her chic fashion style (fig. 7.3). As Mary Lynn Stewart points out, although Lenglen was "playing against a negative stereotype of professional sportswoman, amateur tennis had been accepted as appropriately feminine and bourgeois."[91] Stewart relates how one reporter insisted that the word *sportives* implied "grace, strength, suppleness, beauty, and femininity. Nothing brutal, nothing unattractive, a harmony." Women's bodies in sports were commodified in a way that reinforced gender difference (not unlike today). French culture could accept women's physical strength and athletic virtuosity as long as she remained feminine (i.e., attractive and refined). Stewart writes:

> Between 1880 and 1940, the introduction of cell theory into human biology, of endocrinology into gynecology, and of germ theory into hygiene transformed scientific and medical visions of women's bodies. In these six decades, the implementation of free, compulsory public education, the proliferation of women's self-help literature, and the commercialization of health, beauty, and fitness products disseminated new scientific and commercial representations of the female body. Bodily ideals and aspirations mutated from rounded, plump contours to straighter, slimmer figures and from relatively immobile to more dynamic bodies.[92]

Modern femininity was linked to physical fitness, corporeal mobility, and bodily display. In other words, women's ideal appearance

Figure 7.3 This photograph was published on the cover of *Miroir des Sports*, a major French sports magazine, on 8 July 1920. The sports journal cropped the image to focus on Lenglen with mixed doubles partner Gerald Patterson in the background. Notice the "action" balletic position of Lenglen captured by the photographer. This bears close resemblance to new images of ballet dancers at the time.

transformed to one in which the female body was less shameful, rebuked, or hidden. Like ballet, practice dress became necessary as female activity developed.

The physical culture movement not only brought about a new appreciation for the male dancer, but it also influenced the professionalization of the female dancer. The physical culture movement created new dynamic images of women's bodies; muscularity, coordination, agility, and leanness all became acceptable attributes of feminine beauty and health.[93] This new imagery, which related femininity to exercise and strength, transformed public attitudes towards female bodily movement and its display. As female athletes excelled in a number of sports (e.g., Suzanne Leglen in tennis) and were able to still embody femininity and grace, anxieties about the corporeal nature of ballet lifted.

Certainly, physical culture was a global phenomenon by the interwar years as were the "modern girl," celebrity culture, body politics, cinema, and new forms of professional and work discipline.[94] All these trends had important international and transnational dimensions and all played a vital role in remaking French ballet and its dancers. As physical culture for women became a vehicle for embracing modernity during the interwar years, the French sought to reconcile women's athleticism with clear boundaries of femininity, as we saw in the case of Suzanne Lenglen. Parisian commentary on ballet dancers, as for tennis players, provided an alternative avenue through which to assert new and distinctly French identities of modern womanhood and female corporeality. The fact that the body became the most valued component of ballet dancing (while retaining its feminine beauty) – as the formalism of Levinson and Lifar put forth – indicates some level of acceptance of women as athletes, artists, and professionals, particularly when these bodies were working-class ones.

While such commentary can be seen as reflecting new tastes for physical culture, it can also be understood as expanding the boundaries for modern French womanhood. By educating the public on dance aesthetics and raising awareness of the dancer's rigorous physical training (Levinson described the dancer as "an instrument of precision and daily work"), Levinson and Lifar drew a new type of attention to women's bodies. In this way, dancing bodies not only serve as barometers of cultural transition, but also as vehicles through which to assert new images of womanhood. Suzanne Lenglen, after all, was often described in the interwar period as graceful, strong, beautiful, and feminine in the same manner of the female dancers of the Ballets Russes before the war. By the interwar years, terms such as muscularity, strength, skill, agility, balance, and artistry were attributed to both sportswomen and female dancers in France. Thus images of strong, athletic, modern women took many forms across the globe, including those of dancers. As scholars Carol Osborne and Fiona Skillen point out, these representations, in turn, "invited female audience[s] to wear new types of clothing, perceive their bodies in new ways, and pursue more athletic and physically demanding activities than ever before."[95]

Commercialism and consumer culture also played a role in reshaping images of female ballet dancers. As was the case with theatre actresses and female athletes, images of ballerinas were commodified in new ways in the early twentieth century. They were displayed in women's magazines and postcards, promoted in glamour photography, invited to endorse commercial products, and were even packaged as a type of modern lifestyle of leisure (fig. 7.4). I argue that new images of French ballet dancers offered an alternative representation of modern womanhood, one that was distinct from the *garçonne*. French dancers were able to represent not only professionalism, independence (many were not married), and mobility (they toured around the globe), but also restraint, discipline, industriousness, femininity, and subjection to male authority – the ballet master (fig. 7.5).

Multiple representations of dancers were also made available through historical texts, fiction, fashion, and eventually film. For example, Noel Streatfeild's novel *Ballet Shoes* (1937) followed the lives of three adopted girls who pursue careers in the performing arts: one becomes a successful ballet dancer and another a famous actress in theatre and film. Encouraging women's pursuit of a vocation, the novel revealed what women could accomplish with hard work, persistence, and dedication. Streatfeild was inspired by the technical virtuosity and successful career of English ballerina Ninette de Valois.[96] *Ballet Shoes* launched the author's long career and was reprinted in France almost every year after its first publication, catering to a preteen, ethnically diverse audience.[97] Most interesting are the terms on which the girls accomplish their goals. While the girls do manage to pursue their ambitions, they do so by exhibiting modesty, obedience, politeness, and diligence – traits deemed in the 1920s and 1930s as feminine, respectable, bourgeois, and republican. Popular films also surfaced that concerned women's careers in the performing arts, especially in dance. *La mort de cygne*, or *Ballerina* (1937), starring Paris Opéra star Yvette Chauviré, presented the story of a young girl who aspires to become a ballet dancer.[98] Set in the backstage of the Paris Opéra, the story is told from the girl's perspective. The film attempts to capture the reality, work, and self-sacrifice involved in pursuing a career in ballet. In the end, one of the star dancers gives up her career to get married. The film was distributed internationally, broke box-office records, and was awarded the Grand Prix du Film Français at the 1937 Exposition de Paris. Chauviré was even featured on the cover of *Life* magazine in 1938 (fig. 7.6). By providing a fantasy that steadfast commitment will lead to achievement, ballet narratives such as these offered new images of modern womanhood.[99] Achievement,

Figure 7.4 This photograph of Olga Adabache illustrates the ways in which ballet dancers were represented as strong, athletic, and virtuosic in the 1930s and 1940s.

success, passion, self-discipline, and dedication became traits to which young respectable women could, theoretically, aspire. Images of ballet dancers as legitimate and professional artists authentically

Figure 7.5 Serge Lifar surrounded by female dancers of the Paris Opéra.

captured the hard work, discipline, and intensive training involved in a successful career as a ballet dancer.

However, tensions over the relationship between femininity and achievement and traditional women's roles in society endured and manifested themselves deeply in imagery regarding working women. While the ballerina was still perceived as the epitome of femininity, with her tutus, hair buns, pink tights, and toe shoes, the female dancer also stimulated fears concerning the de-feminization of women insofar as she was professional, unmarried, and without children. The notion that it was necessary for the ballet dancer to free her- or himself from the ties of family in order to reach full potential as a performing artist often appeared in fiction, ballets, and films. Such imagery captured the enduring problem of the conflict between professionalism and family duty for women. Beginning in the 1930s, we find a dualism in popular culture that stated that woman could be a professional or a mother but not both. This dualism is best exemplified in popular films of the 1930s and 1940s in which a professional dancer must choose between marriage and family or her career. The iconic film *The Red Shoes* (1948) is a classic example of this theme: the protagonist, Victoria Paige, must choose between marrying the man she loves or continuing a brilliant career. Tragically, the ballerina's struggle to reconcile her domestic obligations (love for her man) and career ambitions (love for dancing) results in her suicide.[100] In interwar France, we find a nation struggling to negotiate multiple (and sometime vying) images of femininity.[101]

In this brief outline of the alternative images of femininity that circulated during the interwar years, we can understand why changing attitudes toward the body were reflected in dance reviews. The new reverence for the body (female and male) and the new critical vocabulary brought forth by dance experts enabled critics to focus finally on the dancing itself and to recognize choreography as the central component in ballet production. Critics thus became less intrigued with the ballerina's coquetry (as we saw with Fanny Cerrito in the nineteenth century) and more interested in the ballerina's technical virtuosity and individual dancing style. In fact, some critics went to great lengths to emphasize the athleticism of female dancers by highlighting the extent of their discipline and training. This resulted in the de-eroticization of the ballet environment by disseminating new images of female dancers that corresponded with the visions of bourgeois femininity circulating in France. In order to better understand how the female dancer's reputation was improved and her artistry professionalized, it is important to address the ways in which Serge Lifar, as director of the Paris Opéra ballet, managed to revive the integrity of the French ballet dancer and to de-eroticize the ballet environment there.

REDEEMING THE FEMALE DANCER AT THE OPÉRA

André Levinson once stated that technical skill was vital to the success of any dancer (whether female or male). Repeatedly, he argued that ballet was first and foremost a choreographic art form and, as such, should be valued for its quality of dancing. Only in this way, he insisted, would French ballet rise to its former glory. Indeed, Levinson's theories turned out to be prophetic. When Serge Lifar took over the direction of the Paris Opéra ballet, he was devoted to restoring the integrity of the Opéra's dancers. He attempted this through various means: by the professionalization and de-eroticization of the corps

Figure 7.6 Yvette Chauviré, star of the French film *La mort du cygne* (Death of the Swan) (distributed under the English title *Ballerina* in 1937). This film still was chosen as the cover image of *Life* magazine's 5 December 1938 issue. The film helped to make Chauviré an internationally recognized ballerina and enhanced the reputation of the Paris Opéra ballet.

de ballet, which held deep-rooted associations with femininity, promiscuity, and frivolity; by the expansion of choreography for women and men based on a new vision of athleticism and neoclassicism; and by the reconfiguration of gender difference in ballet through distinct laws of technique. The centrality of choreographic form in ballet became the foundation upon which a new national aesthetic was forged at the Opéra. This ballet aesthetic rested on a combination of classical French tradition, neoclassical forms, and modern innovations in music, costume design, and choreography. In his revitalization of the Paris Opéra ballet, Lifar shaped a new ballet ethic and, in time, restored grandeur to the French art form.

As director of the Opéra and as a dance theorist/critic/historian, Lifar attempted to professionalize not only the male dancer, but also the female dancer. He achieved this first through a de-eroticization of the ballet environment, specifically the corps de ballet. When Lifar assumed his position as director, the corps de ballet at the Opéra still reflected the academic traditions of the seventeenth and eighteenth centuries, but its reputation had been tainted by its association with libertinism and its descent into mediocrity in the late nineteenth century. One of Lifar's most critical decisions was to remove the infamous Foyer de Danse, a space in which elite men could "intermingle" with young and vulnerable dancers. The elimination of access to the Foyer was risky politically. In the 1930s, the state offered only limited financial support to the ballet. Therefore, the subscribers could claim a certain amount of influence over what happened at the Opéra. Lifar recalled that shortly after the elimination of access to the Foyer, subscribers accused him "of destroying French choreographic tradition" and argued that the "young 'barbarian' was a serious danger for the French ballet!" By preventing the traditional types of interchange between subscriber and female dancer, however, Lifar offered an opportunity to professionalize the dancer as a legitimate artist:

> Everyone knew that these gentlemen regarded it as their own domain where they intended to make their own ideas prevail ... So, of course, I could not make a frontal attack on positions rooted in "tradition" and powerfully defended. I could not from one day to the next shut the doors of the *Foyer* in their faces. So, in this matter also I decided to proceed more subtly. I arranged for rehearsals to be held at the times the subscribers had the habit of arriving

> in order to turn the *Foyer* into a club. No sooner did I perceive a *danseuse* in close conversation with one of these "balletomaniacs" than I would call out: "Mademoiselle, your variation … quick."[102]

The reconfiguration of the Foyer into a more artistic and professional environment, in the opinion of Lifar, "re-establish[ed] a tradition of work and of artistry." Lifar noticed that this change "gave new courage to the artists" themselves. He recollected: "When the young pupils realized what I demanded of them was rewarded with just and suitable promotion and that their chances of becoming stars were determined by their efforts and their natural ability, the dancing-school of the new generation came right over to my side."[103] He then aimed to showcase their talents and skills as artistic technicians. He accomplished this by publicizing the intensive training of female dancers and promoting the École de Danse de l'Opéra as a vigorous, serious, and exclusive artistic institution. One of its students, Yvette Chauviré (a protégée under Lifar), went on to become the director of the Paris Opéra ballet in 1963. In 1988, she was awarded the Légion d'Honneur, France's highest honour.

Indeed, Lifar's embrace of the "dance for dance's sake" ideology demanded technical proficiency. Neoclassicism as a style served well to showcase the art of dancing. The neoclassical style emphasized linear design, classical themes, symmetry, and the beauty and perfection of the human form. His goal to capture the beauty of corporeal movement in ballet entailed a reworking of choreography as well as roles for both female and male dancers. Regarding the ballet *Sylvia*, he stated in *La danse* that he was resolved, in 1940, to present a new version of the ballet by substituting the ballet's extensive pantomime with choreography based in the neoclassical style. He also expanded choreography for the corps de ballet (thus demanding more from them technically) in his works. He remarked that he would be conferring a greater importance to the corps de ballet not only in *Sylvia* but in all of his subsequent works.[104] In time, Lifar's corps de ballet was made up of vigorously trained French female and male dancers and, eventually, set one of the highest standards for ballet worldwide. Even today, the Paris Opéra dancers are recognized for their meticulous artistry, lyricism, technical brilliance, and unique expressive style. The company is also well known for being almost exclusively composed of French nationals rather than foreign-born dancers.

As this chapter has shown, the status and function of the female ballet dancer in France was reconceptualized in the early twentieth century. Critics, intellectuals, and dance experts all played a vital role in reshaping public opinion about ballet dancers by renegotiating the meanings attached to the female dancing body. They achieved this in a variety of ways. Some highlighted the dancer's ability to transcend bodily form and become the manifestation of poetic metaphor (e.g., the symbolist poets). Others attempted to de-eroticize ballet dancers by praising their potential for dramatic expression and/or illustrating their extraordinary discipline and intensive technical training. Dance experts like André Levinson and Serge Lifar were dedicated to the cultivation of an informed ballet audience. They educated the public on the art of dance by emphasizing the discipline and labours of ballet training, familiarizing the public with dance terminology, and locating choreographic beauty in technical form. By highlighting dancers' technical virtuosity, discipline, athletic prowess, and poetic expression as professional artists, critics attempted to erode the erotic appeal of dancers as performing women. This fostered a new relationship between the ballet and its audiences by recasting ballet as a serious and venerable artistic institution rather than a frivolous entertainment of erotic display. In doing so, they salvaged ballet's status as a high art form and affirmed it as distinct from the other popular entertainments in Paris at the time.

Diaghilev's Ballets Russes played a part in reshaping French ideas about ballet and its dancers by presenting a new type of ballet that was dynamic, energetic, and exotic. Its "new ballet" rested on dramatic expression and the integration of a variety of other arts (e.g., costume design, music, and set decor). The Russian company thus attracted a more diverse and discriminative audience, female patronage, cutting-edge designers and composers, and serious discussion of ballet in respectable Parisian journals. Moreover, it revolutionized roles and choreography for female and male dancers. Diaghilev's dancers (female and male) enthralled Parisian audiences and thus inspired a new type of critical review of ballet.

The Ballets Russes' success in France rested, in part, on the cultural climate in which it found itself. In Paris, dramatic theatre was at its peak, gender identity was unstable, the stigma of women's work and artistic achievement was lifting, and attitudes about female corporeality were changing dramatically. The increasing acceptance of the body as a site through which to assert identity (both female and male) profoundly influenced the way the art of ballet and its dancers were understood. As athleticism and competitive sport were increasingly valorized (particularly in the 1920s), the beauty and expressivity of corporal movement in ballet increasingly captured the attention of the public. While ballet's technical (formal) aspects were disapproved by critics as "mere gymnastics" in the nineteenth century, these qualities became lauded in the interwar years. The revival of the classical idea of the athletic body (whether female or male) as beautiful prompted a new interest in ballet as a choreographic art in the interwar years. In other words, the physical culture movement enabled the French to appreciate the athletic aspects of ballet dancing and the discipline and hard work demanded of its dancers. New tastes for sport and dance enabled the female dancer to be judged by her technical skills, athletic strength, versatility, elegance, and graceful execution of steps. By examining the ways in which critics, intellectuals, theorists, and choreographers reworked older notions about ballet and its dancers, we can see how ballet functioned as a platform through which to articulate ideas about gender identity, artistic practice, and the female body.

In conclusion, the increasing professionalization of the ballet dancer in early twentieth-century France was a gradual process. The positive reception of the Ballets Russes, the physical culture movement, changing ideologies of gender, and critics' attempts to reshape public perceptions of ballet and its dancers all paved the way for Serge Lifar to implement his reforms successfully at the Paris Opéra in the 1940s and to restore credibility to the Opéra ballet and its dancers. Shifts in attitudes towards the body helped not only to instigate changes at the Paris Opéra ballet, but also to reshape understandings of ballet aesthetics. Ultimately, the shaping of a modern and national aesthetic based on corporeal beauty contributed to the professionalization of both the female and male dancer and the legitimization of ballet as a high art in France. Ballet was acknowledged once again as a legitimate art form and reinstated as an art capable of embodying the grandeur of France.

Conclusion

A new fervour for ballet surfaced in France with the arrival of a dynamic Russian ballet company, the Ballets Russes, in Paris in 1909. For the first time, ballet was presented as a vehicle for the expression of modernism and later avant-gardism. This kind of ballet captivated French audiences, who were accustomed to antiquated nineteenth-century Romantic ballet. The spectacle of a Russian ballet in Paris instigated great discussion in reputable Paris journals and newspapers about ballet's relation to national identity, modernism, gender ideologies, and the body. Many critics and intellectuals supported the use of ballet as a vehicle for the expression of modernism and nationalism. In their reviews, they endeavoured to reshape public opinion about ballet and its dancers and to elevate ballet's status as an art form. We have seen some of the reasons why the project to revive ballet became so important to the French between 1909 and 1939. This process was by no means easy. Observers of ballet struggled to define the function of modern ballet, its aesthetic nature, and its relation to French society. In doing so, they attempted to transfigure traditional conceptions of ballet by adorning it with modern republican values.

By the interwar period, critics turned to the state of French ballet and attempted to reshape public opinion about their own ballet and its dancers at the Paris Opéra. Two Russian émigrés played a key role in this process, André Levinson and Serge Lifar. Their attempts to educate the public on the art of ballet, to valorize French classic tradition, and to enunciate the importance of the formal aspects of ballet (e.g., choreographic autonomy) all helped to reaffirm ballet as a high art in France. As one of the few "dance experts" in France (i.e., as a non-dancer and critic), Levinson set the standards for ballet assessment in early twentieth-century France by offering a solid understanding of ballet choreography. He not only became *the* authority in dance (ballet especially) in France, but also helped to redefine and to professionalize the dance critic in French journalism. Levinson proposed "solutions" to the problem of revitalizing French ballet. French ballet, he argued, should showcase classic French technique while becoming modern. The French modern ballet style implemented by Serge Lifar was indeed an amalgam of French technical virtuosity and artistry, and Diaghilevian modernism and expressivity.

The cultural climate of interwar France helped to make all these changes in ballet possible. Postwar fatigue, shifting gender ideologies, and an agenda for national hegemony all contributed to a peaked interest in the arts. New tastes for neoclassicism in the 1920s and 1930s, a new enthusiasm for athleticism in both women and men, and a new comfort with the body all opened a space for a new modern aesthetic of ballet, the return of the male dancer, and a revitalized national cultural institution: the Paris Opéra ballet. Grace, elegance, and virtuosity became grounded in strength and agility rather than decorative or narrative expression. Subsequently, ballet's artistic integrity was reconsidered. Many critics used the ballet as a means through which to assert French cultural pre-eminence and to promote Paris as the centre of modernity in the early twentieth century. Lifar's strategic reforms to renew a national cultural institution came at an opportune time, when France was searching for a strong national identity and for symbols of a distinct cultural hegemony.

As we have seen throughout this book, ballet served as a cultural force that was able to raise some critical questions of the day. Commentary on ballet in reputable Parisian journals reveals not only attitudes towards ballet in this period, but also a wide array of opinions about cultural life in early twentieth-century France. Through critical discussions of ballet, critics and intellectuals addressed modern cultural values at a time of profound change. As this study reveals, the ballet served as a nexus through which issues concerning national identity, modern aesthetics, gender, and the body could be addressed. In doing so, it demonstrates the richness of using ballet as a source through which to understand French culture in the early twentieth century. Dance can serve as a useful resource with which to examine the various ways in which nations embrace aesthetics as a way of asserting cultural identities.

My hope is that this book demonstrates the merits of studying dance as a historical subject and encourages further historical study of ballet in this period and beyond. There is a clear need for further investigation into the Paris Opéra ballet during the Second World War and the subsequent postwar recovery and to place such findings within a historical context. It is truly in the years after the Second World War that the Paris Opéra gained momentum as a national cultural institution. Before then, we see only the foundation upon which the French could build. During the Second World War, the Paris Opéra closed briefly from 1 September to 16 November 1939. Jacques Rouché continued to manage the Opéra but had to face the racist and anti-Semitic laws banning Jews from all jobs in the performing arts. In autumn 1940, Rouché, now a senior civil servant in the service of the state, dismissed around thirty Jewish artists and staff members but managed to continue paying their salaries until December 1942. Under the Nazi occupation, certain works were banned, particular those of Jewish composers. Musicians and stage hands gradually organized resistance movements, which eventually participated in the August 1944 Paris uprising.

The Paris Opéra ballet director, Serge Lifar, was committed to keeping the ballet company operational during the war years. Lifar's activities at the Opéra (and his writings) in occupied France, however, mark a vastly different context (political, social, and cultural) in which to examine ballet's ascendance, and it is for these reasons that they have been omitted in this study. When the Opéra briefly closed in 1939, part of the ballet troupe went on tour, even as far as Australia. In late 1939 when the Opéra reopened, Lifar was asked to serve as director of the Opéra ballet in Nazi-occupied Paris. Under his direction appeared a series of international French ballet stars, including Lycette Darsonval, Yvette Chauviré, Micheline Bardin, Marianne Ivanoff, Paulette Dynalix, Janine Charat, and Jean Babillée. However, Lifar's activities at this time came under scrutiny after the war when he was accused of collaborating with the Germans. These allegations rested, in part, on his social association with high-ranking German officers during the war. Indeed, the Opéra would have been crawling with them. As anti-fascist French intellectual Jean Guéhenno noted in his diary in 1941, "Every evening at the Opera, I am told, German officers are extremely numerous. At the intermissions, following the custom of their country, they walk around the lobby in ranks of three or four, all in the same direction. Despite themselves, the French join the procession and march in step, unconsciously. The boots impose their rhythm."[1]

In late 1944, Lifar was dismissed at the Opéra and forbidden to work in ballet in France for life. In the following year, however, his sentence was reduced to a one-year suspension. Lifar's dismissal was not unique. Long-time Opéra manager Jacques Rouché was also dismissed in 1945 as a collaborator and only reinstated in 1951. The allegation of collaborationism, however, does not cast into doubt the sincerity of Lifar's attempts to make French ballet compatible with republican values before the war. Lifar, as any artistic director in an art that required state support (or even sanction) in France in the 1940s, would either have to give up his post or make compromises that a later generation (ours) might label "collaboration." In fact, there were plenty of republicans who made such compromises at least until the Germans started losing the war.

This ordeal did not hinder Lifar's career for long. After George Balanchine served for six months as ballet master of the Paris Opéra ballet in 1947, Lifar was reinstated as director at the end of the 1947 season. He remained in this position until 1958. The memory of his fraternization with German officers seemed to have faded when, in 1955, Charles de Gaulle awarded him the Chausson d'Or (Golden Shoe), a prestigious dance award, for his twenty-five years at the Paris Opéra. He delivered lectures on dance at the Sorbonne, published a series of books on the theory and history of dance, choreographed and staged ballets for various European companies, and was appointed professor at the École Normale de Musique. He became the first choreographer to be granted full membership in the French Academy of Arts. He even appeared in the film *Le testament d'Orphée* in 1960. When he retired in 1956, he received twelve curtain calls from the Paris audience.

As one can see, the rise of the Paris Opéra ballet under Serge Lifar during and after the Second World War is a rich subject for historical analysis. There are a few studies that may offer a good start to such a task. Claire Paolacci's article "Serge Lifar and the Paris Opera during World War II" (2004) offers a brief description of Lifar's work at the Paris Opéra between 1930 and 1946. The four-page article examines some aesthetic changes that Lifar implemented at the Opéra, but, unfortunately, does not offer any historical or cultural context. Serge

Lifar's autobiography (1965) together with André Levinson's (1934) and Jean Laurent's (1960) biographies of Serge Lifar offer great insight into how Lifar injected a new aesthetic and national spirit into the Paris Opéra ballet. Pierre Michaut also offers a good description of this period of ballet in his *Ballet contemporain, 1929–1950* (1950). Alan Riding's book *And the Show Went On: Cultural Life in Nazi-Occupied Paris* (2010) is an invaluable source that offers a context within which to place the development of the performing arts in occupied France. Likewise, David Ball's translation and annotation of *Diary of the Dark Years, 1940–1944: Collaboration, Resistance, and Daily Life in Occupied Paris* (2014) by Jean Guéhenno offers rich commentary on literary life in France under Nazi rule.

While ballet exists as a performance art, a textual and representational form, and a creator and sustainer of "publics," historians hesitate to rank the ballet at the same level as other expressive forms. It is most surprising how often historical discourse on cultural representation ignores ballet as a subject of analysis. Historians could pay more attention to dance as a subject through which to better understand broader shifts in European culture at this time. And they are beginning to do so. Judith Surkis's article "Carnival Balls and Penal Codes: Body Politics in July Monarchy France" is an encouraging example of how historians are finally turning to dance (in this case, social dancing) as a vehicle through which to analyze French culture.[2] Surkis examines the ways in which public dancing under the July Monarchy was regulated and set strict boundaries for men. She contextualizes these boundaries within shifting attitudes towards male corporeality in which the male body lost its virtuous classical associations and its capacity for public display.

Ballet as an art form continues to hold a distinct place in France due to its French origins. Today, the Paris Opéra Ballet occupies two sites in central Paris: the Opéra-Garnier and the Opéra-Bastille. In France, ballet continues to garner the highest respect and honour. In the words of French critic Louis Laloy, "Alone of all theatre, the Opéra is an institution which trains its own artists, and it is this function that justifies the title of Academy, which in turn has been 'Royal,' 'Imperial,' or 'National,' according to the changes of political regime … Nevertheless, the Opéra has remained the School of Dancing."[3]

ENCORE

At this book's opening, we saw how Degas's exhibition of his now-famous statuette, *Little Dancer Aged Fourteen* (1881), incited fury among his contemporaries because of its vulgarity. The sculpture's realistic depiction of a hard-working, athletic, and vigorously trained dancer drove critics to compare the image to that of monkeys and rats. Nonetheless, the girl who was the model for Degas's statue continues to fascinate museum visitors, art historians, and even choreographers and dancers. In 2003, the Paris Opéra Ballet revived the image of Marie van Goethem, the dancer who posed for Degas's sculpture, in a new ballet, *La petite danseuse de Degas,* which was performed at the Opéra-Garnier. Inspired by research in the late 1990s by the ballet company's cultural director, archivist, and curator, Martine Kahane, and choreographed by Opéra ballet master Patrice Bart, the production was designed to capture the atmosphere of Degas's paintings of ballet dancers. For the first time, it attempted to give Marie's legendary image a life of its own and a place within the history of the Paris Opéra. The ballet opens with a ballerina posed like the Little Dancer, encased in a glass box. The glass descends and the Little Dancer springs to life and tells her story through her own dancing on stage. She articulates her expression by means of her artistic training at the Opéra school, a training founded in the French modern neoclassical style. In the ballet, the Little Dancer becomes an *étoile* before her mother corrupts her and she goes to prison for prostitution. "And then," Bart describes, "I thought I'd make a scene where she becomes a laundress, and the stage is filled with white sheets, and she fades out, as when people die."[4] Degas's presence is echoed only as a mysterious, dark, top-hatted figure, an *abonné,* who wanders through the scenes. "There was no man in that story," Bart points out, "so I added the role of the abonné, the ideal masculine man." As the ballet closes, the glass box ascends from the floor and the Little Dancer is once again trapped inside.

So, as the ballet begins with the statuette in her glass cage, so it ends when she returns to it, driven by Fate, the *abonné,* having been abandoned by the man she loves and dismissed from the Opéra. "Confronted with the real world," as Bart explains, "she breaks." Inspired by Degas's *Le foyer de la danse à l'Opéra, L'examen de danse,* the different versions of *La leçon de danse,* as well as some of his lesser-known works,

Bart explained his aim “to reflect the values of a shifting world, that of the dream confronted with reality.” Bart hoped the ballet would bring Degas to life for young dancers now: “That’s why I created the role of the ‘étoile’ because it’s every little girl starting school, thinking maybe one day … And very few get there.” At last, 122 years later, Marie has been given the tribute she deserves and is truly immortalized as *une étoile*, a star.[5]

Notes

INTRODUCTION

1 Paul Mantz, "Exposition des oeuvres des artistes indépendants," 3.
2 Henry Trianon, "Sixième Exposition de peinture par un groupe d'artistes," 2.
3 See Mantz, "Exposition des oeuvres des artistes indépendants," 3, and Elie de Mont, "L'Exposition du boulevard des Capucines," 2.
4 Huysmann quoted in C.S. Moffett, *The New Painting*, 362.
5 Interview with Martine Kahane, October 2001, Opéra Garnier, Paris, France.
6 In an 1882 newspaper clipping entitled "Paris at Night," Marie was noted to be a regular at two all-night cafes – the Rat Mort and the brasserie des Martyrs – hangouts of artists, models, bohemians, journalists, and young and available women. The writer noted, "Her mother, but no … I don't want to say any more. I'd say things that would make one blush, or make one cry." See Stuart and McLellan's *Paris at Night* (1875). See also miscellaneous newspaper clippings in Bibliothèque de l'Opéra.
7 Marie seems to have disappeared from records after Antoinette's imprisonment and her dismissal from the Opéra.
8 Not only did Charlotte lead a respectable career, she had among her pupils Yvette Chauviré, the most prestigious French ballerina of her time.
9 Certainly, there exist multiple contexts within which to read Degas's work; however, it is the subject matter and its rendering with which I am concerned here.
10 See Griselda Pollock's article, "Modernity and the Spaces of Femininity," 245–68.
11 Previously, ballet criticism had been contained within theatre journals.
12 Jeffrey H. Jackson, *Making Jazz French*, 6.
13 For example, studies by Lynn Hunt, Carolyn J. Dean, Judith Surkis,

Mary Louise Roberts, Christopher Forth, Mary Lynn Stewart, Robert J. Nye, Alan Riding, Herman Lebovics, and Joan Tumblety.

14 L. Berlanstein, *Daughters of Eve*, 1.

15 Ballet companies are invited to tour and perform in venues abroad.

16 Ballet's central role in the struggle for cultural supremacy during the Cold War indicates that the art of ballet had risen from its nineteenth-century degenerative state by mid-century. For example, Khrushchev would not have used ballet as a Cold War cultural weapon if it did not have cultural relevance (status/power) in the West already. See David Caute's *The Dancer Defects.*

17 Benedict Anderson, *Imagined Communities*, 6–7. Hobsbawm's notion of the "invention of tradition" also captures this phenomenon.

18 Some dance scholars, such as Barbara Sparti, have revealed that the earliest texts and practices of early court dance originated in the Italian court in the fifteenth century. Italian dancing masters later dominated the court of Catherine de Medici in France, where similar ballets were created that fused dance, singing, poetry, and music, such as *Le ballet des polonanais* (1573) and the *Ballet comique de la reine* (1581). However, the lines between court "social" dancing and ballet remain debatable. It is clear that ballet found an institutional home and nomenclature in seventeenth-century France.

19 See studies such as James Johnson's *Listening in Paris* and Judith Chazin-Bennahum's *Dance in the Shadow of the Guillotine.*

20 Petipa was not the first French ballet master and dancer to go to Russia. In 1738, the first imperial ballet school was organized by Jean-Baptiste Landé, a French ballet master, during the reign of Anna. However, its survival was uncertain. The future of ballet in Russia was guaranteed under Catherine the Great (Catherine II), who established an imperial theatre system. French master Charles-Louis Didelot (1767–1837) settled in Russia in 1816. Marius Petipa arrived in Russia in 1847. Other French ballet masters involved with the imperial ballet included Jules Perrot, working there from 1848 until 1859, and Arthur Saint-Léon, from 1859 until 1869. Furthermore, Italian Romantic ballerina Marie Taglioni, who trained at and danced for the Paris Opéra, performed in Russia 1837–42. She returned to Paris in 1858.

21 His father Jean Petipa (1796–1855) was a dancer, choreographer, and teacher who founded the Brussels Conservatorie de la Danse, and his brother Lucien (1815–98), also a dancer, was appointed *maître de ballet* of the Paris Opéra in 1865.

22 Petipa's move to Russia was part of a greater project in the policy of foreign borrowing begun under Peter the Great. Such national artistic exchanges are part of the much larger phenomenon occurring through-

out Europe towards the end of the nineteenth and the early twentieth centuries.

23 See Tim Scholl's *From Petipa to Balanchine.* Scholl argues that the roots of modern ballet lie in the modernist works of Marius Petipa not in Diaghilev's Ballets Russes.

24 Louis Véron, *Mémoires d'un bourgeois de Paris,* 3:142. Louis Véron (1798–1867) made a fortune running the Opéra.

25 Petipa's departure in 1845 may have been a result of this commercialization of ballet.

26 John Chapman's study "Jules Janin: Romantic Critic" captures how criticism of this period devalued female dancers as artists by turning them into objects and shows how Romantic ballet was the expression of masculine society's desires.

27 Madame Mariquita was a choreographer who created dances for both these venues. For more information on music hall ballet see Sarah Gutsche-Miller's dissertation, "Pantomime-Ballet on the Music-Hall Stage," Alexandra Carter's *Dance and Dancers in the Victorian and Edwardian Music Hall,* and Ivor Guest's *The Romantic Ballet in England.*

28 Ivor Guest, *The Romantic Ballet in Paris,* 4.

29 Many of the company's early ballets were based on Russian folklore and included collaborations with Russian contemporary composers, set and costume designers, choreographers, and painters. In fact, in some productions, the Ballets Russes abandoned the traditional tutu and replaced it with harem pants, or "Oriental trousers."

30 See Janet Kennedy, *The "Mir Iskusstva" Group and Russian Art,* and Camilla Gray, *The Russian Experiment in Art.* John E. Bowlt describes the World of Art as "a meeting place of ideas essential to the genesis and evolution of Russian modernism," not as an avant-garde or decadent group. See J. Bowlt, *Russian Art of the Avant-Garde,* 41.

31 See studies, such as Patrice Higonnet, *Paris, Capital of the World,* and Charles Rearick, *Pleasures of the Belle Époque* and his *Paris Dreams, Paris Memories.*

32 Johannes Willms, *Paris: Capital of Europe,* 338.

33 Eugen Weber, *France, Fin de Siècle,* 110.

34 Willms, *Paris,* 337.

35 Interestingly, a majority of the company's patrons were wealthy women. Quite ironically, there was also an outpouring of Jewish wealth and support for Diaghilev's enterprise, one which aimed partly at restoring the prestige of a regime so notoriously anti-Semitic as the Russia of Nicholas II. I hypothesize that ballet's emergence in the cultural consciousness of Western societies was determined by the link between this art form and a particularly diverse upper class.

36 See Serge L. Grigoriev, *The Diaghilev Ballet.*

37 The extensive photographic work of Serge Lido offers a good example of this publicity and the glamour attached to ballet stars.

38 After Diaghilev, less attention has been given to the efforts of Serge Lifar, who also helped to restore the male dancer to a position of importance at the Opéra in the 1930s.

39 As cultural historian Robert Nye has noted, "the history of men and masculinity is a comparatively underdeveloped field." Nye has emphasized the importance of examining what French culture decreed men should do, how they should behave, dress, etc. See Robert Nye, *Masculinity and Male Codes of Honor in Modern France.*

40 Wesley Shrum, *Fringe and Fortune,* 12.

41 Ibid., 10.

42 Mary Louise Roberts, *Disruptive Acts,* 2.

43 Ibid.

44 Jane F. Fulcher, *French Cultural Politics and Music,* 5.

45 Herman Lebovics, *True France,* xiii. As Lebovics points out, the new French Right "promoted a deadening hegemony of the idea and practice of a True France as the only hope for national renewal."

46 See David Carroll, "The Aesthetics of Nationalism and the Limits of Culture."

47 Fulcher, *French Cultural Politics and Music,* 6.

48 Ibid. See also Kenneth Silver, *Esprit de corps,* and Christopher Green, *Art in France, 1900–1940.*

49 Jane Fulcher, *The Composer as Intellectual,* 27.

50 Ibid. Fulcher writes that "while literature diffused nationalist ideas, as embodied creatively in fictional form, and the visual arts engaged within politically charged images, music opened up another powerful realm."

51 This explanation should clarify why Lifar would promote "republican ballet" when he, in later years, (allegedly) collaborated with the Nazis.

52 Paul Mantz, "Exposition des oeuvres des artistes indépendants," *Le Temps,* 23 April 1881, 3, and Henry Trianon, "Sixième Exposition de peinture par un groupe d'artistes," *Le Constitutionnel,* 24 April 1881, 2.

53 See L. Berlanstein, *Daughters of Eve,* 231–3.

54 Ibid.

55 Ibid., 233.

56 Ibid., 231.

57 Constance Valis Hall, "Jazz Modernism," 199, 206. Bronislava Nijinska's *Impressions de music-hall* was a one-act ballet performed at the Paris Opéra in 1927. It featured the famous Opéra ballerina Carlotta Zambelli and a corps of dancers who did the "Charleston" on pointe.

58 See Mary Lynn Stewart, *For Health and Beauty.*

59 C. Rearick, *The French in Love and War*, x.

60 These studies include *Modern Girl around the World* (Weinbaum et al., 2008), *Colonial Metropolis* (2010) by Jennifer A. Boittin, and *It's So French* (2007) by Vanessa R. Schwartz.

61 In the mid-eighteenth century, there occurred a shift in dance from merely decorative to the narrative and the dramatic in the new *ballet d'action* of Noverre. In the 1820s, male dancers remained at forefront: Carlos Blasis, Charles-Louis Didelot, Salvadore Vigaro. Pointe work took over and shaped the art form into a feminine one. By the later half of the eighteenth century, ballet became increasingly feminized. In fact, young ballerinas were increasingly fetishized and eroticized by critics (Gautier included), whereupon there was no place for men on stage.

CHAPTER ONE

1 Francis Frascina and Charles Harrison, eds, *Modern Art and Modernism*, 1.

2 "Cultural criticism" here is used to denote criticism on cultural life as defined in nineteenth-century terms: commentary on music, opera, art, dance, philosophy, literature, the sciences, etc.

3 These dailies are all Parisian papers. As Clyde Thogmartin asserts in his book *The National Daily Press of France*, after the First World War "few papers published outside Paris had any national reputation, with the exception of *La Dépêche de Toulouse*, the politically influential voice of the Radical party (really center-left)." Thogmartin, *The National Daily Press of France*, 104.

4 See Orwitz, ed., *Art Criticisms and Its Institutions in Nineteenth-Century France*, 1.

5 See T.J. Clark, *Image of the People* and *The Painting of Modern Life.*

6 Orwitz, ed., *Art Criticisms and Its Institutions in Nineteenth-Century France*, 2.

7 Ibid., 4.

8 Ibid., 5.

9 Ibid.

10 "Acts du Government. Arrêté du 27 Nivôse," *Journal de Paris*, 20 January 1800, 540. Also cited in Susan L. Siegfried, "The Politicization of Art Criticism in the Post-Revolutionary Press," 11.

11 Siegfried, "The Politicization of Art Criticism," 11.

12 Ibid., 12. The custom of printing "letters to the editor" also emerged in this period, offering the opportunity for readers to hold their critics accountable.

13 As a royalist, Geoffroy left Paris just as the country became consumed by republican politics. He returned to Paris in 1799.
14 Siegfried, "The Politicization of Art Criticism," 17.
15 Ibid., 16. Marquis Jean-Baptiste-Bon Boutard worked for the *Journal des Débats* for seventeen years. His replacement, Étienne-Jean Delécluze, worked for the paper for the next forty years.
16 Siegfried, "The Politicization of Art Criticism," 19.
17 Ibid., 22.
18 Ibid., 15.
19 Ibid., 16.
20 The flourishing of specialized presses reflects the atmosphere of the July Monarchy. Article seven from the Charter of 14 August 1830, stated that censorship could never be re-established. Thus, in the early years of the July Monarchy, there was a liberalization of journalism. This was short-lived, however, as the September laws of 1835 reversed this. In addition, with the advances of the printing industry, the prices of the periodicals dropped. The rise of the bourgeois class and increase of its leisure time also expanded readership.
21 Geoffroy's review of Grétry's "La caravane du Caire," *Journal des Débats*, 24 October 1802, as cited in Katherine Ellis, *Music Criticism in Nineteenth-Century France*, 10.
22 Unsigned, *Les Quatre Saisons du Parnasse*, Automne 1805, 291–2, cited in Ellis, *Music Criticism in Nineteenth-Century France*, 12. The *QSP* (1805–9) was a quarterly arts journal that contained occasional opera reviews.
23 Ellis, *Music Criticism in Nineteenth-Century France*, 27.
24 Criticism from this journal offers a valuable source for examining the years leading up to the July Monarchy.
25 Ivor Guest, introduction to Théophile Gautier, *Gautier on Dance*, xxii.
26 See Théophile Gauthier, "La Font, ballet de M. Mazilier," *La Presse*, 10 January 1855, 1, and Jules Janin, "Théâtre de la Gaîté. La Bobémienne de Paris," *Journal des Débats*, 26 February 1844, 1.
27 See Philip Nord, *The Republican Moment.*
28 Many of the 1789 revolutionaries, such as Mirabeau, Marat, Desmoulins, Brissot, and Hébert were themselves journalists who valued above all else the freedom of public opinion.
29 Dominique Kalifa, "The Press," 189.
30 Ibid.
31 Ibid.
32 Ibid.
33 Ibid., 192.
34 Ibid., 191.
35 Ibid., 334.

36 Jane F. Fulcher, *French Cultural Politics and Music*, 4.
37 Eugene Müntz, "L'art et la morale," 738–44. Cited in Robert Allen Jay, "Art and Nationalism in France," 202.
38 Ibid., 203.
39 Between 1900 and the First World War, for example, the image of Joan of Arc was reintroduced by nationalists (particularly those of the Right) as a symbol of French patriotism. This is not surprising as Joan of Arc historically was associated with clerical and royalist sentiment. As Robert Allen Jay points out, in the 1890s "virtually all the most important sculptors of the Société des Artistes Françaises … exhibited sculptures of Joan in the salons." Jay, "Art and Nationalism in France," 193.
40 Henri Baüer, *Le Figaro*, October 1902, cited in Jann Pasler, "'Pelléas' and Power," 261.
41 Cited in Pasler, "'Pelléas' and Power," 261.
42 Ibid., 262.
43 Émile Vuillermoz, "Une tasse de thé," *Mercure Musicale*, 15 November 1905, 505, cited in Pasler, "'Pelléas' and Power," 263.
44 Fulcher, *French Cultural Politics and Music*, 136.
45 Edmond, Got, *Journal d'Edmond Got, sociétaire de la Comédie-française 1822–1901*, 2 vols (Paris 1910), 1:175. Also cited in Berlanstein, *Daughters of Eve*, 17.
46 In France, Parisian theatre criticism carried out two primary functions: first, it reflected the notion that theatre was a representation of Parisian life; and second, theatre reviews were a means by which to connect spectators to the stage.
47 Thogmartin, *The National Daily Press of France*, 64.
48 Ibid., 59. Thogmartin notes that French diplomats read *Le Temps* to gain an understanding of French opinion. On the instigation of General de Gaulle, *Le Monde* was founded in 1944 to replace *Le Temps.*
49 It is also important to address that by the 1920s a growing number of popularized dance periodicals and journals were in circulation in France. In this period, we begin to find a specialized press on dance (social dance and performance): *La Danse* (est. 1921), run by Jacques Hebertot, promoting dance and "les vendredis de danse"; *La Tribune de la Danse* (est. 1923), run by Jean Dorcy as a bulletin of information for dance criticism; *Revue International de Musique et de Danse* (1926), run by Carol-Bérard, the spouse of a librarian at the Opéra; and *Arts et Mouvement* (est. ca. 1926), run by Pierre Conté, addressing theories on dance systems of notation. Other dance magazines included reviews, advertisements, audition notices, news, articles, and other resources for dancers, artistic directors, choreographers, and designers. Their number alone reveals the growing interest in and demand for informa-

tion about dance performance and certainly added to the legitimacy of dance as a profession in its own right.

50 Under the direction of André Gide (1908–14), Jacques Rivière (1919–25), and Jean Paulhan (1925–40), the NRF was known as a Leftist paper. After ceasing publication during the First World War, it reopened in 1919. Its influence steadily grew, and by the interwar years it became the leading literary journal in France and occupied a powerful role in French culture. The NRF's Rightist counterpart was the *Revue Critique des Idées et des Livres*, established in 1908, which associated itself with the Action Française. Also important to note is that the NRF fell under fascist direction from 1940 until 1945 when it was run by Pierre Drieu La Rochelle. After the war, the NRF was banned for collaborationism. It was then relaunched in 1953 by Paulhan, who had been an active member of the French Resistance.

51 Henri Ghéon, "Propos divers sur le Ballet Russe," *La Nouvelle Revue Française,* 199–212.

52 Karen D. Levy, *Jacques Rivière,* 11.

53 Ibid.

54 J. Rivière, "Le sacre du printemps," 726.

55 Ibid., 727.

56 J. Rivière, "Des Ballets Russes et de Fokine," 174.

57 J. Rivière, "Petrouchka, ballet d'Igor Stravinsky," 376–7.

58 Traditionally, there existed in France a battlefield in which two national discourses vied for supremacy under the cover of universalism – one represented Germany, and the other France.

59 Édouard Lalo composed also for the ballet.

60 Louis Laloy, *Claude Debussy.* Laloy wrote about many modern composers, among them Paul Dukas, Maurice Ravel, Igor Stravinsky, and Erik Satie. In addition to Debussy, he was also friends with Georges Auric, Francis Poulenc, Maurice Ravel, Igor Stravinsky, Ricardo Viñes, and critics Romain Rolland and Jean Marnold.

61 Leon Botstein, "Beyond the Illusions of Realism: Painting and Debussy's Break with Tradition," in Fulcher, ed., *Debussy and His World,* 143.

62 Louis Laloy, "La danse à l'Opéra," 1.

63 Prunières had studied music at the Sorbonne from 1906 to 1913 and became a well-respected musicologist and a specialist of seventeenth-century French and Italian music.

64 "Homage à Henry Prunières," brochure from *La Revue Musicale,* 1953, 18.

65 Interview with Prunières conducted by Frédéric Lefèvre, "Nouvelles Littéraires," *La Revue Musicale,* November 1929, 92. Between 1920 and 1926, *La Revue Musicale* was published by *La Nouvelle Revue Française* and shared its pacifist views (e.g., Franco-German reconciliation).

66 "Le ballet contemporain," *La Revue Musicale*, March 1938.
67 Leonid Livak, *Russian Émigrés in the Intellectual and Literary Life of Interwar France*, 7.
68 Ibid. American émigrés in Paris differed in that they could return to their homeland, where their works were never banned. Most Russian intellectuals, on the other hand, did not have that option.
69 Maurice de Waleffe, "Russophile," *Paris-Midi*, 9 March 1922, 2. Cited in Livak, *Russian Émigrés*, 7.
70 Robert H. Johnston, *New Mecca, New Babylon*, 56.
71 James E. Hassell, *Russian Refugees in France and the United States between the World Wars*, 22.
72 Marc Raeff, *Russian Abroad*, 38.
73 Ibid., 37–8.
74 Ibid., 37.
75 Johnston, *New Mecca, New Babylon*, 22.
76 Vassily Yanovsky, *Elysian Fields*, 91, cited in Johnston, *New Mecca, New Babylon*, 22.
77 Boris Schloezer, "Les arts: la danse par Serge Lifar," 329–32.
78 "'Petroushka et Lachete' ou l'histoire vue par le ballet," *Le Figaro*, 24 May 1922.
79 S.C. Summer, introduction to A. Levinson, *Ballet Old and New*, ix–x.
80 L. Garafola, *Legacies of Twentieth-Century Dance*, 126.
81 Ibid.
82 A. Rigaud, "Ce que fut la saison 1922–1923 à l'Opéra," *Comœdia*, 18 July 1922, 1.
83 L. Laloy, "Théâtre de Monte-Carlo: Les Fâcheux, 1923, Ballets Russes," *Comœdia*, 23 January, 1924, 3. He writes: "Dans tous les sens de ce nombre ordinal le premier critique chorégraphique de notre temps" and that he "ne fût pas la pour apprécier de sa haute compétence les mérites de l'interpretation."
84 This text includes photographic plates of Lifar in his various roles and productions and the frontispiece is by Pablo Picasso.
85 A. Levinson, "Stravinsky and the Dance." "Ballet, Painting, Music" appears in his volume of essays, *Ballet Old and New*.
86 Levinson, *Ballet Old and New*, 47.
87 Ibid.
88 Lifar, *Lifar on Classical Ballet*; Lifar, *Le manifeste du chorégraphie*; Levinson, *Ballet Old and New*, 75.
89 Acocella and Garafola, eds, *André Levinson on Dance*, 49.
90 Lifar, *Ma Vie*, 137.
91 Lifar, "La danse et la musique," 182. This article was based on a lecture Lifar delivered at the Sorbonne in Paris.
92 Cited in Ivor Guest, *The Romantic Ballet in Paris*, 156.

93 Lifar, *Lifar on Classical Ballet*, 142.
94 It is interesting to note that Lifar was of French descent.
95 Lifar, "Évolution du ballet au XXeme siècle," 3. Lifar mentioned also that students at the Sorbonne could now choose dance as the subject of their PhD dissertations.
96 Elizabeth Vigée-Lebrun, along with several other women, was admitted into the Royal Academy of Painting and Sculpture as an exception. See Mary D. Sheriff, *The Exceptional Woman.*
97 I am not implying here that women did not critically review art before the 1880s. Wendelin Guentner's *Women Art Critics in Nineteenth-Century France: Vanishing Acts* is an important study that unearths the activities of women art critics in this period.
98 Elizabeth Robins Pennell, "Women's World of London," 772. Also cited in Meaghan Clarke, *Critical Voices*, 155.
99 Linda L. Clark, *Women and Achievement in Nineteenth-Century Europe*, 101.
100 Joachim, *Brief von Joseph Joachim*, 3:42–3, cited in Nancy B. Reich, "Clara Schumann," in *Women Making Music: The Western Art Tradition, 1150–1950*, 275.
101 Nancy B. Reich, "European Composers and Musicians, ca. 1800–1890," 151.
102 Huysmann, quoted in C.S. Moffett, *The New Painting*, 362.
103 Clark, *Women and Achievement in Nineteenth-Century Europe*, 82.
104 Quote in Barbara Ehrlich White, "Renoir's Sensuous Women," 171. Also cited in L. Clark, *Women and Achievement in Nineteenth-Century Europe*, 82.
105 Valentine Gross was married to Jean Hugo, Victor Hugo's grandson.
106 V. Gross, "Le sacre du printemps," *Comœdia*, May 1913, cited in "The Right Stuff," *Independent Online Edition*, 29 April 2002.
107 In 1972, Diaghilev biographer Richard Buckle provided some of her action sketches in his book *Nijinsky on Stage* [with drawings by Valentine Gross] (1971) [orig. 1913].
108 A.V. Coton, "The Critic's Function," in *Writings on Dance*, 5.
109 Ibid., 6.
110 Ibid.
111 Julie Sazonova, "Questions chorégraphiques," 208.
112 Ibid., 209.
113 Ibid., 154–57.
114 American dancer Loïe Fuller, who was extremely successful in Paris, wrote her autobiography *Quinze ans de ma vie* in 1908. In her book, she included a lengthy discussion of her aesthetic of dance.
115 Selma Cohen, "Present Problems of Dance Aesthetics," 19.

CHAPTER TWO

1 This was a security measure that was instituted after Napoleon III's narrow escape from assassination while en route to the old opera house on rue Le Peletier in 1858.

2 Huebner, *French Opera at the Fin-de-siècle,* 10.

3 Édouard Dujardin, "Chronique de Janvier," *Le Revue Wangerienne* 1 (8 February 1885): 1–2. Cited in Verzosa, *The Absolute Limits,* 45.

4 Quoted in Daniel Halévy, *La fin des notables,* 87.

5 See Digeon, *La crise allemande de la pensée française,* and Shattuck, *The Banquet Years.*

6 Alfred Dreyfus, a captain in the French army and a Jew, was accused (falsely) of dealing information to Germany and was found guilty of treason. He was not exonerated until 1906, whereupon his former military rank was restored. Other scandals include the Boulanger affair, the Wilson case, and bribery of government officials and journalists associated with the financing of the Suez Canal.

7 Gordan Wright, *France in Modern Times,* 245.

8 Ibid., 291.

9 Alphonse de Lamartine, *Histoire de la Russie* (1855), cited in C. Corbet, *À l'ère des nationalisms,* 300; Lamartine, cited in Kirill Makhrow, *Russian Paris, 1910–1960,* 3.

10 Ibid., 6.

11 A. Benois, *Reminiscences of the Russian Ballet* (1977), 305.

12 The endurance of the Ballets Russes has been extensively chronicled by dance historians. They have focused almost exclusively on the novelty of the Ballets Russes and its productions. Yet they have neglected to historicize the ballet within broader cultural and social contexts. Those others who have attempted to contextualize the ballet have done so in order to explain the success of the Ballets Russes in France. Some accredit its success to economic, cultural, or artistic factors, or simply timing. Yet, they seldom take into account the historical shifts occurring during its existence, nor do they call attention to the broader consequences of its appearance in France. This chapter reveals the ways in which the Ballets Russes and its performances captured the attention of prominent music critics, who later initiated discussions concerning not only the state of the French ballet, but also its nationalist potential.

13 For example, Russian fur hats, scarves, and muffs became very popular in Paris and were worn by its fashionistas. For more on the influence of the Ballet Russes on Parisian fashion, see Holt, "Style, Fashion, Politics, and Identity."

14 Benois, *Reminiscences of the Russian Ballet,* 140.

15 Lydia Sokolova, *Dancing for Diaghilev*, 97.

16 Benois, *Reminiscences of the Russian Ballet*, 140.

17 Lise-Léon Blum, "Le goût au théâtre," *Gazette du Bon Ton*, July 1914, 253, cited in Davis, *Ballets Russes Style*, 61–2. Lise-Léon Blum was the wife of future French prime minister Léon Blum.

18 Perros, "Après les Ballets Russes," 1.

19 Sokolova, *Dancing for Diaghilev*, 97.

20 Alfred Bruneau, *Musiques de Russie et musiciens de France* (Paris: Bibliothèque Charpentier, 1903), 22–8, cited in Taruskin, *Defining Russia Musically*, 49.

21 Ibid.

22 The idea of "Russianness" in the works of the Ballets Russes has been extensively chronicled by Sally Banes, Richard Taruskin, Dale Harris, and Lynn Garafola. Their thorough analysis of the Ballets Russes' ballets is useful for comparing the responses of critics who did or did not see the company as expressing an authentic Russian national identity. Such work has highlighted the existence of two interwoven currents in many of the Ballets Russes' productions: that of nationalist material and exotica. It also takes note of the complicated nature of Russian identity by locating its mixed Eastern and Western heritage (not a new insight, for this was something frequently addressed by critics of the early twentieth century). For example, Sally Banes notes that Diaghilev's orientalist and Russian folkloric ballets were "two inseparable aspects of a single search for a Russian national identity – a persistent, troubled quest that grew historically out of a resistance both to the epoch of Tatar domination and to the forced Westernization of Russia by Peter the Great, and that posited Russian identity as one of mixed heritage: Eurasian." Banes argues that the Ballets Russes managed to dissolve parts of its Eastern and Western heritage in order to create a "positive unique national identity" and an "ethnic self-conception of Russia." In other words, the Ballets Russes mythologized a Russian national identity to please Parisian audiences. See Banes, "*Firebird* and the Idea of Russianness," 118.

23 Banes, "*Firebird* and the Idea of Russianness," 131. Banes's article does an excellent job in analyzing this particular Ballets Russes production.

24 Sokolova, *Dancing for Diaghilev*, 97.

25 Diaghilev's "Principles of Art Criticism" reveals his ideas on the relationship between nationalism and art. This series of four articles published under the title *Complicated Questions* opened the first issue of the journal *World of Art* (*Mir iskusstva*) in 1898 and 1899. Diaghilev was the editor-in-chief for the magazine. See also the ideas of an "imagined community" in Anderson, *Imagined Communities*, 15–16, and "invented

tradition" in the work of Eric Hobsbawm, "Introduction: Inventing Traditions" in Hobsbawm and Ranger, eds, *The Invention of Tradition*, 1.

26 It must be noted that Diaghilev presented both tradition and innovation in his repertoire of ballets. He presented modernist experimentation in works like *Sacre du printemps* and *Prodigal Son* as well as nineteenth-century classicism in romantic ballets such as *Sleeping Beauty* and *Swan Lake*. This is explored further in chapter 3.

27 Michael Fokine, *Memoirs of a Ballet Master*, 167, cited in Banes, "*Firebird* and the Idea of Russianness," 123.

28 Banes, "*Firebird* and the Idea of Russianness," 119–20, writes: "In reversing the status of Western and non-Western codes of gesture and posture and in bringing previously marginalized aspects of ballet dancing to center stage, the Ballets Russes participated in a longstanding, far-reaching debate about the nature of Russian national identity. The pagan body of both the Islamic Orient and pre-Christian Russia in the above-mentioned ballets, as well as the peasant, folkloric, pre-modern body – epitomized by the familiar figure of the traditional folk-theatre puppet Petrushka – became the site in Western European performances where the assertion of a distinctly Eurasian, non-Western Russian national identity took place, even as the stage was being set for an internationalist political cataclysm at home."

29 In my own international career as a professional ballet dancer, character classes were most often taught by Russian teachers.

30 *Le Figaro*, 24 June 1910, 6.

31 André Levinson, *Ballet Old and New*, 42.

32 Robert Brussel, *Le Figaro*, 27 June 1910, 6.

33 Pierre Lalo, "Au Chatêlet: première spectacle de la saison russe. La musique – Le ballet classique – Les danses caracteristiques – Décors et costumes," *Le Temps*, 22 May 1909, 3.

34 Ibid.

35 P. Lancome, "Les musiciens espagnols," *Le Ménéstral*, September 1878, 320; Jean Lorrain, "Le flamenco," *L'Écho de Paris*, 11 January 1892, 1. Both cited in Rae Beth Gordon, *Dances with Darwin*, 201.

36 Cited in Annegret Fauser, *Musical Encounters at the 1889 World's Fair* (Rochester, NY: University of Rochester Press, 2005), 45.

37 Charles Decours [Charles Réty], "Notes de musique," *Le Figaro*, 26 June 1889, 6, cited in Fauser, "Gendering the Nations: The Ideologies of French Discourse on Music (1870–1914)," 43.

38 A general distrust of Jews had been exacerbated by the Dreyfus affair. James Corbett explains that France "looked with suspicion even on native minority cultures like those of the Basques, Bretons, or [Alsacians]." He adds that foreigners were "expected to fit into the French

mold, French thought processes, the French value system." Corbett, *Through French Windows*, 202–3.

39 Edward R. Tannebaum, *L'Action Française*, 6 January 1909, 261.

40 Maurice Denis, *Journal II* (1957), 133.

41 Gabriel Astruc, who was the owner-manager of the Théâtre du Châtelet where the Ballets Russes routinely performed and who was instrumental in the company's early success in Paris, was often vehemently attacked for being Jewish.

42 Paul Morand, "Paris Letter. May 1925," *Dial*, June 1925, 499, cited in Batson, *Dance, Desire, and Anxiety in Early Twentieth-Century French Theatre*, 132.

43 André Warnod, "Les peintures et les Ballets Russes," *La Revue Musicale*, 1 December 1930, 78–89.

44 Even fellow Russian artist Alexander Benois wrote in a letter: "Bakst is peculiarly Jewish in that he is soft and greedy, *coulant* [compliant] – the combination gives him something slimily predatory, snakelike, i.e., repellant." Benois to Serov (late June) 1911. Cited in Scheijen, *Diaghilev*, 231. Benois's attitude is a reminder of the anti-Semitism that existed in czarist Russia and how Diaghilev's circle would not be impervious to it.

45 Jules Payot, *L'éducation de la volonté* (1893), cited in Christopher Forth, *The Dreyfus Affair the French Crisis of Masculinity*, 122. Forth points out that Payot's book went though thirty-seven editions in twenty years and was translated into most European languages.

46 Léon Daudet, "Les engouements de Paris," *L'Action Française*, 31 May 1912, 1. Daudet was a co-founder of the journal *L'Action Française.*

47 Suarès, "Chronique de Caerdal," 329. Suarès was part of the Jewish community in Marseilles. He sometimes wrote under the name Caerdan and is best known for his *Condottiere* (1910).

48 Abel Bonnard, "Le Ballet Russe," cited in Lifar's *Serge Diaghilev*, 163. Bonnard was a follower of Charles Maurras and a member of the Académie Française who embraced fascism in the 1930s. He served as one of the ministers of national education under the Vichy regime from 1942 to 1944.

49 As Edward Said writes: "The development and maintenance of every culture require the existence of another, different, and competing *alter ego.* The construction of identity … involves the construction of opposites and 'others' whose actuality is always subject to the continuous interpretation and reinterpretation of their differences from 'us'" (*Orientalism*, 331).

50 Lin, "Image (and) Nation: The Russian Exotic in 19th-Century French Travel Narratives," 134.

51 See Gordon, *Dances with Darwin, 1875–1910.*

52 Paulino, *Comœdia,* 22 May 1909, 2. The critical attention to the superiority of Russian dancing and dancers most likely contributed to the success of numerous ballet schools founded in Paris by Russian dancers.
53 Ibid.
54 Ibid.
55 Ibid.
56 Pierre Lalo, *Le Temps,* 20 June 1909, 3.
57 Ibid.
58 Drummond, *Speaking of Diaghilev,* 311–12.
59 Haskell, "Portrait of Serge Lifar," *Lifar on Classical Ballet,* 18.
60 Sokolova, *Dancing for Diaghilev,* 68–9.
61 Ibid., 224.
62 Ibid., 84.
63 Cited in Lifar, *Serge Diaghilev,* 141.
64 Lalo, *Le Temps,* 20 June 1909, 3.
65 A similar notion to that of Wagner's *Gesamtkunstwerk* (the fusion of the arts).
66 Lalo, "La Musique," *Le Temps,* 18 June 1912, 3.
67 Lalo, *Le Temps,* 28 May 1912, 3.
68 Ibid.
69 Essarts, "Est-ce que la fin du tutu?" 1.
70 Ivan Clustine, "Ballets Russes et Ballet d'Opéra, *Musica-Noël* (1912): 245.
71 Debay, "Les Ballets Russes," 341.
72 Louis Laloy, "Article critique concernant *L'Histoire de la Musique* de Camille Mauclair," *Comœdia,* 1914, cited in Davinia Caddy, *The Ballets Russes and Beyond: Music and Dance in Belle-Époque Paris,* 152.
73 Émile Vuillermoz, "La saison russe au Théâtre des Champs-Élysées," *La Revue Musicale,* June 1913, 49.
74 Levinson, *Ballet Old and New,* 14, 16.
75 Ibid., 1, 48.
76 Ibid., 36.
77 R. Brussel, *Le Figaro,* 27 June 1910, 6. This debate about aesthetics is examined in more detail in chapters 4, 5, 6, and 7.
78 Marcel Prévost, "La Danse," *Le Figaro,* 13 June 1910, 1.
79 Ibid.
80 The French novelist Marcel Prévost wrote often about "feminine issues" from a male viewpoint, portraying what he regarded as the moral frailty of modern woman. He caused a sensation in France in the 1890s with stories purporting to show the corrupting effect of Parisian education and Parisian society on young women. He won fame with *The Demi-Virgins* (1894, tr. 1895) in which he attacked feminism. He also wrote on the behaviour of women in the theatre.

81 Prévost, "La Danse," 1.
82 Prévost goes so far as to say that the very training of dancers is linked to an imperial institution. "The school for ballerinas, in St Petersburg, is, if I am not mistaken, an Imperial institution. The young girls who compose it receive an instruction that is quasi-aristocratic (beyond their special art). And it is not rare, I am told, that they end up, thanks to a brilliant marriage, joined definitively to the aristocracy … For a democratic crowd, traditional ballet is not adaptable." Prévost, "La Danse," 1.
83 Ibid.
84 Prévost, as translated in Lifar, *Serge Diaghilev*, 164.
85 C. Mauclair, "L'enseignement de la saison russe," 350–60.
86 Auguste Vestris was a notable dancer and choreographer in the mid-eighteenth century.
87 Cited in Lifar, *Serge Diaghilev*, 177.
88 C. Mauclair, *La Revue*, 1 August 1910, 350–60. Eventually, it was former Ballets Russes dancer Serge Lifar who embarked on and succeeded in such a task.
89 L.P., "Un nouveau maitre de ballet à l'Opéra," *Comœdia*, 24 August 1911, 2.
90 Ibid.
91 Ibid.
92 Ibid.
93 Ibid.
94 Pierre Lalo, *Le Temps*, 22 May 1909, 3.
95 Ibid.
96 Ibid.
97 Ibid.

CHAPTER THREE

1 Cited in Silver, *Esprit de Corps*, 27.
2 Sue Collard, "French Cultural Policy: The Special Role of the State," in Reynolds and Kidd, eds, *Contemporary French Cultural Studies*, 20. In this article, Collard looks at the development of cultural affairs in France and its relationship to the French state. She reveals the close relationship between French culture and political power, and the prominent and visible role of the minister of culture in the French state. As Sian Reynolds points out in *Contemporary French Cultural Studies*, the French state places great importance on having their past define their present.
3 Several academies developed in other European countries in the century that followed. One of the greatest was the Russian Imperial Ballet of St Petersburg, whose school was founded by French dancer Jean-Baptiste Landé in 1738.

4 Collard, "French Cultural Policy," 20.
5 Some ballets were still performed at court, but most were presented at the Opéra.
6 First emerging in the decorative arts, the rococo emphasized pastel colours, delicate, sensuous forms, and patterns based on flowers, vines, and shells. Painters turned from serious religious and historical subjects – though these were never ignored completely – to more intimate mythological scenes, views of daily life, and portraiture.
7 Denis Diderot, *Oeuvres complètes,* 13:222 (Salon de 1761), cited in Melissa Hyde, *Making Up the Rococo,* 3.
8 See Thomas Crow, "Oath of the Horatii in 1785," 424–71.
9 For more information on ballet during the French Revolution, see Judith Chazin-Bennahum's *Dance in the Shadow of the Guillotine.* Also see James Johnson's *Listening in Paris.*
10 Gardel managed to survive as ballet master at the Opéra through the revolution, Napoleon, and the Restoration until 1820.
11 The Opéra changed names many times. Under the Directory, the Opéra was renamed as the Théâtre de la République et des Arts; in 1804, under Napoleon, as the Académie Impériale de Musique; ca. 1870, under the Third Republic, as the Théâtre National de l'Opéra; and in 1994, as the Opéra National de Paris.
12 He was wise to do so as the police kept a vigilant eye on artists. French critic and essayist François Castil-Blaze's first-hand account captures the stringent atmosphere at the Opéra during the Terror: "The members of the Commune exercised an absolute and arbitrary power over the performers and staff, ruling them through a regime of fear … members of the Commune specially charged with the overall supervision of the theatre allowed no excuse, and a performer who was indisposed, even with a doctor's certificate, might be placed on the list of suspected persons as a trouble-making conspirator who was depriving the chiefs of the Republic of their accustomed pleasures and the *sans-culottes* of the free performances that were often an offer." Therefore, like all other aspects of revolutionary society, "transparency" was no stranger to the Opéra. François Castil-Blaze, "*Académie Imperiale de Musique de 1645 à 1855*" (Paris, 1855), cited in Ivor Guest, *Ballet under Napoleon,* 13.
13 Jennifer Homans, *Apollo's Angels,* 110.
14 Susan Leigh Foster, "Dance in the Shadow of the Guillotine," 34. Foster points out that "during the French Revolution, ballets were used as a medium capable of expressing patriotic sentiment, as a propagandistic tool, as an institution with its own structures of power, and as a diversionary entertainment."
15 Homans, *Apollo's Angels,* 110.

16 For example, in September 1792, Gardel and composer François-Joseph Gossec presented the Opéra's first republican spectacle, *L'offrande à la liberté*, which was set to the revolution's national anthem "La Marseillaise," and performed over one hundred times during the First Republic. On the creation and reception of the *Offrande à la liberté*, see Bartlet, "Gossec, *L'Offrande à la Liberté* et l'histoire de la *Marseillaise*," 123–46. *L'offrande* was performed later during the 1848 Revolution to serve a similar function.

17 Ivor Guest, *The Ballet of the Enlightenment*, 341. This chorale dance drama was performed on 27 January 1793.

18 Chazin-Bennahum, *Dance in the Shadow of the Guillotine*, 69.

19 Guest, *Ballet under Napoleon*, 6.

20 Cited in Johnson, *Backstage at the Revolution*, 180.

21 Ibid., 81.

22 Victoria Johnson, *Backstage at the Revolution*, 4.

23 *Les spectacles de Paris et de toute la France, ou Calendrier historique & chronologique des théâtres* (1794), 1:99, cited in Bartlet, "The New Repertory at the Opera during the Reign of Terror," 124.

24 Unlike the fate of twenty-five other theatres in Paris, the Opéra escaped closing but was subject to strict supervision. James Johnson notes that beginning in 1800 "the minister of police approved all ballets before they were danced at the Opera." Subjects deemed appropriate were drawn from either mythology or history "with the main characters 'gods, kings, or heroes.'" Johnson, *Listening in Paris*, 174.

25 Ibid., 166.

26 Madame Mariquita was a choreographer who created dances for both these venues. For more information on music-hall ballet see Gutsche-Miller, *Pantomime-Ballet on the Music-Hall Stage*; Carter, *Dance and Dancers in the Victorian and Edwardian Music*; and Guest, *The Romantic Ballet in England*.

27 The relationship between cultural affairs and national identity remains a close one in France. Even today, the relationship between the state and the arts remains tight. Ballet played and continues to serve a major role in French national identity. In fact, today, it is classical ballet that receives the most government financial support over all other dance forms. In light of this, many contemporary dance companies hide under the guise of a ballet company name for this very reason.

28 Gordan Wright, *France in Modern Times*, 306.

29 Ferro, "Cultural Life in France, 1914–1918," 304 and 295. As Ferro points out, not all aspects of cultural life were affected to the same extent.

30 Pierre de la Rochelle, *La suite des idées* (Paris: Au Sens Pareil, 1927), 125, cited in Mary Louise Roberts, *Civilization without Sexes*, 2.

31 Ibid.

32 As Catherine Hall and Leonore Davidoff observe, "'masculinity' and 'femininity' are constructs specific to historical time and place. They are categories continually being forged, contested, reworked and reaffirmed in social institutions and practices as well as a range of ideologies." Leonore Davidoff and Catherine Hall, *Family Fortunes*, 29.

33 Garafola, "Reconfiguring the Sexes," in Garafola and Baer, eds, *The Ballets Russes and Its World*, 266.

34 By taking "pointe work" away from particular ballets, one wonders whether Fokine attempted to erode or dethrone the "femininity" of ballet dancing by blurring boundaries of gender in ballet production. For example, did androgynous forms work to de-sexualize or "aestheticize" and reveal the dancer as a type of genderless mechanical instrument?

35 See Ulle V. Holt, "Style, Fashion, Politics and Identity."

36 In 1926, Jean Cocteau commissioned the surrealist photographer Man Ray to make a series of photographs of Barbette.

37 Amy Lyford, "'Le Numéro Barbette': Photography and the Politics of Embodiment in Interwar Paris," in Chadwick and Latimer, eds, *The Modern Woman Revisited*, 224.

38 By offering a variety of gender representations in its ballets, Diaghilev's company was no doubt also expanding its audiences and supporters. Were such androgynous images a means through which to assert male and female sexuality upon the ballet stage or to dissolve traditional gender identities? Can androgyny be seen as one of several challenging multiplicities of male identity and how does it relate to the expression of male sexuality? These questions have yet to be explored by gender historians.

39 Paris's popular Nouveau Cirque and Cirque Medrano included a cosmopolitan array of acts – clowns, acrobats, jugglers, magic, and animals – as well as musical plays, pantomimes, and even operettas.

40 Alistair Horne, *To Lose a Battle: France, 1940*, 48.

41 Eksteins, *The Rites of Spring*, 236.

42 Former Ballets Russes dancer Serge Lifar recalled that the Ballets Russes was "Russian" only in the early years of its existence. Only for a decade, he noted, did Diaghilev "displa[y] the works of Russian art to Europe (including that of dance), where he exported from Russia his painters, his musicians, his choreographers, and his male and female ballet stars." Lifar, *Ma Vie*, 90.

43 Leslie Norton, *Léonide Massine and the 20th Century Ballet*, 16.

44 Ibid., 17.

45 Ibid.

46 Lydia Sokolova, *Dancing for Diaghilev*, 97.

47 The Ballets Russes production of *Jeux,* premiered on 15 May 1913 at the Théâtre des Champs-Élysées in Paris, was the first ballet to embrace a contemporary theme – in this case a tennis match.
48 *Le tricorne,* based on Pedro Antonio Alarcón's novel, employed a score by Manuel de Falla and set and costume designs by Pablo Picasso.
49 Lifar, *Ballet Traditional to Modern,* 153.
50 Levinson, "Où en sont les 'Ballets russes'?" *Comœdia* 18 June 1923, 4.
51 Levinson, "A Crisis in the Ballets Russes," *Theatre Arts Monthly* (ca. 1926), 787.
52 Ibid.
53 See Garafola, "The Making of Ballet Modernism," in *Diaghilev's Ballets Russes,* 76–97.
54 See Clive James, *Cultural Amnesia,* 169.
55 The production required a huge contingent of artists: a few French (pianists Auric and Meyer and conductor Ansermet), and others mostly Russian (composer Igor Stravinsky, choreographer Bronislava Nijinska [Vaslav Nijinsky's sister], designer Natalia Goncharova, all principal singers, Vasily Kibalchich's Russian chorus, and many of the dancers).
56 On the whole, the ballet reflected Diaghilev's yearning to continue his depiction of Russia in one form or another. The ballet opened with the "Consecration of the Bride," a lament of the peasant bride's loss of her virginity, which is often interpreted as symbolizing the loss of the Holy Mother Russia after the 1917 revolution. This is followed by the "Consecration of the Bridegroom," which contained elements of Russian religious symbolism (such as dancing around an altar and prayer gestures). The manner of dancing was reflective of Stravinsky's score, which evoked a sombre and pensive atmosphere, far from that of a merry wedding, but as might be imagined for an arranged marriage of this kind. See Robert Craft and Vera Stravinsky, *Stravinsky in Pictures and Documents.*
57 Drue Fergison, "Bringing *Les Noces* to the Stage" in Garafola and Baer, eds, *The Ballets Russes and Its World,* 183.
58 Ibid., 172–4.
59 Ibid.
60 J.R.F., "La grande semaine de Paris," *Vogue* (Paris), 1 August 1923, 56, cited in Davis, *Ballets Russes Style,* 104.
61 Ibid.
62 Grigoriev, *The Diaghilev Ballet, 1909–1979,* 185–6.
63 Émile Vuillermoz, "Premières, Ballets Russes: 'Les Noces d'Igor Stravinsky,'" *Excelsior,* 18 June 1923.
64 Raymond Charpentier, "Les Ballets Russes à la Gaîté-Lyrique. 'Noces.' Ballet de M. Igor Stravinski," *Comœdia,* 16 June 1923.

65 Cited in Robert Johnson, “Ritual and Abstraction in Nijinska’s Les Noces,” 147–59.

66 Natalia Goncharova, “The Metamorphoses of the Ballet ‘Les Noces,’” 137–43. Goncharova, the designer for *Les noces*, recalled “weddings of necessity” involving boys “being called up for military service.” She described later seeing very similar young men marching through cities, “holding a rifle in their hand, too heavy for those brown, fragile, child’s hands, their heads resigned and weighed down by their caps, which seemed too big for their heads, like the nuptial crowns that had been held over their own heads before their departure for the army.”

67 Roland-Manuel, “La Quinzaine musicale, Les Ballets Russes à la Gaîté Lyriques – Les Noces d’Igor Stravinsky,” *L’Éclair*, 23 June 1923, cited in Kelly, *Music and Ultra Modernism in France*, 215.

68 E. Vuillermoz, *Excelsior*, 18 June 1923.

69 Boris Kochno, *Diaghilev and the Ballets Russes*, 189.

70 Levinson, “Les Ballets Russes à la Gaîte-Lyrique. ‘Noces.’ Ballet de M. Stravinski. Le décor, la chorégraphie,” *Comœdia*, 16 June 1923; “La Danse. Où sont les ‘Ballets russes’?” *Comœdia*, 18 June 1923.

71 Nijinska Archives (clipping), cited in D. Fergison, “Bringing *Les Noces* to the Stage,” 187.

72 Fergison, “Bringing *Les Noces* to the Stage.”

73 Cited in Volkov, *St. Petersburg*, 227.

74 See art journals *Arts and Decoration* 25 (A. Budge, 1926) and *The Studio* 117–18 (1939).

75 Beaumont, *The Diaghilev Ballet in London*, 245.

76 As described by the ballet’s composer Francis Poulenc in “Francis Poulenc on His Ballets,” *Ballet* 2, no. 4 (September 1946): 57.

77 Garafola, *Diaghilev’s Ballets Russes*, 129–30.

78 Poulenc, “Francis Poulenc on His Ballets.”

79 Jean Cocteau, *Théâtre Serge de Diaghilev: Les Biches*, 6.

80 Florence E. Grenfell, unpublished diaries, Monte Carlo, 6 January 1924, cited in Schouvaloff, *The Art of the Ballets Russes*, 243.

81 Francis Poulenc, *Correspondence* (from Monte Carlo, Tuesday, 8 January 1924), 68, cited in Schouvaloff, *The Art of the Ballets Russes*, 243.

82 “Sitter Out,” *The Dancing Times* (London), August 1927, 498, cited in Schouvaloff, *The Art of the Ballets Russes*, 243.

83 Louis Laloy, “Les Biches – Ballet de M. Francis Poulenc, chorégraphie de Mme Nijinska. Décor et costumes de Mme Marie Laurencin,” *Comœdia*, 11 January 1924, 3.

84 Ibid.

85 Bronislava Nijinska, “Reflections about the Production of *Les Biches* and *Hamlet* in Markova-Dolin Ballets,” *Dancing Times*, February 1937, 618–19.

86 Boris Schloezer, "Les Arts: Serge de Diaghilev," *La Nouvelle Revue Française,* October 1929, 572–5.

87 Rolf de Mare was devoted to dancing. In 1932, he founded the Archives Internationales de la Danse – the largest documentation centre of dance in the world at the time. In 1950, he donated the archives to the Bibliothèque Nationale de Paris, where it was transferred to the Bibliothèque Nationale de l'Opéra.

88 Cited in Wilson, *Les Ballets Suédois,* 60.

89 J. D'Argency, *La Revue Mondiale* 12 (1920), and A. Coeuroy, "Théâtre des Champs-Élysées: Ballets Suédois," *L'Ère Nouvelle* (Paris), 21 November 1920, cited in Pascale de Groote, *Ballets Suédois,* 12.

90 Levinson, *La danse d'aujourd'hui,* 400–1.

91 Levinson, "Quelques lieux communs sur la Danse II," *Comœdia* 10 September 1923, 3.

92 Ibid. After the 1917 Russian Revolution, Petipa's works had fallen out of favour because of their outdated themes and their association with the imperial court. Susan Au, *Ballet and Modern Dance,* 103.

93 Levinson, *Comœdia,* 10 April 1922, 3.

94 Levinson, *Comœdia,* 10 September 1923, 3.

95 Levinson, "Quelques lieux communs sur la danse II," *Comœdia,* 10 September 1923, 3.

96 Ibid.

97 Levinson, "Pour le ballet français," *Comœdia,* 5 March 1923, 3.

98 Ibid.

99 See his review in *Comœdia,* 23 November 1923.

100 Levinson, "La Danse," *Comœdia,* 8 January 1923, 5.

101 Emma Livry has often been remembered in a tragic sense. During one performance, her tulle skirt came in contact with the gas jet and caught fire. Two male dancers tried to extinguish the flame, but were unsuccessful. She suffered severe burns and died eight months later from complications.

102 Ibid. "*Ballon*" was defined then as the ability of a dancer to suspend herself/himself in the air.

103 Guest, *The Romantic Ballet in Paris,* 57. Referring to Livry's performance in *Papillon,* this critic remarked that "the Butterfly would not be possible [without Livry]" and that she was "so ethereal, and diaphanous, an intangible [and] imperative artist, an artist with *ballon.*"

104 Interestingly, Levinson commended Mlle Craponne's professionalism and "formal beauty" (plastic arts) as he also (somewhat hypocritically) denied her any exceptional qualities. It appears as though Levinson was implying that such qualities as that of Mlle Craponne were nothing extraordinary to a professional ballet dancer. In other words, he seems

to have been wary of giving too much praise to qualities that should be expected of a professional ballet dancer. In doing so, he thus establishes a new standard of ballet criteria.

105 Before becoming director of the Paris Opéra, Rouché wrote his *Art théâtral moderne* in 1910, following time spent in Russia and Germany studying their respective theatrical innovations. From 1910 to 1913, he directed the Théâtre des Arts and hoped to continue the reforms he had begun there when he took over direction at the Palais Garnier in 1914. Rouché is a good example of the nature of art exchange in this period.

106 Rigaud, "Ce que fut la saison 1922–1923 à l'Opéra," *Comœdia*, 13 July 1923, 1.

107 The collections of the Bibliothèque nationale de France conserve a record of the three centuries of the Opéra's past. Rigaud's article "Le véritable Musée de la Danse" applauded this new cultural institution.

108 André Rigaud, *Comœdia*, 19 July 1923, 1.

109 Rigaud, *Comœdia* 13 July 1923, 1.

110 Rigaud, "Ce que fut la saison 1921–22 à l'Opéra," *Comœdia*, 18 July 1922, 1.

111 Ibid.

112 The Paris Opera ballet repertory for the season included *Artémis troublée* (P. Paray), *Frivolant* (J. Poueigh), *La petite suite* (C. Debussy), *Sylvia* (L. Delibes), *Daphnis et Chloé* (M. Ravel), *La maladetta* (P. Vidal), and *La tragédie de Salomé* (F. Schmitt). Other productions of the season were *Le mariage de la belle au bois dormant (Aurora's Wedding), Giselle, Les sylphides, Coppélia, Taglioni chez Musette,* and *Cydalise* – all representing French tradition and talents. *Le mariage de la belle au bois dormant,* choreographed by Bronislava Nijinska and staged at the Opéra in 1922, was based on French folklore and had its roots in the Romantic classical ballet. The ballet was first performed in France by Italian ballerinas Marie Taglioni, Fanny Elssler, and Fanny Cerrito and originally choreographed by the legendary Marius Petipa for Taglioni in 1829. One critic wrote of the work: "*Le Mariage de la belle au bois dormant* is borrowed from French folklore but, in our country, goes by a different title. It is effectively set to French choreography created long ago. The work is indeed a classical ballet, one of those ballets which has had such great popularity in Russia as in France over the last century, and which brought glory to the likes of Taglioni, Fanny Elssler, and Fanny Cerrito." *Comœdia* 18 May 1922, 3.

113 André Messager, *Figaro-Théâtre,* 19 June 1925, 3.

114 Garafola, "Forgotten Interlude," 70.

115 Levinson, "Propos de ballet," *Comœdia,* 17 April 1922, 3.

116 Rigaud, "Ce que fut la saison 1921–22 à l'Opéra," *Comœdia*, 18 July 1922, 1. One performance was a benefit for Russian refugees in France.
117 Rigaud, "La seconde saison de ballets français à l'Opéra," *Comœdia*, 14 July 1923, 1.
118 Ibid.
119 Grigoriev, *The Diaghilev Ballet*, 186–7.
120 Levinson, "Le paradoxe de Saison Française," *Comœdia* 16 July 1923, 3. *This was the last ballet in which Louis XIV appeared. He was costumed as Apollo, god of the sun. It is considered the most famous example of a *ballet de cour.*
121 Levinson, "Le paradoxe de Saison Française," *Comœdia*, 16 July 1923, 3.
122 Ibid.
123 Levinson, "Propos de ballet," *Comœdia*, 17 April 1922.
124 Levinson, *Comœdia*, 16 July 1923, 3. Levinson may have been responding to an earlier claim that Rouché was attempting to "conquer" the Russian ballet in Paris.
125 Horner, *To Lose a Battle: France, 1940*, 517.
126 Lifar, *Ma Vie*, 107.
127 Ibid.
128 Ibid.
129 André Rigaud published an article on the Foyer de la Danse entitled, "Le foyer de la danse à l'Opéra," *Comœdia*, 19 January 1924, 1.
130 Lifar, *Ma Vie*, 139.
131 Ibid. Lifar notes that "from 1940 onwards ballet 'Wednesdays' were established and it became necessary to organise 'a month of the Dance' to which foreigners flocked This 'Ballet Month' became so much of a tradition that one cannot imagine the Paris Opera being able to do without it. The art of Dance had won its place in France. Now what must be done was to spread this French message to the rest of the world."
132 Boris Schoelzer, "Les arts: la danse par Serge Lifar," *La Nouvelle Revue Française*, August 1938, 329–32.
133 These were short ballooning breeches that extended from the waist to mid-thigh. Also called slops.
134 B. Schloezer, "Les arts: la danse par Serge Lifar," 107–18.
135 Georgiana Gore and L. Louppe, "France: Effervescence and Tradition in French Dance," 41.
136 Serge Lido, *30 ans de ballets français*, 5.
137 The photographs of Serge Lido played an important role in glamorizing and publicizing the Opéra's dancers.
138 See Lebovics, *True France.*
139 Ruth Bereson, *The Operatic Stage*, 51.

140 Raymond Soubie, *Rapport au Ministre de la Culture et de la Communication sur la situation et les perspectives de l'Opéra* (1987), quoted in Bereson, *The Operatic Stage*, 53.

141 Lebovics, *True France*, 198.

CHAPTER FOUR

1 Grigoriev, *The Diaghilev Ballet*, 9; my emphasis.

2 From 1920 to 1940, ballet was largely an affair for the elite.

3 For more information on sixteenth-century dance in France, see Margaret M. McGowan, "Dance in Sixteenth- and Early Seventeenth-Century France," 94–114. Using the arts for such purposes was common during the Italian Renaissance.

4 Susan Au, *Ballet and Modern Dance*, 11.

5 Yates, *The French Academies of the Sixteenth Century*, 240.

6 Beaujoyeulx, *Le ballet comique de la reine*, 33.

7 Beyond its aesthetic innovations, however, it is clear that the primary intent of the *Ballet comique* was political. In the preface to the ballet, Beaujoyeulx declared, "So, after many disorders that you have experienced, to see so great an affluence of good humour, vitality, a disposition of goodwill and such kind understanding to bring about that which you desired – this [the ballet] will serve as a true and infallible sign of the good and solid establishment of your kingdom." As a grand spectacle designed to enhance the glory of France, the *Ballet comique* provides a good example of how court ballet served the needs of the state. Nine years after the brutal St Bartholomew's Day massacre, desperate religious struggles remained and the kingdom of France was politically and economically weak. Beaujoyeulx, aware of this, used myth and metaphor in his ballet to represent the power of the French monarch to redress ills and to restore order to the state. Beaujoyeulx, *Le ballet comique de la reine*, 28.

8 "Turnout" is the ability of the dancer to turn her or his feet and legs out from the hip joints to a 90-degree position. Turnout is one of the essential principles of classical ballet, giving the dancer freedom of movement in every direction.

9 Ballet's expressive potential served well in the years between 1620 and 1636, when "satirical ballet" became very popular: these were "court ballets" which mocked the manners, pretensions, and customs popular at the time. Later in the 1660s, court composer Jean-Baptiste Lully (1632–1687) and ballet master Pierre Beauchamps (1631–1705) joined with Molière to explore a new form of ballet – one distinct from the traditional court ballet. Influenced by the comic and improvised tendencies

of the *commedia dell'arte*, which had gained popularity in France, they created the *comédie-ballet*, which integrated dance with drama. In 1670, they incorporated satire and wit in the *comédie-ballet* entitled *Le bourgeois gentilhomme*, which ridiculed bourgeois aspirations of ascendancy. Thus we can see here how ballet's development was shaped to a certain extent by foreign influences; in this case, the Italian theatre.

10 Beaujoyeulx, *Le ballet comique de la reine*, 17.

11 The power of wealth in facilitating social mobility was a major concern of the aristocrats in Molière's time. In referring to the bourgeoisie's attempts to emulate the rules and behaviours of the court (here court dancing), the character of the ballet master in *Le bourgeois gentilhomme* makes it clear that dance is an art form that should not be denigrated by the lowly bourgeoisie. As he offers the dance lesson to his pupil, a bourgeois gentleman (an oxymoron in his eyes), he asserts the superiority of dance as an art: "Man can do nothing at all without dancing ... All the misfortunes of mankind, all the dreadful disasters of which history is full, the blunders of politicians and the negligence of great commanders, all this comes though not knowing how to dance." He later insists that "dance is a science to which one cannot do enough honor." Ironically, this *comédie-ballet* concluded with the *Ballets des nations*, performed by professional dancers rather than ranking nobility.

12 In the late 1670s, Louis XIV encouraged French court dancer Pierre Beauchamps to devise a system of dance notation which was published and popularized later by Raoul-Auger Feuillet (ca. 1650–1709) in his book *Chorégraphie* (1700) – choreography then meant dance notation not the art of making dance. This work included the five canonical ballet positions: "coupe," "pirouette," "entrechat," "sissone," and "turnout." See Raoul-Auger Feuillet, *Chorégraphie: ou l'art de décrire la danse par caractères, figures, et signes demonstratifs.*

13 Louis XIV probably stopped dancing around 1670 when he was thirty-two-years old. He had also grown rather fat.

14 Other women involved in the ballet as dancers were Mesdemoiselles Caré, Pesant, and Leclerc. See the edited work by Lynn Brooks, *Women's Work: Making Dance in Europe Before 1800*, specifically the essay by Nathalie Lecompte, "The Female Ballet Troupe of the Paris Opera from 1700–1725," trans. Régine Astier, 99–122.

15 Sarah Cohen, *Art, Dance and the Body in French Culture of the Ancien Régime*, 10.

16 Ibid., 134

17 Ibid., 134–5.

18 Nonetheless, other major ballet texts continued to be written in the early eighteenth century such as Pierre Rameau's *Le maître à danser* (*The*

Dancing Master) in 1725. Rameau used stage dancers as models of perfection of form. His work provides one of the best sources of knowledge of eighteenth-century dance and reveals the widening gulf between social and theatrical dance.

19 Jean-Jacques Rousseau, *Dictionnaire de musique*, 28.

20 Jeffrey Giles, "Dance and the French Enlightenment," 258.

21 Ibid.

22 Ibid.

23 Cited in ibid., 259.

24 Ibid. 258.

25 Aristotle, *Poetics*, 1–5.

26 Levinson, *André Levinson on Dance*, 77. Levinson attacked this statement as a "fatal text [which] assigns to the dance an aim *outside of itself* and creates confusion between saltatory motion and expressive or descriptive gesture, using the dance as a substitute for words."

27 Abbé Jean Baptiste Dubos, *Réflexions critiques sur la poésie et sur la peinture* (1719), cited in Giles, "Dance and the French Enlightenment," 246.

28 Ibid., 249.

29 Louis-Sébastien Mercier, *Du théâtre; ou, Nouvel essai sur l'art dramatique* (Amsterdam: E. Van Harrevelt, 1773), 133n, cited in Hyde, *Making Up the Rococo*, 45.

30 Ibid., 47.

31 Jean Georges Noverre, *Lettre I*, cited in André Levinson, "The Idea of Dance: From Aristotle to Mallarmé," in Copeland and Cohen, eds, *What Is Dance?* 48.

32 Noverre, *Lettres sur la danse et sur les ballets, Lettre X*, 99.

33 Ibid., *Lettre I*, 30.

34 Dance historian Dorothy Samachson writes that "among other improvements, Noverre introduced the *pas d'action*, the step of action, or pantomime, used to advance the story of the ballet. This and other innovations helped break the rigid formula of court dances and led to the development of the dramatic possibilities of the ballet." "Noverre," she writes, "helped change the ballet from a divertissement, a mere pastime, into a *ballet d'action*, a ballet of action that told a story of human emotions." See Samachson, *Let's Meet the Ballet*, 9.

35 Noverre, *Lettres sur la danse et sur les ballets, Lettre IX*, 98.

36 For more information on ballet during the French Revolution, see Chazin-Bennahum, *Dance in the Shadow of the Guillotine.* Also see James Johnson, *Listening in Paris.*

37 J. Geoffroy, "Les prétendus," *Journal des Débats*, 28 June 1807, 3. Also cited in John Chapman's "Jules Janin: Romantic Critic," in Garafola, ed., *Rethinking the Sylph*, 198.

38 Pointe shoes at this time were merely non-heeled, ribboned ballet shoes, heavily darned at the tip and providing little reinforced support.

39 While Marie Taglioni danced in the full-length ballet *La sylphide* on pointe in 1832, almost certainly other dancers before her rose onto the tips of their toes. Mme Camargo may have done so one hundred years earlier. There are references in newspaper accounts of various ballerinas with "fantastic toes" or "falling off her toes."

40 Blasis was well educated with a background in music, architecture, drawing, geometry, and anatomy. In 1820, he wrote *De l'origine et des progrès de la danse ancienne et moderne* (*An Elementary Treatise upon the Origin and Progress of the Art of Dancing*) and, in ca. 1830, *Code de Terpsichore* (*The Code of Terpsichore*), an official codification of ballet which brought him recognition in French literary circles. It is also at this time that choreographer Arthur Saint-Léon invented a system of dance notation in his book *La sténochorégraphie, ou Art d'écrire promptement la danse,* published in 1852. His system used a five-line staff for leg positions, with a single line above it for head and arm positions, over which were notated modified stick figures. This system of notation was matched to the score by being printed above the music and aligned with its musical bars. His was the first system to record movements of the upper body.

41 For example, Didelot combined the dances of soloists and the corps de ballet to create an ensemble dance. Didelot is considered to be the "father of the Russian ballet." He was invited to St Petersburg by Paul I in 1811 and settled there in 1816. Perrot also worked with the Russian Imperial Ballet, residing there from 1848 until 1859. It was at this time that ballet's developments in technique and staging were exported to Russia.

42 It is interesting to note that early twentieth-century ballet critic André Levinson referred to Romantic ballet as the peak of the classic ballet tradition. He did so because he felt that classical dance had developed significantly in this period and that it shifted focus on to the dancing itself and the beauty of "static and dynamic forms" (corporeal movement). See Levinson, *Ballet Old and New,* 87.

43 Théophile Gautier, "Opéra: Rentrées de la Cerrito," *La Presse,* 9 October 1848, translated by John V. Chapman, cited in Chapman, "Silent Drama to Silent Dream: Parisian Ballet Criticism, 1800-1850," 375.

44 Victor Dandré, *Anna Pavlova in Art and Life,* 365.

45 Gautier, *The Romantic Ballet as seen by Théophile Gautier.* Gautier's writings on dance were made accessible by Cyril Beaumont in this translated collection of 1932.

46 Ramsey Burt, "The Trouble with the Male Dancer," in Dils and Albright, eds, *Moving History/Dancing Cultures,* 46.

47 Walters, *The Nude Male*, 8.
48 Jules Janin, *Journal des Débats*, 2 March 1840, cited in J. Chapman, "Jules Janin: Romantic Critic," 204.
49 In his own attempt to formulate a philosophy of dance years later, the poet Paul Valéry asked, "What then is the dance? See Valéry, "Philosophy of the Dance," in *Aesthetics*, 206.
50 Mallarmé, *Oeuvres complètes*, 304.
51 When Mallarmé uses the word dancer, he is referring to the female dancer.
52 See Mary Lewis Shaw, *Performance in the Texts of Mallarmé*, 67.
53 Mallarmé, "Ballets," 107.
54 See Sherry B. Ortner, "Is Female to Male as Nature Is to Culture?" 67–87.
55 Here Mallarmé is referring to the ballet *Les deux pigeons*, in which the dancers represent lovebirds. See *Oeuvres*, 304.
56 Ibid., 309.
57 Mallarmé, "Ballets," 109.
58 Susan P. Kozel, "Athikte's Voice," 17.
59 Paul Valéry retained this vision of dance as metaphoric, transcendent, and feminine in the early twentieth century. In his *l'âme et la danse* (The Soul and the Dance, 1921), dance is defined narrowly as a representational art and serves only as a metaphor for the intellect.
60 Émile Vuillermoz, "Les Ballets Russes," *Musica-Noël* (1912), 157, cited in Caddy, *The Ballets Russes and Beyond*, 150.
61 Svetlov, *Le ballet contemporain*, 29.
62 However, a new relationship between theatre and avant-garde painters had already been established in France almost a decade earlier. Joan Acocella writes: "By the 1890s, Parisian avant-garde theatres such as Paul Fort's Théâtre d'Art and its longer-lived successor, Lugne-Poe's Théâtre de l'Oeuvre, both of them closely allied to literary symbolism, were commissioning sets from experimental painters, particularly the Nabis." Acocella, "The Reception of Diaghilev's Ballets Russes by Artists and Intellectuals in Paris and London, 1909–1914," 4–5.
63 Weber, *France, Fin de Siècle*, 146.
64 He forged collaborations with modern Russian artists such as Bakst, Benois, Golovine, Roerich, Larionov, Goncharova, Tchelitchev, Stravinsky, Prokofiev, Rimsky-Korsakov, Borodin, Dukelsky, Liadov, and Nabokov; and non-Russian artists such as Picasso, Matisse, Derain, Laurençin, Miró, Dalí, Dufy, Satie, Braque, Roualt, Leger, Weber, Debussy, Auric, Poulenc, Ravel, Sauguet, De Falla, and Milhaud. Ballets Russes scholars, including Nancy Van Norman Baer, Joan Acocella, and John E. Bowlt have intricately examined these collaborations.

65 After the Ballets Russes' initial associations with Russian folk culture, orientalism and exoticism, it turned its attention to Russian and French avant-gardism (ca. 1912–29).

66 Myers, *Modern French Music: From Fauré to Boulez*, 20: "It is significant that the phrase 'avant-garde' began to be used of the arts in a new sense in the 1880s. It showed that a growing area of cultural experience was inaccessible, even to educated people, because of its novelty and complexity. It is partly for this reason that developments in the arts which, in retrospect, seem symptoms of important psychological and spiritual changes, were little noticed at the time."

67 In fact, critics were often so astonished by Ballet Suédois productions that they labelled some productions as "anti-ballets."

68 Lifar, *Serge Diaghilev*, 165.

69 Fokine noted how Svetlov captured well his own theories and artistic temperament.

70 Diaghilev once wrote of Fokine that "Duncan's influence on him was the very foundation of all his creative activity" (cited in Lifar, *Serge Diaghilev*, 140), although Fokine insisted that his concept of the "new ballet" was developed well before that of Duncan.

71 Music historian Rollo Myers argues that composers regarded ballet, with its ability to convey emotion through suggestion, to be more appealing than opera. Myers suggests that this is one reason why modern composers were writing more ballets than operas in early twentieth-century France. Myers, *Modern French Music*, 9.

72 Massine, *My Life in Ballet*, 86.

73 Massine's ballets emphasized the deep connection between ballet and music. By highlighting the dancer's bodily movements and their correspondence to qualities in music, he drew attention to corporeal expression rather than dramatic expression. The work can be seen as one of the first "abstract" ballets performed in France. George Balanchine, another dancer of the Ballets Russes, also began to create plotless ballets in which the primary motivation was movement to music.

74 Quoted in Massine, *My Life in Ballet*, 194–5.

75 Quoted in ibid.

76 *Vogue*, 2 January 1926.

77 For that matter, it also drew increasing attention to the art of ballet.

78 The manifesto included two articles entitled "The Search for Beauty" and "Principles of Art Criticism."

79 Fokine, "The New Ballet," Serge Diaghilev Correspondence, Dance Collection, New York Public Library (NYPL), 107.

80 Fokine was once outraged by the lack of attention given to his choreography in a review in *Comœdia Illustré* from 1 June 1910. In her mem-

oirs, Bronislava Nijinska noted that when the next edition of *Comœdia* came out on 15 June, "in a special supplement devoted to the Saison Russe considerable attention was given to the creation of the new ballet Schéhérazade, but the emphasis was on the artist Bakst and not on the choreographer Fokine." Nijinska, *Early Memoirs*, 295.

81 Lifar, *Serge Diaghilev*, 158.

82 Guillaume Apollinaire, program notes to *Parade*, 18 May 1917, 69. Also cited in Judi Freedman, "Fernand Leger and the Ballets Russes," in Garafola and Baer, eds, *The Ballets Russes and Its World*, 145.

83 Pierre Lalo, "La musique," *Le Temps*, 3 June 1913, 3.

84 Henry Ghéon, *La Nouvelle Revue Française*, August 1913, 306.

85 Ghéon, *La Nouvelle Revue Française*, August 1910, 208.

86 Robert Brussel, "Les Théâtres: La Saison russe à l'Opéra," *Le Figaro*, 6 June 1910, 6. Writing for *Vogue* magazine in 1951, Jacqueline Lee Bouvier described Diaghilev as an "alchemist unique in art history" whose specialty was achieving "an interaction of the arts [and] an interaction of cultures East and West … taking the best of the arts and molding it into a unified yet transient ballet masterpiece." See J. Bouvier, "People I Wish I Had Known," Prix de Paris submission, *Vogue*, Summer 1951.

87 Brussel, "La saison russe à l'Opéra," *Le Figaro*, 27 June 1910, 6.

88 Ghéon, *La Nouvelle Revue Française*, August, 1913, 306–7.

89 Jacques Rivière, *La Nouvelle Revue Française*, August 1913, 311.

90 Boris Schloezer, *La Nouvelle Revue Française*, October 1929, 574.

91 V. Debay, "Les Ballets Russes," *Le Courrier Musical*, 1 July 1910, 502.

92 J. Vaudoyer, "Variations sur les Ballets Russes," *La Revue de Paris*, Paris 1910. Vaudoyer wrote the plot for *Le spectre de la rose* after Theophile Gautier's poem for the Ballets Russes in 1911.

93 Cited in Lifar, *Serge Diaghilev*, 163.

94 L. Laloy, "La musique: Les Ballets Russes – Igor Stravinski," *La Grande Revue* 73 (25 June 1912): 845.

95 P. Lalo, "La musique. La saison Russe," *Le Temps*, 28 May 1912, 3.

96 Furthermore, how does this idea relate to gesture in silent film and its status in France?

97 Interestingly, Cocteau does not seem to ever address Diaghilev's position as an entrepreneur.

98 Jean Cocteau, preface to Serge Lido, *Ballet: 3*, 1.

99 Ibid.

100 Robert Brussel, *Le Figaro*, 27 June 1910, 6.

101 Cocteau, *Le coq et l'arlequin*, cited in Myers, *Modern French Music*, 125.

102 Levinson, *Ballet Old and New*, 64.

103 Ibid., 41.

104 Ibid., 44.

105 Ibid., 72.
106 Ibid., 42.
107 Ibid., 35–6. Here Levinson opens with a citation from Ernest Schur's *Der moderne Tanz* (Munich: Brustmann and Martin, 1910).
108 Ibid.
109 Théophile Gautier, preface to *Mademoiselle de Maupin* (1835), 39.
110 Émile Zola, "Un nouvelle manière en peinture: M. Édouard Manet," *Revue du XIXe. Siècle*, 1 January 1866.
111 Merrill, *A Pot of Paint*, 82.
112 Despite all the attention the trial attracted, when it reached the courts in 1878, the official record of the proceedings was unaccountably discarded.
113 Diaghilev had put forth his own art-for-art's-sake argument in "The Eternal Conflict" in his manifesto *Complicated Questions* (1898) in which he advocated freedom in art. He wrote, "The great strength of art lies precisely in the fact that it is an end in itself, that is serves only itself, and above all that it is free." Diaghilev, "The Eternal Conflict," in Garafola and Baer, eds, *The Ballets Russes and Its World*, 72. Yet in another article he wrote contrarily that "beauty in art is temperament expressed in images and therefore it is of no concern to us where those images are taken from, as a work of art is not important in itself, except as an expression of the personality of its creator … For us what is essential is the expression of the human spirit." It is interesting to note that Diaghilev described the *Ruskin v. Whistler* trial and noted that it was a battle over principles, a battle in which he would later find himself with Levinson. Diaghilev, "Principles of Art Criticism," *Complicated Questions*, 85.
114 Merrill, *A Pot of Paint*, 6.
115 Richard Ellmann and Charles Feidelson Jr, eds, *The Modern Tradition*, 883–4. The *Symbolist Manifeste* was published in 1886 by Jean Moréas.
116 It is important to note that, at the turn of the century, anti-art-for-art's-sake campaigns emerged across Europe due to fears of national and moral degeneration; symbolists and aesthetes were, at times, viciously attacked.
117 Igor Stravinksy, "Quelques confidences sur la musique" (1935), reprinted in Eric White, *Stravinsky: The Composer and His Works*, 539.
118 André Coeuroy, "The Esthetics of Contemporary Music," trans. Theodore Baker, *Musical Quarterly* 15 (1929), 246. Also cited in Verzosa, *The Absolute Limits*.
119 Levinson, *Ballet Old and New*, 15.
120 Boris Schloezer, *La Nouvelle Revue Francaise*, October 1929, 574.
121 Jacques Rivière, *La Nouvelle Revue Française*, 1 March 1920, 462.
122 Boris Schloezer, *La Nouvelle Revue Française*, October 1929, 575.

123 Lifar, *Ma Vie*, 90.
124 Ibid.
125 Cited in Levinson, "The Idea of Dance," in Acocella and Garafola, eds, *Andre Levinson on Dance: Writings from Paris in the Twenties*, 82.
126 Paul Valéry, "La philosophie de la danse" (1936), 3. http ://www.uqac.uquebec.ca/zone30/Classiques_des_ sciences_sociales/index.html.
127 Jean Cocteau, preface to Serge Lido, *Ballet*, 13.
128 Diaghilev once wrote the "the only possible nationalism is the unconscious nationalism of the blood." Diaghilev, "The Eternal Conflict," in Garafola and Baer, eds, *The Ballets Russes and Its World*, 73.
129 In this period, dance troupes from such places as Cambodia, Bali, and Japan performed in Paris. Dance schools were being founded by Russian ballerinas, Argentine tango dancers, and English ballroom teams.
130 Henry Prunières, *La Revue Musicale* 126 (May 1932): 396. He writes, "à dissiper l'obscurité dont s'enveloppe ce noble art." Prunières prided himself on having an apolitical stance.

CHAPTER FIVE

1 Both Fokine and Levinson came from prosperous, middle-class families.
2 Serge Lifar makes an important point in asking, "To what extent did Fokine's ballets owe their artistic mastery to Fokine himself, or to those who guided him – Diaghilev and the young choreauthor's young friends?" Lifar, *Ballet Traditional and Modern*, 155.
3 Valerian Svetlov, "Balet," *Peterburgskaia gazeta*, 27 February 1909, 4. Cited in Elizabeth Souritz, "Isadora Duncan and Prewar Russian Dancemakers," 114. On June 1909, one year after *Egyptian Nights* was performed in St Petersburg, the Ballets Russes presented *Cléopâtre*, which was based on the earlier work. Principle dancers included Vaslav Nijinsky and Anna Pavlova.
4 Au, *Ballet and Modern Dance*, 72.
5 Michel Fokine, "The New Russian Ballet," *Times* [London], 6 July 1914, 6, Fokine Papers, Dance Collection, NYPL. The entire letter is reprinted in Beaumont, *Michel Fokine and His Ballets*, 144–7.
6 Lincoln Kirstein, *Fokine*, 64.
7 Fokine, "The New Russian Ballet," 6.
8 Ibid.
9 Many misconceptions surfaced in the press. His letter to the *Times* of London was a response to such misconceptions.
10 Fokine Papers, Dance Collection, NYPL. Fokine wrote an article about his reservations about central European modern dance. Fokine's essays

and papers in this collection mention Mary Wigman and Isadora Duncan, the evolving modern dance, and his commentary upon it as well as statements on his ideals in the new ballet.

11 Fokine, "The New Russian Ballet," 6.

12 Ibid.

13 Ibid.

14 Robert Brussel, "À l'Opéra: Saison de Ballets russes, l'Oiseau de feu," *Le Figaro*, 22 June 1910, 24 June 1910.

15 Brussel, "À l'Opéra: Saison de Ballets russes, l'Oiseau de feu," *Le Figaro*, 27 June 1910.

16 Pierre Lalo, "La Musique," *Le Temps*, 11 June 1912, 3.

17 Cited in Lifar, *Serge Diaghilev*, 195.

18 During this time, opera and virtuoso performance flourished in Paris. One could hear and see the likes of the Italian opera composers Rossini, Donizetti, and Verdi. In addition, program music, often associated with poetic, descriptive, or narrative subject matter, gained popularity. Program music sought to capture the composer's interest in literature and in instrumental music's expressive power.

19 Susan Bernstein, *Virtuosity of the Nineteenth Century*, 10. See also Alan Walker, *Franz Liszt*.

20 Camille Saint-Saëns, *Germanophile*. It is interesting to note that Saint-Saëns permitted the Russian choreographer Michel Fokine to use his *Le cygne* for Anna Pavlova's signature solo dance *The Dying Swan* (1905). His collaboration reflects the escalating status of ballet as distinguished nationalist composers were increasingly willing to collaborate with the ballet.

21 Jane Fulcher, ed., *Debussy and His World*, 10.

22 Debussy was greatly influenced by the modernist trends in literature and painting. His works also reflected the new thematic parallels between music and painting.

23 Fulcher, *Debussy and His World*, 12. See also Dietschy, *A Portrait of Claude Debussy*, and Lockspeiser, *Debussy: His Life and Mind*. In this respect, he was often viewed as an "impressionist' – a musical equivalent of Monet. Although he shied away from being associated with the impressionists, Debussy did place great importance on capturing fleeting impressions and moods in his compositions. Debussy's collaborations with the Ballets Russes accentuated ballet's poetic qualities, as so often addressed by the symbolist poets.

24 Fauré and Ravel publicly voiced their admiration for his works, including his ballet scores such as *La prêtresse de Korydwen*, his stage music such as *Tristan et Iseut* (1918), and his opera, *Myrdin* (1921). Scholar Paul-André Bempéchat points out that Breton artists "attempted to create

their own distinct cultural patrimony through the revivals of ancient, modal Church canticles, folk melodies, and traditionally Celtic instruments." See Bempéchat, "Toward a Breton Musical Patrimony," 2.

25 As chief music critic for *Comœdia, Le Courier Musical, Paris-Soir,* and *La Lanterne* for many years, Vuillemin was one of the first to discover Maurice Ravel (1875–1937). He also often wrote reviews of ballet.

26 Bempéchat, "Toward a Breton Musical Patrimony," 2. As Bempéchat notes, violently repressive measures were taken after the First World War to outlaw the speaking of the Breton language and the holding of Mass in Breton.

27 As music historian Rollo Myers points out, French music had been predominately aristocratic and there existed a "distrust of folk-music as a source for the 'serious' composer." Myers, *Modern French Music,* 7.

28 Debussy's compositions were first used by the Ballets Russes in 1912 for the production of *L'après-midi d'un faune,* which was based on a poem by Stéphane Mallarmé. His music was also later used for the ballet *Jeux.*

29 Cited in Myers, *Modern French Music,* 7.

30 Ibid.

31 Ibid., 9.

32 Ibid.

33 Yet another group of modern musicians to assert French nationalism were Les Six – six young composers who strongly reacted against the heavy German Romanticism of Richard Wagner and Richard Strauss, as well as the lush impressionism of Claude Debussy. Les Six consisted of Darius Milhaud, Francis Poulenc, Arthur Honegger, George Auric, Louis Durey, and Germaine Tailleferre (the group's only woman). The official manifesto of Les Six, a group with very disparate personalities, was enunciated by Jean Cocteau, who had ignored German music (with the exception of Bach) but who also rejected the music of Debussy and the Russians. He contended that the new generation of French composers should derive their inspiration from the witty and worldly art of music hall and circus, that is from popular culture. The group desired to align their work with painting and literature, and often associated themselves with the French writers Aragon, Claudel, Gide, Apollinaire, and Cocteau. The only actual collaboration between the members of Les Six was limited to a single ballet, conceived by Jean Cocteau for the Ballet Suédois, *Les mariés de la Tour Eiffel* (The Wedding on the Eiffel Tower) (1921). Cocteau once claimed that the music of Les Six was "une musique française de France." He expressed his nationalist stance when he stated that the avant-garde composers would "guide France towards greater and stronger self-expression and subjecthood, no longer bound to discourses imposed from outside." See Cocteau,

Le coq et l'arlequin, 58. Yet, individually, Les Six often collaborated with the Ballets Russes and achieved much success. The French critic Henri Collet originated the label Les Six in his article "The Russian Five, the French Six, and M. Erik Satie" (*Comœdia,* 16 January 1920).

34 *La Baïonnette,* 18 April, 1918, cited in Silver, *Esprit de Corps,* 20–1.

35 Myers, *Modern French Music,* 70.

36 The term "neoclassicism" was first coined by Russian émigré Boris de Schloezer in a review of a concert given in 1923. Schloezer was a well-respected music critic who often reviewed the ballet.

37 See Scott Messing, *Neoclassicism in Music,* 129–32.

38 Several members of the Parisian avant-garde embraced neoclassicism, such Jean Cocteau, Pablo Picasso, Fernand Léger, Paul Valéry, André Gïde, and Igor Stravinsky, who strove for more simplicity and formalism in their work. See Marion Schmid, "À bas Wagner!" 89.

39 Levinson, "The Idea of Dance," 81.

40 Pridden, *The Art of Dance in French Literature,* 65.

41 "L'âme et la danse," 221.

42 Valéry, *Aesthetics/Paul Valéry* 196.

43 Ibid., 12.

44 Ibid., 197.

45 Levinson, *La danse d'aujourd'hui,* 9.

46 All contributed ballet libretti to Ballets Russes' productions in the 1920s and early 1930s.

47 Aschengreen, *Jean Cocteau and the Dance,* 12.

48 Ibid.

49 Roger Lannes, "Poésie de la danse," *La Revue Musicale,* March 1938, 191–7.

50 Cited in Lifar, *Serge Diaghilev,* 161.

51 Rivière, "Des Ballets Russes et de Fokine," *La Nouvelle Revue Française,* July 1912, 174.

52 Rivière, "Petrouchka, ballet d'Igor Stravinski, Alexandre Fokine et Alexandre Benois," *La Nouvelle Revue Française,* September 1911, 377.

53 Levinson, "The Spirit of the Classic Dance," 43.

54 H. Malherbe, *Le Temps,* 10 January 1834, and *Candide,* 6 December 1934, translated in Acocella and Garafola, eds, *Levinson on Dance,* 19.

55 Levinson, "The Spirit of the Classic Dance," 42.

56 As Lynn Garafola, in *André Levinson on Dance,* and others have also noted.

57 Levinson praised English balletomane Cyril Beaumont for his "ballet manual" and even suggested a French translation. *Comœdia,* 3 March 1924, 5.

58 Levinson, "The Spirit of the Classic Dance," 43.

59 Levinson defined "classic dance" as "a term designating the style of dancing that is based on the traditional ballet technique – which has prevailed in the Western world." Levinson, "The Spirit of the Classic Dance," 44.
60 Ibid.
61 Ibid.
62 Ibid., 46.
63 Ibid., 47.
64 Ibid., 48.
65 Levinson, "Some Commonplaces on the Dance," 32. The essay was originally published in English in the American expatriate journal *Broom* in 1922. It was based on his first book on dance, *Ballet Old and New.*
66 Levinson, "The Spirit of Classic Dance," 46–7.
67 Levinson, "The Idea of Dance," *Theatre Arts Monthly*, August 1927. Also translated in *André Levinson on Dance*, 76–7.
68 Levinson, "Some Commonplaces on the Dance," 30.
69 Greenberg, "Modernist Painting," 6.
70 Fokine, *Memoirs of a Ballet Master*, 35.
71 Ibid.
72 Ibid., 38.
73 Fokine, *Michel Fokine Papers, 1914–1941*, Jerome Robbins Dance Division, NYPL.
74 Levinson may also be differentiating social dance from artistic dance in that social dance is the embodiment of an idea through its gestural means of communications, while artistic dance such as the ballet relates to the movements of the dancers themselves and their choreographic expression. See Levinson, *André Levinson on Dance*, 23, where Levinson discusses Spanish dance and Asian dance.
75 As often recalled by his students; see D. Horwitz, *Michel Fokine*, 156.
76 Lifar, *Ballet Traditional to Modern*, 153.
77 Lifar, *Ma Vie*, 132–3; italics in original.
78 Levinson, *Ballet Old and New*, 75.
79 Rebay, "The Beauty of Non-Objectivity," 145.
80 Levinson, "A Crisis in the Ballets Russes," in *André Levinson on Dance*, 64.
81 Levinson, *Ballet Old and New*, 47.
82 Levinson, "Stravinsky and the Dance," in *André Levinson on Dance*, 38.
83 Levinson, "Some Commonplaces on the Dance," in *André Levinson on Dance*, 34.
84 Levinson, *Ballet Old and New*, 75.
85 Levinson, "The Spirit of Classical Dance," in *André Levinson on Dance*, 44.
86 Louis Laloy, "La danse à l'Opéra," *Comœdia*, 23 January 1924, 1.

87 Levinson's insistence on the centrality of choreography in criticism had a profound effect on critics abroad as well as in France. For example, the embrace of his new standard of assessing ballet resonates in the writings of British dance critic A.V. Coton later in 1938. Coton was the leading dance critic in England from the late 1930s through the 1970s. He once wrote, "I still believe that an important art should be discussed and analyzed and evaluated with scrupulous care – that is why I have continued to assess any new work on, first, its choreography, and only after that, on its degree of success as regards music, decor, idea and dancing. Without good choreography there can be no good standard of dancing ... One judges the whole ballet by calculating exactly how the choreography expresses its creator's intentions *apropos* that ballet, and through this analysis of the choreography one sees all the contributory parts (idea, music, decor, costume, staging, dancing) in correct perspective." Throughout most of his writings, Coton underlined the importance of dance as a major art form and acknowledged repeatedly that ballet dancing was one of the most demanding forms of self-expression. Coton, "The Critic's Function," in *Writings on Dance,* 8–9.

88 In his position as ballet master and director of the Paris Opéra ballet, Lifar crossed paths with powerful and influential people in the government, in the diplomatic corps, in the arts, in the aristocracy, and in society. Biographers Gillian Freeman and Edward Thorpe note that Lifar was "friendly" with the Duke and Duchess of Windsor, met Mussolini and Prince Umberto, and was presented with an inscribed gold cigarette by King George VI and Queen Elizabeth after he danced before them. See Freeman and Thorpe, *Ballet Genius,* 70.

89 Lifar, *Lifar on Classical Ballet,* 31.

90 Lifar's letter to Bonnard, June 1942, AN.F17.13368, Cabinet du Ministre de l'Instruction publique (État français), Papiers provenant du cabinet d'Abel Bonnard, 1942–1944. Bibliothèques; beaux-arts; spectacles et musique; bâtiments civils et palais nationaux; architecture, 1942–1944.

91 Lifar, *La danse: Les grands courants de la danse académique,* 49.

92 Ibid.

93 Lifar, *Ma Vie,* 112–14.

94 Ibid., 114.

95 Ibid., 117.

96 A. Haskell, "Portrait of Serge Lifar," in *Lifar on Classical Ballet,* 23.

97 Lifar, *Ma Vie,* 126.

98 Lifar, *La danse: La danse académique et l'art chorégraphique,* 22. Also cited in his article, "La danse et la musique" published in *La Revue Musicale,* March 1938, 182. Lifar's article "La danse et la musique" originated

in his lectures at a conference at the Sorbonne run by the Congrès d'Esthetique et de Science et l'Art in 11 August 1937.

99 Particularly, biographers such as Arnold Haskell, Florence Poudru, and Jean-Pierre Pastori.

100 Lifar, *Ma Vie,* 92.

101 Ibid., 116.

102 Ibid., 127.

103 Lifar, *La danse: La danse académique et l'art chorégraphique,* 115.

104 See Serge Lifar, *Le manifeste du chorégraphie.*

105 Lifar, *Ma Vie,* 132.

106 Lifar, *Lifar on Classical Ballet,* 142.

107 André Boll, "Pour ou contre une chorégraphie autonome," *La Revue Musicale,* March 1938, 187.

108 Lifar, *Ma Vie,* 132.

109 Ibid., 132–3.

110 Lifar, "La danse et la musique," *La Revue Musicale,* March 1938, 174.

111 Boll, "Pour ou contre une choregraphie autonome," 189. J.E. Szyfer was the conductor of the ballet, not the composer. Arthur Honegger was the actual composer but preferred to remain anonymous. See Harold Halbreich, *Arthur Honegger.*

112 Lifar, *Ma Vie,* 136–7.

113 Ibid., 138.

114 Ibid., 139.

115 Ibid., 107–8.

116 Lifar, *La danse: La danse académique et l'art chorégraphique,* 145.

117 Lifar, *Lifar on Classical Ballet,* 30.

118 Lifar, *Ma Vie,* 125.

119 Lifar, "La danse et la musique," 176.

120 Lifar, *La danse: La danse académique et l'art chorégraphique,* 142.

121 Lifar, *Lifar on Classical Ballet,* 204.

122 Lifar, "Appendices," *Lifar on Classical Ballet.*

123 Delibes achieved great fame for his ballet *Coppélia.*

124 Henriette Blond, "La danse: Les inconnue dans la saison," *La Chronique de Paris,* November 1943, 82–4, cited in Leslie A. Sprout, *Musical Legacy of Wartime France,* 9–10.

125 Arthur Hoérée, "À l'Opéra: spectacle de danse," *Comœdia,* 19 July 1941, 6.

CHAPTER SIX

1 Cited in Rose Eichenbaum, *The Dancer Within,* 24.

2 It even offered an education through the exposure of art, music, poetry, etc. Diaghilev insisted that his dancers visit the museums of the

countries in which they toured. Many former dancers noted that the Ballets Russes offered them such an education.

3 Émile Vuillermoz, *Les Ballets Russes*, cited in Jean-Pierre Pastori, *L'homme et la danse*, 82.

4 Both women and men (heterosexual and homosexual) were attracted to Nijinsky's talents and beauty on stage.

5 There remains little historical research on the relationship between the status of modern ballet and the changing notions regarding gender politics, sexuality, and the body in early twentieth-century French culture and society. Discourse that addresses the relationship between modernism and gender, although insightful in comparative analysis, has neglected to draw attention to the profession of ballet or to ideas about dance as a profession. For example, Mary Louise Roberts's *Civilization without Sexes* (1994) is very helpful in understanding postwar anxieties about changing gender boundaries and definitions. However, she does not discuss how the professional woman, specifically the theatre woman, fits within the new order of social relationships that developed after the First World War. Roberts does not address the position of performing women within natalist postwar propaganda or the complexity of their professionalism. Moreover, there is no analysis of how such anxieties manifested themselves in ballet and its discourse. Other studies, such as those of Robert Nye and Christopher Forth, are also useful in their attempts to examine changing ideals of masculinity in the early twentieth century. Yet such studies do not address the increasing legitimization of the vocation of the male dancer, the discourse stimulated by him, or his relationship to the aggrandizing of a national artistic institution: the Paris Opéra.

6 "Lettres patentes du roi pour l'établissement de l'Académie royale de danse en la ville de Paris" in *Danseurs et Ballet de l'Opéra de Paris depuis 1671: exposition*, 27.

7 Chandra Mukerji, *Territorial Ambitions and the Gardens of Versailles*, 245.

8 Ibid.

9 Ibid. Mukerji notes that as the professional soldier gained power the eighteenth century, the "physicalized aristocratic body" lost its strength "by the emphasis on physical passivity" (ibid.).

10 It is important to note that there did not exist a connection between ballet and homosexuality in the popular imagination in this period. In fact, contemporaries testify that Louis XIV was extremely homophobic. Yet he had a homosexual father (Louis XIII), a homosexual uncle (César de Vendôme), a homosexual brother (Philippe d'Orléans), and a son (the Comte de Vermandois) whom he punished for his affairs with other young men.

11 Jennifer Neville, "Introduction and Overview," in *Dance, Spectacle, and the Body Politick, 1250–1750*, 21.
12 Georgia J. Cowart, *The Triumph of Pleasure*, xvi.
13 Sarah R. Cohen, *Art, Dance, and the Body in French Culture of the Ancien Régime*, 10.
14 Ibid., 15. Beauchamps was ballet master at the Royal Academy of Music from 1669 to 1689.
15 Ibid., 134.
16 Ibid., 17.
17 Jean-Jacques Rousseau, *Dictionaire de musique* (1768), 28.
18 Jean-Georges Noverre, *Lettres sur la danse et sur les ballets* (1760), 50.
19 "Ballet d'action" was a term that described ballets that told a story. Other terms used (sometimes interchangeably) were "heroic ballet," "tragic ballet," and "pantomime ballet."
20 A leading proponent of this style was Jacques-Louis David, who developed a distinctly French neoclassical aesthetic. Formally, French neoclassicism offered a new understanding of the use of space in painting and sculpture. In painting, for example, poignant sculptural lines, a subdued palette, spatial delineation through linear recessession and divergent planes were all aspects of this new aesthetic style.
21 Eventually, neoclassicism ushered in new imagery of ideal manhood that linked itself to republicanism.
22 Thomas Crow, *Emulation*, 2.
23 Horace Walpole, "Letter to the Countess of Ossory," 17 December 1780, in *Letters of Horace Walpole: Earl of Orford*, 7:477. Horace Walpole was the son of the first prime minister Sir Robert Walpole.
24 *Public Advertiser*, 7 December 1783.
25 Noverre, *Lettres sur la danse*, 2:125, and Julien-Louis Geoffroy, *Journal des Débats*, 20 May 1804, both cited in John V. Chapman, "Auguste Vestris and the Expansion of Technique," 12.
26 *The Examiner*, 16 August 1809, cited in Chapman, "August Vestris and the Expansion of Technique," 12.
27 Margaret Walters, *The Nude Male*, 213.
28 Walters, *The Nude Male*, 233, 237. Walters writes that "From a whole series of 'realists' from Courbet to Degas, the naked woman, rather than the naked man, emerges as central theme." She goes on to write that "by the fifties, female models were more or less a fixture in private studios and jokes about sexual relations between models and artists had become commonplace."
29 Judith Surkis, "Carnival Balls and Penal Codes," 60.
30 Ibid.
31 Ibid., 78.

32 As film theorist Steve Neale proposes, "Masculinity, as an ideal, at least, is implicitly known. Femininity is, by contrast, a mystery." Neale, "Masculinity as Spectacle: Reflections on Men and Mainstream Cinema," 19.
33 Lynn Garafola, "Reconfiguring the Sexes," in Garafola and Baer, eds, *The Ballets Russes and Its World*, 248.
34 Théophile Gautier, *Gautier on Dance*, 53. See also Michael Gard, *Men Who Dance*, 50.
35 Ramsey Burt, *The Male Dancer*, 25.
36 *Journal des Débats*, 2 March 1844, 41, translated by Ivor Guest in *The Romantic Ballet in Paris*, 21.
37 Alexandre Benois, *Reminiscences*, 145.
38 Pierre Lalo, "La musique," *Le Temps*, 20 June 1909, 3.
39 André Rigaud, *Comœdia*, 28 July 1922, 1. "Les danses du prince Igor furent une sorte de revelation."
40 Anna Elisabeth de Noailles, "Adieux aux Ballets Russes" [Farewell to the Ballets Russes], *La Revue Musicale*, 1 December, 1930, 3–7.
41 Romola de Pulszky Nijinsky, *Nijinsky*, 46.
42 Lynn Garafola, *Legacies of Twentieth-Century Dance*, 179.
43 Garafola, "Reconfiguring the Sexes," 246.
44 "La Danse et la Mimique" par Ricciotto Canudo, *Comoedia*, 24 July 1911.
45 Serge Grigoriev, *The Diaghilev Ballet*, 79.
46 Ibid.
47 Gaston Calmette, "Un faux pas," *Le Figaro*, 30 May 1912, 1.
48 Richard Buckle provides details of this exchange in *Nijinsky*, 243–45.
49 Cyril Beaumont, *The Diaghilev Ballet in London*, 54.
50 Pierre Lalo, *Le Temps*, 11 June 1912, 3.
51 Gaston de Pawlowski, "Troisième série des Ballets Russes," *Comœdia*, 30 May 1912, 1.
52 Louis Vuillemin, "Troisième série des Ballets Russes," *Comœdia*, 30 May 1912, 2.
53 Louis Schneider, "Les Ballets Russes," *Comœdia*, 30 May 1912, 8. Debussy, in a letter to Nijinsky, proclaimed him a "genius" of choreography, thanking him for adding "a new dimension of beauty" to his music. Letter reprinted in *Daily Mail*, 21 February 1913, cited in Buckle, *Diaghlev*, 244.
54 A. Rodin, "La rénovation de la danse," *Le Matin*, 30 May 1912, 1.
55 Valentine Gross, *Comœdia Illustré*, June 1909, 2.
56 Henri Ghéon, "Propos divers sur le Ballet Russe," *La Nouvelle Revue Française*, 1910, 202.
57 While some dance scholars argue that Diaghilev and his company accentuated the connection between homosexuality and ballet, critics

avoided addressing this issue in their reviews in respectable journals. This may be seen as part of a broader attempt on the part of the French to exorcize homosexuality from French culture.

58 Cocteau admitted the disappointment he felt when he saw Nijinsky offstage for the first time. "I remember … having felt sadness to see him smoking in a restaurant after the show," he recalled. "Vaslav Nijinsky," *Comœdia*, 2 July 1910, 1.

59 Ibid.

60 There has been much study of Nijinsky and his sexuality, and debates remain over whether he was bisexual or homosexual. Evidence seems to indicate that he was bisexual. Nijinsky described his crushes on female dancers, particularly on Tamara Karsavina, who dismissed his advances. This is a topic that lies beyond the scope of this book.

61 J. Rivière, "La Musique," *La Nouvelle Revue Française*, July 1914, 159–60.

62 J. Rivière, *La Nouvelle Revue Française*, September 1911, 377. Fokine danced with and choreographed for the Ballets Russes between 1909 and 1912. Two years later, he collaborated with the company on four ballets, *Papillon, La légend de Joseph, Le coq d'or*, and *Midas*.

63 Robert Brussel, *Le Figaro*, 18 June 1910, 4.

64 Henri Ghéon, "Propos divers sur le Ballet Russe," *La Nouvelle Revue Française*, 1910, 190, 205.

65 Ibid., 203.

66 Ibid., 1910.

67 Christopher Breward, *The Hidden Consumer*, 24.

68 Robert A. Nye, *Masculinity and Male Codes of Honor in Modern France*, 97.

69 Jacques Bertillon, "Mariage," in *Dictionnaire encyclopédique des sciences médicales*, 2nd series, 5 (1872): 67, cited in Nye, *Masculinity and Male Codes of Honor in Modern France*, 97.

70 Cited in Christopher S. Thompson, *The Tour de France*, 29.

71 Baron P. de Coubertin, "We Want to Go Ever Forward. The 'Trustees' of the Olympic Idea," *Olympic Review*, July 1908, 23, cited in Gertrud Huidberg-Hansen, "Hellas under Northern Skies," in *The Spirit of Vitalism*, 75.

72 Also see *Les Athlètes de la République*, 41–62, 63–86.

73 George Mosse, *Image of Man*, 24–50.

74 *Le Culture Physique* served as an avenue for male bodybuilding and commercialized physical culture.

75 See Christopher Forth, *The Dreyfus Affair and the Crisis of French Manhood.*

76 Ibid., 205.

77 Forth, *The Dreyfus Affair.* See also Robert Nye, "Fencing, the Duel, and Republican Manhood in the Third Republic," 365–77.

78 Ibid.
79 Rachel Chrastil, *Organizing for War*, 118.
80 Since the French Revolution, masculinity had played a vital role in the establishment of a national "imagined community" in France. Nationalism was defined in masculine terms, and, as such, legitimized male dominance over women. "Imagined community" was coined by Benedict Anderson in *Imagined Communities.*
81 Joan Tumblety, *Remaking the Male Body*, 4.
82 Mosse, *Image of Man*, 108.
83 Tumblety, *Remaking the Male Body*, 11.
84 Thompson, *The Tour de France*, 144.
85 See Mark Meyers, "Feminizing Fascist Men: Crowd Psychology, Gender, and Sexuality in French Antifascism, 1929–1945," 109–42.
86 Henri Pollès, *L'opéra politique* (Paris 1937), 183, cited and translated in Meyers, "Feminizing Fascist Men," 109.
87 Henri Ghéon, "Propos divers sur le Ballet Russe," *La Nouvelle Revue Française*, August 1910, 190, 205.
88 André Levinson, *Ballet Old and New*, 87. Levinson came from a Russian cultural background in which male dancing was valued and less problematic. His allusion to "ephebic grace" relates to the ephebic training included in the athletic preparation for the Olympics of ancient Greece.
89 Jacques Rivière, *La Nouvelle Revue Française*, 1 March 1920, 463.
90 Ibid.
91 Julie Sazonova, "Mlle Semenova à l'Opéra," *La Nouvelle Revue Française*, February 1936, 471.
92 H. Ghéon, "Propos divers sur le Ballet Russe," *La Nouvelle Revue Française*, August 1910, 202.
93 A. Levinson, "Le danseur et le préjugé au travesti," *Comœdia*, 30 October 1922, 3.
94 Ibid.
95 André Rigaud, "La classe de danse des hommes à l'Opéra: 'Renaissance d'un Art,'" *Comœdia*, 28 July 1922, 1.
96 Ibid.
97 Ibid.
98 There are numerous dance studies that examine the develoment of choreography for men in Europe and in the United States. Michael Gard's *Men Who Dance: Aesthetics, Athletics, and the Art of Masculinity* is particularly informative.
99 Léonide Massine, *My Life in Ballet*, 191.
100 Ibid.
101 Serge Lifar, *Lifar on Classical Ballet*, 36.

102 Chauviré was to become one of the most famous French dancers of her time.
103 Lifar, *Lifar on Classical Ballet*, 103. These boundaries have eroded since then (1980s) – contemporary ballet now breaks the boundaries of gender that Lifar delineated.
104 Ibid.
105 During an interview with the director of the National School of Dance at the Paris Opéra, I was told that there was absolutely no relationship between homosexuality and ballet. She then went on to emphasize that the Paris Opéra's highest enrolment of boys occurred in the 1950s.
106 Interestingly, Jean Babilée joined the French Resistance and, being Jewish on his father's side, narrowly escaped being sent to the concentration camps in July 1942. His career and work are explored in the documentary *Le mystère de Jean Babilée* [*The Mystery of Jean Babilée*] (2001), conceived and directed by Patrick Bensard.
107 Philip and Whitney, *Danseur: The Male in Ballet*, 14.

CHAPTER SEVEN

1 *European Review* (1970), 20–3.
2 Women's activity in civic culture partly involved the denial of sexual identity.
3 Stewart, *For Health and Beauty*, 153.
4 Schiebinger, *The Mind Has No Sex?* 190–1.
5 Stewart, *For Health and Beauty*, offers a comprehensive examination of this phenomenon in France.
6 See reviews such as Paul Mantz, "Exposition des oeuvres des artistes indépendents," *Le Temps*, 23 April 1881, 3; Henry Trianon, "Sixième Exposition de peinture par un groupe d'artistes," *Le Constitutionnel*, 24 April 1881, 2; and Elie de Mont, "L'Exposition du Boulevard des Capucines," *La Civilization*, 21 April 1881, 2.
7 Berlanstein, *Daughters of Eve*, 112.
8 Ibid., 117.
9 The first female dancers to perform professionally in a theatre production appeared in a ballet called *Le triomphe de l'amour* (The Triumph of Love) (1681).
10 Parmenia Migel, *The Ballerinas*, 37.
11 *Mercure de France*. 1726, cited in Edmund Fairfax, *The Styles of Eighteenth Century Ballet*, 223.
12 Cohen, *Dance as a Theatre Art*, 40. Marie inspired significant costume reforms by disregarding the conventional skirt and corset and wearing a simple muslin robe draped like a Greek statue in her performance of *Pygmalion*, which she also choreographed. In fact, she is considered one

of the first women choreographers in France. The staging of Sallé's ballet was remarkable for a time in which women were expected to merely interpret, not create. For more information on Marie Sallé, see Sarah McCleave, "Marie Sallé, a Wise Professional Woman of Influence," in *Women's Work*, 160–82.

13 Voltaire, *Mercure de France*, January 1732, cited in Moore, *Artists of the Dance*, 27.

14 Its successor, *Giselle* (1841), also contrasted the human and supernatural worlds. In its second act the ghostly spirits, called willis, wear the white tutu popularized in *La sylphide. Giselle* was the last great event of the period of romantic ballet. Théophile Gautier wrote the scenario, with choreography of Jean Perrot and Jean Coralli.

15 Cohen, *Dance as a Theatre Art*, 67.

16 *L'Illustration*, 21 December 1844, 247, cited in Berlanstein's *Daughters of Eve*, 215.

17 Quoted in Guest, *The Ballet of the Second Empire*, 15.

18 This practice was strictly forbidden in the early years of the nineteenth century. See Martine Kahane, ed., *Le Foyer de la Danse*, 5.

19 See Robert L. Herbert, "Chapter Four: Theatre, Opera and Dance," in *Impressionism*, 107.

20 J. Geoffroy, "Les prétendus," *Journal des Débats*, 28 June 1807, 3, cited in John Chapman, "Jules Janin: Romantic Critic," in Garafola, ed., *Rethinking the Sylph*, 198.

21 Gautier, *The Romantic Ballet*, 23.

22 Théophile Gautier, *La Presse*, 13 October 1836, cited in Gautier, *Gautier on Dance*, 2.

23 Théophile Gautier, "La Font, ballet de M. Mazilier," *La Presse*, 10 January 1855, 1.

24 Cited in Chapman, "Jules Janin: Romantic Critic," 204.

25 Ibid., 202.

26 Ibid.

27 See Cyril Beaumont, *Ballet Design*.

28 Berlanstein, *Daughters of Eve*, 118–21.

29 From *La Vie Parisienne*, 19 September 1891, 528–9, cited in Berlanstein, *Daughters of Eve*, 130.

30 Although, as Selma Cohen notes in *Dance as a Theatre Art*, some artists and intellectuals such as Degas, Arthur Symons, Mallarmé, Ford Madox Ford, and Walter Sickert still enjoyed the ballet for artistic subjects or for pleasure.

31 Cited in Herbert, *Impressionism*, 93.

32 Arnold Haskell, "Portrait of Serge Lifar," *Lifar on Classical Ballet*, 18.

33 Quoted in Guest, *The Ballet of the Second Empire*, 15.

34 Valéry, *Aesthetics*, 197.
35 Ibid., 198.
36 "A poem," Valéry explains, "is *action* because a poem exists only at the moment of being spoken … this act, like the dance, has no other purpose than to create a state of mind; it imposes it own laws; it, too, creates a time and a measurement of time which are appropriate and essential to it: we cannot distinguish it from its form of time. To recite poetry is to enter into a verbal dance" (*Aesthetics*, 208).
37 Mallarmé, "Ballets," 109.
38 Susan P. Kozel, "Athikte's Voice," 17; and Mallarmé, "Ballets," 107.
39 Berlanstein, *Daughters of Eve*, 105.
40 Ibid., 235.
41 Ibid., 226.
42 Ibid., 153.
43 Ibid., 9.
44 Octave Uzanne, *The Modern Parisienne*, 147. Uzanne was a journalist and publisher who collaborated closely with the symbolists and early art nouveau artists. His book *The Modern Parisienne* was a widely circulated neo-sociological study of French women.
45 Ibid., 153.
46 Interestingly, Uzanne discouraged women from pursuing a career as professional artists (i.e., painter or sculptor) in his chapter on "Artists and Bluestockings."
47 Berlanstein, *Daughters of Eve*, 131.
48 Ibid., 181.
49 Ibid.
50 Ibid., 117.
51 Ibid., 237, 240.
52 Ibid.
53 Even though there was a new acceptance of the public woman and a new regard for the performing woman, each theatrical profession carried its own unique set of ideologies and values. Women performed in different types of venues, for different audiences, were critiqued by different journals and presses, and engaged in art forms with different historical traditions.
54 André Mangeot, "La danse à l'Opéra et le ballet 'Le lac des aulnes,'" *Le Monde Musicale*, 30 November 1907, 331.
55 Mangeot's and Zambelli's correspondence surfaced in a series of articles in *Le Monde Musicale*: 30 November, 15 December, and 30 December 1907. It was not until the 1930s (e.g., Merlyn Severn in England) and 1940s (e.g., Serge Lido in France) that photographers experimented with "dance action" stills.

56 Mangeot, "La danse à l'Opéra et le ballet 'Le lac des aulnes,'" 331.
57 Tilburg, *Collette's Republic*, 142.
58 This representation of the body on stage differs from those bodies imaged in painting in that the dancer's body is the creative expression itself, whereas the painterly image does not actively participate in the creation process.
59 Davis, *Ballets Russes Style*, 8.
60 Ibid.
61 Ibid., 9.
62 For more information on Fokine's "new ballet" aesthetic, see Garafola, "The Liberating Aesthetic of Michel Fokine," in *Diaghilev's Ballets Russes*, 3–49. Garafola notes how Fokine "exalted the meaning rather than the metaphor of movement" and advocated "'a mimetic of the whole body.'" "Man can ... and should see expression from head to foot," Fokine once wrote (24).
63 R. Brussel, *Le Figaro*, 13 June 1910.
64 Ibid.
65 Isadora Duncan's new modern dance significantly influenced modern attitudes towards the art of bodily movement. Dance, for Duncan, represented the discovery and liberation of the human body. She also related modern dance to ancient dance, which was known as "free dance" or "danse libre." See Isadora Duncan, *My Life* (1927).
66 This term first appeared in Victor Margueritte's bestselling novel *La Garçonne* (1922) in which the protagonist, Monique, embodies the modern woman.
67 Garafola, *Diaghilev's Ballets Russes*, 15.
68 Sokolova, *Dancing for Diaghilev*, 203.
69 Levinson, "The Spirit of the Classic Dance," in Acocela and Garafola, eds, *André Levinson on Dance*, 48.
70 A. Levinson, *Comœdia*, 27 November 1922, 5.
71 Levinson, *Comœdia*, 27 November 1922.
72 Antoine Banes, "Théâtre National de l'Opéra," *Le Figaro*, 17 May 1920.
73 L. Laloy, *Comœdia*, 11 January 1924, 3.
74 Quoted in Garafola, "Reconfiguring the Sexes," in *The Legacies of Twentieth-Century Dance*, 200.
75 Levinson, *Comœdia*, 2 July 1922, 1.
76 Levinson, Comœdia, 29 January 1923, 5.
77 I am not arguing that the classical ballet body is itself transgressive. This classical ideal in many ways has reinforced a denial of the female body in favour of an alternate ideal. Here, I am concerned with the profession of ballet, its substance as an art of bodily movement, and, as such, its association or disassociation with ideologies surrounding the body as "Woman" and as a "marginal" zone.

78 Levinson, *Ballet Old and New*, 87.
79 Levinson, "L'école du critique," *Comœdia*, 27 Novembre 1922, 5.
80 Ibid.
81 See Levinson's review in *Comœdia*, 23 November 1923.
82 Levinson, "La Danse," *Comœdia*, 8 January 1923, 5.
83 Levinson, *Comœdia*, 24 December 1923, 4.
84 Ibid.
85 Levinson, *Comœdia*, 8 January 1923, 5.
86 Many married women continued to work during the economic depression of the 1930s.
87 See Roberts, *Civilization without Sexes*.
88 As Roberts points out, such changes inevitably created new notions of the feminine.
89 Julie Sazonova's article in *La Nouvelle Revue Française* entitled "La saison chorégraphique: Ballet Joos, Ballets 1933, Ballets de Monte-Carlo" is a good example of how some women were being acknowledged as experts on choreography and the art of dance (July 1933, 154–7).
90 Lenglen became a professional tennis player in 1926.
91 Stewart, *For Health and Beauty*, 169.
92 Ibid., 1.
93 Ibid.
94 See Modern Girl around the World Research Group, *Modern Girl around the World: Consumption, Modernity, and Globalization*.
95 Carol Osborne and F. Skillen, "Women and Sport in Interwar Britain," in Hargreaves and Anderson, eds, *Routledge Handbook of Sport, Gender, and Sexuality*, 55.
96 Bull, *Noel Streatfeild*, 52.
97 Streatfeild's book may be placed in the tradition of Frances Hodgson Burnett's *The Little Princess* (1905). The story is set in the 1920s and 1930s and its plot is about three orphans, one of whom becomes a brilliant dancer.
98 It is interesting to look at film in the context of gender. Films about dancers surfaced in great numbers in the 1930s, 1940s, and 1950s. The most common plot involved a female dancer having to choose between her profession or her lover. If she chose her profession, she inevitably went mad or died in the end (*Limelight, Red Shoes*). The film *Rainbow Dance* concerned a heterosexual dancer who ultimately goes insane from enforced homosexuality.
99 For an interesting discussion of how ballet narratives create such fantasies see Angela McRobbie, "Fame, Flashdance, and Fantasies of Achievement" in Gaines and Herzog, eds, *Fabrications: Costume and the Female Body*, 45.
100 Inspired by Hans Christian Anderson's fairy tale and Diaghilev's Ballets Russes, *The Red Shoes* was a British feature film about a young woman

of aristocratic descent who wants to become a professional ballerina. It was distributed in Britain, the US, France, and later globally when Universal Studios took over its distribution. It became the highest-grossing British film of its time.

101 Even later films, such as the successful *The Turning Point* (1977), starring Anne Bancroft and Shirley MacLaine, and professional dancers Leslie Brown and Mikhail Baryshnikov, embraced the idea that a dancer had to sacrifice her career to have a family (MacLaine's character Deedee).

102 Lifar, *Ma Vie*, 109.

103 Ibid.

104 Ibid., 160.

CONCLUSION

1 Jean Guéhenno, *Diary of the Dark Years*, 58.

2 Judith Surkis, "Carnival Balls and Penal Codes," 59–83.

3 Louis Laloy, "La danse à l'Opéra," 4.

4 Interview with Patrice Bart, Conservatoire de Ballet de l'Opéra, Palais Garnier, June 2003.

5 Also in April 2003, curators Jill DeVonyar and Richard Kimball gathered one of the largest collections of Degas's ballet-inspired art. The joint production of the American Federation of Arts, the Detroit Institute of Art, and the Philadelphia Museum of Art offered more than the traditional focus on the formal and thematic innovations in Degas's work. It turned instead to the subjects themselves: the dancers. *Degas and the Dance* not only emphasized Degas's place in the larger history of art, but it also made a case for looking at Degas's ballerinas as dancers. Organized into themes such as the classroom, the stage, the wings, portraits, the exhibition represented Degas's dancers as modern women workers not necessarily creative artists in their own right. Two years later in 2005, the fictionalized autobiography of Marie van Goethem entitled *Marie, Dancing* by Carolyn Meyer, was published as a book for young teens.

Bibliography

ARCHIVAL COLLECTIONS

New York

Fokine Papers, Dance Collection, New York Public Library
Gabriel Astruc Papers, Dance Collection, New York Public Library
Serge Diaghilev Correspondence, Dance Collection, New York Public Library

France

Archives Nationales, Paris: Series AJ13 (Opéra)
Boris Kochno Papers, Bibliothèque de l'Opéra

San Francisco

Inventory of Ballets Russes Material, San Francisco Performing Arts Library and Museum

NEWSPAPERS AND JOURNALS

Apollon
Comœdia
Comœdia Illustré
Le Courier Musical
Femina
Le Figaro
L'Illustration
Journal des Débats
Journal de Paris
Mercure Musicale
Musica Nöel

La Nouvelle Revue Française
La Presse
La Revue Musicale
Revue de Paris
Le Temps
Vogue

PUBLISHED SOURCES

Acocella, Joan. "The Reception of Diaghilev's Ballets Russes by Artists and Intellectuals in Paris and London, 1909–1914." PhD diss., Rutgers University, 1984.

Acocella, Joan, and L. Garafola, eds. *André Levinson on Dance: Writings from Paris in the Twenties.* Wesleyan, CT: Wesleyan University Press, 1991.

Adshead-Lansdale, Janet, and June Layson. *Dance History: An Introduction.* New York: Routledge, 1983.

Anderson, Benedict. *Imagined Communities: Reflections on the Origin and Spread of Nationalism.* London: Verso, 1983.

Anderson, Jack. *The One and Only – Ballet Russes de Monte Carlo.* New York: Dance Horizons, 1981.

Archives nationales, Bibliothèque nationale, Musée de l'histoire de France. *Danseurs et ballet de l'Opéra de Paris depuis 1671: exposition.* Exhibition catalogue. Paris: Archives nationales, 1988.

Aristotle. *Poetics.* Translated and introduced by Kenneth McLeish. New York: Theatre Communications Group, 1998.

"Les arts: La danse par Serge Lifar (Denoel)." *La Nouvelle Revue Française,* August 1938, 331.

Aschengreen, Erik. *Jean Cocteau and the Dance.* Translated by Patricia N. McAndrew and Per Avsum. Copenhagen: Gyldendal, 1986.

Au, Susan. *Ballet and Modern Dance.* London: Thames and Hudson, 1998, 2002.

Auric, Georges. "Jeux, de Claude Debussy, au Théâtre des Champs Élysées." *La Nouvelle Revue Française,* January 1921, 101–3.

– "Théâtre Des Champs-Élysées – Les Ballets Russes: À propos de Parade." *La Nouvelle Revue Française,* February 1921, 224–7.

Baer, Nancy Van Norman, ed. *The Art of Enchantment: Diaghilev's Ballets Russes, 1909–1929.* San Francisco: Fine Arts Museum of San Francisco, 1988.

– *Bronislava Njinska: A Dancer's Legacy.* San Francisco: Fine Arts Museum of San Francisco, 1986.

Banes, Sally. *Dancing Women: Female Bodies on Stage.* New York: Routledge, 1998.

– "*Firebird* and the Idea of Russianness." In *The Ballets Russes and Its World*, edited by Lynn Garafola and N. Baer. New Haven, CT: Yale University Press, 1999.

– *Writing Dancing in the Age of Postmodernism.* Middletown, CT: Wesleyan University Press, 1994.

Bartlet, M. Elizabeth C. "Gossec, *L'Offrande à la Liberté* et l'histoire de la *Marseillaise*." In *Le Tambour et la Harpe: Oeuvres, pratiques et manifestations musicale sous la Révolution, 1788–1800*, edited by Jean-Rémy Julien and Jean Mongrédien. Paris: Éditions du May, 1991.

– "The New Repertory at the Opera during the Reign of Terror: Revolutionary Rhetoric and Operatic Consequences." In *Music and the French Revolution*, edited by Malcolm Boyd. Cambridge: Cambridge University Press, 1992.

Batson, Charles R. *Dance, Desire, and Anxiety in Early Twentieth-Century French Theatre: Playing Identities.* London: Ashgate, 2005.

Beaujoyeulx, Baltasar de. *Le ballet comique de la reine.* Paris 1582.

Beaumont, Cyril W. *Ballet Design: Past and Present.* London: The Studio, 1946.

– *The Diaghilev Ballet in London: A Personal Record.* London: Putnam, 1940; reprint, London: Adam and Charles Black, 1951.

– *Michel Fokine and His Ballets.* London: The Author, 1945.

Becker, Jean-Jacques, and Serge Bernstein. "Victories et frustrations, 1914–1929." *Nouvelle histoire de la France contemporaine*, 12. Paris: Seuil, 1990.

Bempéchat, Paul-André ."Toward a Breton Musical Patrimony: Symbiosis and Synthesis of the Folkloric, the Classical and the Impressionistic." In *Proceedings of the 22nd Harvard Celtic Colloquium* (2002), 1–38. Cambridge, MA: Harvard University Press, 2008.

Benois, Alexandre. *Reminiscences of the Russian Ballet.* Translated by Mary Britneira. London: Putnam, 1941; reprint, New York: Da Capo Press, 1977.

Berenson, Edward, V. Duclert, and C. Prochasson, eds. *The French Republic: History, Values, Debates.* Ithaca, NY: Cornell University Press, 2011.

Bereson, Ruth. *The Operatic Stage: Cultural Policy and the Opera House.* London and New York: Routledge, 2002.

Berlanstein, Lenard. *Daughters of Eve: A Cultural History of French Theatre Women from the Old Regime to the Fin de Siècle.* Cambridge, MA: Harvard University Press, 2001.

Bernstein, Susan. *Virtuosity of the Nineteenth Century: Performing Music and Language in Heine, Liszt, and Baudelaire.* Stanford, CA: Stanford University Press, 1998.

Boittin, Jennifer A. *Colonial Metropolis: The Urban Grounds of Anti-Imperialism and Feminism in Interwar Paris.* Lincoln: University of Nebraska Press, 2010.

Boll, André. "Pour ou contre une chorégraphie autonome." *La Revue Musicale,* March 1938, 187–90.

Bowlt, John E. *Russian Art of the Avant-Garde: Theory and Criticism: 1902–1934.* New York: Viking, 1976.

– *The Silver Age: Russian Art of the Early Twentieth Century and the "World of Art" Group.* Newtonville, MA: Oriental Research Partners, 1979.

Breward, Christopher. *The Hidden Consumer: Masculinities, Fashion and City Life, 1860–1914.* Manchester: Manchester University Press, 1999.

Brooks, Lynn, ed. *Women's Work: Making Dance in Europe Before 1800.* Madison: University of Wisconsin Press, 2007.

Brussel, Robert. *Le Figaro,* 27 June 1910, 6.

– "Les théâtres: La saison russe à l'Opéra." *Le Figaro,* 6 June 1910, 6.

Buckle, Richard. *Diaghilev.* London: Weidenfeld and Nicolson, 1979.

– *In Search of Diaghilev.* New York: Thomas Nelson, 1956.

– *In the Wake of Diaghilev.* New York: Holt, Rinehart, and Winston, 1982.

– *Nijinsky.* New York: Simon and Schuster, 1971.

Bull, Angela. *Noel Streatfeild: A Biography.* Glasgow: Collins, 1984.

Burt, Ramsay. *The Male Dancer: Bodies, Spectacle, Sexualities.* London: Routledge, 1995.

Caddy, Davinia. *The Ballets Russes and Beyond: Music and Dance in Belle-Époque Paris.* Cambridge: Cambridge University Press, 2012.

Carroll, David. "The Aesthetics of Nationalism and the Limits of Culture." In *Politics and Aesthetics in the Arts,* edited by Salim Kemal and Ivan Gaskell. Cambridge: Cambridge University Press, 2000.

Carter, Alexandra. "Blonde, Bewigged, and Winged with Gold: Ballet Girls in the Music Halls of Late Victorian and Edwardian England." *Dance Research Journal of the Society for Dance Research* 13, no. 2 (Autumn 1995): 28–46.

– *Dance and Dancers in the Victorian and Edwardian Music Hall Ballet.* London: Ashgate, 2005.

Caute, David. *The Dancer Defects: The Struggle for Cultural Supremacy during the Cold War.* Oxford: University of Oxford Press, 2005.

Chapman, John V. "August Vestris and the Expansion of Technique." *Dance Research Journal* 19, no. 1 (Summer 1987): 11–18.

– "Jules Janin: Romantic Critic." In *Rethinking the Sylph: New Perspectives on the Romantic Ballet,* edited by Lynn Garafola. Hanover, NH: University Press of New England/Wesleyan University Press, 1997.

– "Silent Drama to Silent Dream: Parisian Ballet Criticism, 1800–1850." *Dance Chronicle* 11, no. 3 (1988): 365–80.

Chazin-Bennahum, Judith. *Dance in the Shadow of the Guillotine.* Carbondale: South Illinois University Press, 1988.

Chrastil, Rachel. *Organizing for War: France, 1870–1914.* Baton Rouge: Louisiana State University Press, 2010.

Clark, Linda L. *Women and Achievement in Nineteenth-Century Europe.* Cambridge: Cambridge University Press, 2008.

Clarke, Meaghan. *Critical Voices: Women and Art Criticism in Britain, 1880–1905.* Burlington: Ashgate, 2005.

Clustine, Ivan. "Ballets Russes et Ballet d'Opéra." *Musica-noël* (1912): 245.

Cocteau, Jean. *My Contemporaries.* London: Peter Owen, 1967.

Cocteau, Jean. *Le coq et l'arlequin: Notes autour de la musique.* Paris: Éd. de la Sirène, Collection des tracts, 1, 1918.

Cocteau, Jean et al. *Théâtre Serge de Diaghilev: Les biches.* Paris: Éditions des Quatre Chemins, 1924.

Cohen, Sarah R. *Art, Dance and the Body in French Culture of the Ancien Régime.* Cambridge: Cambridge University Press, 2000.

Cohen, Selma Jeanne, ed. *Dance as a Theatre Art.* New York: Dodd, Mead, 1974.

– "Present Problems of Dance Aesthetics." *Dance Research: The Journal of the Society for Dançe Research* 1, no. 1 (Spring 1983): 12–20.

Copeland, Roger, and Marshall Cohen, eds. *What Is Dance?* Oxford: Oxford University Press, 1983.

Corbet, Charles. *À l'ère des nationalisms: l'opinion française face à l'inconnue russe, 1799–1894.* Paris: M. Didier, 1967.

Corbett, John. *Through French Windows.* Ann Arbor: University of Michigan Press, 1994.

Coton, A.V. *A Prejudice for Ballet.* London: Methuen, 1938.

– *Writings on Dance, 1938–68.* London: Dance Books, 1975.

Cowart, Georgia J. *The Triumph of Pleasure: Louis XIV and the Politics of Spectacle.* Chicago: University of Chicago Press, 2008.

Craft, Robert, and Vera Stravinsky. *Stravinsky in Pictures and Documents.* New York: Simon and Schuster, 1978.

Crow, Thomas. *Emulation: Making Artists for Revolutionary France.* New Haven, CT: Yale University Press, 1995.

– "Oath of the Horatii in 1785: Painting and Pre-Revolutionary Radicalism in France." *Art History* 1 (1978): 424–71.

Dandre, V. *Anna Pavlova in Art and Life.* London: Cassell, 1932.

Darlow, Mark. *Staging the French Revolution: Cultural Politics and the Paris Opéra, 1789–1794.* Oxford: Oxford University Press, 2012.

Davidoff, Leonore, and Catherine Hall, eds. *Family Fortunes: Men and Women of the English Middle Class, 1780–1850.* London: Routledge, 1987; reprinted 1992, 1994.

Davis, Mary E. *Ballets Russes Style: Diaghilev's Dancers and Paris Fashion.* London: Reaktion, 2010.

Debay, V. "Les Ballets Russes." *Le Courrier Musical,* 1 July 1910, 502.

De Groote, Pascale. *Ballets Suédois.* Ghent: Academia Press, 2002.

Denis, Maurice. *Journal II.* Paris: La Colombe, 1957.

Desmond, Jane C., ed. *Meaning in Motion: New Cultural Studies of Dance.* Durham, NC: Duke University Press, 1997.

Dietschy, Marcel. *A Portrait of Claude Debussy.* Edited and translated by William Ashbrook and Margaret G. Cobb. Oxford: Clarendon Press, 1990; French edition, 1962.

Digeon, Claude. *La crise allemande de la pensée française, 1870–1914.* Paris: Presses Universitaires de France, 1959.

Dils, Ann, and Ann Cooper Albright, eds. *Moving History/Dancing Cultures: A Dance History Reader.* Middletown, CT: Wesleyan University Press, 2001.

Dolin, Anton. *Autobiography: A Volume of Autobiography and Reminiscence.* London: Oldbourne, 1960.

Drieu la Rochelle, Pierre. "Chroniques des spectacles." *La Nouvelle Revue Française,* November 1923, 588–96.

Drummond, John. *Speaking of Diaghilev.* London: Faber and Faber, 1997.

Duchesne-Guillemin, J., *Introduction à l'âme et la danse de Paul Valéry.* Liege: Editions Hesoer, 1946.

Duncan, Isadora. *My Life.* New York: Liveright, 1927.

Eichenbaum, Rose. *The Dancer Within: Intimate Conversations with Great Dancers.* Edited by Aron Hirt-Manheimer. Middletown, CT: Wesleyan University Press, 2008.

Eksteins, Modris. *The Great War and the Birth of the Modern Age.* New York: First Anchor Books, 1990.

Ellis, Katherine. *Music Criticism in Nineteenth-Century France: La Revue et Gazette musicale de Paris, 1834–80.* Cambridge: Cambridge University Press, 1995.

Ellmann, Richard, and Charles Feidelson, eds, *The Modern Tradition: Backgrounds of Modern Literature.* New York: Oxford University Press, 1965.

Essarts, F.D. des. "Est-ce que la fin du tutu?" *Comœdia,* 19 September 1911, 1.

Fairfax, Edmund. *The Styles of Eighteenth Century Ballet.* Lanham, MD: Rowman and Littlefield, 2003.

Fauser, Annegret. "Gendering the Nations: The Ideologies of French Discourse on Music (1870–1914)." In *Musical Constructions of Nationalism: Essays on the History and Ideology of European Musical Culture, 1800–1945,* edited by Michael Murphy and Harry White. Cork: Cork University Press, 2001, 72–103.

– *Musical Encounters at the 1889 World's Fair.* Rochester, NY: University of Rochester Press, 2005.

Fergison, Drue. "Bringing *Les Noces* to the Stage." In *The Ballets Russes and Its World,* edited by Lynn Garafola and N. Baer. New Haven, CT: Yale University Press, 1999.

Ferro, Marc. "Cultural Life in France, 1914–18." In *European Culture in the Great War: The Arts, Entertainment, and Propaganda, 1914–1918*, edited by Ariel Roshwald and R. Stites. Cambridge: Cambridge University Press, 1999.

Feuillet, Raoul-Auger. *Chorégraphie: ou l'art de décrire la danse par caractères, figures, et signes demonstratifs*. Paris, 1701.

Fokine, Michel. *Memoirs of a Ballet Master*. Boston: Little, Brown, 1961.

Forth, Christopher. *The Dreyfus Affair and the Crisis of French Manhood*. Baltimore: Johns Hopkins University Press, 2004.

Foster, Susan Leigh, ed. *Choreographing History*. Bloomington: Indiana University Press, 1995.

– "Dance in the Shadow of the Guillotine." Review of *Dance in the Shadow of the Guillotine* by Judith Chazin-Bennahum. *Dance Research Journal* 22, no. 1 (Spring 1990): 34.

Fulcher, Jane F. *The Composer as Intellectual: Music and Ideology in France, 1914–1940*. Oxford: Oxford University Press, 2005.

– ed. *Debussy and His World*. Princeton, NJ: Princeton University Press, 2001.

– *French Cultural Politics and Music: From the Dreyfus Affair to the First World War*. New York: Oxford University Press, 1999.

– *A Nation's Image: French Grand Opera as Politics and Politicized Art*. Cambridge: Cambridge University Press, 1987.

Frascina, Francis, and Charles Harrison, eds. *Modern Art and Modernism: A Critical Anthology*. London: Harper and Row, 1982.

Fuller, Loïe. *Quinze ans de ma vie*. Paris: Société d'Éditions et de Publications, 1908.

Garafola, Lynn. *Diaghilev's Ballets Russes*. New York: Oxford University Press, 1989.

– "Forgotten Interlude: Eurhythmic Dancers at the Paris Opéra." *Dance Research: The Journal of the Society for Dance Research* 13, no. 1 (Summer 1995): 70.

– *Legacies of Twentieth-Century Dance*. Middletown, CT: Wesleyan University Press, 2005.

– "The Making of Ballet Modernism." *Dance Research Journal* 20, no. 2 (Winter 1989): 23–32.

– "Politics in Paradise: André Levinson's Classicism." *New Dance Review* 6, no. 3 (Spring 1994): 12–18.

– ed. *Rethinking the Sylph: New Perspectives on the Romantic Ballet*. Hanover, NH: University Press of New England/Wesleyan University Press, 1997.

Garafola, Lynn, and Baer, Nancy Van Norman, eds. *The Ballets Russes and Its World*. New Haven: Yale University Press, 1999.

Garber, Marjorie. *Vested Interest: Cross Dressing and Cultural Anxiety*. New York: Harper Collins, 1993.

Gard, Michael. *Men Who Dance: Aesthetics, Athletics and the Art of Masculinity.* New York: Peter Lang, 2006.

Gautier, Théophile. *Gautier on Dance: Selected, Translated, and Annotated by Ivor Guest.* London: Dance Books, 1986.

– *Mademoiselle de Maupin.* Paris, 1835.

– *The Romantic Ballet as Seen by Théophile Gautier.* Translated by Cyril W. Beaumont. New York: Dance Horizons, 1932.

Ghéon, Henri. "Culture physique, Hellenisme et sculpture." *La Nouvelle Revue Française,* June 1913, 1041–3.

– "Propos divers sur le Ballet Russe." *La Nouvelle Revue Française,* August 1910, 199–212.

– "La saison 'Russe' au Chatelet." *La Nouvelle Revue Française,* July 1911, 250–1.

– "Sur quelques ballets de transition (Daphnis et Chloé, La tragédie de Salomé, Jeux)." *La Nouvelle Revue Française,* August 1913, 306–9.

Gide, André. A Jean Cocteau." *La Nouvelle Revue Française,* June 1919, 125–8.

Giles, Jeffrey. "Dance and the French Enlightenment." *Dance Chronicle* 4, no. 3 (1981): 245–63.

Goncharova, Natalie. "The Metamorphoses of the Ballet *Les noces.*" *Leonardo* 12 (1979): 137–43.

Goncharova, Natalie, et al. *Les Ballets Russes, Serge de Diaghilew et la décoration théâtrale.* Belves, Dordogne, France: Pierre Vorms Éditeur d'Art, 1955.

Goodman, Lizbeth, ed. *The Routledge Reader in Gender and Performance.* London: Routledge, 1998.

Gordon, Rae Beth. *Dances with Darwin, 1875–1900: Vernacular Modernity in France.* Surrey: Ashgate, 2009.

Gore, Georgiana, and Laurence Louppe with Wilfride Piollet. "France: Effervescence and Tradition in French Dance." In *Europe Dancing: Perspectives on Theatre Dance and Cultural Identity,* edited by Andrée Grau and S. Jordan. London: Routledge, 2000.

Got, Edmond. *Journal d'Edmond Got, sociétaire de la Comédie-francaise 1822–1901.* 2 vols. Paris: Plon-Nourrit et Cie, 1910.

Grau, Andrée, and Stephanie Jordan, eds. *Europe Dancing: Perspectives on Theatre Dance and Cultural Identity.* London: Routledge, 2000.

Gray, Camilla. *The Russian Experiment in Art, 1863–1922.* New York: Harry N. Abrams, 1962.

Green, Christopher. *Art in France, 1900–1940.* New Haven, CT: Yale University Press, 2003.

Greenberg, C. "Modernist Painting." In *Modern Art and Modernism: A Critical Anthology,* edited by Francis Frascina and Charles Harrison. London: Harper and Row, 1982.

Grigoriev, S.L. *The Diaghilev Ballet 1909–1929*. London: Constable, 1953.

Guéhenno, Jean. *Diary of the Dark Years 1940–1944: Collaboration, Resistance, and Daily Life in Occupied Paris*. First published in 1947. Reprint edition. Translated and annotated by David Ball. London: Oxford University Press, 2014.

Guentner, Wendelin, ed. *Women Art Critics in Nineteenth-Century France: Vanishing Acts*. Newark: University of Delaware Press, 2013.

Guest, Ivor. *The Ballet of the Enlightenment: The Establishment of Ballet d'Action in France, 1770–1793*. London: Dance Books, 1996.

– *Ballet under Napoleon*. Hampshire: Dance Books, 2002.

– *Le ballet de l'Opéra de Paris: Trois siècles d'histoire et de tradition*. Paris: Theatre National de l'Opéra, 1976.

– *The Ballet of the Second Empire*. London: Pitman; Middletown, CT: Wesleyan University Press, 1974.

– *Fanny Cerrito*. Middletown, CT: Wesleyan University Press, 1970.

– *The Romantic Ballet in England: Its Development, Its Fulfillment, and Decline*. Middletown, CT: Wesleyan University Press, 1972.

– *The Romantic Ballet in Paris*. Middletown, CT: Wesleyan University Press, 1966.

– *Victorian Ballet-Girl: The Tragic Story of Clara Webster*. New York: Da Capo, 1980.

Gutsche-Miller, Sarah. "Pantomime-Ballet on the Music-Hall Stage: The Popularisation of Classical Ballet in Fin-de-Siècle Paris." PhD diss., McGill University, 2010.

Halbreich, Harold. *Arthur Honegger*. Paris: Fayard, 1992.

Halévy, Daniel. *La fin des notables*. Paris, 1930.

Hall, Constance Valis. "Jazz Modernism." In *Moving Words: Re-Writing Dance*, edited by Gay Morris. New York: Routledge, 1996.

Hall, M. Ann, ed. *Feminism and Sporting Bodies: Essays on Theory and Practice*. Champaign, IL: Human Kinetics, 1996.

Hanna, Judith Lynne. *Dance, Sex, Gender: Signs of Identity, Dominance, Defiance, and Desire*. Chicago: University of Chicago Press, 1988.

Haskell, Arnold L. *Balletomania: The Story of an Obsession*. New York: Simon and Schuster, 1934.

– *Diaghileff: His Artistic and Private Life*. New York: Simon and Schuster, 1935.

– "Portrait of Serge Lifar." In *Lifar on Classical Ballet*, edited by Arnold L. Haskell. London: Allan Wingate, 1951.

– *Prelude to Ballet: An Analysis and a Guide to Appreciation*. London: T. Nelson and Sons, 1947.

Hassell, James E. *Russian Refugees in France and the United States between the World Wars*. Transactions of the American Philosophical Society, vol. 81, part 7. Philadelphia: American Philosophical Society, 1991.

Herbert, Robert L. *Impressionism: Art, Leisure, and Parisian Society*. New Haven, CT: Yale University Press, 1988.

Higonnet, Patrice. *Paris, Capital of the World.* Translated by Arthur Goldhammer. Cambridge, MA: Belknap Press of Harvard University Press, 2002.

Hill, Edward Burlingame. *Modern French Music.* Boston: Houghton Mifflin, 1924.

Hobsbawm, Eric. "Introduction: Inventing Traditions." In *The Invention of Tradition*, edited by E. Hobsbawm and T. Ranger. Cambridge: Cambridge University Press, 1983.

Holmes, Olive, ed. *Motion Arrested: Dance Reviews of H.T. Parker.* Middletown, CT: Wesleyan University Press; New York: Harper and Row, 1982.

Holt, Ulle V. "Style, Fashion, Politics, and Identity: The Ballets Russes in Paris from 1909 to 1914." PhD diss., Brown University, 2000.

Homans, Jennifer, *Apollo's Angels: A History of Ballet.* New York: Random House, 2010.

Horne, Alistair. *To Lose a Battle: France 1940*. London: Macmillan, 1969.

Horwitz, Dawn Lille. *Michel Fokine.* Boston, MA: Twayne, 1985.

Huebner, Steven. *French Opera at the Fin-de-Siècle: Wagnerism, Nationalism, and Style.* Oxford: Oxford University Press, 1999.

Hunt, Lynn, ed. *The New Cultural History*. Berkeley: University of California Press, 1989.

Hyde, Melissa. *Making Up the Rococo: François Boucher and His Critics.* Los Angeles: Getty Publications, 2006.

Jackson, Jeffrey H. *Making Jazz French: Music and Modern Life in Interwar Paris.* Durham, NC: Duke University Press, 2003.

James, Clive. *Cultural Amnesia: Necessary Memories from History and the Arts.* New York: W.W. Norton, 2007.

Jay, Robert Allen. "Art and Nationalism in France, 1870–1914." PhD diss., University of Minnesota, 1979.

Johnson, James. *Listening in Paris: A Cultural History*. Berkeley: University of California Press, 1995.

Johnson, Robert. "Ritual and Abstraction in Nijinska's Les Noces." *Dance Chronicle* 10, no. 2 (1987): 147–59.

Johnson, Victoria. *Backstage at the Revolution: How the Royal Paris Opera Survived the End of the Old Regime.* Chicago: University of Chicago Press, 2008.

Johnston, Robert H. *New Mecca, New Babylon: Paris and the Russian Exiles, 1920–1945*. Montreal and Kingston: McGill-Queen's University Press, 1988.

Kahane, Martine. *Les Ballets Russes à l'Opéra de Paris.* Paris: Hazan, Bibliothèque nationale, 1992.

– *Le Foyer de la Danse.* Paris: Musée d'Orsay/Bibliothèque Nationale, 1988.

Kalifa, Dominique. "The Press," translated by Renée Champion and Edward Berenson. In *The French Republic: History, Values, Debates*, edited by Edward Berenson, V. Duclert, and C. Prochasson. Ithaca, NY: Cornell University Press, 2011.

Karsavina, Tamara. *Theatre Street. The Reminiscences of Tamara Karsavina.* London: Heinemann, 1930.

Kelly, Barbara L. *Music and Ultra Modernism in France: A Fragile Consensus, 1913–1939.* Rochester, NY: Boydell and Brewer, 2013.

Kemal, Salim, and I. Gaskell, eds. *Politics and Aesthetics in the Arts.* Cambridge: Cambridge University Press, 2000.

Kennedy, Janet. *The "Mir Iskusstva" Group and Russian Art, 1898–1912.* New York: Garland, 1977.

Keynes, Milo, ed. *Lydia Lopokova.* London: Weidenfeld and Nicolson, 1983.

Kirstein, Lincoln. *Fokine.* London: British-Continental Press, 1934.

Kochno, Boris. *Diaghilev and the Ballets Russes.* New York: Harper and Row, 1971.

Kodicek, Ann, ed. *Diaghilev. Creator of the Ballets Russes. Art. Music. Dance.* London: Barbican Art Gallery/Lund Humphries, 1996.

Koritz, Amy. *Gendering Bodies/Performing Art: Dance and Literature in Early-Twentieth-Century Culture.* Ann Arbor: University of Michigan, 1995.

– "Moving Violations: Dance in the London Music Hall, 1890–1910." *Theatre Journal* 42, no. 4 (December 1990): 419–31.

Kozel, Susan P. "Athikte's Voice: Listening to the Voice of the Dancer in Paul Valéry's 'L'âme et la danse.'" *Dance Research Journal* 27, no. 1 (Spring 1995): 16–24.

Lalo, Pierre. "La Musique." *Le Temps*, 22 May 1909, 3.

– "La Musique." *Le Temps*, 20 June 1909, 3.

– "La Musique." *Le Temps*, 28 May 1912, 3.

– "La Musique." *Le Temps*, 11 June 1912, 3.

– "La Musique." *Le Temps*, 18 June 1912, 3.

– "La Musique." *Le Temps*, 3 June 1913, 3.

Laloy, Louis. "Article critique concernant *L'histoire de la musique* de Camille Mauclair." *Comœdia*, 1914.

– *Claude Debussy.* Paris: Les Bibliophiles fantaisistes, 1909. Reprint, Paris: Aux Armes de France, 1944.

– *Comœdia*, 11 January 1924, 3.

– "La danse à l'Opéra," *Comœdia*, 23 January 1924, 1.

– "Théâtre de Monte-Carlo: Les Fâcheux, 1923, Ballets Russes." *Comœdia*, 23 January 1924, 3.

Lannes, Roger. "Poésie de la Danse." *La Revue Musicale*, March 1938, 191–7.

Lebovics, Herman. *True France: The Wars over Cultural Identity, 1900–1945.* Ithaca, NY: Cornell University Press, 1992.

Lehman, A.G. *The Symbolist Aesthetic in France 1885–95*. Oxford: Basil Blackwell, 1950.

Leoussi, Athena S. *Nationalism and Classicism: The Classical Body as National Symbol in Nineteenth-Century England and France.* Hampshire: MacMillan, 1998.

Levinson, André. *Ballet Old and New* (1918). Translated by Susan Cook Summer. New York: Dance Horizons, 1982.

– *Ballet romantique.* Paris: Éditions du Trianon, 1929.

– *Comœdia,* 10 April 1922, 3.

– *Comœdia,* 10 September 1923, 3.

– *Comœdia,* 23 November 1923.

– *Comœdia,* 24 December 1923, 4.

– "A Crisis in the Ballets Russes." *Theatre Arts Monthly,* ca. 1926, 787.

– "La Danse." *Comœdia,* 8 January 1923, 5.

– *La danse d'aujoud'hui.* Paris: Duchartre and Van Buggenhoudt, 1929.

– "Le danseur et le préjugé au travesti." *Comœdia,* 30 October, 1922, 3.

– "The Idea of Dance from Aristotle to Mallarmé." In *André Levinson on Dance: Writings from Paris in the Twenties,* edited by Joan Acocella and Lynn Garafola. Hanover, NH: Wesleyan University Press, 1991.

– *Marie Taglioni* (1804–84). Translated by Cyril W. Beaumont. London: Dance Books, 1930.

– "Ou en sont les Ballets russes?" *Comœdia,* 18 June 1923, 4.

– "Le paradoxe de la Saison Francaise," *Comœdia,* 16 July 1923, 3.

– *Paul Valéry: Philosophe de la danse.* Les Cahiers Valéry. Paris: La Tour d'Ivoire, 1927.

– "Propos de ballet." *Comœdia,* 17 April 1922.

– "Pour le ballet français." *Comœdia,* 5 March 1923, 3.

– "Some Commonplaces on the Dance." In *André Levinson on Dance: Writings from Paris in the Twenties,* edited by Joan Acocella and Lynn Garafola. Hanover, NH: Wesleyan University Press, 1991.

– "The Spirit of the Classic Dance." In *André Levinson on Dance: Writings from Paris in the Twenties,* edited by Joan Acocella and Lynn Garafola. Hanover, NH: Wesleyan University Press, 1991.

– "Stravinsky and the Dance." *La Revue Musicale,* December 1923.

Levy, Karen D. *Jacques Rivière.* Boston: Twayne, 1980.

Lido, Serge. *Ballet: 3. Photographies par Serge Lido.* Preface by Jean Cocteau, commentaries by Irène Lipova. Art et industrie N° spécial. Paris: Société Française du Livre, 1953.

Lido, Serge, and Irène Lidova. *30 ans de ballets français.* Paris: Vilo, 1969.

Lieven, Prince Peter. *The Birth of the Ballets Russes.* London: George Allen and Unwin, 1936.

Lifar, Serge. *Ballet Traditional to Modern.* Translated by Cyril W. Beaumont. London: Putnam, 1938.

– *Carlotte Grisi.* Paris: Albin Michel, 1941.
– *La danse: La danse académique et l'art chorégraphique.* Genève [Paris]: Gonthier, 1965.
– *La danse: Les grands courants de la danse académique.* Paris: Denoël, 1938.
– "La danse et la musique." *La Revue Musicale,* March 1938, 182–6.
– "Evolution du ballet au XXème siècle: Du ballet imperial russe au ballet sovietique, 1906–1956." Bulletin No. 1 de l'Institut Chorégraphique, 1957, 3.
– *Lifar on Classical Ballet.* Ed. Arnold L. Haskell. London: Allan Wingate, 1951.
– *Le manifeste du chorégraphie.* Paris: Étoile, 1935.
– *Ma Vie: From Kiev to Kiev.* Translated by James Holman Mason. London: Hutchinson, 1970.
– *Pensées sur la danse.* Préface de Paul Valéry. Dessins d'Aristide Maillot. Paris: Bordas, 1946.
– *Serge Diaghilev: His Life, His Work, His Legend. An Intimate Biography.* New York: Da Capo, 1976.

Lin, Stephanie. "Image (and) Nation: The Russian Exotic in 19th-Century French Travel Narratives," *Dialectical Anthropology* 27, no. 2 (2003): 121–39.

Livak, Lenard. *Russian Emigres in the Intellectual and Literary Life of Interwar France: A Bibliographical Essay.* Montreal and Kingston: McGill-Queen's University Press, 2010.

Lobet, Marcel. *Le ballet français d'aujourd'hui de Lifar à Béjart.* Paris: Librairie Théâtrale, 1958.

Lockspeiser, Edward. *Debussy: His Life and Mind.* London: Cassell, 1962.

Lyford, Amy. "'Le Numéro Barbette': Photography and the Politics of Embodiment in Interwar Paris." In *The Modern Woman Revisited: Paris between the Wars,* edited by Whitney Chadwick and T. Latimer. New Brunswick, NJ: Rutgers University Press, 2003.

MacDonald, Nesta. *Diaghilev Observed by Critics in London and the United States, 1911–1929.* New York: Dance Horizons, 1975.

Makhrow, Kirill. *Russian Paris, 1910–1960.* St Petersburg: Palace Editions, 2003.

Mallarmé, Stéphane. "Ballets." Translated by Evlyn Gould. *Performing Arts Journal* 15, no. 1 (January 1993).
– *Oeuvres complètes.* Paris: Gallimard, 1945.

Mangeot, André. "La danse à l'Opéra et le ballet 'Le lac des aulnes,'" *Le Monde Musicale,* 30 November 1907, 331–2.

Manning, Susan. *Ecstasy and the Demon: Feminism and Nationalism in Dancing of Mary Wigman.* Berkeley: University of California Press, 1993.

Mantz, Paul. "Exposition des oeuvres des artistes indépendants." *Le Temps,* 23 April 1881.

Massine, Léonide. *My Life in Ballet.* London: Macmillan, 1968.

Mauclair, C. "L'enseignement de la saison russe." *La Revue,* 1 August 1910, 350–60.

McCleave, Sarah. "Marie Sallé, a Wise Professional Woman of Influence." In *Women's Work: Making Dance in Europe before 1800,* edited by Lynn Brooks. Madison: University of Wisconsin Press, 2007.

McGowan, Margaret M. "Dance in Sixteenth- and Early Seventeenth-Century France." In *Dance, Spectacle, and the Body Politick, 1250–1750,* edited by Jennifer Nevile. Bloomington: Indiana University Press, 2008.

McLean, Adrienne. "The Image of the Ballet Artist in Popular Films." *Journal of Popular Culture* 25, no. 1 (Summer 1991): 1–19.

McQuillan, Melissa A. "Painters and the Ballet 1917–1926: An Aspect of the Relationship between Art and Theatre." PhD diss., New York University, 1979.

McRobbie, Angela. "Fame, Flashdance, and Fantasies of Achievement." In *Fabrications: Costume and the Female Body,* edited by Jane Gaines and C. Herzog. New York: Routledge, 1990.

Merrill, Lynda. *A Pot of Paint: Aesthetics on Trial in Whistler v. Ruskin.* Washington: Smithsonian, 1992.

Messager, André. *Figaro-Théâtre,* 19 June 1925, 3.

Messing, Scott. *Neoclassicism in Music: From the Genesis of the Concept through the Schoenberg/Stravinsky Polemic.* Rochester, NY: University of Rochester Press, 1996.

Meyers, Mark. "Feminizing Fascist Men: Crowd Psychology, Gender, and Sexuality in French Antifascism, 1929–1945." *French Historical Studies* 29, no. 1 (2006): 109–42.

Michaut, Pierre. *Le ballet contemporaine 1929–1950.* Paris: Éditions Plon, 1950.

– "Souvenir de Diaghilev." *La Revue Musicale,* March 1938, 163–72.

Migel, Parmenia. *The Ballerinas: From the Court of Louis XIV to Pavlova.* New York: MacMillan, 1972.

Moffett, C.S., ed. *The New Painting: Impressionism 1874–86.* San Francisco: Fine Arts Museum of San Francisco, 1986.

Mont, Elie de. "L'Exposition du boulevard des Capucines." *La Civilization,* 21 April 1881, 1–2.

Moore, Lilian. *Artists of the Dance.* New York: Thomas Y. Crowell, 1938.

Morris, Gay, ed. *Moving Words: Re-Writing Dance.* London: Routledge, 1996.

Mosse, George L. *Image of Man: The Creation of Modern Masculinity.* Oxford: Oxford University Press, 1996.

Mukerji, Chandra. *Territorial Ambitions and the Gardens of Versailles.* Cambridge: Cambridge University Press, 1997.

Myers, Rollo. *Modern French Music: From Faure to Boulez.* New York: Praeger, 1971.

Neale, Steve. "Masculinity as Spectacle: Reflections on Men and Mainstream Cinema." In *Screening the Male: Exploring Masculinities in Hollywood Cinema*, edited by Steven Cohan and I.R. Hark. London: Routledge, 1993.

Neville, Jennifer. "Introduction and Overview." *Dance, Spectacle, and the Body Politick, 1250–1750*. Bloomington: Indiana University Press, 2008.

Nijinska, Bronislava. *Early Memoirs*. New York: Holt, Rinehart, and Winston, 1951.

Nijinsky, Romola de Pulszky. *Nijinsky*. London: V. Gollancz, 1933.

Nijinsky, Vaslav. *The Diary of Vaslav Nijinsky*. Edited by Romola Nijinsky. Berkeley: University of California Press, 1968.

Nord, Philip. *The Republican Moment*. Cambridge: Harvard University Press, 1998.

Norton, Leslie. *Léonide Massine and the 20th Century Ballet*. Jefferson, NC: McFarland, 2004.

Noverre, Jean-Georges. *Lettres sur la danse et les ballets*. 8 vols (1760). Translated by Cyril Beaumont. Reprint. Brooklyn: Dance Horizons, 1975.

Nye, Robert A. "Fencing, the Duel, and Republican Manhood." *Journal of Contemporary History* 25, nos 2/3 (1990): 365–77.

– *Masculinity and Male Codes of Honor in Modern France*. New York: Oxford University Press, 1993.

Ortner, Sherry B. "Is Female to Male as Nature Is to Culture?" In *Woman, Culture, and Society*, edited by M.Z. Rosaldo and L. Lamphere. Stanford, CA: Stanford University Press, 1974.

Orwitz, Michael R., ed. *Art Criticisms and Its Institutions in Nineteenth-Century France*. Manchester: Manchester University Press, 1994.

Osborne, Carol, and F. Skillen. "Women and Sport in Interwar Britain." In *Routledge Handbook of Sport, Gender, and Sexuality*, edited by Jennifer Hargreaves and E. Anderson. New York: Routledge, 2014.

Pasler, Jan. "Pelléas and Power: Forces behind the Reception of Debussy's Opera." *19th-Century Music* 10, no. 3 (Spring 1987): 243–64.

Paulino. *Comœdia*, 22 May 1909, 2.

Pennell, Elizabeth Robins. "Women's World of London." *Chautauquan: A Weekly Newsmagazine*, 1 March 1893.

Perros, Jean. "Après les Ballets Russes." *La Critique Independante*, 15 June 1913, 1.

"'Petroushka et Lachete' ou l'histoire vue par le ballet." *Le Figaro*, 24 May 1922.

Philip, Richard, and Mary Whitney. *Danseur: The Male in Ballet*. New York: McGraw-Hill, 1977.

Pollock, Griselda. "Modernity and the Spaces of Femininity." In *The Expanding Discourse: Feminism and Art History*, edited by Norma Broude and Mary D. Garrard. New York: IconEditions, 1992.

Prévost, Marcel. "La danse." *Le Figaro*, 13 June 1910, 1.

Pridden, Deidre. *The Art of Dance in French Literature*. London: Adam and Charles Black, 1952.

Prunières, Henry. *La Revue Musicale*, May 1932, 396.

Raeff, Marc. *Russian Abroad: A Cultural History of the Russian Emigration, 1919–1939*. New York: Oxford University Press, 1990.

Rameau. Pierre. *Le maître à danser* (The Dancing Master). Paris 1725.

Rearick, Charles. *The French in Love and War: Popular Culture in the Era of the World Wars*. New Haven, CT: Yale University Press, 1997.

– *Paris Dreams, Paris Memories: The City and Its Mystique*. Palo Alto, CA: Stanford University Press, 2011.

– *Pleasures of the Belle Époque*. New Haven, CT: Yale University Press, 1997.

Rebay, Hilla. "The Beauty of Non-Objectivity." In *Modern Art and Modernism: A Critical Anthology*, edited by F. Frascina and C. Harrison. London: Harper and Row, 1982.

Reich, Nancy B. "Clara Schumann" and "European Composers and Musicians, ca. 1800–1890." In *Women and Music: A History*, edited by Karin Pendle. Bloomington: Indiana University Press, 1999, 2001.

Reynolds, Sian, and William Kidd. *Contemporary French Cultural Studies*. London: Arnold; New York: Oxford University Press, 2000.

Riding, Alan. *And the Show Went On: Cultural Life in Nazi-Occupied Paris*. New York: Vintage; Reprint edition, 2011.

Ries, Frank W.D. *The Dance Theatre of Jean Cocteau*. Ann Arbor, MI: UMI Research Press, 1986.

Rigaud, André. "Ce que fut la saison 1921–22 à l'Opéra." *Comœdia*, 18 July 1922.

– "La classe de danse des hommes à l'Opéra: 'Renaissance d'un Art.'" *Comœdia*, 28 July 1922, 1.

– *Comœdia*, 19 July 1923, 1.

– "Le foyer de la danse à l'Opéra." *Comœdia*, 19 January 1924, 1–3.

Rivière, Jacques. "Des Ballets Russes et de Fokine." *La Nouvelle Revue Française*, July 1912, 174–80.

– "Les Ballets Russes à l'Opéra: La Boutique Fantasque, le Tricorne, Le Chant du Rossignol." *La Nouvelle Revue Française*, 1 March 1920, 462–7.

– "La Musique." *La Nouvelle Revue Française*, July 1914, 150–62.

– "Petrouchka, ballet d'Igor Stravinski, Alexandre Fokine et Alexandre Benois." *La Nouvelle Revue Française*, September 1911, 376–7.

– "Le sacre du printemps." *La Nouvelle Revue Française*, November 1913, 706–30.

– " Le sacre du printemps, ballet par Igor Stravinsky, Nicholas Roerich et Vaslav Nijinski (Théâtre des Champs Elysées)." *La Nouvelle Revue Française*, August 1913, 309–13.

Roberts, Mary Louise. *Civilization without Sexes: Reconstructing Gender in Post-war France, 1917–1927*. Chicago: University of Chicago Press, 1994.
– *Disruptive Acts: The New Woman in Fin-de-Siècle France.* Chicago: University of Chicago Press, 2002.
Rodin, Auguste. "La rénovation de la danse." *Le Matin*, 30 May 1912, 1.
Roshwald, Ariel, and Richard Stites, eds. *European Culture in the Great War: The Arts, Entertainment, and Propaganda, 1914–1918*. Cambridge: Cambridge University Press, 1999.
Rousseau, Jean-Jacques. *Dictionnaire de musique.* Paris. 1768.
Rubin-Challan, Louise. "Social Conditions of Ballet Dancers at the Paris Opera in the Nineteenth Century." *Choreography and Dance* 2, no. 1 (1992): 17–28.
Said, Edward. *Orientalism.* New York: Vintage Books, 1979.
Saint-Saëns, Camille. *Germanophile.* Paris: Dorbonne, 1916.
Samachson, Dorothy. *Let's Meet the Ballet.* New York: Schuman, 1951.
Sazonova, Julie. "Mlle Semenova à l'Opéra." *La Nouvelle Revue Française*, February 1936, 470–1.
– "Questions chorégraphiques." *La Revue Musicale*, March 1938, 208.
– "La saison chorégraphique: Ballets Joos, Ballets 1933, Ballets de Monte Carlo." *La Nouvelle Revue Française*, July 1933, 154–7.
Scheijen, Sjeng. *Diaghilev: A Life.* Translated by Jane Hedley-Prôle and S.L. Leinbach. Oxford: Oxford University Press, 2009.
Schiebinger, Londa. *The Mind Has No Sex? Women in the Origins of Modern Science.* Cambridge, MA: Harvard University Press, 1991.
Schloezer, Boris. "Les arts: La danse par Serge Lifar." *La Nouvelle Revue Française*, August 1938, 329–32.
– "Les arts: Serge de Diaghilev." *La Nouvelle Revue Française*, October 1929, 572–5.
– "Chronique Musicale." *La Nouvelle Revue Française*, July 1928, 104–8.
– "Stravinsky; Quelques reprises: Le sacre du printemps, Petrouchka, Contes risses, L'après-midi d'un faune." *La Nouvelle Revue Française*, July 1922, 116–20.
– "La musique: Ballets." *La Nouvelle Revue Française*, February 1938, 506–8.
– "La musique: Jeu de cartes, par Igor Stravinsky." *La Nouvelle Revue Française*, February 1938, 149–51.
Schmid, Marion. "À bas Wagner! The French Press Campaign against Wagner during World War I." In *French Music, Culture, and National Identity*, edited by Barbara L. Kelly. Rochester, NY: University of Rochester, 2008.
Scholl, Tim. *From Petipa to Balanchine: Classical Revival and the Modernization of Ballet.* New York: Routledge, 2014.
Schouvaloff, A. *The Art of the Ballets Russes: The Serge Lifar Collection of Theatre Designs, Costumes, and Paintings at the Wadsworth Atheneum, Hartford, Connecticut.* New Haven, CT: Yale University Press, 1997).

Schwartz, Vanessa R. *It's So French: Hollywood, Paris, and the Making of Cosmopolitan Film Culture.* Chicago: University of Chicago Press, 2007.

Shattuck, Roger. *The Banquet Years: The Origins of the Avant-Garde in France 1885 to World War I.* New York: Vintage, 1968.

Shaw, Mary Lewis. *Performance in the Texts of Mallarmé: The Passage from Art to Ritual.* University Park: Pennsylvania State University Press, 1992.

Sheriff, Mary D. *The Exceptional Woman: Elisabeth Vigée-Lebrun and the Cultural Politics of Art.* Chicago: University of Chicago Press, 1996.

Showalter, Elaine. *Sexual Anarchy: Gender and Culture in the Fin-de-Siècle.* New York: Penguin, 1990.

Shrum, Wesley. *Fringe and Fortune: The Role of Critics in High and Popular Art.* Princeton, NJ: Princeton University Press, 1996.

Siegfried, Susan L. "The Politicization of Art Criticism in the Post-Revolutionary Press." In *Art Criticisms and Its Institutions in Nineteenth-Century France,* edited by Michael R. Orwitz. Manchester: Manchester University Press, 1994.

Silver, Kenneth E. *Esprit de Corps: The Art of the Parisian Avant-Garde and the First World War, 1914–1925.* Princeton, NJ: Princeton University Press, 1989.

Silverman, Deborah L. *Art Nouveau in Fin-de-Siècle France: Politics, Psychology, and Style.* Berkeley: University of California Press, 1992.

Sokolova, Lydia. *Dancing for Diaghilev: The Memoirs of Lydia Sokolova.* London: John Murray, 1960.

Solomon-Godeau, Abigail. *Male Trouble: A Crisis in Representation.* London: Thames and Hudson, 1997.

Souritz, Elizabeth. "Isadora Duncan and Prewar Russian Dancemakers." In *The Ballets Russes and Its World,* edited by Lynn Garafola and N. Baer. New Haven, CT: Yale University Press, 1999.Sparti, Barbara, ed. *De Practica Seu Arte Tripudii: "On the Practice and Art of Dancing."* Oxford: Oxford University Press, 1995.

Spencer, Charles. *The World of Diaghilev.* Chicago: Henry Regnery, 1974.

Sprout, Leslie A. *Musical Legacy of Wartime France.* Berkeley; University of California Press, 2013.

Stewart, Mary Lynn. *For Health and Beauty: Physical Culture for Frenchwomen, 1880s–1930s.* Baltimore: Johns Hopkins University Press, 2000.

Stravinsky, Igor. *Stravinsky: An Autobiography.* New York: Simon and Schuster, 1936.

Stuart and McLellan. *Paris at Night: Sketches and Mysteries of Paris High Life and Demi-monde. Nocturnal Amusements; How to Know Them! How to Enjoy Them!! How to Appreciate Them!!!* Boston: Boston and Paris Publishing Company, 1875.

Suarès, A. "Chronique de Caerdal, VII: Beauté de la danse." *La Nouvelle Revue Française,* 1 August 1912, 329.

Surkis, Judith. "Carnival Balls and Penal Codes: Body Politics in July Monarchy France." *History of the Present* 1, no. 1 (Summer 2011): 59–83.

Svetlov, Valerian. *Le ballet contemporaine.* With the collaboration of Léon Bakst. Translated by M.D. Calvocoressi. Paris: de Brunoff, 1912.

– "The Diaghileff Ballet in Paris," part 1. *Dancing Times,* December 1929, 263–74.

– "The Diaghilev Ballet in Paris," part 2. *Dancing Times,* January 1930, 460–3.

– "The Diaghilev Ballet in Paris," part 3. *Dancing Times,* February 1930, 569–74.

Swinson, Cyril, ed. *Dancers and Critics.* London: Adam and Charles Black, 1950.

Tannebaum, Edward R. *The Action Française: Die Hard Reactionaries in Twentieth-Century France.* New York: Wiley, 1962.

Taruskin, Richard. *Defining Russia Musically: Historical and Hermeneutical Essays.* Princeton, NJ: Princeton University Press, 2000.

Thogmartin, Clyde. *The National Daily Press of France.* Birmingham, AL: Summa, 1998.

Thomas, Helen. *Dance, Gender, Culture.* New York: St Martin's, 1993.

Thompson, Christopher S. *The Tour de France: A Cultural History.* Berkeley: University of California Press, 2006.

Tilburg, Patricia A. *Collette's Republic: Work, Gender, and Popular Culture in France, 1870–1914.* New York: Berghahn Books, 2009.

Trianon, Henri. "Sixième Exposition de peinture par un groupe d'artistes." *Le Constitutionnel,* 24 April, 1881.

Tumblety, Joan. *Remaking the Male Body: Masculinity and the Uses of Physical Culture in Interwar and Vichy France.* Oxford: Oxford University Press, 2012.

Uzanne, Octave. *The Modern Parisienne.* London: Heinmann, 1912. Originally published in France in 1910 by *Mercure de France* as "Études de sociologie féminine: Parisiennes de ce temps et leurs divers milieux, états et conditions."

Valéry, Paul. *Aesthetics/Paul Valéry.* Translated by Ralph Manheim. New York: Pantheon, 1964.

– "L'Âme et la danse." *La Revue Musicale* 3, no. 2, special number *Le Ballet au XIXe siècle* (December 1921): 3–32/99–128.

Valois, Ninette de. *Come and Dance with Me: A Memoir, 1898–1956.* Cleveland: World Publications, 1957.

Vaudoyer, Jean-Louis. "Variations sur les Ballets Russes." *La Revue de Paris,* 15 July 1910.

Véron, Louis. *Mémoires d'un bourgeois de Paris.* 6 vols. Paris: G. de Gomet, 1856.

Verzosa, Noel Orillo, Jr. *The Absolute Limits: Debussy, Satie, and the Culture of French Modernism, ca. 1860–1920.* Berkeley: University of California, 2008.

Volkov, Solomon. *St. Petersburg: A Cultural History.* New York: Simon and Schuster, 1995.

Volodina, Tatiana, and Militsa Pozharskaya. *The Art of the Ballets Russes: The Russian Seasons in Paris, 1908–1929.* New York: Abbeville, 1990.

Walker, Alan. *Franz Liszt.* Ithaca, NY: Cornell University Press, 1989.

Walker, Kathryn Sorley. *De Basil's Ballets Russes.* New York: Athenaeum, 1983.

Walpole, Horace, "Letter to the Countess of Ossory," 17 December 1780, in *Letters of Horace Walpole: Earl of Orford,* 7 . London: Richard Bentley, 1840.

Walters, Margaret. *The Nude Male: A New Perspective.* New York: Paddington Press, 1978.

Warnod, A. "Les peintures et les Ballets Russes." *La Revue Musicale,* 1 December 1930, 78–89.

Weber, Eugen. *France, Fin de Siècle.* Cambridge, MA: Harvard University Press, 1986.

– *The Hollow Years: France in the 1930s.* New York: W.W. Norton, 1994.

Weinbaum, Alys Eve, et al. *Modern Girl around the World: Consumption, Modernity, and Globalization.* Durham, NC: Duke University Press, 2008.

Werth, Léon. *Danse, Danseurs, Dancings.* Paris: F. Rieder, 1925.

White, Barbara Ehrlich. "Renoir's Sensuous Women." In *Women as Sex Objects: Studies in Erotic Art, 1730–1970,* edited by Thomas B. Hess and Linda Nochlin. London: Allen Lane, 1973.

White, Eric Walter. *Stravinsky: The Composer and His Works.* Berkeley: University of California Press, 1966.

Willms, Johannes. *Paris: Capital of Europe.* Translated by Eveline L. Kanes. New York: Holmes and Meier, 1997.

Wright, Gordan. *France in Modern Times: From the Enlightenment to the Present,* 5th ed. New York, London: W.W. Norton, 1995.

Yanovsky, Vassily. *Elysian Fields: A Book of Memory.* Translated by Isabella and Vassily Yanovsky. DeKalb: Northern Illinois University Press, 1987.

Yates, Frances A. *The French Academies of the Sixteenth Century.* New York: Routledge, 1947.

Zeldin, Theodore. *France 1848–1945: A History of French Passions, Ambition, Love and Politics,* vol. 1. Oxford: Oxford University Press, 1993.

Index

Page numbers in italics indicate figures